NARRATIVE VOICES
IN MODERN FRENCH FICTION

Valerie Minogue

NARRATIVE VOICES
IN MODERN FRENCH FICTION

STUDIES IN HONOUR OF
VALERIE MINOGUE
ON THE OCCASION OF HER RETIREMENT

Edited by

Michael Cardy, George Evans and Gabriel Jacobs

UNIVERSITY OF WALES PRESS
CARDIFF
1997

© The Contributors, 1997

British Library Cataloguing-in-Publication Data
A catalogue record for this book is available from the British Library.

ISBN 0-7083-1394-9

All rights reserved. No part of this book may be reproduced, stored in a retrieval system, or transmitted, in any form or by any means, electronic, mechanical, photocopying, recording or otherwise, without clearance from the University of Wales Press, 6 Gwennyth Street, Cardiff, CF2 4YD.

Typeset at the University of Wales
Printed in Great Britain by Dinefwr Press, Llandybïe

Contents

List of Contributors	vii
Valerie Minogue: A Tribute	ix
Valerie Minogue: Bibliography	xi
Introduction *Michael Cardy, George Evans, Gabriel Jacobs*	1
Lettre *Nathalie Sarraute*	6
L'Ordre du Poème *Monique Wittig*	7
Orchestrated Voices: Selves and Others in Nathalie Sarraute's *Tu ne t'aimes pas* *Sheila M. Bell*	13
Nathalie Sarraute – Criticism and the 'Terrible Desire to Establish Contact' *Ann Jefferson*	37
The Voice on the Page and the Voice from the Stage: Contemporary Dramatic Adaptations of the Works of Balzac and George Sand *F. W. J. Hemmings*	57
'Voilà le poëte hystérique': Flaubert, Frédéric and Emma *Naomi Segal*	79

Flaubert and Semanalysis: Rereading *L'Éducation sentimentale*
  Brian Nelson — 101

Description et psychologie: génétique et poétique
de l'indice dans *L'Éducation sentimentale*
  Éric Le Calvez — 113

Dressed/Undressed: Objects of Visual Fascination
in Zola's *L'Assommoir*
  Susan Harrow — 143

Hitting the Mine: Modulations in Narrative Voice
in Proust's *A la recherche du temps perdu*
  Robin MacKenzie — 165

Proust and Politics
  Malcolm Bowie — 183

'Le Renégat': An Ironic Re-enactment of Camus's Djihad?
  Valerie Howells — 215

Le « je » durassien féminin: un miroir aux alouettes?
  Catherine Rodgers — 239

List of Subscribers — 259

The Contributors

Michael Cardy is Professor of French at the University of Wales, Swansea

George Evans is Senior Lecturer in French at the University of Wales, Swansea

Gabriel Jacobs is Senior Lecturer in European Business Management at the University of Wales, Swansea

Sheila M. Bell is Senior Lecturer in French at the University of Kent at Canterbury

Malcolm Bowie is Professor of French at the University of Oxford

Susan Harrow is Lecturer in French at the University of Wales, Swansea

F. W. J. Hemmings is Emeritus Professor of the University of Leicester

Valerie Howells is Lecturer in French at the University of Wales, Swansea

Ann Jefferson is a Fellow of New College, University of Oxford

Éric Le Calvez is Associate Professor of French at Georgia State University

Robin MacKenzie is Lecturer in French at the University of Wales, Swansea

Brian Nelson is Professor of French at Monash University

Catherine Rodgers is Lecturer in French at the University of Wales, Swansea

Naomi Segal is Professor of French at the University of Reading

Monique Wittig is Professor of French at the University of Arizona

Valerie Minogue: A Tribute

Valerie Minogue was born and received her primary and secondary education in Wales, at Llanelli. She went to Girton College, Cambridge in 1949, and was awarded a 1st-Class Honours degree in French and Italian in 1952. In that same year she was awarded the Mary Elizabeth Ponsonby Prize for French Literature. As a recipient of the Maria Degani Research Scholarship, she worked on Tristan L'Hermite with Odette de Mourgues, for which she received a Cambridge M. Litt. in 1956. She undertook part-time work while raising her children in the second half of the 1950s, and in 1962 was appointed Temporary Assistant Lecturer at what was then Queen Mary College, London, where she stayed until 1981, having been promoted to Senior Lecturer in 1975. In 1981 she was appointed to the Chair of French at the University College of Swansea, as it then was. There, she was also Head of the Department of Romance Studies until July 1988, when she became Research Professor in French, a post she held until she was confirmed Emeritus Professor of the University of Wales in April 1996.

Her acceptance of the Chair at Swansea coincided with the start of the extraordinary internal and external administrative pressures which impose such a heavy burden on Heads of Department, yet a glance at her bibliography shows that her scholarly output has been consistent since the early 1960s. Throughout her career, Valerie has retained her enthusiasm for and commitment to the true purposes of academic life – research and teaching. That enthusiasm and that commitment are among her most enduring qualities, and the ones which have had the most impact on all those who have worked with her, whether as colleagues (one of the editors of this volume owes her a particular debt of gratitude for having taught him the value of concise and accurate expression) or postgraduate and undergraduate students who have enjoyed the benefit of encountering those same qualities which have marked her published research.

Her scholarly work is destined to last. It is characterized by perceptive engagement with texts, by a desire to penetrate beyond their surface, by a punctilious and incisive concern with the expression of ideas. And her critical work is quite simply a pleasure to read. With the exception of the occasional incursion into the area of nineteenth-century poetry, it has been prose fiction of the past 150 years that has retained her attention. She would recognize Flaubert as the *fons et origo* of a tradition of fictional writing that leads in France through Zola and Proust to the *nouveau roman*. She has ranged widely in this domain. Her published studies of Proust and Zola are important contributions to the fields, and her shorter pieces on a variety of twentieth-century writers are all of major significance. But one writer above all others, Nathalie Sarraute, has come to be central to her scholarly preoccupations. With her 1981 book, with a series of ground-breaking articles, and very recently with her massive contributions to the Pléiade edition of Sarraute's complete works, Valerie has become one of the principal advocates, both in Britain and abroad, of a writer with whom she is linked through intense admiration of the writings and ties of personal friendship.

Typical of Valerie's energy and enthusiasm was the foundation in 1982 of the journal *Romance Studies*, in collaboration with Brian Nelson, who was then at Aberystwyth. She has been General Editor of the journal since 1986, a task which has been extremely demanding of time and commitment. Not only has *Romance Studies* provided scholars in the United Kingdom and elsewhere with a high-level outlet for their research, but it has also afforded Valerie the opportunity to show her mettle as an editor of great talent. Her sure sense of the quality of the work submitted, even when it has dealt with topics outside her own area of specialization, her exacting demands with regard to both substance and style, and her ability to inculcate these qualities in colleagues associated with the enterprise, have combined to make the journal one of very high standing. Chief among the concerns that have activated the editors of this *Festschrift* has been the fear, terror even, that they might not attain Valerie's own exceptionally high editorial standards.

This tribute has so far dealt with Valerie in her professional capacity, but it would be wholly remiss of us to omit the personal. At a time when the Department of French at Swansea has experienced a growth spurt in its personnel, mainly of young academics, Valerie has been the soul of hospitality, welcoming new colleagues to her home, encouraging their scholarly ambitions, and taking a genuine, helpful interest in their careers. Above all, Valerie cares. And her house in Eaton Crescent, Swansea, has been the centre of the French Department's social life, whether this has involved receiving foreign visitors, celebrating individual achievements such as the award of doctorates or the publication of books, or simply for the pleasure of one another's company outside the confines of the Department. The latter occasions have often brought to light colleagues' secret talents. It was, for example, on one such occasion that Valerie herself revealed that she might easily have made a second career as an impersonator of Edith Piaf.

Valerie Minogue's contribution to the culture of the Department of French and the School of European Languages at Swansea has been immense, and it is a matter of considerable gratification to her friends and colleagues that she intends to spend her retirement in the locality, though all who know her are also certain that she will not retire from scholarly work.

Michael Cardy
George Evans
Gabriel Jacobs
Swansea, 1997

Valerie Minogue: Bibliography

I. Books

Proust: 'Du côté de chez Swann' (London: Edward Arnold, 1973, reprinted 1976), 68 pp.

Nathalie Sarraute: The War of the Words (Edinburgh: Edinburgh University Press, 1981), viii, 230 pp.

Zola: 'L'Assommoir' (London: Grant & Cutler, 1991), 100 pp.

Nathalie Sarraute, *Œuvres complètes*, sous la direction de Jean-Yves Tadié (Paris: Gallimard [Bibliothèque de la Pléiade]), 1996, xlvi, 2128 pp. [*Notices* and *Notes* for *Tropismes, Portrait d'un inconnu, Martereau, Le Planétarium, Vous les entendez?, "disent les imbéciles", L'Usage de la parole* and *Tu ne t'aimes pas*].

II. Editorship

Co-editor (and co-founder with Brian Nelson) of *Romance Studies*, 1982–1985. General Editor 1986– .

III. Contributions to academic journals, edited books and other works

'Philosopher, go home!', *The Twentieth Century* (March 1960), 26–34.

'Taking care of the caretaker', *The Twentieth Century* (September 1960), 226–234. Reprinted in A. Ganz (ed.), *Pinter: A Collection of Critical Essays* (Englewood Cliffs, NJ: Prentice-Hall, 1972), 72–77.

'Jean Cocteau, Orpheus in the modern world', *France-Britain* 20 No. 80 (Summer 1964), 7–9.

'The tableau in Vigny's "La Colère de Samson"', *Modern Language Review* 60 (July 1965), 374–378.

'Paths and feet in Vigny's *Les Destinées*', *Modern Languages* (December 1965), 131–139.

'The workings of fiction in Robbe-Grillet's *Les Gommes*', *Modern Language Review* 62 (July 1967), 430–442.

'*Les Liaisons dangereuses*: a practical lesson in the art of seduction', *Modern Language Review* 67 (October 1972), 775–786.

'The imagery of childhood in Nathalie Sarraute's *Portrait d'un inconnu*', *French Studies* 27 (April 1973), 177–186.

'Nathalie Sarraute's *Le Planétarium*: the narrator narrated', *Forum for Modern Language Studies* 9 (July 1973), 217–234.

'Distortion and creativity in the subjective viewpoint: Robbe-Grillet, Butor and Nathalie Sarraute', *Forum for Modern Language Studies* 12 (January 1976), 37–49.

'The housekeeper's Proust', *Quadrant* (April 1977).

'Picasso and the apple: the French new novel', *Quadrant* (August 1977).

'The creator's game: some reflections on Robbe-Grillet's *Le Voyeur*', *Modern Language Review* 72 (October 1977), 815–828.

'Presumptuous girls', *Quadrant* (December 1977).

'Zola's mythology: that forbidden tree', *Forum for Modern Language Studies* 14 (July 1978), 217–230.

'Victorious women', *Quadrant* (June 1978).

'Pinter-size Proust', *Quadrant* (July 1979).

'Parody in Proust and Robbe-Grillet', *Southern Review* (March 1980), 53–65. Translated into Japanese by Shigekazu Kishimoto in *Structure of Parody* (Tokyo: Otori Shobo Press, 1989), 161–194.

'Nathalie Sarraute: an assessment', *The Literary Review* 20 (11–24 July 1980), 11–24.

'Roquentin's self-conscious narrative: *La Nausée* and the *nouveau roman*', *Forum for Modern Language Studies* 17 (July 1981), 230–244.

'Fiction and the facts of life', *Quadrant* (January–February 1982).

'Realism and the *nouveau roman*', *Romance Studies* 1 (Winter 1982), 77–94.

'Trials of life', Inaugural Lecture, University College of Swansea (Swansea, 1982), 16 pp.

'Nathalie Sarraute: l'usage de la parole', *Romance Studies* 2 (Summer 1983), 35–52.

Entry 'Nathalie Sarraute' in J. Vinson and D. Kirkpatrick (eds.), *Contemporary Foreign Language Writers* (New York: St. James Press, 1984), 306–308.

'Nathalie Sarraute's *Enfance*: fragments of a childhood', *Romance Studies* 9 (Winter 1986), 71–83.
'Sticks and stones: the weaponry of words in *Vous les entendez?*' in D. G. Coleman and G. Jondorf (eds.), *Words of Power: Essays in Honour of Alison Fairlie* (Glasgow: University of Glasgow Studies in French Language and Literature, 1987), 243–265.
'Ironie et réalité dans les romans de Nathalie Sarraute', *Cahiers du CERF* (Brest) 20 No. 3 (1987), 7–22.
'Nathalie Sarraute's *Enfance*: from experience of language to the language of experience' in R. Gibson (ed.), *Studies in French Fiction in Honour of Vivienne Mylne* (London: Grant & Cutler, 1988), 209–224.
'Sarraute, Auden and the great tall tailor', *Modern Language Review* 84 (April 1989), 331–336.
'Rimbaud's Ophelia', *French Studies* 43, no. 4 (1989), 423–436.
'Virtualities of the self: Nathalie Sarraute's *Tu ne t'aimes pas*', *French Studies Bulletin* 33 (Winter 1989/1990), 18–20.
'Le Cheval de Troie: à propos de *Tu ne t'aimes pas*', *Revue des Sciences Humaines* 93 No. 217 (January–March 1990), 151–161.
'Nathalie Sarraute', *Guardian* (18 July 1990).
'The lady and the whore: the inscription of the heroine in the text in Zola's *Nana* and James's *Portrait of a Lady*', in B. Nelson (ed.), *Naturalism in the European Novel* (New York and Oxford: Berg, 1992), 245–264.
'Voices, virtualities and ventriloquism: Nathalie Sarraute's *Pour un oui ou pour un non*', *French Studies* 49 (April 1995), 164–177.
'Venus observing – Venus observed: Zola's *Nana*' in P. Pollard (ed.), *Émile Zola Centenary Colloquium 1893–1993* (London: The Émile Zola Society, 1995), 57–72.
'The child, the doll, and the hands that hold: *Tropismes 1* as a paradigm in the work of Nathalie Sarraute', *New Novel Review* 3 (October 1995), 22–34.
'L'Enfant et les sortilèges ou l'Enfant d'Éléphant au pays des mythes', in S. Raffy (ed.), *Autour de Nathalie Sarraute* (Besançon: Annales Littéraires de l'Université de Besançon, 1995), 49–62.
'Nathalie Sarraute anti-terrorist: a reading of *"disent les imbéciles"*', *L'Esprit Créateur* 36 (Summer 1996), 75–88.
'The hand and the child: a basic figure in the work of Nathalie Sarraute', *Romance Studies* 27 (Spring 1996), 73–83.
Entries for Michel Butor, Alain Robbe-Grillet and Nathalie Sarraute in J. Julliard et M. Winock (eds.), *Dictionnaire des*

intellectuels français (Paris: Éditions du Seuil, 1996), 200–201, 992–993, 1026–1027.

IV. Reviews

Reviews in numerous journals including *British Book News, France-Britain, French Studies, The Literary Review, Modern Language Review, New Novel Review, Quadrant, Quinquereme, The Times, Times Higher Education Supplement*, and *Times Literary Supplement*.

V. Translation

'The Inside of the Glove' ('Le Gant retourné'), text of a talk given by Nathalie Sarraute, *Romance Studies* 4 (Winter 1984), 1–7.

VI. Poetry

Valerie Minogue's poetry has appeared in *Poems 89*, edited by John Stuart Williams (Llandysul: Gwasg Gomer, 1969), and in *John Bull, Wales, Anglo-Welsh Review, Envoi, Outposts, English* and *Contemporary Review*.

VII. Broadcast talk

'The French New Novel', BBC Radio 4, first broadcast 26 January 1982.

Introduction

This volume, published in honour of Valerie Minogue, contains essays on French writers who are especially close to her heart. The primary focus, which is on the narrative voice in fiction of the second half of the nineteenth century to the present, reflects not only a Cambridge tradition within which Valerie's literary enthusiasms were fostered, but also the field in which she herself has made major contributions. That the essays are contributed both by colleagues of long standing and by some relatively newer ones bears witness to the continuing richness of this field and to Valerie's enduring capacity to stimulate.

There is no attempt to be narrowly ideological in critical stance. Barthes's concept of *disponibilit*é – the idea that great texts will constantly generate new forms of critical discourse – now seems unassailable. Nevertheless, and allowing for one or two contributions of high quality which have a more tangential relationship with the central focus, the essays seek to highlight the insights to be gained from a critical approach involving close attention to textual detail, an undogmatic openness to new possibilities, and a particular sensitivity to tone of voice and its implications. Such an approach forms the basis of Valerie's own critical practice and her considerable achievements as a reader of texts and an inspiring colleague and teacher. It also helps to explain why Nathalie Sarraute became Valerie's author of predilection: for Sarraute too, criticism becomes, in the words of Ann Jefferson's highly original treatment of her critical writings contained in this volume, 'narratives of encounters' with texts. In these encounters readers are called upon to demonstrate those very qualities exemplified by Valerie in her own reading. Hence the decision to break what is otherwise a chronological ordering of the essays by starting with the three devoted to Sarraute's work, which are in their own ways homages to Sarraute and, now directly, now indirectly, to Valerie.

Monique Wittig provides a concise survey of Sarraute's massive achievement, showing how Sarraute's original and poetic use of language enables her to explore uncharted fictional territory. Sheila M. Bell illustrates Sarraute's preoccupation with narratorial voice, before engaging directly with the multiplicity of voices to be found in *Tu ne t'aimes pas* that is the principal focus of her study. Bell notes that Sarraute 'sets out to deconstruct the discourses of autobiography'. As in much of her work, Sarraute eschews the fixity of character, and liberates the virtualities of the self that have always been one of her principal artistic concerns. Bell's exploration of the clashing, sometimes tentatively self-narrating, voices of *Tu ne t'aimes pas* shows us how those virtualities find expression in Sarrautean discourse.

In *L'Ère du soupçon*, Sarraute noted with approval the 'rude coup' delivered to traditional fictional dialogue by Ivy Compton-Burnett. This reminds us of the sharp blows Sarraute herself has directed at a variety of targets, and of the creativity of her criticism. Ann Jefferson, in her contribution, establishes close links between Sarraute's criticism and her fiction: the same aesthetic impulses are at work motivated by the same aspiration for contact. Jefferson highlights the undogmatic, anti-authoritarian stance that seeks above all to retain direct contact between the reader and the text.

F. W. J. Hemmings combines scholarly theatre history and perceptive literary analysis in his review of the popular nineteenth-century practice of adapting contemporary novels for the theatre, a practice which authors found less and less resistible (of major figures, only Stendhal and Flaubert stand out). Hemmings also highlights the fact that the prevailing tastes of theatre audiences, rather than technical considerations, tend to explain the nature of the changes that occur in the novels' passage from book to stage.

There is a sense in which, without falsification of a sane historical perspective, modern art can be envisaged as having engaged in significant new directions in the 1850s. No one could deny the centrality of Flaubert in the movement to explore fresh aesthetic possibilities. As Robbe-Grillet declared: 'Dès Flaubert, tout commence à vaciller'. It is not therefore surprising that a number of contributors should have decided to offer pieces on this author. Naomi Segal looks at Baudelaire's characterization of Emma

Bovary, and studies Flaubert's authorial paternity of two of his major characters, together with the questions and issues implicit in the ambivalent relationship between author and character. Taking up the theme of gender ambiguity as it had been developed by Gautier and Baudelaire, Segal's wide-ranging study contrasts the mother/son relationship in *Le Rouge et le noir* with what she calls the 'negative procreation' of *L'Éducation sentimentale*, the two sick boys of the latter novel and the anguish experienced by their mothers being envisaged as Flaubert's self-inflicted punishment for having created such a supine and contemptible character as Frédéric. In studying Emma, Segal discusses Flaubert's use of *style indirect libre* and the heroine's relationship with her daughter to illustrate how much more complex is the author's stance when faced with the fictional body of a woman. On the other hand, Brian Nelson applies the theoretical approach of Julia Kristeva to produce an 'integrated reading' of *L'Éducation sentimentale*. He shows how the development of the Kristevan concepts of the symbolic and the semiotic enable the reader to gain access to an inner coherence that seems belied by Flaubert's deliberate undermining of the reader's desire for certainties. Finally, the starting point chosen by Éric Le Calvez is Flaubert's own claim that there existed no gratuitous descriptions in his work, since description always related to characterization and influenced the fictional action. Le Calvez exploits his close study of the manuscripts of *L'Éducation sentimentale* in order to verify Flaubert's claim and to illustrate the constant interaction between the particularization of space and psychic states. The manuscripts reveal, in an especially interesting fashion, the movement from the explicit to the implicit, from mimesis to semiosis.

Zola is treated here in Susan Harrow's detailed reading of the topos of clothes in *L'Assommoir*, a novel which has been the subject of a typically perceptive study by Valerie herself. Harrow illustrates how, in Valerie's words, 'the physical and the concrete become, in Zola's hands, rich vehicles for the moral and the psychological'.[1] Harrow shows how clothes become texts that lend themselves to interpretation by the attentive reader, as do the bodies they cover or reveal, and express the ambivalence of the authorial voice when confronted with the details of the characters' degradation.

The two contributions on Proust's *A la recherche du temps perdu* take different approaches but reveal aspects of the same polyphony in the multiple voices of the narrator. Robin MacKenzie studies a single episode, while Malcolm Bowie covers the whole work. The episode chosen by MacKenzie occurs in the early part of *La Prisonnière*, when Marcel wakes to find that his will to work has vanished with the change in the weather. The long passage which follows reveals dramatic shifts in tone and style, shifts which MacKenzie examines in order to show not only that the identity of the narrator is fragmented, but also that the narrative voice is modified as a result of the emotional impact of different modes of reminiscence. MacKenzie explores the passage in terms of the complicated interaction between memory and discourse, and as a prime example of the multiplicity of Proust's narrative voice. Bowie shows that while Proust is apparently interested in political events only in so far as they affect social relationships or his narrator's self-analysis, a closer inspection reveals that *A la recherche* is in fact shot through with political awareness and concerns, especially with respect to class relations and the socio-political complexities of aristocratic society, for example as reflected in reactions to the Dreyfus affair which represents for Proust's narrator a grand experimental laboratory. In a masterly way, Bowie explores the elaborate network of political attitudes and opinions revealed through the narrator, and shows that while the latter is able to release himself from class identities, he is also able to remain fascinatingly mobile throughout the novel, and to speak with many different, sometimes opposing voices, such that his political position is fragile, to say the least. Bowie demonstrates that when seen in this light, many of the seeming oddities of *A la recherche* begin to make sense, but also that the novel offers a pessimistic view of politics as 'an art of the impossible', leaving us 'with ample reason for despair'.

Valerie Howells, one of Valerie Minogue's former postgraduate students, shows how well she has acquired her mentor's characteristic habits, and offers a convincing demonstration of the beneficial consequences in her alert reading of one of Camus's most enigmatic and 'difficult' tales, 'Le Renégat'. Howells pays particular attention to the richness and effects of the narrative techniques, the role played by description and the interplay of time frames, in order to bring out the ironies of a tale in which a 'mute' speaks so much, and also to reveal the ways in which the text reflects the narrator's torments and Camus's own underlying (and unresolved) conflicts arising out of his inevitable involvement with the Algerian crises of the 1940s and 1950s.

In the concluding essay, Catherine Rodgers contends that Marguerite Duras's entire *œuvre* represents an eventually successful struggle to achieve a genuinely feminine form of expression, giving the lie to the Lacanian view of the feminine 'I' as an inevitable, pale reflection of its masculine counterpart. Rodgers shows that the 'I' which Duras constructs, in her series of increasingly autobiographical texts, is multiple and changing: Duras produces similar but nevertheless differing images of herself, images which resist categorization. Rodgers suggests that, in the final account, this very multiplicity of subjective positions is what constitutes Duras's rejection of the phallocratic 'I', thus characterizing a feminine way of writing.

As many of the writers dealt with in this volume have been at the heart of the literary experimentation and critical debate over the past 150 years, it is perhaps not surprising that the attention given to voice in fiction has provided insights into such a wide variety of issues – gender, politics, genre, the complexities of human personality, the nature of criticism – issues which Valerie herself has so incisively addressed in her own writing. Although this collection of essays does not do justice to the full range of her literary interests, in presenting this volume to her, the editors and contributors trust that she will recognize in it and through it the profound intellectual respect she has so deservedly earned as a critic and scholar of great distinction, and the personal affection she has inspired.

Note

[1] Valerie Minogue, *Zola: 'L'Assommoir'* (London: Grant & Cutler, 1991), 96.

Comme il est difficile de parler de ce qui vous tient au cœur et pourtant comme je suis contente d'avoir cette occasion de dire combien a compté pour moi tout ce que m'a apporté Valerie Minogue, son constant et généreux soutien depuis tant d'années, sa très grande, toujours pénétrante et délicate attention à mon travail.
 Les liens déjà forts ont été encore renforcés par ceux de l'amitié et de l'affection. Mes séjours chez elle, dans son beau pays, dans sa lumineuse et accueillante maison sont des souvenirs auxquels j'aime retourner. A tant de douceur s'ajoute la présence tout près, dans la maison voisine, de sa délicieuse maman, à mes yeux une vraie maman de conte anglais.
 Peut-être que la réserve, la grande modestie de Valerie pourraient s'offusquer de ces 'épanchements', n'est-elle pas d'un pays où l'on préfère les 'understatements'? Qu'elle se rassure, moi aussi je les aime, et c'est vraiment un 'understatement', tout ce que je dis là.

              Nathalie Sarraute

L'Ordre du Poème*

MONIQUE WITTIG

> Un cheval haut comme une montagne, de Pallas le divin artifice, / [ils] édifient, et de troncs de sapin lui façonnent les côtes [...] [Parmi les Troyens] les uns s'étonnent de l'offrande sinistre à la vierge Minerve, / et du Cheval ils admirent la masse [...] [Quelqu'un] nous exhorte de le conduire dans nos murs et de le loger dans la citadelle / [...] il faut amener le simulacre dans le temple. / A grands cris tous le réclament. / Nous abattons nos murs, nous pratiquons une brèche dans les remparts de la ville. / Tous de se mettre à l'œuvre et aux pieds du Cheval, pourvu de roues, assurent le glissement, et des cordes de chanvre à l'encolure / ils tendent; elle monte vers nos maisons la fatale machine [...][1]

Quoi, est-ce une machine de guerre?

Toute œuvre de forme nouvelle fonctionne comme une machine de guerre. Son sens est de démolir les formes vieillies, les règles et les conventions. Tout travail littéraire important est au moment de sa production comme un Cheval de Troie. Toujours il s'effectue en territoire hostile dans lequel il apparaît étrange, inassimilable, non conforme. Puis sa force (sa polysémie) et la beauté de ses formes l'emportent. La cité fait place à la machine dans ses murs. Il faut qu'elle soit adoptée pour accomplir son travail de minage et de sape des conventions littéraires et sociales et les dévoiler comme périmées, incapables d'opérer des transformations. Telle est l'œuvre de Sarraute auprès de laquelle je ne nommerai aucune autre.

> Il est impossible qu'ils ne le voient pas. C'est là, surgi du néant. Cela se dresse, se déploie avec assurance, avec une audace tranquille.
> Au centre de cela il y a quelque chose d'indestructible. Un noyau qu'il n'est pas possible de désintégrer, vers lequel toutes les particules convergent, autour duquel elles gravitent à une vitesse si énorme qu'elle donne à l'ensemble l'apparence de l'immobilité. Autour de cela des ondes

se répandent, tout oscille, tout vibre autour, si on s'en approche on se met à vibrer...

Il y a dans la façon dont cela a poussé une violence contenue, une agressivité toujours maîtrisée qui lui a permis de mordre sur la grisaille ambiante.

C'est là. On ne sait pas ce que c'est... Est-ce beau ou laid, on n'en sait rien ... Une merveille? Un monstre? Peu importe... [...] Leurs regards passent et repassent distraitement sans le voir.[2]

Le texte sarrautien, on le voit (typographiquement, grammaticalement, syntaxiquement), est scindé, éclaté, bourré de points, de tirets, de guillemets, coupé en anneaux vivants qui glissent, ou encore multiplié à l'infini, comme un ciel brillant d'été avec ses constellations et ses étoiles isolées. Ou plus proche, un planétarium.

C'est le texte qui, quand il touche le lecteur, lui fait prendre connaissance, comme celui de Rimbaud ou d'autres poètes, de ce que c'est que le choc des mots. Il s'agit ici d'un choc à la fois physique et abstrait, introduisant brutalement à ce que Sarraute appelle « un univers sensible d'ordre intellectuel ». Quand je parle de ce contact violent avec le texte, on s'y trouve dedans au plus extrême de ce que Barthes a appelé le « plaisir du texte ».[3] C'est une sorte d'éblouissement comme quand on perd la vue et l'ouïe dans l'acte carnal. Dans cet éblouissement, ce corps à corps du lecteur avec le texte, il y a quelque chose du désir d'écrire qui se manifeste. En parlant ainsi, je parle du point de vue du lecteur, c'est-à-dire de l'effet du texte. Du point de vue de l'écrivain, il n'y a qu'une loi, celle de Flaubert, rappelée dans *L'Ère du soupçon* : « découvrir de la nouveauté ».[4]

La plupart des innovations littéraires ont à voir avec des formes nouvelles et en ce qui concerne le roman visent à produire des structures inconnues jusqu'alors. Elles touchent des modifications de surface et d'apparence, ce qui est déjà énorme. Mais dans le cas de Sarraute la nouveauté des formes est le résultat d'une révolution beaucoup plus radicale qui est la transformation de la matière romanesque elle-même. C'est-à-dire que c'est en ce qui concerne la matière du roman et sa substance (et non pas seulement sa forme) que Sarraute inaugure dans l'histoire littéraire une perspective nouvelle. Elle opère un déplacement à la fois dans la manière de travailler un texte et un déplacement de la relation de la littérature au réel. Cette révolution a été préparée mais non pas complètement accomplie par Proust. Car ces « actions » de la conscience, nouvelles et inconnues pour l'art du roman, « il les a considérées comme un enchaînement d'effets et de causes qu'il s'est efforcé d'expliquer » (*ES*, p. 98). Il leur a donné « une grande distance », il les a « figées », au lieu de faire « ce qui a toujours été et ce qui est encore le propre de toute œuvre romanesque » (*ES*, p. 98), il a fait accomplir au lecteur lui-même ces actions : « Des drames intérieurs faits d'attaques, de triomphes, de reculs, de défaites, de caresses, de morsures, de viols, de meurtres, d'abandons généreux ou d'humbles soumissions » (*ES*, p. 99). Ces « actions souterraines », qui « se révèlent brusquement au dehors dans une parole en apparence insignifiante, dans une simple intonation ou un regard » (*ES*, p. 97), Proust en a manqué l'aventure, sinon pour lui, pour le lecteur.

Quant au monologue intérieur, il n'est pas une technique étrangère à Sarraute (mais dans une autre organisation), puisqu'on a pu parler en ce qui la concerne de « dialogues intérieurs ». Ce qui l'intéresse dans le monologue intérieur, c'est sa composition avant qu'il soit formalisé, sa teneur. Et je cite « Conversation et sous-conversation », comme dans mes citations précédentes concernant Proust, « ce qui se dissimule derrière le monologue intérieur », c'est

> un foisonnement innombrable de sensations, d'images, de sentiments, de souvenirs, d'impulsions, de petits actes larvés qu'aucun langage intérieur n'exprime, qui se bousculent aux portes de la conscience, s'assemblent en groupes compacts et surgissent tout à coup, se défont aussitôt, se combinent autrement et réapparaissent sous une autre forme, tandis que continue à se dérouler en nous pareil au ruban qui s'échappe en crépitant de la fente d'un téléscripteur le flot ininterrompu de mots. (*ES*, pp. 96–97)

Pour cette masse d'événements qui se bousculent à la porte de la conscience avant que le langage ait eu le temps de leur donner forme, Sarraute a adopté l'appellation de « tropismes ».

Avec les tropismes on se trouve dans un art poétique du roman, c'est pourquoi il est si difficile de les comprendre et d'en parler. Il faut les prendre à la fois du côté du poème et du côté du mental. Et quand je dis à la fois, je veux dire qu'ils sont indissociables en même temps du mental auquel ils appartiennent et du poème qu'ils forment. Cette opération simultanée rend compte de la révolution littéraire qui est du fait de Sarraute et exclusivement de son fait.

« Le gant retourné », cette expression heureuse dont s'est servie Sarraute pour parler de ses pièces,[5] peut décrire aussi la geste sarrautienne, le bouleversement de la relation écrivain/réalité. Il n'y a plus dans les romans de Sarraute mimesis ou prétendue représentation d'un réel physique ou sociologique — fussent-ils imaginaires ou métaphoriques. Tout ce qui en est connu nous est rendu en quelque sorte par le dedans, par le creuset de la conscience où advient le langage.

La plupart des écrivains partent du plus simple et se dirigent vers le plus complexe, y compris s'il s'agit de formes rhétoriques. Pour Sarraute tout se passe à l'envers, à rebours, puisqu'elle part d'un texte social déjà élaboré, de plusieurs formes de discours, que ce soit des métaphores, des morceaux d'intrigues connus provenant de films, romans, pièces de théâtre connus et classiques, de lieux communs, de récits, de contes de fée, de proverbes, de dictons, d'idées reçues, pour transporter le lecteur au lieu où le langage s'agite, se fait violence, non encore dégangué de ses attaches avec la conscience, comme un marron encore poisseux. On avance de l'ordre vers le désordre, de la mort vers la vie. On dépasse le sens figuré, on va au-delà du littéral, car tous deux sont également conventionnels et rigides. On va au lieu où mots et sensations de mots ne sont pas séparables (et entre parenthèses on est renvoyé à ce qui fait la nature du langage, un corps hétérogène, à la fois abstrait et concret, matériel et symbolique, réel et irréel).

La geste sarrautienne met en scène tout ce qui se passe avec, autour du langage : « Mes véritables personnages, mes seuls personnages, ce sont les mots », phrase extraite d'une interview avec la *Quinzaine littéraire*. Et dans *Entre la vie et la mort* ces deux extraits :

> Plus de Ballut, Chenut, Dulud, Tarral, Magnien ou autres. On s'en passera. Plus besoin de personne. Les mots seuls. Des mots surgis de n'importe où, poussières flottant dans l'air que nous respirons [...] Des mots que des inconnus ont échangés à une table de restaurant voisine, marchant devant vous dans la rue ou dans une allée de jardin, assis près de vous dans l'autobus, et que vous avez absorbés, parfois sans même vous en rendre compte. (*EVM*, p. 56)

> Les mots sont ses souverains. Leur humble sujet se sent trop honoré de leur céder sa maison. Qu'ils soient chez eux, tout est à eux ici, ils sont les seuls maîtres... (*EVM*, pp. 70–71)

Sarraute est le premier écrivain, unique dans son genre, à être écrit tout du côté du langage. Partout le référent qu'on cherche dans la vie est ici dans la vie du langage et dans ces situations de mot, qui tout à coup en lisant Sarraute, nous deviennent si familières qu'on ne sait plus si elles ont toujours existé à notre insu, ou si c'est Sarraute qui les a inventées. On a tout d'un Monsieur Jourdain quand il découvre que ce qu'il parle c'est de la prose et qu'il s'émerveille et trouve ça beau. C'est-à-dire que tout à coup, en Sarraute, on s'aperçoit qu'on vit en langage, sans cesse, sans un instant de repos, nuit et jour, quand on dort et quand on veille. Toutes les situations pratiques qu'on connaît, ce qu'on appelle la vie, la mort, ce qui appartient à la tragédie, à la comédie, aussi bien qu'aux situations les plus banales, sont vécues dans le langage ou plutôt en langage.

Chez Sarraute, tous ces morceaux rapportés, toutes ces pièces qui sont semblables aux bâtis du narrateur de Proust cousus feuille à feuille par Françoise, la cuisinière, mettent en présence, comme je l'ai déjà fait remarquer, des fragments de discours les plus divers, relevant d'instances connues des romans et des pièces classiques (de ceux que Sarraute appelle les Anciens par opposition aux Modernes), fragments de conversation réelle ou imaginaire, fragments de mots, onomatopées, mentions de soupirs et de sons (scories du langage formalisé), mentions de gestes. C'est dans ces gisements qu'on trouve les formes romanesques nouvelles, les dialogues, les drames, les sautes de temps. Et aussi des personnages qui apparaissent et qui disparaissent comme vus d'un train.

A leur tour ces formes nous permettent d'aller vers les tropismes, vers des gisements plus souterrains. Je dirais que Sarraute est le premier écrivain abstrait, comme on dit un peintre abstrait, pour qui la pâte et la couleur seules comptent. La pâte et la couleur de Sarraute, c'est le matériau langage. Comme on peut le dire d'un peintre abstrait, Sarraute ne détruit pas la forme pour aller vers l'informe. Car ce que Sarraute appelle « l'innommé » a besoin de formes très précises pour apparaître en littérature.

C'est un art poétique du roman que Sarraute élabore du côté des tropismes, dans une sorte de métaphore à l'envers, en ce qu'ils nous transportent dans un texte où les mots travaillés, devenus ce que Sarraute après Mallarmé appelle « essentiels », émergent des tropismes, tiennent encore aux tropismes, y tiennent par un bout et, tels quels, partagent des deux versants de la littérature, celui de l'avant du travail et celui de l'après. De sorte qu'on ne peut plus faire de distinction entre le poème et le roman. Ce transport poétique est le résultat d'une conjonction sans cesse menacée. Et je cite « Ce que je cherche à faire » :

Entre le non nommé et le langage qui n'est qu'un système de conventions extrêmement simplifié, un code grossièrement établi pour la commodité de la communication, il faudra qu'une fusion se fasse pour que, patinant l'un contre l'autre, se confondant et s'étreignant dans une union toujours menacée, ils produisent un texte.[6]

Ou peut-être il s'agit d'un transport poétique double, simultané, car à fleur de texte, vivent encore dans le produit fini, les « mouvance[s], virtualités, [les] sensations vagues et globales, [...] ce non nommé qui oppose aux mots une résistance et qui pourtant les appelle, car il ne peut exister sans eux ».[7]

Notes

* Ce texte a déjà paru dans S. Raffy (éd.), *Autour de Nathalie Sarraute* (Besançon: Annales Littéraires de l'Université de Besançon, 1995), 31–36.

[1] Virgile, *L'Énéide*, tr. Pierre Klossowski (Paris: Gallimard, 1990).

[2] Nathalie Sarraute, *Entre la vie et la mort* (Paris: Gallimard [Livre de poche], 1968), 95–96.

[3] Roland Barthes, *Le Plaisir du texte* (Paris: Seuil, 1976).

[4] Nathalie Sarraute, *L'Ère du soupçon* (Paris: Gallimard, 1956), 77. Les références à ce texte renvoient à cette édition.

[5] « Le Gant retourné », *Cahiers Renaud-Barrault*, 89 (1975), 70–79.

[6] Nathalie Sarraute, « Ce que je cherche à faire » in *Nouveau Roman: Hier, aujourd'hui*, II, *Pratiques* (Paris: UGU, 1972), 32–33.

[7] « Ce que je cherche à faire », 32.

Orchestrated Voices: Selves and Others in Nathalie Sarraute's *Tu ne t'aimes pas*

SHEILA M. BELL

> maintenant qu'on est entre nous, ici, dans notre for intérieur (*Tu ne t'aimes pas*)

If *Tropismes* on its publication in 1939 provoked little in the way of reaction, one response at least was appropriate: a letter from Max Jacob saluting its author as 'un profond poète'.[1] Nathalie Sarraute's œuvre has both the particularity of vision and the density of language which characterize poetry. Each new work takes us further into her chosen domain and the exploration of subject matter is inseparable from an exploration of the resources of language. The world she explores is that of the 'for intérieur'. This, she maintains, is what set her apart from the other *nouveaux romanciers* of the 1950s.[2] The critical essays, published between 1947 and 1956 and collected under the title *L'Ère du soupçon*, sought to defend this inner world in a context in which it had become unfashionable: 'Le "for intérieur", "l'ineffable intimité avec soi" n'avait été qu'un miroir à alouettes. "Le psychologique", source de tant de déceptions et de peines, n'existait pas'.[3] At the same time, Sarraute set forth her distinct understanding of 'cette immense masse mouvante qu'on nomme notre "for intérieur"'[4] and the means by which it can be rendered in fiction. *Tu ne t'aimes pas* tackles this subject more directly than ever before by placing the reader within the 'for intérieur' and making him experience it as 'une énorme masse mouvante... où il y a de tout... où tant de choses dissemblables s'entrechoquent, se détruisent'.[5] Speaking with Claude Régy of the theme of *Tu ne t'aimes pas*, 'cette immensité des moi, cette diversité des moi, qui ne sont même plus des moi', Nathalie Sarraute agrees with his suggestion that it is perhaps the dominant theme of her work: 'Finalement je crois que c'est ce qui m'a toujours préoccupée'.[6]

As well as identifying Nathalie Sarraute's particular subject matter, the essays *of L'Ère du soupçon* reflect her engagement with issues of form over a number of years, and one of the major questions they address is that of voice. If, for whatever reason, the writer and reader of novels is no longer receptive to the phrase 'la marquise sortit à cinq heures', it is the novel's traditional narrative form as much as its content which has become outmoded and lacking in life. In the essay of 1950, and for her first two novels published in 1948 and 1953, the first-person mode is to be the solution. Examples abound of novels ('depuis *A la recherche du temps perdu* et *Paludes* jusqu'au *Miracle de la rose*, en passant par *Les Cahiers de Malte Laurids Brigge*, *Le Voyage au bout de la nuit* et *La Nausée*')[7] which derive their substance from the author's inner life and which choose as their central focus 'un je anonyme' who in some way or other acts as the author's spokesman or reflection. The narrator of *Portrait* – Sarraute prefers the description 'celui qui cherche les tropismes'[8] – undoubtedly acts in some measure as spokesman for his creator. He may none the less represent an obstacle, standing between his subject matter and the reader's awareness of it. As mediator of tropisms, he is nearest to success when he is at his most transparent. In *Martereau*, Sarraute went some way towards solving the problem of the narrator as obstacle by making him an active participant in the tropismic dramas of the family. It is *Le Planétarium*, however, which represented a turning-point, as Valerie Minogue argued in an important early study of Sarraute's fiction.[9] Sarraute subjects the figure of the narrator to critical scrutiny, at the same time as she takes leave of him. Alain Guimiez (or Guimier, as in later editions of the novel) has much in common with the first-person narrators of *Portrait* and *Martereau*. However, his role is that of a 'displaced narrator'; he has given up any special status and become 'just another narrator among others, one whose self-projections will have no more and no less validity than all the others'.[10] According to Nathalie Sarraute, the device in the first two novels of 'une conscience qui cherchait' was a product of her initial lack of confidence in her readers' ability to understand.[11] With not only character and plot but also the narrator figure submitted to critical scrutiny, she was ready for the major new departure represented by *Les Fruits d'or*.[12] There, in the absence of a narratorial figure, a series of anonymous minds enter into dialogue with one another (concerning 'Les Fruits d'or') and, more rarely, with the novel itself. This was the technique which had been evoked in the well-known passage from the essay of 1956, 'Conversation et sous-conversation':

> Il est donc permis de rêver – sans se dissimuler tout ce qui sépare ce rêve de sa réalisation – d'une technique qui parviendrait à plonger le lecteur dans le flot de ces drames souterrains que Proust n'a eu le temps que de survoler et dont il n'a observé et reproduit que les grandes lignes immobiles: une technique qui donnerait au lecteur l'illusion de refaire lui-même ces actions avec une conscience plus lucide, avec plus d'ordre, de netteté et de force qu'il ne peut le faire dans la vie, sans qu'elles perdent cette part d'indétermination, cette opacité et ce mystère qu'ont toujours ses actions pour celui qui les vit.[13]

In the novels after *Les Fruits d'or*, one voice in particular may dominate – that of the writer(s) in *Entre la vie et la mort* or the father in *Vous les entendez?* – but the privileged narrative voices of *Portrait* and *Martereau* continue to be absent. Isolated fragments of what might be identified as third-person narrative persist but are hardly detectable among the discourses which compete for the reader's attention. Thus, one may argue, authorial voice does succeed in giving way to the voices that speak to one another in the text. It remains true of course that authorial presence makes itself felt by stylistic means (for example, by irony and the absence of irony), or is heard at points through comments made by the anonymous voices on the subject matter of the text.[14]

If the narratorial voice is written out, or at least goes underground, in the fictional texts of the 1960s and 1970s, it resurfaces dramatically in the works of the 1980s, in what might be called the third period of Sarraute's creative endeavour. In *L'Usage de la parole*, a narrator, reminiscent of the narrative personae of eighteenth-century fiction, addresses the reader directly and acts as master of ceremonies. Nathalie Sarraute comments: 'Dans *L'Usage de la parole*, comme pour une opération chimique, je m'efforce de réunir les conditions dans lesquelles le texte va fonctionner. Je montre au lecteur à quoi on va jouer, je lui donne les règles du jeu'.[15] The narrator, then, who is explicitly identified as a writer here ('Et voilà que ces mots prononcés sur ce lit [...] viennent... poussés par quel vent... se poser ici, une petite braise qui noircit, brûle la page blanche...'),[16] represents Sarraute as director of operations within the text and we, as real readers, are placed in the position of the narratee. Another dialogue – this time between two narrating voices – plays a crucial role in structuring the 'souvenirs d'enfance' of *Enfance*.[17] The device develops out of the relationship between the writer and his double in *Entre la vie et la mort* and at first seems to reproduce that relationship. The first narrator[18] initiates the process of remembering and recording. The second narrator appears to stand aside from the project; a critical alter ego, grammatically masculine as commentators have noted (like the writer and his double in *Entre la vie et la mort* and the narrator of *L'Usage de la parole*), he queries the validity of such a venture. In fact, as the venture gets under way, this secondary voice is encouraging as well as critical, and even contributes in an active way. Moreover, though the principal narrator appears as feminine later in the text (as the adult version of the child: 'Je me suis longuement contentée, quand il m'arrivait plus tard de repenser à cet instant...'),[19] in the initial discussion (s)he is neutral and joins forces with the grammatically masculine voice in a collective 'nous': 'Ce qui nous est resté des anciennes tentatives nous paraît toujours avoir l'avantage sur ce qui tremblote quelque part dans les limbes...'.[20] The two figures together are to represent the writer at work in this text; their dialogue provides the text with a structure which links the fragments without imposing a continuous narrative and, above all perhaps, gives it a certain rhythm, making possible the stressing of particular episodes, or particular pieces of information, by more insistent interventions – the text concerning 'femme et mari sont un même parti',[21] for example, or the precision of age and date when the separation from the mother took place: 'Huit ans et demi exactement, c'était en février 1909'.[22] Thus the processes of memory and the attempt at retrospective understanding are dramatized for us, and both past experience and present endeavour are enacted in the text. In *Tu ne t'aimes pas*, a similar orchestration of plural voices will once again be central.

The Plural Self

Tu ne t'aimes pas once more has the label *roman* on the cover of the Collection Blanche edition – the covers of both *L'Usage de la parole* and *Enfance* are free of any suggestion as to genre affiliation – and it may be seen as taking up again and pursuing further one of the main themes of the novel, *"disent les imbéciles"*, which precedes it: 'que chacun de nous est à lui seul l'univers entier, qu'il se sent infini, sans contours'.[23] In the opening section of *Tu ne t'aimes pas*, the theme is presented to us in inverted commas, an imagined response to an interlocutor for whom 'deux êtres contradictoires' are already too much to encompass: ' "je suis l'univers entier, toutes les virtualités, tous les possibles... l'œil ne perçoit pas, ça s'étend à l'infini..." ' (pp. 17–18).[24] The inverted commas also suggest self-quotation and a statement which is here to be unpacked in characteristic Sarrautean fashion. *Tu ne t'aimes pas* places us firmly within one self, 'maintenant qu'on est entre nous, ici, dans notre for intérieur' (p. 11), and seeks to convey to us the sense of its plurality of being: 'Nous si nombreux... incernables... incommensurables...' (p. 29). The images or descriptions of the self, which the novel offers us, stress its plural, diverse, constantly shifting nature. Above all, the sense of the self as multifarious and constantly in motion is conveyed in *Tu ne t'aimes pas* by the use of voice.

The self speaks itself and in place of the two relatively distinct narrators of *Enfance*, we have here a medley of voices. In speaking of the 'self' and 'it', we come up against the problems caused by paraphrase and, indeed, by the shift from French to English. The French expression *le moi* – 'ce "moi", [...] ce qu'on nomme ainsi' (p. 12) – raises the issue of pronoun, which is sidestepped by the English term 'self'. Furthermore, to speak of 'the self' and of 'it' is to make an assumption about number, if not gender. How can the shifting, multifarious self express itself though pronouns, given the assumptions which already attach to their use? The problem was already formulated in *"disent les imbéciles"*, where pronouns were seen as suggestive of a *personnage* who might endanger the free movement of the idea:

> Voyons un peu ce qu'il nous montre... – Oh non, ne dites pas cela: pas "il"... qui "il"?... c'est un espace sans limites qu'aucun "il" ne peut contenir... – Ah bon, donc "nous montre" ou plutôt "montre"... Pas à "nous" non plus, sans doute?... – Non, il ne faut pas de "nous"... ce sont des espaces infinis... sans contours...[25]

In *Tu ne t'aimes pas*, the text immediately raises these problems of nomenclature in a series of exchanges. In the opening phrase, "Vous ne vous aimez pas" (pronounced by another but quoted by the self), the content of the 'vous' is queried: 'Qui n'aime pas qui?' The plural was not a real one but only the polite form. Thus the remark was addressed to a particular incarnation of the self – 'Toi, bien sûr' – but the self is in fact plural: 'A moi? Moi seul? Pas à vous tous qui êtes moi... et nous sommes un si grand nombre...'. On first mention, the pronoun 'je' is put in inverted commas – 'tu as dit "je"' – to suggest its quality as label: 'Chaque fois que l'un de nous se montre au-dehors, il se désigne par "je", par "moi"... comme s'il était seul, comme si vous n'existiez pas...' (pp. 9–10). The 'je' is a representative, an ambassador, a 'délégué', sent out by the self to engage with the other. By definition, this 'je' is singular and an impoverishment, compared to the plural nature of the self. The self can thus be perceived as 'une multitude de "je" disparates' (p. 86), all of whom can be called on to negotiate with the outside world, any of whom may indeed rush into action without consulting the others. At first, the 'je' and the 'tu' are also used without inverted commas in exchanges between different tendencies of the self, but later the practice ceases: 'nous ici, entre nous, ces "moi", ces "je", nous ne les employons pas...' (p. 86). The 'pas' is corrected to 'plus'; gradually, a voice states, the use of 'tu' and 'je' within the self has stopped and 'nous' and 'vous' have taken their place:

> Comme des bancs de poissons de même espèce, des vols d'oiseaux qui se déplacent d'un même mouvement, des groupements dont les membres ont les mêmes tendances... Leur appliquer un "tu", un "je"... non, nous ne le pouvions plus... il fallait un "nous", un "vous" (p. 87).

The 'nous' has to become 'je' in order to enter into contact with others – 'Il le faut bien, sinon comment arriveraient-ils à se faire entendre?' (p. 87) – but within the self, the "je" is a travesty. The 'nous' who speak in the text are themselves plural and represent particular groupings, more or less sizeable: 'Pas nous tous [...] Ce n'est pas à nous tous que ce "nous" s'applique... Nous ne sommes jamais au grand complet...'. Any given 'nous' will refer to 'ceux qui étaient là'. There are always some tendencies of the self which are absent for whatever reason, 'qui sommeillent, paressent, se distraient, s'écartent...' (p. 10). The variety of possible motives reinforces the sense of unpredictability: these other selves may intervene at any point to disrupt a pattern apparently firmly established by the majority of the 'nous'. One may argue that there is also a 'nous totalisateur'[26] in the text, who speaks for the collective self, but no specific characteristics can be attributed to it (except perhaps the awareness that it lacks any). Thus the play of pronouns too is made to undermine any notion of a fixed identity and to create an impression of movement, of constant flux. Here, one might argue, Sarraute pushes one stage further her resistance to naming.[27] Pingaud's statement: ' "Je" n'est jamais un personnage, "il" l'est toujours',[28] no longer applies and Benveniste's categories, whereby the 'je' and the 'tu' are the only truly personal pronouns,[29] are given an ironic twist.

Thus it is through dialogue that the plural self is enacted for us. The text is presented very consciously as dialogue, a series of utterances, relatively brief for the most part, each punctuated with a dash and separated by a blank line from the following one, giving the impression at once of a series of voices. Voices, speaking for different representatives or groupings of the self, question one another, agree or disagree, explain, remonstrate, criticize, justify themselves.[30] The effect is to convey a sense of the mobility of the self ('Chez nous aussitôt on s'agite...', p. 141), and the rhythms of the dialogue further this aim. The connections between one utterance and the next are always close, and short interventions contribute to the sense of pace. Even where there is no disagreement or change of pronoun to indicate a change of voice, the impression of dialogue is maintained (a series of like-minded 'nous' passing the baton?). In the context of such a dialogue, in which the speakers are long familiar with their interlocutors and quickly sensitive to differing moods and points of view, it is not surprising that attempts at self-definition are gently mocked:

– Tu as eu le front de dire: "Moi, vous savez, je suis plutôt d'une nature insouciante..." Alors quel déchaînement...

– Tous les porteurs d'angoisse assoupis, ceux pour qui nous absorbons des calmants, se sont dressés... leurs chuchotements partaient de toutes parts... insouciante? tu as dit insouciante? Quand par moments des raz de marée d'angoisse déferlent sur nous, nous roulons suffoqués... (p. 37).

If the will to know and to understand temporarily creates a collective self, the old disarray finally resurfaces: 'Une même curiosité, un même effort nous avait unis, nous l'avions oublié, et ça revient aussi fort qu'avant, les tiraillements entre nous, les reproches, les rancunes...' (p. 208). This, then, is the way the self functions, experienced from within.

Rival Voices

The self, however plural, does not monopolize the dialogue to the exclusion of all other speech. As always in Sarraute, the self is perceived as living not in a vacuum but in relation to others. Within the dialogue of the self (or selves) are to be heard the voices of others and through them is articulated an alternative way of experiencing and speaking the self. An encounter between self and other is, as we have seen, the text's point of departure. The encounter takes the form of a critical (or pitying or reproachful) remark: the phrase 'Vous ne vous aimez pas', which has been addressed by an outside speaker to the self and is now internalized and explored by the self.[31] At once the gulf between the language of the other and that of the self is underlined: the 'vous' means different things, singular for the other, plural for the self. But there is more to the phrase than this. Its power to generate the text of the fiction derives from a further meaning discovered in it by the plural voices of the self. It does apply in a significant way to the self as a whole: 'Et cette masse, comment peut-elle s'aimer? ni d'ailleurs se détester?... C'est vraiment difficile à comprendre' (p. 13). In contrast, 'others' – those who operate in the social world outside – become 'ceux qui s'aiment'. It is not a question of a particular psychological trait, bearing the label 'la satisfaction de soi'; this 'poupée de cire peinte' ('Rose et rond. Joufflu et comme tout gonflé...', p. 19) is set aside at the outset. What is at issue is something more radical. The self-love of the other is linked to a view of the self as character, a belief in subject identity. Others, unlike the self, claim to know who they are: 'ils savent qui ils sont' (p. 95). They may in fact be constituted in the same way as the self: 'Ils sont pourtant comme nous, chacun d'eux...' (p. 30). Such is not, however, what they appear to believe or the impression they create. It is as if they are able to view themselves from outside: 'Celui qui s'aime se scinde en deux... projette au-dehors son double... le place à une certaine distance de lui-même...' (p. 138). Thus their way of speaking about themselves has a particular ring of self-regard, of self-confident assertion. In contrast, therefore, to the self, 'un espace ouvert de tous côtés' (p. 26), the other is perceived as 'cet ensemble compact' (p. 14), 'un tout très compact et uni' (p. 17) or even, in his most impressive form, 'Un énorme bloc d'un seul tenant' (p. 181). To pursue another of the text's metaphors, the other is ruled by a strong central government, whereas the self, while it attempts to gather its various tendencies together in committees, and sends out ambassadors to speak for it, is basically anarchic and has great difficulty in operating as a united force for any length of time.

Selves and others are seen in opposition to each other: within the self, we are 'ici parmi nous', 'entre nous, ici'; the other is to be found 'chez eux', 'là-bas', 'au-dehors'. Both, however, are to be explored in terms of this opposition. The novel continues, as it began, as a series of encounters between self and other, provoked by the utterances of the other and prolonged by the efforts of groupings of the self: 'vous qui arrivez parfois à si bien vous transporter "chez les autres" '(p. 84). In a rare case, that designated by the unsatisfactory label of "amour partagé", the other is not perceived as different, but as coextensive with the self: 'Comme si nous étions seuls entre nous... comme s'il n'y avait ici avec nous personne d'autre...' (p. 122). Difference can only be measured after loss and then in terms of an enhanced self that was and is no longer: 'On dirait que notre immense masse mouvante s'était encore accrue... était plus dense, plus vibrante... elle s'épandait, elle couvrait de plus vastes espaces, elle les enserrait de plus près, elle adhérait à eux avec plus de force...' (p. 122). In such a case, then, the social dimension is transcended and the life of the self is enhanced. At the opposite end of the spectrum of human contact, encounters with complete strangers constitute light relief after the demands made on the self by a month spent in the company of 'une de ces personnalités conquérantes' (p. 71): the people on the train are perceived as 'des gens libres, des gens dignes, des gens comme nous, comme aussitôt nous redevenons... Entre eux et nous les paroles volettent, nous effleurent...' (p. 77). In most cases, however, the other is perceived as separate, different, even threatening.

To convey the sense that the other is indeed other and a social being, the encounters often take place in some kind of minimal setting (as in *L'Usage de la parole*): 'cette promenade à la campagne' (p. 76); 'sur une terrasse, entourés de gens' (p. 80); 'quelques personnes assises en cercle, en train de parler... [...] une réunion d'amis' (p. 104). For the same reason, the other may be perceived as a physical presence (only briefly, and in no way particularized, lest we be distracted into focusing on what is ancillary). In one case, we are told, 'celui qui s'aime s'affale sur son siège, l'air hébété... [...] il s'éponge le front...' (p. 46); in another: 'Il s'étire, il redresse la tête, le dos, il fait craquer ses doigts...' (p. 142). It is significant that the first example of a self-regarding other to be evoked in detail is perceived in loving contemplation of his hand. This physical presence supports our sense that 'ceux qui s'aiment' belong in every way 'au-dehors'. It is the sign of what is their distinguishing characteristic, their ability to identify with the way others see them: 'ce pli de se sentir tel qu'on les voit' (p. 31).[32] The selves, on the other hand, are described in movement ('vous vous élancez, nous vous retenons, nous nous accrochons à vous...', p. 82) but are otherwise disembodied: 'Si nous avions des corps, des visages, on pourrait nous voir en foule nous bousculant, nous serrant les uns contre les autres' (p. 108). The selves only assume physical properties when they venture outside themselves and engage with the other; then they may have a face, a shoulder or even 'le torse bombé' (p. 208). The sudden and dramatic assumption of a physical exterior marks the point at which that other, who is normally coextensive with the self, becomes a stranger: 'Le voici qui se renverse dans son fauteuil, croise les jambes, balance son pied avec assurance et lance ces mots dont ils se servent...' (p. 125).

As a category, 'ceux qui s'aiment' are always 'ils', but they are also singular beings, each embodying in a different way essential characteristics of the phenomenon, and as such they are referred to as 'il' and 'elle'. Gender is, however, played down: in a number of cases – though not all – the 'elle' derives from a grammatically feminine noun.[33] There is at least one occasion where the text appears to play with the reader's expectations in these matters: 'une présence... / – Mais comme à l'écart... très effacée...' (p. 97; feminine?) becomes on next mention 'cette présence effacée... mais stimulante... un témoin' (p. 99; masculine?). Even if the 'elle' comes without an alibi and is there simply for the sake of variety or as a convenient and minimally 'characterizing' way to distinguish between speakers, the presence of such devices tends to discourage the reader from attaching too much significance to the gender of the pronoun. However the other may see himself as particular, he is not of interest to us in his particularity, but as an example of a general phenomenon, a mode of being, a way of experiencing selfhood.

This mode of being is revealed above all in discourse. Others have, according to the narrating selves, 'une façon de parler qu'on reconnaît aussitôt' (p. 86). One distinguishing feature of this discourse is the use that is made of pronouns. The other speaks in a singular voice, using 'je' and 'moi' with all the confidence the self lacks. "J'ai été froissé. Il m'a blessé. Ça m'a été désagréable" (p. 87): the communication is rephrased by the self to bring out the importance of the pronouns. The same emphasis is to be found when the other explains how he would react: "Si c'était moi, voilà ce que je ferais..." (p. 141); "Ce qu'il y a de certain, c'est que si c'était moi..." (p. 142). According to the self, 'nous ici, entre nous, ces "moi", ces "je", nous ne les employons pas...' (p. 86), but others, unlike the self, know who they are and appear to boast of that knowledge by frequent use of the first person singular. When the self sets out to think itself into their way of seeing, its first move is to adopt the first person singular: 'Je suis "un" au-dedans de moi-même. [...] Il suffit de m'écarter un peu... je me regarde: me voici' (p. 59). Thus it is confirmed that the singular pronouns are to be aligned with proper names and belong properly in the sphere of social intercourse.[34]

The other, who speaks as "je", speaks in a discourse which is immediately familiar, made up of banal phrases and commonplaces: "Vingt ans de bonheur... Eh oui... j'ai eu ça..." (p. 47); "Moi, vous savez, je suis soupe au lait" (p. 88); "un amour partagé" (p. 121); "Oh moi, vous savez, ces choses-là... ça me dépasse..." (p. 146); "Non. Ce n'est pas bien" (p. 168). Thus he makes himself recognizable both to others and to himself.[35] Such remarks, and the exchanges between self and other, are identified as *other* by the use of inverted commas. At the same time, both are firmly contained within an utterance of the self and accompanied by a reaction: '"Vingt ans de bonheur... Eh oui... j'ai eu ça..." une pierre précieuse qu'ils sortent de leur coffret à bijoux et nous font admirer... "Vingt ans de bonheur"...' (p. 47). Do we have then an invasion of self by other, the commonplace penetrating within the citadel of the self: 'la présence de tout le monde en moi'?[36] In a number of ways, it is suggested that the self feels pressurized, invaded, out-manœuvred by the other. One of the characteristics of the self is its vulnerability, its lack of protective barriers: 'chez nous entre qui veut...' (p. 40). Related images of the self have a negative ring: 'Nous ne sommes qu'un espace vide où il peut se déployer...' (p. 24); 'un espace ouvert de tous côtés' (p. 26). The self may trip over the discourse of the other ("Vraiment? Vous pensez que Robert... oui... est... quoi?... dissimulé!", p. 42), or dispense with the proper name, but cannot rid itself of the sensations which the words have provoked. Its moral sensibilities can be questioned, its aesthetic sense undermined by a confident other. The 'être exceptionnel', 'celui qui s'aime avec tant de génie' (p. 194) can take over entirely: 'Il nous a entièrement envahis, occupés...' (p. 176); the length of this particular fragment is testimony to the difficulty experienced by the self in breaking free. In response to outside pressure, the self will attempt to play the game, to present to the outside world 'un beau "je" présentable, bien solide...' (p. 37). If one does not take, another will be substituted: 'Nous ne nous décourageons pas... le défilé de délégués se poursuit...' (p. 114). The self can be surprised by its own resources, even ironically proud of its showmanship ('d'assez étonnantes performances', p. 71), but it is conscious at the same time of being forced into a series of roles in the attempt to please or to placate, or indeed to engage in any way at all with the other. This sense of plurality (the obverse side of openness), of being 'une multitude de "je" disparates', is equally disturbing: 'Peut-être étaient-ce des choses qui se trouvaient chez nous et que nous n'avions pas vues... Nous ne faisons jamais l'inventaire... / – Comment pourrions-nous le faire dans cet immense bric-à-brac, cet entassement, ce désordre?' (p. 112). According to the other, these two opposing ways of perceiving the self – as empty or as cluttered – have tags which can be attached to them (and which of course defuse the challenge they might represent): "ce genre de perte du sentiment du moi... ou alors cette hypertrophie..." (p. 18). The sufferer, like the narrator of *Portrait*, requires the attention of a specialist. The initial comment, "Vous ne vous aimez pas", is seen as implying sickness: lack of self-love is 'une tare, une maladie... Chacun d'eux est sain, normal, chacun d'eux s'aime, et nous... on ne s'aime pas' (p. 12). Later, when the self tries to react as the other does and fails, the idea recurs: 'c'est toujours ce vice dans notre construction... cette malformation...' (p. 57). Towards the end, when one of the selves makes an attempt to see itself from the outside as the others do, this is the image which is adopted: "Chez moi c'est pathologique" (p. 208). We return to the 'personnage' of the first fragment, 'un pitre, un clown grotesque' (p. 11), but the move is doubtfully profitable: it is too easy for the others to turn the tables on the self and to leave it stranded, turning their eyes from 'l'image du clown triste resté seul au milieu de l'estrade' (p. 211). Negative feelings as to the selves' identity are accompanied by a measure of envy regarding the other. The latter's initial comment, "Vous ne vous aimez pas", was provoked by an expression of these ambivalent feelings: "Ah que voulez-vous, je suis ainsi fait, je n'en fais jamais d'autres... Incorrigible... Depuis que j'étais petit, j'ai toujours admiré, j'ai contemplé avec envie ceux qui ont cette chance... qui ne sont pas comme moi..." (p. 11). After all, 'ceux qui s'aiment vivent mieux' (p. 14); if the self is critical, 'C'est que par moments on les envie tellement...' (p. 51). Thus the other is present within the self throughout, tempting, or forcing it to foreground one facet of itself at the expense of others, and producing a sense of dissatisfaction and unease with regard to its own plurality.

Narrating Voices

The plural selves in *Tu ne t'aimes pas* speak in conflicting voices and react to the voices of others; they also function collectively as narrators in a way which is reminiscent of the two narrators of *Enfance*, even if here the numbers involved are greater: 'Nos chercheurs aussitôt fouillent partout, rapportent... et nous nous rassemblons pour regarder...' (p. 44). The front man, at a number of points, is 'toi notre dénicheur, notre détective' (p. 24), but it is the 'nous' who have commissioned him to bring his particular talents to bear. The 'nous' are engaged in 'un même effort', an exploration which has been stimulated by the initial remark and which reaches some kind of tentative conclusion in the brief final fragment. The difference discovered between self and other provokes the question, 'Mais comment font-ils donc?' (p. 14). The question cannot be put directly, so the 'nous' set out to explore the matter themselves: 'On devrait s'efforcer de trouver par nous-mêmes...' (p. 19). Like the two narrators of *Enfance*, the narrative voices of the self support one another, query each other's statements, correct or amplify. A 'je' is attempting to penetrate the mode of being of the other and to grasp what is meant by "Bonheur": 'Vous me suivez? / – Nous faisons de notre mieux...' (p. 60). One group wants to pursue a line of questioning, another is impatient to bring it to an end: 'Oh vous! Avec vous on n'en finira jamais...' (p. 97). For much of the time, however, it is as if a group of like-minded 'nous' were conversing with one another, agreeing ('C'est juste', p. 25), making minor corrections ('Non, là s'arrête la comparaison', p. 115), reassuring ('Enchantement... est-ce bien ce mot qui a été prononcé? on a du mal à se rappeler... / – Si si, c'était bien enchantement', p. 161) and simply taking turns to advance the narrative. The dialogue form therefore serves not only to embody the idea of plurality, but also to create the sense of a collaborative endeavour taking place in the present. As a narrative form, it proves highly flexible: it can enact shifts of feeling and of tone with great sensitivity, pause for reflection on its own activity and give emphasis to particular moments or utterances. Above all, it dramatizes the process of imaginative understanding (and of writing, since the two are here synonymous): a tentative affair of stops and starts, of sudden illuminations and gradual progress. The perspective of the narrating selves is a present one: 'Essayons d'abord'; 'Regardons-le'; 'Imaginons que nous sommes, nous aussi, dedans...' Very often, however, the evidence lies in past experience: 'nous étions stupéfaits...' (p. 172); 'C'était si inattendu' (p. 156). Sometimes – as in the last example cited – the dramatic present is used in a reliving of the episode. Sometimes, the recounting of a past incident (in the past tense) prompts the self to imagine a contrasting one in the present tense (pp. 161–165). The point of departure can also be a sense of sudden discovery in the present (which may, however, relate to past experience): 'c'est une illumination, une révélation...' (p. 166). Thus interconnections of past and present are foregrounded by the narrative strategies.

Tu ne t'aimes pas maintains the characteristic Sarrautean division of the text into untitled, unnumbered fragments, each with its own subdivisions and its self-contained development.[37] At the same time, the perspective of the narrating selves provides a structuring framework. Each fragment contributes some additional insight into the enterprise in hand.[38] Frequently, a fragment will seem to pick up a train of thought where the preceding one left off. Some sequences are grouped together but even where the fragments do not appear to have any necessary order, the sense of an ongoing endeavour is maintained by references forward, as with the theme of "amour partagé" ('Là où un jour il faudra bien que nous tentions d'aller...', p. 117), or back, to previous examples of 'ceux qui s'aiment' (see, for example, pp. 137, 156). The last fragment of all returns to the text's point of departure: the gathering of evidence is over and a tentative conclusion has been reached.

The plural self, as we have seen, registers the other as challenging and invasive. Yet the tone of the narrative is ironical, even buoyant at points (very different in fact from that of *Portrait*): the selves are not after all defenceless. From the beginning, the other's discourse is undermined by parody. In the first section, there is an exchange with a speaker who is rather proud both of his inner complexities and of his ability to understand them: "vous voyez, c'est assez complexe... il y a deux hommes en moi, je suis tantôt l'un tantôt l'autre, pas les deux à la fois". The reference to Dr Jekyll and Mr Hyde underlines the familiarity of this psychological insight, and the irony is pushed further by the speaker's unease at being compared with Mr Hyde: "évidemment personne n'est parfait... mais je ne crois pas..." (p. 17). The other's account of his morning routine is equally parodic:

> "Ensuite coup sur coup deux cigarettes... après la seconde seulement l'effet se produit... Il pose la main sur son ventre, il sourit... complice de son intestin qui agit im-man-qua-ble-ment... il étire le mot, il appuie, sur le ton de la satisfaction, de la reconnaissance sur chaque syllabe... Im-man-qua-ble-ment... Jamais de ratés..." (pp. 22–23).

The self-deprecating irony of the narrating selves at their readiness to be impressed ('Pourtant en nous aussi deux cigarettes... et même une seule parfois... C'est sans doute un effet plus fréquent qu'on ne croit...', p. 23) only serves to undermine the speech still further. As the exploration proceeds, the criticism becomes more serious. The other's discourse is made to suggest self-deception, hollowness, a failure of sensitivity or even of intelligence. The self-knowledge laid claim to by the other is shown to be a way of dressing up disagreeable realities: "J'étais jeune, très chien fou..." (p. 155); "Pour dire la vérité, j'ai plutôt un tempérament de chasseur..." (p. 160). The 'elle' who lays claim to an innate moral sense can deploy no argument in support of her "Non. Ce n'est pas bien" (p. 168); the "être exceptionnel" (p. 173) who, by his authority, annihilates the aesthetic responses of anyone else, is deflated by a final hostile image. The certainties of the other are seen as limitations: "Oh moi, vous savez, ces choses-là... ça me dépasse..." (p. 146); the father–son relationship is reduced to a few familiar labels: 'Père. Pitié. Respect...' (p. 149). The phrase "Vingt ans de bonheur' conjures up images of travel brochures: 'Une mer toute lisse, toute bleue, un ciel sans nuage...' (as one says of happiness, p. 48). The fragment which occupies the central position in the text, and which follows the piece on "amour partagé", points to the inadequacy of the discourse of the other in communicating authentic feelings:

> Quand nous étions emportés, suffoqués, aveuglés, incapables de regarder en nous-mêmes... nous n'avions pas l'impression d'exister... lui ne se perdait pas de vue, il a su trouver que ce qui se passe en lui se nomme 'souffrance'... (p. 130)

> Ce qui était fragile, périssable, qui se serait décomposé, aurait disparu... elle a su le sauvegarder... Elle l'a embaumé, elle l'a exposé dans un

cercueil de verre, elle le contemple en hochant la tête d'un air nostalgique, attendri... "Ce que je me serai amusée..." (p. 133).

The narrating voices do not therefore simply absorb examples of the 'façon de parler' of the other; they unpack these utterances and re-enact the mental movements which accompany them and which are provoked by them. The idea that the self is thereby reinvesting language with meaning is further supported by the self's own use of consecrated phrases at a number of points in the text: "il n'y en a que pour lui" (p. 24), "Je lui ai sorti ses quatre vérités" (p. 40), "C'est un monde!" (p. 135), "ce sont des choses qui ne s'expliquent pas" (p. 169), "c'est impensable" (p. 206). The text as a whole, one might say, is bounded by two such phrases. At the beginning, as we saw, the self is invaded by the voice of others but understands their words in its own way. The conclusion of the whole endeavour returns to this point of departure: the phrase ' "Vous ne vous aimez pas" qui nous avait tant surpris, il y a déjà assez longtemps' (p. 216). Would it not be better for all concerned if the self too could experience 'cet amour de soi'? There comes in reply, and in support of such an idea, the consecrated phrase: 'On ne demanderait pas mieux...' The *points de suspension* which follow it, however, suggest a pause and hesitation. The phrase is then repeated by another voice within the self but turned into a query: 'On ne demanderait pas mieux?' The effect is reinforced by two further question marks: 'Pas mieux? Vraiment?'. It is highly appropriate that this transgressive text should end on a series of questions, querying, it seems, both sentiment and familiar phrase.

The Voice of the Author

Nathalie Sarraute is suspicious of autobiographical writing and fond of quoting Freud's dictum about its falsity. Her comments on particular works echo this view: 'l'ensemble des *Mots*, bien que très beau, sonne faux'.[39] Where her own works are concerned, she has often stressed how separate they are from her life, for example in a recent interview with Isabelle Huppert: 'je ne pense jamais à moi quand j'écris. Quand je suis devant ma feuille, je n'existe pas'.[40] The 'prière d'insérer' of *Entre la vie et la mort* (signed N.S.) insists: 'Ce livre où il est question d'écrivains et d'écriture n'est cependant pas, comme on pourrait le croire, une autobiographie'.[41] In the Folio edition, the possibility is not even discussed; only the key phrase of the original blurb survives: 'Là où une œuvre littéraire prend naissance, grandit, ou meurt'. On its first publication, Nathalie Sarraute's one 'autobiographical' work, *Enfance,* had no label, and no 'prière d'insérer' other than a sober account of its author's career as a writer. In discussing the text of *Enfance* in interview, Sarraute is repeatedly anxious to stress its fragmentary, incomplete nature. To Viviane Forrester, after publication, she says: 'j'ai vraiment choisi certains moments, comme toujours, proches de mon travail, de ma recherche, de mon écriture [...] Il ne s'agit pas d'un rapport sur toute ma vie. Pas même sur toute l'enfance'.[42] To Pierre Boncenne:

> Aujourd'hui comme hier à l'école communale, je n'aime pas ces étalages de soi-même et je n'ai pas l'impression qu'avec *Enfance* je me suis laissée aller. Comme dans *Tropismes*, ce sont plutôt des moments, des formes de sensibilité [...] Je n'ai pas essayé d'écrire l'histoire de ma vie.[43]

Tu ne t'aimes pas represents a return to fiction – it comes with the label *roman* on its cover – and there is no coincidence of proper names (of author and protagonist) to suggest any kind of pact with the reader. Its principal theme is, however, the activity of self-portraiture, as social skill and, by extension, as literary genre. It mounts a critique of an autobiographical discourse based on the idea of a coherent and individually interesting self (however complex and difficult to pin down in practice) and at the same time, one might argue, offers an even more radical rewriting of that discourse than did *Enfance*.[44] One of the first exchanges with the other is concerned with the response to the self's question: "Est-ce qu'en vous-même, enfin dans votre for intérieur, vous avez l'impression... mais je dis bien: tout au fond de vous, vous arrivez à vous voir avec une certaine netteté... vous avez l'impression de savoir qui vous êtes..." (p. 16). It is not the biographical details which are at issue but the sense of a character:

> "Ce que je voulais savoir c'est... c'est difficile à expliquer... si vous sentez que vous êtes un tout très compact et uni, doté de telles ou telles qualités et, bien sûr, de défauts... mais formant un ensemble... nettement délimité, que vous pouvez regarder du dehors... enfin que vous projetez devant vous..." (p. 17)

The reply is, as we have seen, a parody, and the target in a number of respects is autobiographical discourse: biographical origins, the claim to psychological complexity, the desire to present a good image to the world. The belief that a preoccupation with the individual self can be taken seriously is even more radically undermined in the following:

> Celui qui s'aime avec assez d'intensité transforme tout ce qui émane de lui en richesses... tout sans exception... ses moindres manifestations, esquisses, brouillons, bavardages, radotages, balbutiements, cartes de vœux, nom écrit de sa main, livres de comptes, effets des cigarettes sur son intestin... (p. 25)

The two contrasting images of statue and snowman relate to this theme of self-portraiture and make the stance of the text very clear. One example of 'ceux qui s'aiment', with whom the self is already familiar, possesses 'une statue de lui-même qu'il a toujours portée en lui... [...] Cette statue de lui-même l'occupe tout entier, il n'y a de place en lui que pour elle' (p. 33). The notion refers us implicitly to any autobiography or *autoportrait* which sees the self in terms of one unifying tendency. Sartre makes use of this belief, albeit ironically, in *Les Mots*: 'Or voici qu'on m'avait sondé et que la sonde avait rencontré le roc; j'étais écrivain comme Charles Schweitzer était grand-père: de naissance et pour toujours'.[45] In François Jacob's autobiography (published two years before *Tu ne t'aimes pas*), the idea of a 'statue intérieure', which its owner continues to model throughout his life, is sufficiently important for it to give the work its title: 'Je porte ainsi en moi, sculptée depuis l'enfance, une sorte de statue intérieure qui donne une continuité à ma vie, qui est la part la plus intime, le noyau le plus dur de mon caractère'.[46] For Nathalie Sarraute, the statue, like the mechanical doll or the waxwork, is an image for the *personnage*: 'L'important, c'est de savoir comment on édifie un personnage, et comment ce personnage apparent, cette statue parfaitement contournée, masque l'immensité de la vie intérieure, l'infini que chacun de nous est pour lui-même'.[47] In the passage from *Tu ne t'aimes pas*, the idea is mocked by the phrasing: 'Ils ne faisaient qu'un, sa statue et lui. Alors ensemble ils ont grandi... / – Et ils sont devenus plus tard, sa statue et lui, un grand génie' (p. 34). The self's equivalent of the statue is the snowman, decked out with felt hat and pipe to give it an air of verisimilitude (shades of 'l'ami', 'l'étranger', 'l'autre' in *Vous les entendez?*), exciting to build, but short-lived and never intended to be taken seriously. It is the possession of a 'statue' – even a modest one – which makes self-narration easy. If, however, driven by fear of what others will think ('Cela me gêne au point que je ne tiens plus... je me mets à "me raconter"...'), the plural self, in one of its incarnations, attempts a self-portrait, the result is 'des contrevérités' (pp. 35–36), and a series of highly comical ones at that.

Tu ne t'aimes pas sets out then to deconstruct the discourses of autobiography: 'Connais-toi toi-même, n'est-ce pas? vous le prescrivez...' (p. 209). At the same time, as has been seen, it offers a view of the self as bereft of identity, and it demonstrates a way of narrating such a self. Sarraute's comments in interview suggest that her point of departure is her own sense of self (or the lack of it):

> Il m'a toujours été extrêmement difficile de me dire je suis ceci ou cela. On me le dit du dehors mais je ne le sens pas. [...] Quand on me dit que j'ai une certaine qualité cela m'étonne beaucoup parce que je vois presque toujours l'opposée qui est aussi là.[48]

In particular, the conversations with Simone Benmussa, recorded while she was working on *Tu ne t'aimes pas*, contain many such affirmations: 'Mais moi, j'ai l'impression, que là où je suis, il y a comme une place vide'; 'Dès que je dis "je", j'ai l'impression de ne jamais parler de moi, ou très rarement. Je ne dis jamais comment je suis parce que ce serait faux'. She distinguishes here, as always, between external 'character' and the domain which interests her, that of the 'sensation intérieure': 'Nous avons à l'extérieur certains comportements, une certaine personnalité marquée etc. mais je parle, moi, de cette sensation profonde – et je crois que beaucoup de gens l'ont – de n'être rien, rien, rien'.[49] Not only is the sense of self 'autobiographical', but the enterprise of the narrating selves mirrors a similar enterprise on the part of the author:[50]

> Prends donc ce que tu fais en ce moment... Quand tu cherches à retrouver cette sensation de Bonheur... [...]
>
> —Je me tends de toutes mes forces... pour l'éprouver je donnerais n'importe quoi... je vais l'avoir... je l'ai... non, je ne l'ai pas... ce n'est pas ça... pas le Bonheur... (p. 64)

The selves' defence of their vision becomes a restatement of Sarraute's faith in her own creation: it is an advantage 'de ne pas être obligés de plaquer ce nom de Bonheur sur toute sensation encore intacte, vivante... de l'écraser...' (p. 65). It would be pleasant to have a sense of certainty as to who one is, but ultimately, despite the discomfort, the lack of definition is a source of pride. To be labelled is to be 'réduits à cela' ('celui qui a eu l'honneur de rencontrer...'), 'Nous si nombreux... incernables... incommensurables...' (pp. 28–29); 'Nous, il n'y a pas moyen d'en venir à bout...' (p. 110). We have here a statement of how the self may be portrayed, if Nathalie Sarraute is true to herself as writer: this is how it seems, 'là où je travaille, où je me place',[51] 'au niveau où je me place'.[52] To describe *Tu ne t'aimes pas* as 'autobiographical' or even as a self-portrait may involve an extension of what is understood by each term (as *Portrait* did with the novel).[53] However, the impression of coincidence between narrating selves (neutral and plural) and author is such that one is tempted to speak of a reinvention of autobiography. In *Enfance*, a special status is given to Mark Twain's *The Prince and the Pauper*: 'Je crois qu'il n'y a aucun livre dans mon enfance, où j'aie vécu comme j'ai vécu dans celui-là'. However much the child may have identified with the life of David Copperfield or that of the hero of *Sans famille*: 'elles n'ont pas laissé en moi ces sillons... deux sillons que deux images, et elles seules, ont creusés...'.[54] In context, it seems appropriate to draw a parallel with the experience of the child, moving between two households and belonging to neither ("femme et mari sont un même parti" and "Ce n'est pas ta maison"). But the images could be given a rather different emphasis: each child might be seen as caught in a persona imposed by the group surrounding him, a persona with which he is not at ease, but which he cannot escape. A similar opposition appears in *Tu ne t'aimes pas*. In two complementary fragments, the self finds itself enclosed in a 'moi' not of its own making, an image imposed by the other, and is seen as being first in a prison, 'inculpé, arrêté et emprisonné' (p. 115), then in a golden cage, 'préservé, arrangé, nettoyé, frotté, poli...' (p. 120).[55] If *Enfance* is the story of a liberation, in that it celebrates the child's achievement of 'une complète et définitive indépendance',[56] *Tu ne t'aimes pas* also celebrates the deliverance of the self (and of the author) from the '"moi" personnage' and its/her resumption of 'notre précieux bonnet... / – Ce bonnet magique qui rend invisibles les héros des contes de fées' (p. 116).

Notes

[1] The letter is reproduced as an illustration in Mimica Cranaki and Yvon Belaval, *Nathalie Sarraute* (Paris: Gallimard [Bibliothèque Idéale], 1965). There were two other letters, one from Charles Mauron and one from Sartre, and one critical review by Victor Moremans in *La Gazette de Liège*.

[2] 'Mon domaine c'était le for intérieur': Pierre Boncenne, 'Interview: Nathalie Sarraute', *Lire* (June 1983), 92. The colloquium on Sarraute's work, organized by Monique Wittig and held in Tucson, Arizona, in April 1994, took as its title: *Nathalie Sarraute ou le texte du for intérieur*. A selection of the papers has been published in *L'Esprit Créateur* 36 (Summer 1996).

[3] *L'Ère du soupçon* (Paris: Gallimard, 1965), 12. The ironic tone of Nathalie Sarraute's comments was not always understood. In 1959, she felt impelled to write to the *Times Literary Supplement* in order to set the record straight regarding her admiration for Proust, Joyce and Virginia Woolf: Valerie Minogue prints this letter in an appendix to her book, *Nathalie Sarraute and the War of the Words* (Edinburgh: Edinburgh University Press, 1981).

[4] *L'Ère du soupçon*, 137.

[5] *Tu ne t'aimes pas* (Paris: Gallimard, 1989), 16. Subsequent page references in the text of this article are to this edition.

[6] *Conversations avec Claude Régy* (Paris: La Sept/INA, 1989).

[7] *L'Ère du soupçon*, 58.

[8] Simone Benmussa, *Nathalie Sarraute. Qui êtes-vous?* (Lyon: La Manufacture, 1987), 58.

[9] Valerie Minogue, 'Nathalie Sarraute's *Le Planétarium*: the narrator narrated', *Forum for Modern Language Studies* 9 (1973). The substance of this article reappears in modified form in idem, *Nathalie Sarraute and the War of Words*.

[10] Minogue, 'Nathalie Sarraute's *Le Planétarium*', 226.

[11] Benmussa, *Nathalie Sarraute*, 60.

[12] Among critics who have emphasized the significance of the shift which takes place with *Les Fruits d'or*, see A. S. Newman, *Une poésie des discours* (Geneva: Droz, 1976), 62. Monique Wittig is perhaps the most categorical in seeing the novel as marking 'une transformation si totale de la matière romanesque, qu'il est difficile de la saisir comme telle', 'Le Lieu de l'action', *Digraphe* 32 (March 1984), 69.

[13] *L'Ère du soupçon*, 117–118.

[14] In a paper given at the Tucson colloquium, 'Nathalie Sarraute, anti-terrorist: a reading of *"disent les imbéciles"'*, Valerie Minogue pointed to such traces of a 'quasi-authorial presence' in *"disent les imbéciles"*.

[15] Carmen Licari, '"Qu'est-ce qu'il y a, qu'est-ce qui s'est passé? mais rien." Entretiens avec Nathalie Sarraute', *Francofonia* 9 (1985), 4.

[16] *L'Usage de la parole* (Paris: Gallimard, 1980), 10–11.

[17] The phenomenon of the two narrators in *Enfance* has received particular attention in critical studies of the text: see my article, 'The conjurer's hat: Sarraute criticism since 1980', *Romance Studies* 23 (1994), 92–93.

[18] It is in fact the second narrator who speaks first in the text but he speaks in response to an earlier utterance: in Sarraute's work, every utterance acknowledges the existence of a 'partenaire', past, present or imagined.

[19] *Enfance* (Paris: Gallimard, 1983), 90.

[20] Ibid., 11.

[21] Ibid., 71–74.

[22] Ibid., 232.

[23] 'Prière d'insérer', *"disent les imbéciles"* (Paris: Gallimard, 1976). See the chapter: 'Je n'existe pas' in Roger Pierrot, *Nathalie Sarraute* (Paris: Corti, 1990) for a tracing of the theme through the fiction prior to *Tu ne t'aimes pas*.

[24] Where double inverted commas are used in the text, these are reproduced in quotation and single inverted commas dispensed with.

[25] *"disent les imbéciles"*, 71.

[26] Lucie Jauvin, 'L'Autoportrait virtuel et universel de Nathalie Sarraute', *Études Françaises* 29 (1993), 186.

[27] For a discussion of the use of name and pronoun in Sarraute's fiction up to *Vous les entendez?*, see Ann Jefferson, 'What's in a name? From surname to pronoun in the novels of Nathalie Sarraute', *PTL: A Journal for Descriptive Poetics and Theory of Literature* 2 (1977), 203–220.

[28] Bernard Pingaud, 'Le Personnage dans l'œuvre de Nathalie Sarraute', *Preuves* 154 (December 1963), 21.

[29] Emile Benveniste, 'La Nature des pronoms' in *Problèmes de linguistique générale* (Paris: Gallimard, 1966).

[30] The great variety of these voices is evoked in Valerie Minogue, 'A propos de *Tu ne t'aimes pas*', *Revue des Sciences Humaines* 93 (1990), 152–153.

[31] Here too the text's first utterance is a reaction to an earlier one, which itself was a response to 'Ah que voulez-vous, je suis ainsi fait' (11).

[32] For an account of the role of the body in self–other relations, see Ann Jefferson, 'Bodymatters: self and other in Bakhtin, Sartre and Barthes' in Ken Hirschkop and David Shepherd (eds.), *Bakhtin and Cultural Theory* (Manchester: Manchester University Press, 1989). See also the same author's 'Materialism and the mind: Nathalie Sarraute', *Romance Studies* 20 (Summer 1992), 31–43.

[33] Valerie Minogue draws attention to this point in 'A propos de *Tu ne t'aimes pas*' (see n. 30 above), 157. Examples are 'La victime [...] elle voyait notre effort... elle refusait de nous suivre' (67–68) and 'une de ces personnalités conquérantes qui, elle, ne sait que trop bien qui elle est' (71).

[34] Proper names themselves, of which there are two examples in *Tu ne t'aimes pas*, Galion and Robert, appear, as one would expect, in quoted speech and connote, as elsewhere in Sarraute, the artificiality of 'character' (Louis Dumontet and Martereau). The memory of a presence becomes Galion, when served up in conversation ('pour qu'il puisse se présenter à tous ces gens rassemblés...', 108), and Robert loses his name, when contemplated by the self ('Ici, entre nous, nous ne prononçons pas son nom...', 43).

[35] On the commonplace in Sarraute, see Celia Britton, 'The function of

the commonplace in the novels of Nathalie Sarraute', *Language and Style* 12 (1979), 79–90. See also, on the empty self and its lack of a language, the same author's 'The self and language in the novels of Nathalie Sarraute', *Modern Language Review* 77 (1982), 577–584.

[36] J.-P. Sartre, preface to *Portrait d'un inconnu* (Paris: Gallimard, 1956), 9.

[37] *Vous les entendez?* is the only novel in which there are no chapter-like divisions, only gaps of varying size in the print.

[38] In a paper given at the Tucson colloquium, 'La Forme du dialogue', Françoise Asso argued that the fragments of both *Enfance* and *Tu ne t'aimes pas*, like the texts of *L'Usage de la parole*, should be seen as exemplary, 'des moments prélevés dans une série'.

[39] Boncenne, 'Interview' (see n. 2 above), 90.

[40] Isabelle Huppert, 'Rencontre: Nathalie Sarraute', *Cahiers du Cinéma* 477 (March 1994), 10.

[41] *Entre la vie et la mort* (Paris: Gallimard, 1968).

[42] 'Portrait de Nathalie', *Magazine littéraire* 196 (June 1983), 19.

[43] Boncenne, 'Interview', 90.

[44] It might also be seen as extending further the boundaries of 'autofiction': see S. Doubrovsky, J. Lecarme and P. Lejeune (eds.), *Autofictions & Cie* (Paris: RITM, Université Paris X, 1993).

[45] J.-P. Sartre, *Les Mots* (Paris: Gallimard, 1964), 142. In contrast, *Enfance* explicitly rejects the idea that either child or father perceived in Natacha 'des dons d'écrivain'.

[46] *La Statue intérieure* (Paris: Éditions Odile Jacob, Seuil, 1987), 24.

[47] 'Nathalie Sarraute: ' "Sartre s'est trompé à mon sujet". Propos recueillis par Jean-Louis Ezine', *Nouvelles littéraires* (30 September 1976), 5. Sarraute is speaking about *"disent les imbéciles"*, for which an earlier title was 'Le Jeu des statues'.

[48] *Conversations avec Claude Régy*.

[49] Benmussa, *Nathalie Sarraute*, 75, 82, 163.

[50] It would of course be possible to discover in the text a number of personal references, but this would be to reconstruct what the text deconstructs and to create an 'identity' out of 'des bribes de sensations' (Huppert, 'Rencontre', 14).

[51] *Conversations avec Claude Régy*.

[52] Benmussa, *Nathalie Sarraute*, 113.

[53] Lucie Jauvin suggests such an extension in the title of her article cited above (n. 26).

[54] *Enfance*, 77.

[55] As Alan Clayton has pointed out in his article ' "Coucou... attrapez-moi" ', *Revue des Sciences Humaines* 93 (1990), 17–18, the leitmotif appears with this sense in *"disent les imbéciles"*: 'Oh je vous prie, je vous assure, vous vous trompez... Moi je suis... Mais justement je ne suis pas... je vous l'ai toujours dit, il n'y a pas de "je"... C'est vous qui... oui, vous me comprenez, il n'y a pas moyen de coïncider avec ça, avec ce que vous avez construit...' (82–83).

[56] *Enfance*, 131.

Nathalie Sarraute – Criticism and the 'Terrible Desire to Establish Contact'*

ANN JEFFERSON

L'Ère du soupçon is one of the most cited critico-theoretical accounts of the novel in the post-war period. On its publication in 1956 it was read as a timely diagnosis of an entire genre which had come to be perceived as being in crisis, and as a programme for its renewed development.[1] Subsequently and more specifically, it was seen as articulating some of the basic premises of the *nouveau roman* as it emerged in the late 1950s. And it has provided critics and readers of Nathalie Sarraute's novels with cues and handles on what might otherwise have seemed a perplexing and difficult literary phenomenon. It is as hard to imagine reading Sarraute's fiction without *L'Ère du soupçon* as it is to read *Madame Bovary* without the *Correspondance*, or *A la recherche* without *Contre Sainte-Beuve*, and over the years the book has been allowed to settle without contest into the theoretical half of a theory-and-practice approach to the novel. In short, its status has largely been that of 'un traité du roman' (as Jean-Yves Tadié has called it),[2] and the ideas contained in this 'treatise' have become familiar and crucial points of reference in the critical landscape that surrounds Sarraute's fiction: the attack on Balzacian characterization, the defence of a new so-called 'tropistic' view of psychology based on anonymity, the discussion of dialogue in the novel with its attendant specifically Sarrautean terminology of 'conversation' and 'sous-conversation', the redefinition of realism as a preoccupation with form, and, finally, the general conception of the novel as essentially innovatory and experimental.

There is little point, then, in rehearsing once again the critical and theoretical content of these essays. Instead, I want to change the terms of the discussion and ask not what Nathalie Sarraute's critical writing *says*, but rather what it *does*. The question then becomes: what kind of function do the essays fulfil, rather than what kind of argument do they contain? This is, of course, already a very Sarrautean approach to the question: according to *L'Ère du soupçon* itself, words are a form of action, whether it be as the agent of 'innumerable small crimes' ('Conversation', p. 122), or more neutrally as the medium for the 'jeu d'actions et de réactions' by means of which language becomes for the novelist 'le plus précieux des instrûments' (p. 123).[3] In attempting to explore this view of Sarraute's criticism as something that 'does' as well as something that 'says', I propose to look first at how criticism is represented and defined as an activity within Sarraute's work as a whole (fictional and critical), and then go on to examine more precisely what role it can be seen to have in relation to the novels themselves. I shall be basing my comments not just on *L'Ère du soupçon* but on all Sarraute's published essays, as well as three of her unpublished lectures, which together form the corpus for the criticism section of the Pléiade volume. The point behind this is not only to establish a more complete picture of a body of Sarrautean theory, but, more importantly, by approaching her critical writings as a sequence of essays, to make the issue of their doing present from the start, and highlight their status as *interventions*.

Until now, I have used the terms *criticism* and *theory* more or less interchangeably when talking about Sarraute's non-fictional writing; but though the essays are not strictly critical in the sense that they are not primarily concerned with the works of other writers, they are equally not purely theoretical to the extent, precisely, that they set themselves up against the *ex nihilo*, programmatic or magisterial manner of theory. While I would not wish to undersell the theoretical import of Sarraute's work in this domain, it makes better sense when looking at what this kind of writing does, to regard them as critical essays rather than theoretical pronouncements. For time and again, Sarraute's essays define themselves as a riposte to instances of what in *Les Fruits d'or* she terms 'des arguments d'autorité';[4] and this may be seen as the first of the ways in which Sarrautean criticism is something that does, as well as something that says. From the very beginning – indeed, on the very first page of her very first essay devoted to Paul Valéry – Nathalie Sarraute's critical voice emerges as that of the 'Enfant d'Éléphant [...] qui posait toujours des questions et qui se faisait partout rabrouer' ('PV', p. 9), daring to question the 'vérités premières' ('L'Ère du soupçon', p. 67) of the literary establishment by asking sacrilegious questions. Like the subsequent essays, 'Paul Valéry et l'Enfant d'Éléphant' is presented as a challenge to the *status quo* of a literary dogma whose authority rests only on the unreflecting consensus of its adherents. In the aftermath of Valéry's death, Sarraute is taking on the defenders of the view that he was 'un grand poète' (p. 9); and in the process she is also calling into question his view of literature as a matter of intellect rather than feeling, contemplation rather than contact. The issues raised by this redefinition are important ones, and I shall be returning to them later; but for the meantime, there remains more to be said about the way in which Sarraute's critical voice repeatedly appears as a heretical intervention in a literary orthodoxy.

This is certainly how her comments on psychology in the novel are staged in her next essay, 'De Dostoïevski à Kafka'. First published in *Les Temps Modernes*, it offers itself once again as a form of 'parole sacrilège' ('PV', p. 9), daring to contest a conception of the novel that was closely identified with *Les Temps Modernes* itself, the so-called 'roman de l'absurde' (i.e. Camus's *L'Étranger* and the kind of American fiction exemplified by Hemingway and Caldwell), which she presents as both misguided in its refusal of psychological interiority and profoundly conformist in its principles of composition. The third essay, 'L'Ère du soupçon', opens with an attack on the conventional critical dogma that a novel is 'une histoire où l'on voit agir et vivre des personnages' (p. 67); and 'Ce que voient les oiseaux' continues in a similar vein in its provocative reversal of the traditional opposition between formalism and realism. In short, these first essays are each targeted at a series of critical orthodoxies, and repeatedly present Sarraute as a critical heretic.

This stance is maintained throughout the 1960s as she contests a certain line of thinking in the *nouveau roman* (and for which Jean Ricardou was the spokesman), summed up by her as 'l'idée que la "réalité" d'une œuvre tient à la seule exploration du langage' and which she dismisses quite simply and peremptorily as 'évidemment insoutenable' ('La Littérature, aujourd'hui', p. 49). This characteristic critical contrariness culminates in her talk at the Cerisy colloquium on the *nouveau roman* in 1971, where she begins by describing herself once again as a lone voice at odds with the beliefs and assumptions of the group she finds herself in. In admitting to her initial reluctance to participate in the colloquium, she says:

Si j'ai tant hésité, c'est que je savais que je me trouverais ici de nouveau, comme je l'ai été si souvent au cours de ma vie, dans une situation assez singulière. Dans un certain isolement dont d'ailleurs je ne me plains pas –

il m'a probablement été nécessaire – mais enfin il n'est pas assez agréable pour que j'aille délibérément le chercher. ('Ce que', p. 25)

This remark acknowledges, as both recurrent and necessary to her, her role of renegade amongst a group of believers. The underlying nature of this group as a 'bande de croyants' remains the same, whether they be defenders of the reputation of Paul Valéry, the proponents of a behaviourist representation of human experience, the guardians of a traditional view of fiction, or the theorists and practitioners of ludism and the freeplay of the signifier. For this reason, it is no accident that the vocabulary of orthodoxy and sacrilege, dogma and heresy, pervades *Les Fruits d'or* (the novel which deals most directly with the nature of critical activity), and that so much of the book consists of imaginary scenes which act out scenarios based on the terms of these oppositions. For example:

> Qu'est-ce que c'est? Qui trouble l'ordre? Qu'est-ce que c'est que cette folle, cette illuminée qui parcourt la terre, pieds nus et en haillons, crie sur les places publiques, se frappe la poitrine, appelle à la pénitence, prêche la parole du Christ, pointe son doigt crochu sur les grands de cette terre, nargue l'ordre établi, annonce le Jugement dernier ... On l'entoure. Leurs regards la lapident. Elle est repoussée, expulsée. Le cercle des fidèles se referme. (p. 124)

As a critic Sarraute always implicitly casts herself as a version of 'cette folle [...] qui crie sur les places publiques ... [et] nargue l'ordre établi'.

However, *Les Fruits d'or* makes it very clear that the established order is also a critical order, so that criticism in Sarraute's world must be seen as taking two very different forms: dogma as well as heresy. I should therefore like to turn now to the way in which she depicts what one might call criticism-as-dogma which her own interventions so provocatively thumb their nose at. Criticism of the type practised by 'les cercles des fidèles' is invariably represented as a form of 'argument d'autorité', and is consequently treated by Sarraute with the deepest suspicion. It appears as a self-justifying orthodoxy that simultaneously saps the life-blood of the literary text and destroys the reader's relation with it. This implication is clearly visible in one of her earliest fictional characters, the anonymous professor of *Tropismes* XII who lectures on literature at the Collège de France:

Il se plaisait à farfouiller, avec la dignité des gestes professionnels, d'une main implacable et experte, dans les dessous de Proust ou de Rimbaud, et étalant aux yeux de son public très attentif leurs prétendus miracles, leurs mystères, il expliquait 'leur cas'.[5]

His destructive achievement is ironically summed up in his concluding claim: 'je les ai vidés pour vous de leur puissance et de leur mystère, j'ai traqué, harcelé ce qu'il y avait en eux de miraculeux' (p. 77). The practice of criticism-as-dogma is always presented as this kind of power game where its objects are expertly and implacably emptied of their 'puissance' for the sole benefit of the critic.

The language of this type of criticism is extensively parodied in *Les Fruits d'or* so as to appear as an aggressively mystificatory nonsense which never brings critical illumination to the text, and which merely bolsters the authority of the critic: ' "Oui. Évidemment. Il y a là un envol qui abolit l'invisible en le fondant dans l'équivoque du signifié ..." ', is the comment of one of the parodied critics (p. 93). Readers 'qui avaient eu pendant un bref instant l'espoir de se fixer dans les pays riants qu'ils avaient entrevus' find themselves having instead to bow to a regime of forced labour imposed by the vacuous but nevertheless repressive critical authorities: '[ils] reprennent leur marche, morne troupe captive traînant ses chaînes, chassée vers quelles immensités marécageuses, quelles étendues sans fin de toundras glacées' (p. 94). The dogmatic critic is someone who seeks to promote his own status at the expense of both the text and its readers. His discursive currency is the 'argument d'autorité', a self-generating critical discourse with no relation to the text it supposedly describes, and which interposes itself to deadly effect between the reader and that text: 'Les arguments d'autorité. Rien d'autre. Jamais aucun contact vrai, aucun sentiment spontané' *(FO*, pp. 58–59).

For Sarraute, in criticism as in human relations, contact is all. In fact, contact appears often as the very opposite of criticism, with criticism almost invariably standing in the way of contact. In recounting her attempt to make up her own mind about Valéry's poetry, Sarraute describes herself as first needing to shut out the world ('Je n'avais qu'à m'enfermer dans ma chambre; fermer ma porte à tous les bruits du dehors' ('PV', p. 11), and then having to prise the text free of its surrounding commentary in order for an authentic encounter to be possible:

> Quelle couche chaque jour plus épaisse de vernis protecteur ne fallait-il pas gratter, quelle gangue solide et dure, chaque jour plus solide et plus dure, de paroles louangeuses et de commentaires enthousiastes ne fallait-il pas briser autour de chaque ligne, de chaque strophe, de chaque vers, pour les faire apparaître à la lumière! ('PV', p. 12)

This solitary meeting between reader and text is for Sarraute the only valid relation between the two.

The immediacy and spontaneity of readerly contact are evoked in very similar terms by Sarraute nearly twenty-five years after the Valéry article, in her talk at Cerisy, where she describes the way she reads the critical essays of others. Her habit, she says, is to reverse the normal sequence of reading this kind of writing, and to defer the commentary until she has made independent contact with the cited literary text. The effect is to render even the best instances of critical comment marginal or ultimately superfluous:

> Quand je lis un article critique, c'est aux citations que je vais d'abord, puis, ayant pris contact avec le texte – un contact si direct et si spontané qu'aucun commentaire venu du dehors ne pourra le modifier – je lis avec intérêt ce qu'en dit le critique, je relis les citations à cette lumière, je cherche à retrouver ce qu'il y a vu – ce qui parfois enrichit ma relecture, sans jamais me faire perdre ma première impression. ('Ce que', p. 28)

These two accounts of reading demonstrate that for Sarraute criticism is anathema to contact, and that there is an important distinction to be made between reading and criticism. To the extent that reading can be defined as a form of contact (and in Sarraute the two terms are virtually synonymous), her own so-called critical writing is not so much a form of criticism as a defence of reading, which frequently takes the form of what Jonathan Culler (admittedly in a rather different context) has called 'stories of reading'.[6] There is a sense in which for Sarraute all criticism tends ultimately to become dogma (the present essay would be no exception), and the article on Valéry is not intended as a better critical account than those proposed by existing commentaries, but is offered quite explicitly as a story about the experience of reading his work. It begins with a description of the various responses elicited by her question about whether Valéry was really 'un grand poète' (which, incidentally, recalls the very similar scene which opens *Portrait d'un inconnu*),[7] goes on with her decision to see for herself as she shuts herself away in her room, and above all confronts the text as an *event* in its own right: '[l'œuvre de Paul Valéry] serait pour moi ce que toute œuvre d'art, comme le dit si bien Thierry Maulnier, "peut être à chaque moment et pour tout lecteur qui se place en face d'elle, un événement neuf et un commencement absolu"' ('PV', p. 11). Contact is made possible by the status of works of art as events, a status which means that the only valid sort of commentary about them are narratives of the reader's experience of them. This, at any rate, is the formula which Sarraute adopts when writing about the works of other authors such as Dostoevsky, Kafka and Flaubert: 'Je vous ai prévenus que je regarderais cette œuvre [here, Flaubert's *Salammbô*] comme un événement neuf et sans idée préconçue. Ici soyons sincères, et disons ce que font surgir en nous ces belles descriptions ciselées et cadencées ...' ('Flaubert', p. 71). What she is proposing here is not an interpretation, nor an analysis, nor a judgement, but an account of the response that the work provokes in its reader.

For this reason 'criticism' does indeed turn out to be as much of a misnomer as 'theory' when one talks about Sarraute's essays. Although, for Sarraute, Barthes is just the kind of critic who gives criticism a bad name (and whose particular kind of critical language is heavily parodied in *Les Fruits d'or*), his discussion of the difference between criticism and reading in *Critique et vérité* seems to echo very closely her own feeling on the question, and may help to explain where the problem about criticism might lie:

> [...] le critique ne peut en rien se substituer au lecteur. C'est en vain qu'il se prévaudra – ou qu'on lui demandera – de prêter une voix, si respectueuse soit-elle, à la lecture des autres, de n'être lui-même qu'un lecteur auquel d'autres lecteurs ont délégué l'expression de leurs propres sentiments, en raison de son savoir ou de son jugement, bref de figurer les droits d'une collectivité sur l'œuvre.[8]

The critic, says Barthes, can never be a spokesman for the reader, because, as he goes on to explain, reading implies a relation with the text, criticism inevitably and only a relation with critical language: 'Passer de la lecture à la critique, c'est changer de désir, c'est désirer non plus l'œuvre, mais son propre langage' (p. 79). This is exactly the view which we have seen amply and repeatedly reflected in Sarraute's own representation of criticism. Reading for, in, and, ideally, of Sarraute is very much a matter of desire – and, more especially, of desire as identification – which takes the form described here by Barthes: 'Seule la lecture aime l'œuvre, entretient avec elle un rapport de désir. Lire, c'est désirer l'œuvre, c'est vouloir être l'œuvre, c'est refuser de doubler l'œuvre en dehors de toute autre parole que la parole même de l'œuvre' (pp. 78–79). It is precisely because criticism is so inevitably deflected from its object by its investment in its own language that Sarrautean heresy never aspires to the status of criticism as such. Sarraute's essays aim, instead, to be an expression of the desire embodied in reading: they speak in the name of that desire, or, as in the case of the stories of reading, offer narratives of Sarraute's encounters with works that have to a greater or lesser degree responded to its identificatory thrust.

In other words, the 'terrible desire to establish contact' applies as much to the relations between the reader and the text as it does to the psychology of the tropism ('Dostoïevski', p. 43). The desire that drives Dostoevsky's characters towards 'une impossible et apaisante étreinte' also drives the reader on in the same search for an ideal relation – but in this case with the text. This, at least, is the presupposition behind the essays; it is also the response that the novels would like to elicit from their real readers; and it is an experience that is occasionally represented within the novels themselves. For instance, the lone reader at the end of *Les Fruits d'or* is depicted in just such a relation: unable to express the textual 'étreinte' by means of critical comment and 'le vocabulaire perfectionné [des] savants docteurs' (p. 218), he articulates his contact and expresses his readerly desire by speaking directly to the work itself:

> Ce silence où vous baignez, dépouillé de tous les vêtements et ornements dont vous aviez été affublé, nu, tout lavé, flottant à la dérive, avec moi cramponné à vous, rend très étroit notre contact. Nous sommes si proches maintenant, vous êtes tellement une partie de moi, qu'il me semble que si vous cessiez d'exister, ce serait comme une part de moi-même qui deviendrait du tissu mort. (pp. 224–225)

The text is regarded here by its reader not as a linguistic construct that might lend itself to contemplation or analysis, but as a kind of being that has an existence beyond language, and this is precisely what makes contact possible: 'ce silence [...] rend très étroit notre contact'.

What, then, does all this imply about Sarraute's own so-called criticism? It is certainly something very different from my own commentary which in a Sarrautean schema is bound to appear uncomfortably like the lectures of the professor at the Collège de France as I try to explain the 'case' in hand. But at the risk of seeming to have been deaf to the values I have been elucidating, the discussion so far has established that Sarraute's essays take the form of a heretical intervention into systems of critical orthodoxy, and that they speak in the name of readerly contact with the text rather than with the aim of providing critical interpretation. In other words, they seek to do what Barthes has argued that the contradictory logics of readerly versus critical desire make impossible when he says that, because he uses a language other than that of the text, the critic can never act as spokesman for a collectivity of readers. Nevertheless, and logic notwithstanding, Sarraute writes precisely in the hope that

> la réponse que je me ferais à moi-même ne vaudrait pas pour moi seule. Elle serait peut-être aussi la réponse timide de quelques-uns de ces lecteurs inconnus qui, isolés les uns des autres, enfermés dans leurs chambres solitaires, en face de '[l']œuvre' s'interrogent avec inquiétude et s'étonnent. ('PV', pp. 11–12)

There remains more to be said about the paradoxical nature of the essays as criticism that speaks in the name of reading, and I shall return to this question later. In the meantime, I want to consider the use that the essays make of the critical capacity which they have – as it were – in spite of themselves for the benefit of the reader of Sarraute's own fiction. For the essays are addressed not to other critics but to a reader, a lone individual and not a member of a critical sect, in short, to the 'lecteurs inconnus [...] enfermés dans leurs chambres solitaires' from the Valéry essay. More particularly, the reader of the essays is treated as an actual or potential reader of Sarraute's own fictional œuvre, and thus as someone who may be trusted not to take critical language at face value.[9]

It is a striking feature of the essays that their literary and technical concerns are almost exclusively with those aspects of writing which bring reader and fictional text into closer contact. This is the case, for example, with the first issue that Sarraute confronts in *L'Ère du soupçon*: character. The exterior representation of character promoted by the 'roman de l'absurde' is already a barrier to contact, and Sarraute speaks of 'sa dureté [...] et son opacité' (p. 21). So too is the outmoded form of Balzacian characterization: in Balzac's time, the portrayal of a figure like Père Grandet represented '[un] terrain d'entente' between author and reader, but its anachronism in the modern era has opened up a breach between author and reader and character has become '[un] terrain dévasté où ils s'affrontent' (p. 74). In order to restore 'entente' between the two, character has to adapt to the reader's new-found knowledge of human psychology which is the legacy of the work of Joyce, Proust and Freud.

Furthermore, the manner in which that psychology is depicted in writing is just as urgent a critical question as is its content for Sarraute: no longer a matter of 'la vieille analyse des sentiments' *(ES*, p. 11), psychology becomes 'la substance vivante de tous mes livres' (p. 9), and the essays explain that this is by virtue of the fact that psychology is represented as contemporary with the writing of the text. In an interview in 1967, she sums up the point as follows: 'Chez moi, il s'agit de montrer des actions intérieures en train de se faire, des actes en train de se produire qui ne sont pas analysés mais seulement donnés'.[10] The gap implied by retrospect is closed through this simultaneity of writing – and consequently of reading – with the action itself. However, this would still leave open the gap implied by the depiction of psychology in the form of a spectacle which the reader merely observes, if Sarraute's conception of writing were not designed to shift the action from an imaginary stage in the novel to an inner space located within the reader himself – as she explains in the same essay: '[...] il n'était possible de communiquer [les tropismes] au lecteur que par des images qui en donnent des équivalents et lui fassent éprouver des sensations analogues' *(ES*, p. 9). Sarraute's reflections on the novel in these essays are about the technical means of bringing about this shift of scene, so that critical self-consciousness is not incompatible with this ultimate goal:

> Il est donc permis de rêver [...] d'une technique qui parviendrait à plonger le lecteur dans le flot de ces drames souterrains que Proust n'a eu le temps que de survoler, [...] qui donnerait au lecteur l'illusion de refaire lui-même ces actions. ('Conversation', pp. 139–140)

If this dream could be technically realized, the reader would be moved up so close to the action of the novels that the boundary which separates him from the text would be dissolved, and the symbiosis imagined by the figure at the end of *Les Fruits d'or* might become a guaranteed literary reality. It is as if Sarraute is prepared to take a detour through a potentially alienating critical awareness, to rummage around in her own literary 'dessous' explaining her own technical 'case', in order to formulate fantasies about this ideal 'étreinte' between reader and text.

The discussions of first-person narration and of dialogue represent two further aspects of this project. The first person is conceived of as a device to draw the reader on to a version of the 'terrain d'entente' provided by character in the traditional realist novel:

> Tout est là, en effet: reprendre au lecteur son bien et l'attirer coûte que coûte sur le terrain de l'auteur. Pour y parvenir, le procédé qui consiste à désigner par un 'je' le héros principal, constitue un moyen à la fois efficace et facile. ('L'Ère', pp. 90–91)

The use of dialogue is similarly designed to lure the reader into the universe of the text. The purpose behind Sarraute's preoccupation with the *modus* ('dit-il', 'répondit-elle') is to bring author and reader into direct contact with each other.[11] These little phrases undermine the novelist's aim because they maintain the distance which traditionally separates author from character and character from reader in a novel:

> Elles marquent la place à laquelle le romancier a toujours situé ses personnages: en un point aussi éloigné de lui-même que des lecteurs; à la place où se trouvent les joueurs d'un match de tennis, le romancier étant à celle de l'arbitre juché sur son siège, surveillant le jeu et annonçant les points aux spectateurs (en l'occurence les lecteurs) installés sur les gradins. ('Conversation', pp. 128–129)

Dispensing with the *modus* is a means of closing this gap and bringing author, reader and character into mutual contact.

The use of dialogue in the form of the combined effect of *conversation* and *sous-conversation* is viewed by Sarraute as a further device for involving the reader in the action of the novel and creating a contact which elicits his active response: 'Le lecteur, sans cesse tendu, aux aguets, comme s'il était à la place de celui à qui les paroles s'adressent, mobilise tous ses instincts de défense, tous ses dons d'intuition, sa mémoire, ses facultés de jugement et de raisonnement' ('Conversation', pp. 144–145). The dialogic nature of the novels obliges the reader to call on all his human resources as if he were himself directly implicated as their addressee.

The essays that deal with realism ('Ce que voient les oiseaux', and the two lectures 'Roman et réalité' and 'Forme et contenu dans le roman') go further than the previous ones by claiming that awareness of formal and technical issues is essential to the reader's grasp of the reality the author is trying to represent. Realism for Sarraute is not a matter of accurate resemblance, but of a joint involvement between author and reader in a quest for the real. The reality which the novelist seeks is by definition new and uncharted: 'c'est toujours du réel qui n'a pas été pris dans des formes convenues'. Forms have constantly to be renewed and revised: 'Il est nécessaire que les formes se déplacent continuellement. On ne peut plus reprendre les formes anciennes sans retrouver une substance romanesque ancienne, elle aussi connue'.[12] This means that critical awareness becomes a condition of the realism in the novels. If the reader is to share in the pursuit of an elusive reality, he must go through the same critical education as the novelist, unlearning old habits, and participating in the discovery of new ones. First of all, he needs to undertake a thorough rethinking of characterization, a project which is so vital that critical lessons are sometimes included in the novels themselves. Indeed, *Portrait d'un inconnu* could be seen as one long lesson on the subject. But, in addition, the book contains some quite overtly critical moments, such as the discussion of the character of Prince Bolkonsky in *War and Peace*. These moments are virtually indistinguishable from the essays, and the reading of Tolstoy is more or less identical to the account of Dostoevsky in 'De Dostoïevski à Kafka'. The critical enterprise is inseparable from the creative one, and the reader's participation in the text requires a degree of critical awareness that it is the essays' special task to promote, but which is not their exclusive preserve.

If the reader's contact with the text is so urgently sought by Sarraute that critical lessons must sometimes be included in the fiction, this implies the possibility of a reluctance or failure on his part to make the contact he is assumed so terribly to desire. And, at times, the essays do seem to anticipate potential resistance from the reader. Far from being shut off from the world in solitude and perplexity, awaiting endorsement of his own uncertain responses in the form of Sarraute's spokesmanship, he is also depicted as someone in need of some quite firm handling: having to be stripped of his possessions and drawn 'coûte que coûte' on to the author's ground. But these signs of his occasional reluctance merely draw attention to the *mutual* nature of the desire for contact: if – in principle, at least – the reader desires contact with the text, the text is equally desiring of its readers. Signs of a recourse to technical force and pedagogical self-commentary are proof of the fact that the text can no more stand the resistance and opacity of its readers than can the characters they portray. It is as desperate as they are to 'essayer par n'importe quel moyen de se frayer un chemin jusqu'à autrui, de pénétrer en lui le plus loin possible, de lui faire perdre son inquiétante, son insupportable opacité ('Dostoïevski', p. 43). And like these same characters, this desire for contact with the other 'le [...] pousse à s'ouvrir à lui à [son] tour, à lui révéler [ses] plus secrets replis'. In so far as the essays are part of this desire to break down the terrifying opacity of the other and draw him into the orbit of the novels, the function of their critical awareness is to *remove* any obstacles (outmoded assumptions, readerly resistance) that might stand between reader and text, and not to add to them in the manner of the sort of critical commentary ('la gangue solide et dure [...] de commentaires enthousiastes') that surrounds the work of Paul Valéry. In short, the essays both contain an inventory of the devices used by the novels to draw the reader into their embrace, and themselves constitute just such a device: offering explanations that help to reduce the opacity of the work, and inviting the reader behind the scenes, and into their most intimate recesses, to share the author's creative preoccupations and concerns.

Nevertheless, nothing guarantees this transparency, and Sarraute appears very conscious of the risk of her own commentaries becoming an impediment to contact ('gangue' rather than 'étreinte'); and in interviews she frequently attempts to divert the attention of potential readers away from the essays and back to the fictional texts:

> [...] je suis entièrement d'accord avec Roland Barthes quand il nie la possibilité pour un écrivain de communiquer aux lecteurs par des discours ou des écrits autres que son œuvre elle-même les sens différents, le plus souvent ignorés de lui, qu'elle contient, de renforcer par des articles ou par des déclarations l'impression que seule l'œuvre elle-même, dans la forme particulière qu'il a choisie, peut donner.[13]

The reason she gives for the impossibility of critical communication with the reader is that critical self-commentary requires of the writer 'un langage [...] très différent de celui qu'il emploie dans son œuvre écrite'. Critical language is, however, not only different, but positively dangerous, since it brings with it a degree of 'lucidity' which undermines the creative impulse: 'Une grande lucidité, une conscience trop claire au cours du travail seraient, me semble-t-il, assez dangereuses; je crois que l'impulsion créatrice trouve au départ sa source dans l'inconscient' (p. 28). One solution to the threat posed by the excessive lucidity and the linguistic difference of critical commentary is to efface or eclipse it before the literary text by directing the reader to set it aside and return to the text, as Sarraute does here. But another means of achieving this would be to create maximum homology between the two forms of discourse, and actively work against the difference between the two. I have already discussed how critical language forms a necessary part of the fiction; so I should like now to look at the homology from the reverse perspective, and examine the ways in which the critical essays repeat the fictional strategies found in the novels.

Much of this repetition consists in a miming of scenarios that appear in the novels. I began by suggesting that the essays themselves are staged in the terms of a particular scenario which is a recurrent feature in the novels: the lone figure ('le voyou qui trouble l'ordre' of *"disent les imbéciles"*,[14] as well as the 'folle' of *Les Fruits d'or*) who deliberately or inadvertently comes up against the concerted opposition of established opinion, social and cultural as well as specifically literary. In miming this relation, then, the essays are strongly identifying themselves with the fiction from the outset. Similarly – if somewhat paradoxically – the *prise de conscience* and the lucidity associated with criticism, and whose pernicious effects Sarraute condemns in the remarks quoted above, are none the less an integral element of the fiction. In describing her essays as a retrospective attempt to understand her own writing, Sarraute is repeating a gesture that is fundamental both to the experience of the characters in her novels and to the work of the novelist: 'J'ai été amenée ainsi à réfléchir – ne serait-ce que pour me justifier ou me rassurer ou m'encourager – aux raisons qui m'ont poussée à certains refus, qui m'ont imposé certaines techniques' *(ES,* p. 10). Not only does this account of the genesis of the essays establish an order of events which preserves the spontaneity of the creative impulse in the unconscious, but it also follows the course that events tend to take in the fictional and dramatic work. Action in Sarraute very frequently appears as a spontaneous or unconscious phenomenon which can be grasped only by a retrospective unpacking of the moment in response to the question: 'que s'est-il passé?', which is asked both by the characters and by the novelist/narrator: 'Vous me dites quelque chose, je sens un malaise ou je rougis, il est impossible que je l'empêche, et c'est là que commence mon travail: que s'est-il passé? Quel mouvement avez-vous accompli pour produire en moi cet autre mouvement?'[15] In other words, as well as being stories of reading, the essays also become stories of writing which, by turning back to the novels and treating them as a similar sort of spontaneous or unconscious event, re-enact the plot-forms of the novels whose writing they narrate.

This mimicry goes very deep and it is reinforced by a number of more localized rhetorical and stylistic effects.[16] In particular, the essays make extensive use of the irony, metaphor and dialogue which characterize so much of Sarraute's fictional work. For example, 'Conversation et sous-conversation' opens with a heavily ironic dismissal of Virginia Woolf: 'Qui songerait aujourd'hui à prendre encore au sérieux ou seulement à lire les articles que Virginia Woolf, quelques années après l'autre guerre, écrivait sur le roman? Leur confiance naïve, leur innocence d'un autre âge feraient sourire' (p. 98). It was a risky piece of rhetoric and even some of the most well-disposed critics missed the ironic intent,[17] but it does illustrate the extent to which the language of the novelist comes naturally to the critic. This is even more evident in the essays' use of imagery, some of which also appears in near-identical form in the novels. For example, in the Valéry article Sarraute uses a highly metaphorical passage to describe the effect that reading 'La Jeune Parque' has on her: 'Je venais de reconnaître cette vieille odeur aigrelette de chiffon humide et de craie, cette vieille odeur rassurante et familière d'encre et de poussière qui flotte autour des souvenirs d'exercices et d'efforts scolaires' (p. 16). The same image returns in *Vous les entendez?* some twenty-five years later where the father reluctantly submits to the verdict passed on his children as 'des cancres':

> Se levant, prenant congé, prenant la fuite, fuyant à travers les tristes cours couvertes de gravier, de ciment, le long des hideux couloirs à l'odeur de poussière humide, de désinfectants, le long des mornes salles vitrées où des médiocres ingurgitent docilement des bouillies insipides.[18]

In both essay and novel, the dreary atmosphere of the classroom is evoked to convey a sense of enforced mediocrity and obligatory conformism. The fact that the image appears in the essay so long before the novel is yet another sign of the extent to which the language of the essays repeats and mimes – even to the extent of anticipating – that of the novels.

Jean-Yves Tadié has drawn attention to the widespread use of spoken language and dialogue in the essays,[19] but there is also a way in which, above and beyond this use, the essays are fundamentally conceived as components of a dialogue. In their heretical guise, they appear as a retort or a challenge to existing views, a posture which of itself already implies dialogue of sorts. A somewhat more conciliatory version of this confrontation is sketched by Sarraute in one of her lectures where she accepts the possibility of critical difference in asking: 'L'essentiel, n'est-il pas, dans une rencontre comme celle-ci, de discuter, de confronter les points de vue?' ('Roman et realité', p. 1). More frequently and more consistently, however, the essays adopt a distinctly complicitous tone of address, as if they were one half of a dialogue with a silent and largely assenting reader. For instance, the reading of Camus in 'De Dostoïevski à Kafka' is presented as a shared undertaking: 'Enfin! Nous y voilà donc. Ce dont nous nous étions timidement doutés se trouve d'un seul coup confirmé' (p. 29). And the ironic comment on Virginia Woolf cited above clearly presupposes an addressee who knows how to interpret it correctly.

The implicitly dialogic nature of the essays becomes overt in the lectures, and after *L'Ère du soupçon* (with the single exception of the essay on Flaubert) all Sarraute's critical work started life in lecture form.[20] Although the lectures were written out in full and delivered from a script, Sarraute always had beside her a set of what she has called 'notes de plaidoirie', consisting of a list of headings corresponding to the different points she intended to cover, and designed above all to lend the lectures as much of a spoken air as possible.[21] The lectures testify to a powerful awareness of their audience whom Sarraute frequently addresses in the second person: 'Je *vous* ai proposé de *vous* parler aujourd'hui du langage dans l'art du roman. Et à ce propos je *vous* ferai part de quelques opinions', etc. ('Le langage dans l'art du roman', p. 1, my italics). Elsewhere she describes the occasion as a 'causerie' ('Forme'), and in fact from the 1970s onwards she abandoned the lecture proper in favour of the 'rencontre' or 'causerie' which took (and still takes) the form of question and answer sessions, so making explicit the underlying dialogue contained in the more traditional lectures.

All this would seem to confirm that through dialogue, irony and metaphor, the writing of the essays mimes the fiction to a very considerable degree. But another point also emerges from the orientation of the essays as dialogue, for the effect of this slant is to figure the reader in a way which has important implications for his role in relation to the fictional texts. In an interview (and, incidentally, the interview format is, of course, yet another version of the dialogue in which critical ideas are expressed) Sarraute has talked about her conception of the audience of her lectures as a collective instance of the silent but assenting reader postulated in the essays: 'Quand je suis devant un auditoire, je ne vois que des gens *grosso modo* sympathisants et qui sont comme moi. Il n'est pas question d'hostilité ni de résistance: ils sont comme moi'.[22] The lectures, like the early essay on Valéry, conjure up adressees 'qui sont comme moi', beings whose sensibilities ultimately make them ideal readers of the novels. The very overt and direct forms of address used in the lectures, and heavily implied in the critical writings, work towards creating this ideal reader for the fiction.

Sarraute goes on to describe the critical self-commentary contained in *L'Usage de la parole* as a means of creating the reader of her desires: 'Je montre au lecteur à quoi on va jouer, je lui donne les règles du jeu'. This device works, according to her, because the reader is a figure whom she conceives of as 'like her': 'Dans ma naïveté, je crois toujours que le lecteur est exactement comme moi, que celui qui me lit a les mêmes sensations que moi' (p. 4). This is the counterpart to the process of identification through which the reader's desire for the text manifests itself: just as the reader desires the text by wishing to become the text, so the author desires the reader as a self-projection with whom she too can in turn identify.

One of the purposes of the critical writing is to create such a figure from whom real readers of the novels may take their cue. This is perhaps not so much a matter of miming as of projecting, but the reader called up by means of this projection in the criticism constitutes a crucial link between the essays and the fiction. He is also a figure who fits in multiple ways into the 'terrible desire to establish contact', being the object of the author's desire for contact through the text, and imagined as the subject of a reciprocal desire. The reader's contact with the text is made possible, first by a critical self-commentary which spells out the rules of the game so that nothing may stand in the way of maximum participation; and second, by turning that commentary into a rehearsal of the scenarios and the rhetoric of the novels themselves. The essays are thus both precept and example, both a saying and a doing, and as such, they put the reader through a dual apprenticeship for the fictional corpus. There seems, in other words, to be no limit to the 'terrible desire to establish contact' in Sarraute, and the essays constitute a particularly intense – if risky – instance of it, adopting the potentially alienating language of critical lucidity in the hope of making the reader experience the text as a living and non-linguistic part of his own self and capable of addressing it in the words of the figure depicted in *Les Fruits d'or*: 'Nous sommes si proches maintenant, vous êtes tellement une partie de moi, que si vous cessiez d'exister, ce serait comme une part de moi-même qui deviendrait du tissu mort'.

Abbreviations

The critical corpus referred to is as follows:

'Paul Valéry et l'Enfant d'Éléphant' (first published in *Les Temps Modernes* 2 No. 16 (January 1947). Full version published in *Paul Valéry et l'Enfant d'Éléphant, Flaubert le précurseur* (Paris: Gallimard, 1986), 9–57 ('PV' and *PV* respectively in my text).
'De Dostoïevski à Kafka', first published in *Les Temps Modernes* 3 No. 25 (October 1947). Reprinted in *L'Ère du soupçon* (Paris: Gallimard, 1956). I shall be referring to the Collection Idées edition (Paris: Gallimard, 1964, 15–66) which includes a preface by Sarraute ('Dostoïevski' and *ES* respectively in my text).
'L'Ère du soupçon', first published in *Les Temps Modernes* 5 No. 52 (February 1950). Reprinted in *ES*, 67–94 ('L'Ère' in my text).
'Conversation et sous-conversation', first published in the *Nouvelle Revue Française* 7 Nos. 37–38 (January–February 1956), and reprinted in *ES,* 97–147 ('Conversation' in my text).
'Ce que voient les oiseaux' in *ES*, 149–184.
'La littérature, aujourd'hui – II', *Tel Quel* 9 (1962), 48–53.
'Flaubert le précurseur', first published in *Preuves* 15 No. 168 (1965), reprinted in *PV*, 61–89 ('Flaubert' in my text).
'Roman et réalité', unpublished lecture first delivered at the University of Lausanne in 1959 (page references are to the manuscript version).
'Forme et contenu du roman', unpublished lecture (page references are to the manuscript version).
'Le langage dans l'art du roman', lecture first delivered at the

University of Seinan-Gakuin in Japan in 1970. A slightly abbreviated version is included in Simone Benmussa, *Nathalie Sarraute: Qui êtes-vous?* (Lyon: La Manufacture, 1987), 183–202. References are to the manuscript version.

'Ce que je cherche à faire', lecture given at Cerisy-la-Salle in 1971 in Jean Ricardou and Françoise van Rossum-Guyon (eds.), *Le Nouveau Roman: Hier, aujourd'hui* (Paris: Union Générale d'Éditions, 1972), II, 25–40 ('Ce que' in my text).

'Le Gant retourné', lecture first delivered at the University of Wisconsin at Madison in 1974, *Cahiers Renaud-Barrault* 89 (1974), 70–79.

Notes

* This essay has already appeared, dedicated to Valerie Minogue, in *L'Esprit Créateur* 36 (Summer 1996), 44–62.

[1] Reviewing the volume in 1956, Paul de Man sums up *L'Ère du soupçon* as 'le diagnostic sur l'état actuel d'un genre littéraire devenu problématique', *Monde Nouveau* 12 No. 101 (June 1956), 57–61. See also Claude Mauriac, 'Nathalie Sarraute et le nouveau réalisme', *Preuves* 7 No. 72 (February 1957), 76–81, for a similar view.

[2] Jean-Yves Tadié, 'Un traité du roman', *L'Arc* 95 (1984), 55–59. Tadié's is the only discussion of *L'Ère du soupçon* known to me that treats the work as a text in its own right.

[3] No one has argued more clearly for this kind of reading of Sarraute's language than Valerie Minogue. See her *Nathalie Sarraute and the War of the Words* (Edinburgh: Edinburgh University Press, 1981).

[4] *Les Fruits d'or* (Paris: Gallimard, 1963), 58. Henceforward referred to as *FO* in the text.

[5] *Tropismes* (Paris: Éditions de Minuit, 1957), 76.

[6] Jonathan Culler, *On Deconstruction* (London: Routledge & Kegan Paul, 1983), 64–83.

[7] I owe this observation to Mark Lee.

[8] Roland Barthes, *Critique et vérité* (Paris: Éditions du Seuil, 1966), 76. See also n. 13 below.

[9] I shall continue to refer to the reader as 'he' in compliance with Sarraute's positive refusal to take gender into consideration. On this subject see S. Benmussa, *Nathalie Sarraute: Qui êtes-vous?* (Lyon: La Manufacture, 1987), 139–145.

[10] Interview with Nicole Zand, *Le Monde* (18 January 1967), 18.

[11] For a full discussion of this aspect of Sarraute's writing, see A. S. Newman, *Une poésie des discours: essai sur les romans de Nathalie Sarraute* (Geneva: Droz, 1976).

[12] Interview with Serge Fauchereau and Jean Ristat, *Digraphe* 32 (March 1984), 9–18 (16).

[13] Interview with Geneviève Serreau, *Lettres Nouvelles* 29 (April 1959), 28–30 (28). In the light of the remarks I have quoted from *Critique et vérité*, it is interesting to see Sarraute put her seal of approval on Barthes's views on the matter. Since *Critique et vérité* did not appear until 1966, one can only speculate about what essay or work by Barthes Sarraute might be referring to here.

[14] *"disent les imbéciles"* (Paris: Gallimard, 1976), 9.

[15] Interview with François Poirier, *Art Press* (July–August 1983), 28–30 (29).

[16] Some of these have been briefly noted by Tadié, 'Un traité', 58–59.

[17] See, for example, Claude Mauriac in his review of *L'Ère du soupçon*, 'Nathalie Sarraute et le nouveau réalisme'.

[18] *Vous les entendez?* (Paris: Gallimard, 1972), 53–54.

[19] 'Le langage parlé et le langage pensé sont le sujet de la fiction; ils envahissent la critique du roman'. But the explanation for this phenomenon ('l'essai se fragmente en dialogue et devient un roman d'idées') does not explain why Sarraute's critical writing needs to take the form of fiction. See Tadié, 'Un traité', 59.

[20] In addition to the three unpublished lectures, there are the two articles – 'Ce que je cherche à faire' and 'Le Gant retourné' – which were both delivered as lectures before appearing in written form. The interview with *Tel Quel* is a special case since, although it takes the form of a dialogue, the answers were provided in writing in reponse to written questions. It is, however, quite manifestly a dialogue, if not a spoken one.

[21] Information gleaned from a conversation with Nathalie Sarraute.

[22] Interviews with Carmen Licari, *Francofonia* 9 (August 1985), 3–16 (15).

The Voice on the Page and the Voice from the Stage: Contemporary Dramatic Adaptations of the Works of Balzac and George Sand

F. W. J. HEMMINGS

Ever since Shakespeare borrowed the plot of Thomas Lodge's romance *Rosalynde* for *As you like it* and of Robert Greene's *Pandosto* for *The Winter's Tale*, dramatists have never scrupled to exploit the inventions of fiction writers of their day. Richardson gave Goldoni the idea of *Pamela nubile*, and Defoe's *Robinson Crusoe*, well known to the French, delighted them in Pixérécourt's stage version (1805), a very free one indeed; as one of his biographers commented: '[...] jamais île déserte ne fut plus peuplée que celle du Robinson de Pixérécourt'. It would indeed be difficult to imagine a faithful reworking of this novel for the stage other than by a succession of monologues in the first part and of halting dialogue after the discovery of Man Friday; but Pixérécourt 'ne se contentait jamais d'employer une intrigue telle quelle. Il se délectait à créer des complications inédites et des personnages nouveaux'.[1]

The ideas for a number of Pixérécourt's melodramas were taken not from older novelists like Defoe, whose works were in the public domain, but from his contemporaries. Nodier had no sooner published his *Jean Sbogar* than Pixérécourt busied himself with dramatizing it, turning the brigand chief into the leader of a band of pirates and shifting the action from the Adriatic to Sicily. Under the title *Le Belvéder ou la Vallée de l'Etna*, Pixérécourt's play was a sensational hit when put on at the Ambigu-Comique, a bare twelve months after the novella appeared; there is no evidence that he sought Nodier's permission to use his work as the basis for his melodrama. Such permission would have been deemed altogether superfluous at the time, and an action for breach of copyright would have been laughed out of court. However, as time went by, the shameless plundering of fictional successes by writers for the stage reached such proportions that protests began to be voiced, though not originally by the novelists who may have been quite flattered by the extra publicity given to their work, but rather by their publishers, who reckoned that the popularity of these stage adaptations was doing serious damage to the sale of the original novels. Jules Janin relates a conversation he had had with an 'honnête libraire' who stated that he had brought out five successive novels the previous year with very little profit:

> On me les a pris tout chauds et à peine publiés, pour les mettre sur la scène [...] Comment faire, je vous prie, et comment tolérer ce brigandage? d'autant plus que ces drames, faits sur des livres, dégoûtent souvent du livre: on croit que c'est là le roman, on n'a pas grand empressement à le lire; et moi, pauvre éditeur, me voilà placé entre deux Belgiques qui contrefont mes livres, impunément.[2]

Belgium, at the time, had no copyright convention with France, and Belgian publishers were waxing rich on the profits made by producing cheap reprints of current French best sellers.

Balzac

Balzac may have suffered to some extent from the loss of income that these unauthorized transfers of his work to the stage represented, though it is possible that what he resented most was the deliberate distortions introduced in the original by the dramatists. The first of his novels to attract their attention was *La Peau de chagrin* which, published in August 1831, excited immediate interest among the reading public thanks to its strange blending of contemporary allusion and social comment with an underlying theme of oriental mystery. The first stage version was that by A. J. B. Simonnin and Théodore Nézel, which was produced at the Gaîté on 4 November 1832 as a 'comédie-vaudeville' with a subtitle *La Peau de chagrin ou le Roman en action, extravagance romantique.* Unlike all the others we shall be considering here, this was never intended as a true adaptation where the salient incidents in a novel are presented on the stage much as they had been on the printed page; it would be better described as one of the numerous efforts around this time to deflate and ridicule the pretensions of the Romantic movement. Raphaël is still the central character, but instead of being an impoverished marquis, he is now a mere *commis-marchand* living in poorly appointed bachelor's lodgings rented to him by Gaudin, now transformed into an *ouvrier-gainier*; Pauline, Gaudin's sister, is first seen tidying his room in his absence. She has clearly set her cap at Raphaël who, however, is indifferent to her charms; but she also knows his weaknesses: 'O Dieu! aime-t-il les romans, mon jeune homme ... surtout les romans – romantiques ... Il en a la tête farcie et je crois un peu timbrée'. When her brother speaks of him contemptuously as 'un gaillard qui se figure être toujours le héros du dernier roman qui paraît', she cannot but agree with him: 'C'est pourtant vrai: quand il a lu *Le Dernier Jour d'un condamné*, il y avait des moments où il croyait avoir perdu la tête'. It is clear that the authors of this extravaganza had not only Balzac in their sights, but Hugo too and probably all the *chefs de file* of the young Romantic movement.

Should their *extravagance romantique* be seen not so much as a dramatization of *La Peau de chagrin* as a parody? To be parodied was, under the Restoration, the ultimate consecration of a theatrical success. Dumas actually collaborated with two friends in the confection of *La Cour du roi Pétaud*, a parody of his own *Henri III et sa cour*. Juste Olivier, arriving in Paris from Switzerland in 1830, went straight to the Théâtre-Français to regale himself with *Hernani* and then, on 12 May, records seeing *Harnali ou la Contrainte par cor* at the Vaudeville. The author was a certain F. A. Duvert, to whom a member of the cast of *Hernani* had smuggled a copy of the original which Duvert used as the basis of his parody, advertised on the playbills only a month after the celebrated first night of *Hernani*.

But these were all parodies of theatrical hits; there is no record of a novel, no matter how popular, being guyed in this way on the stage. Simonnin and Nézel were nevertheless counting on the phenomenal success of Balzac's *La Peau de chagrin* to attract an audience which they proceeded to keep amused with various in-jokes. The scenario they devised was to have all the marvels described in the book brought about by Pauline, with the help of an occasional stroke of luck: it is Pauline, not any magic talisman, who arranges that all Raphaël's wishes should be granted. When she overhears him sighing for the miraculous shagreen skin he has read about, she procures a piece from her brother – shagreen being one of the commoner articles of his trade – and places it where Raphaël will find it when he wakes up after a nap. She also, from her own savings, orders him a fine new suit of clothes and purchases a winning lottery ticket by means of which she can announce to him that he has come into a fortune. During one of Raphaël's absences, Gaudin returns for his shagreen skin but, deciding the piece is too large for his purposes, shears off a portion and returns to his shop with it. Thus the skin shrinks, exactly as in the novel; on a later occasion a couple of billiard players, needing to mend a cue, take the remnant of the shagreen skin and cut away a further piece.

Balzac had shown his hero as infatuated initially with Foedora and only later turning to Pauline. The two adapters, giving Pauline credit for a good deal more initiative than she displays in the novel, show her hiding in Foedora's house where, running into her unexpectedly one night and mistaking her for Foedora, Raphaël exclaims: 'Je vais faire la fin du 3e acte d'*Antony*', and so consummates his passion off-stage. (It will be recalled that the third act of Dumas's *Antony* ends when the hero, who has secretly followed Adèle Hervey to an inn, covers her mouth with a handkerchief and carries her off into the bedroom.) Having made love to Pauline, Raphaël is under an obligation to marry her, as her brother Gaudin points out to him quite fiercely. In a final explanation, Raphaël is made to understand that the progressive shrinking of the supposedly magical skin does not betoken his approaching death, for it was not the piece of shagreen but Pauline who was responsible for ensuring that all his wishes come true. As was customary, the actor addressed his last words to the audience: 'Oui, mes amis, je suis guéri! je suis raisonnable; et pourtant, je vais me marier, c'est ma dernière extravagance. Celle-là, du moins, elle est *classique*'.

A more faithful stage adaptation of *La Peau de chagrin*, in which the supernatural element, explained away as we have seen in the 1832 version, is restored and even reinforced, was attempted by Louis Judicis in 1851, where it was described as a 'drame fantastique ... tiré du roman de M. H. de Balzac' – Balzac having died the previous year. The opening scene in the gambling den is passed over, but otherwise the first act follows the original narrative quite closely. Raphaël, penniless, desperate, and waiting only for nightfall when he can throw himself into the Seine without risk of rescue, enters the antique dealer's shop and is shown round by a young assistant, who later summons the proprietor – nameless in the novel but here called M. Job. Having understood that Raphaël is proposing to commit suicide rather than face destitution, Job promises to make him an instant millionaire; the expressions he uses are much the same as those we find in the novel: 'Sans que je vous donne un centime de

France, un maravédis d'Espagne, une gazetta de Venise, un farthing d'Angleterre, je puis vous faire plus riche, plus puissant, plus considéré qu'un roi constitutionnel'; whereupon he shows him the magic shagreen skin. Raphaël deciphers correctly the Sanskrit inscription and, despite the antiquary's warnings, grasps the talisman and utters his first trivial wish: to participate in an orgy. There follows a transformation scene (one of the *changements à vue* which were still at this time a fascinating novelty on the French stage) and the audience is transported to the banquet given to celebrate the inauguration of a new periodical. Raphaël realises his first wish has been granted, but he also makes the sinister discovery that the shagreen skin has shrunk, as foretold.

There seems to be no reason why Judicis should not have continued in this way, giving shape and reality to the various incidents in Raphaël's remaining short span of life, and omitting only such as would have been difficult to stage (the attempt to restore the shagreen skin to its original dimensions by applying hydraulic pressure, an experiment which causes the machine to explode without enlarging the piece of leather by a hair's breadth). Instead, wanting no doubt to even up the parts taken by the two principal actresses, he gave a much more important role to Foedora who is at most a shadowy figure in Balzac's novel. At a ball, Raphaël shows the company the ignoble origins of Foedora's fortune, supposedly thanks to his mysterious powers, but in fact probably by a display of *ombres chinoises*, cut-out figures moving behind a translucid screen with lights shining behind them. To avenge herself, Foedora persuades one of her admirers to insult Raphaël who, by another piece of sleight of hand, diverts the blow aimed at his cheek so that it falls on Job's. In the fourth act Foedora, reduced now to her original trade of streetwalker, threatens Raphaël with reprisals for having revealed the secret of her infamous past. But Raphaël, making further use of the famous talisman, expresses one last wish: 'Je veux qu'à ton tour tu subisses les tortures d'un amour méprisé, foulé aux pieds. Je le veux ... cela sera'; whereupon Foedora, choking out the words: 'Raphaël, je te h ... Je t'aime', sinks to her knees before him.

The fifth act transports us to the Auvergne. In a last reminiscence of Balzac's story, Judicis introduces the episode where Raphaël, in a vain attempt to rid himself of the talisman, throws it down a well only to have it restored to him, to his consternation, by the gardener who had noticed it floating in a bucket of water he had drawn. More importantly, he completely alters the ending. In the novel, it will be remembered, Raphaël dies in Pauline's arms, his teeth buried in her breast, in a final frenzy of desire. For this scene, which propriety would never have permitted on the stage in 1851, Judicis substituted a string of incidents of his own invention. It emerges that a codicil had been added in Chaldean to the Sanskrit inscription on the skin, which Job interprets as reading: 'Qu'un mortel, homme ou femme, consente à donner sa vie pour ta vie, et je perds toute ma puissance'. The last scenes of this act take place in gathering darkness. Raphaël tells Foedora that he has, in Marlowe's words, 'but one bare hour to live', unless she consents to die in his place. Foedora hesitates, whereupon Pauline grasps the talisman, now a mere scrap of leather, and utters the fatal words: 'A moi la mort, à lui la vie!' and falls dead on the spot, Raphaël crying out in despair: 'c'est moi qui l'ai tuée'. That is not, however, how the play ends, for there is an epilogue, in which all the events in the preceding drama are shown to be the hallucinations Raphaël has been subject to while suffering from an attack of brain fever. It was all a dream, except that Raphaël's uncle has died, leaving him no millions but 'une honnête aisance', sufficient at any rate to allow Raphaël to propose to Pauline. The closing words, given to Rastignac to speak, are improbably sententious considering what we know of Rastignac's character: 'Ton rêve t'aura du moins prouvé ceci: que la véritable sagesse consiste à ne pas user sa vie à courir après le bonheur' – to which Raphaël adds smugly: 'lorsqu'il suffit d'étendre la main pour le saisir'. Balzac was no longer around to protest at the monstrous liberties taken with his work; and the honest artisans who composed the bulk of the audience at the Ambigu-Comique were no doubt quite satisfied with the banality of this ending.

The 1830s saw several other dramatizations of the novels and short stories that poured from Balzac's pen over that decade: they were all undertaken by professional writers for the stage, and for the most part figured on the playbills shortly after the originals were published – incidental testimony to the rapid growth of Balzac's reputation. Thus, a version of *Le Colonel Chabert* was produced at the Vaudeville in July 1832, having been drawn not from the book but from the serialized story which had appeared in *L'Artiste* over the previous February and March. The text of the play, published by Barba the same year, contains no reference to the originator of the story but prints on the title-page simply the names of the two adapters, Jacques Arago and Louis Lurine. It probably had a short run and Balzac, who had gone down to Saché on 8 June 1832 and did not return to Paris until the following December, may not even have seen a performance. One reason why the play may have commended itself to the management of the Vaudeville is that, under the Restoration, any reference to Napoleon, his battles or his campaigns, was pitilessly proscribed by the censorship; and the July Revolution was followed by a positive avalanche of plays concerned with the events that had occurred under the Empire.

As so often in these adaptations, the dramatists made no attempt to improve on the novelist's opening scenes which are, here as elsewhere, sufficiently dramatic not to need any touching up. Accordingly, when the curtain went up, the audience was shown the impertinent reception of the ragged officer by the copy-clerks in Derville's office; taking down his name, Chabert, one of them asks jokingly: 'Ce n'est pas le colonel mort à Eylau?' and is confounded by the flat answer: 'Lui-même'. Derville, entering at this point, sends the clerks packing and invites his strange client to tell his story; Chabert does so, making much of the difficulties he has found since his return to Paris to establish his identity, and concluding with the same words virtually as Balzac had given him to speak: 'Je me suis vu enterré sous des morts et voilà qu'on m'enterre sous des vivants'. It is only in the second of the two acts, which takes place at the countess's country estate, that the adapters diverged to any great extent from Balzac's story line. In the novella Chabert finally abandons the attempt to secure legal restitution of his rights, in sheer despair at the thought of the endless struggles that lie ahead; or, as Balzac puts it: 'Il touchait à l'une de ces maladies pour lesquelles la médecine n'a pas de nom [...] affection qu'il faudrait nommer le *spleen* du malheur'. But a novelist, in the days when authorial comment was not only tolerated but expected, is free to explain matters which a playwright has to pass over in silence. In the stage adaptation, seeing the havoc that his return to respectability would cause, Chabert acknowledges that 'les morts ont bien tort de revenir', and is on the point of abandoning his lawsuit and returning to obscurity. But when his wife presses him, asking that he should sign a document in due form to confirm this, he flares up: 'Ma parole ne vous suffit-elle pas?' and he positively refuses to declare himself an impostor trying to extort money by blackmail.

This was not an ending that would have satisfied an audience at the Vaudeville, nor would they have been happy with an epilogue such as Balzac appended, showing Derville discussing the case with a friend and comparing it with others he has come across in the course of his legal career: 'J'ai vu des crimes contre lesquels la justice est impuissante. Enfin, toutes les horreurs que les romanciers croient inventer sont toujours au-dessous de la vérité'. In the story, the countess, once Chabert has assured her he would trouble her no longer, had allowed him to leave, satisfied, 'avec la profonde perspicacité que donne une haute scélératesse ou le féroce égoïsme du monde, elle crut pouvoir vivre en paix sur la promesse et le mépris de ce loyal soldat'. But the spectators would never have tolerated this: they needed to see the countess punished for refusing to acknowledge her rightful husband and to allow him to take his proper place in society. So the play brings on Ferrières, who never appears in person in the novella, and culminates in an admittedly dramatic encounter between the countess's legal husband and the other, who married her bigamously, believing her to be a widow. Chabert tells the full story to Ferrières in the presence of the countess who has not a word to say in her defence; then he storms out. Ferrières rounds on her, declaring himself shamed and dishonoured by her conduct, and insists that she leave Paris and never see the two children she has had by him again. In the short scene before the final curtain, the two men both bid her farewell, Ferrières addressing her as 'madame la comtesse Chabert' and Chabert addressing her as 'madame la comtesse Ferrières': humiliation could go no further.

Suiting Balzac to the requirements of a boulevard audience under the July Monarchy posed playwrights the same basic problem whatever the novel they undertook to adapt: that of dispensing with the tragic or sordid ending and substituting an upbeat denouement that would allow the spectators to leave the theatre reassured and in a cheerful frame of mind. Neither *Eugénie Grandet* nor *Le Père Goriot* could be dramatized with the painful resolution devised by the novelist; no theatre director would have entertained for a moment the idea of a faithful transcription of the march of events as the novelist had given them. *La Fille de l'avare*, under which title the adaptation of *Eugénie Grandet* was launched in January 1835, was described on the playbills as a 'comédie-vaudeville en deux actes' and was put on at the Gymnase-Dramatique which had some seasoned troupers in its company: Léontine Fay, who had swept the boards as a child prodigy and who acted now under her married name, Volnys, was given the part of Eugénie, and Bouffé, the celebrated comic actor who had joined the Gymnase in 1831, played

Grandet. The other characters were Charles Grandet, Nanon, and a notary (Menu) with his nephew Isidore, representing approximately Cruchot and his nephew. Delestre-Poirson, the redoubtable director of the Gymnase, was evidently sufficiently confident in the version (the work of Jean-François Bayard and Paul Duport) to invite the novelist to the first night.[3] What Balzac thought of the dramatization is not known; but he had, in the course of writing the book, almost invited some such a transmutation, referring at one point to 'la prodigieuse curiosité qu'excitent les avares habilement mis en scène'.[4] The question whether Balzac's Grandet, however fascinating a character, could figure properly in a light comedy was hardly resolved by *La Fille de l'avare*. It is towards the end of the first act that Eugénie's father hands her the letter Charles has brought him from his father. In the novel this letter announced the banker's impending suicide, and requests only that Grandet should advance Charles sufficient capital to allow him to start trading in India. In the play we are given to understand that there would still be time to save Charles's father if the miser would come to his rescue; but this, of course, is what Grandet will not do.

Essentially, what Bayard and Duport did was to substitute for Balzac's denouement that of Molière's in *L'Avare*. Eugénie, whose sympathy has been aroused by Charles's desperate grief, breaks into Grandet's locked room and removes his treasure, the heavy 'valise' corresponding to Harpagon's 'cassette'; she entrusts it hastily to Isidore who takes it at top speed to Paris. Charles, knowing nothing of her plan, saddles a horse and gallops off in the same direction. Grandet, on discovering his loss, leaps to the mistaken conclusion that Charles, who has so inexplicably disappeared, must be the thief, and dispatches Menu to fetch him back. This *chassé-croisé* obviously represents the comic scenes at the end of Act IV and the beginning of Act V of *L'Avare*, but a further scene in the adaptation, when Eugénie confesses to the theft but refuses to say what she has done with the gold and is locked in her room by her enraged father, is clearly inspired by a much later episode in *Eugénie Grandet*. The play ends happily, as it had to, with Isidore returning from Paris having arrived in time to prevent the banker's threatened suicide, and Eugénie accepting Charles's proposal of marriage.

La Fille de l'avare went through a respectable number of performances in Paris and subsequently in the provinces; rather less successful, and deservedly so, was the dramatization of *Le Père Goriot* later the same year by the three 'fournisseurs attitrés' at the

Théâtre des Variétés: Jaime, Decomberousse and Théaulon. Balzac seems to have thought but little of their work, while appreciating the efforts of their interpreters: according to a story related by Charles Monselet in the first chapter of his *Souvenirs littéraires* (1888), he sent carriages for the cast after the first performance to take them to a fashionable restaurant, but pointedly did not include in the invitation any of the three playwrights. Balzac might well have been irritated at the liberties taken with his masterpiece, having himself applied the word *drame* to it in the opening paragraph ('en quelque discrédit que soit tombé le mot drame par la manière abusive et tortionnaire dont il a été prodigué dans ces temps de douloureuse littérature, il est nécessaire de l'employer ici'). A few pages further on, after introducing the various lodgers in the Pension Vauquer, he uses the word again: 'Ces pensionnaires faisaient pressentir des drames accomplis ou en action; non pas de ces drames joués à la lumière des rampes, entre des toiles peintes, mais des drames vivants et muets, des drames glacés qui remuaient chaudement le cœur, des drames continus' – suitable, however, only for enactment before the solitary reader ensconced in his armchair.

The principal change introduced by Jaime & Co. was to transform Victorine, the motherless girl unjustly disinherited by her father and living in the *pension* with Mme Couture as sole companion, into a foundling adopted by Goriot and far prettier than either of the Goriot daughters, at least in the eyes of Rastignac. The enormous dowries intended by their doting father to help them marry above their station are settled on them in an early scene. Thus the play starts by showing on stage what was conveyed to Rastignac very concisely by the Duchesse de Langeais: 'Ce père avait tout donné. Il avait donné, pendant vingt ans, ses entrailles, son amour; il avait donné sa fortune en un jour'. However, it appears that Goriot has hidden resources. Turned out of the Pension Vauquer for non-payment of rent at the end of Act II, he is discovered in Act III having taken refuge in a *maison de santé* together with Victorine, his sole support, and Rastignac, as staunchly determined as ever to marry her despite her apparent poverty. Almost at the end of the play, Goriot, enraged at learning that his daughters are planning to have him confined to Bicêtre as a lunatic, reveals that Victorine is in reality his third daughter; he has invested 500,000 francs in her name, intending the sum should be paid over to her on her marriage. As for Delphine and Anastasie, they will not get a penny more, nor will he have any further truck with them; the final curtain falls on the line uttered by the implacable *père de famille*: 'Sortez! les portes de Bicêtre nous séparent pour toujours'.[5] It is clear that the adapters made up their minds from the start that Balzac's novel, a modernized *King Lear*, was meat far too strong for audiences at the Variétés; so the decision was taken to turn it into a variant on the Cinderella story, complete with the two ugly sisters and a Prince Charming, the role filled by Rastignac.

Shortly before viewing this irritating travesty of what was his major work to date, Balzac had published his 'Lettre adressée aux écrivains français du XIXe siècle':[6] basically a call to arms in which he argued eloquently that authors were being scandalously defrauded of their dues which were being pocketed by the shameless playwrights who made a living by cribbing from the latest best seller. 'A peine l'écrivain a-t-il publié un livre, créé des personnages, inventé des ressorts, dessiné un drame; ce drame, ces ressorts, ces personnages, ce livre est pris et devient pièce de théâtre' without reference to the author and with no acknowledgement to him; and a major work of fiction, adapted for the stage, is in nine cases out of ten a mere travesty of the original, the idea informing the book having been 'découpée, tirée, déshabillée, écartelée, mise sur le gril d'une rampe et servie aux habitués d'un théâtre comme un mets aux dandies du Rocher de Cancale'. Balzac concludes by appealing to his fellow novelists to form an authors' rights society, as the dramatists had formed theirs; and it is possible that his words did not fall on deaf ears. In 1838, four years after the article appeared, Louis Desnoyers founded the Société des Gens de Lettres, initially as a pressure group to achieve the reforms Balzac had been urging. But it took time for this to happen. As late as 1849, a five-act vaudeville called *Madame Marneffe ou le Père prodigue* was put on at the Gymnase, in which the characters bore the same names as Balzac had given them in *La Cousine Bette* but where the liberties taken with the plot were of the grossest, according to Jules Lemaître's review of the play: 'Mme Marneffe est devenue un ange de pureté, qui se donne les apparences d'un monstre parce qu'elle a une double vengeance à poursuivre. Elle veut venger sa sœur, autrefois séduite par Hulot, et son père, autrefois dépouillé par Crevel [...] Mais, à la fin, elle pardonne à tout le monde'.[7]

George Sand

Balzac was no doubt right in saying that in his day a novelist whose work was transferred to the stage was awarded no part in the profits it might make: these were shared by the director of the theatre concerned and by the playwrights who adapted it. But at least the fact that a version could be seen on the stage was proof of the popularity of the novel. *Indiana*, the first of Sand's numerous works of fiction (if we discount *Rose et Blanche*, co-authored with Jules Sandeau) gave her instant celebrity, which was confirmed the year following its publication by two stage versions, one devised by Scribe in collaboration with J. F. A. Bayard and put on at the Gymnase on 11 March 1833, the other the work of Léon Halévy and Francis Cornu which could be seen in November that year at the Gaîté and later at a revival in 1842 at the Théâtre de la Porte-Saint-Martin. The Halévy–Cornu play bore the title *Indiana* while the earlier version, described as a 'comédie-vaudeville en deux actes, tirée du roman d'*Indiana*' was retitled *Le Gardien*, with no other reference to Sand or her sensational novel.

This title suggests that the originality of Sand's early work of fiction, at least as perceived by Scribe and his collaborator, lay in the strange situation of Ralph, the phlegmatic Englishman secretly in love with Indiana, who interposes himself whenever the heroine is threatened by the bullying of her jealous husband or the machinations of her would-be seducer. He is her unacknowledged 'guardian', and to make his presence in the household more credible to a theatre audience, they decided he should change his social position from that of a foreigner of independent means to that of secretary and *homme de confiance* of Indiana's husband. It should be noted that none of the characters bears the same name as in the novel, and that this husband, the irascible Delmare of the novel, is spoken of in the play but never actually appears, since he is away looking after the running of his factory while Daniel (= Ralph) looks after the morals of his wife. Aurélie (= Indiana) is a pleasure-loving flibbertigibbet, with nothing of Indiana's proto-feminism apart from her occasional reference to her husband as 'mon maître'. Varades (= Raymon de Ramières), besides courting Aurélie, is also conducting an intrigue with her maid Zoé (= Noun), though his thoughtlessness does not have the same catastrophic results as it had in the novel. All ends well, with Daniel relieved finally of his awkward charge and Aurélie delivered back to her husband 'pure et chaste', as he says in the curtain line. In avoiding what might have been thought scabrous in Sand's first major work of fiction, Scribe demonstrated once more his well-known tact in judging where the line had to be drawn between what could be tolerated in a novel and what would outrage a theatre audience of the period. But it does also mean that the play was less a transposition of *Indiana* than an *embourgeoisement* of the work to make it more acceptable to the *habitués* of the Gymnase who had been accustomed over the years to associate Scribe's name with the propagation of sound middle-class values.

The Halévy–Cornu adaptation sticks rather more closely to the original, though we notice at the start that Noun has been eliminated and replaced by a much more serious rival for Raymon's affections, namely Laure de Nangy, the aristocratic young lady who, in the novel, had been simply the woman he had married finally, *faute de mieux*. What is remarkable about this version is the number of conversational passages that are directly lifted from the novel and incorporated bodily in the play; this is particularly noticeable in scenes 1 to 7 of the first act, which contain long passages of dialogue copied word for word from the first part of the novel. One is tempted to speculate that the author herself, recognizing how well her dialogue withstood the test of the footlights, might have been encouraged to start writing plays on her own (*Cosima*, the first of these, was produced in 1840). However, there is no evidence that George Sand visited the Gaîté in 1833 to discover how her novel had fared at the hands of Halévy and Cornu. When Paul Meurice approached her – admittedly thirty-five years later – with the suggestion that he and she should work together on a dramatization of *Indiana*, neither of them seems to have been aware that this would be the third time the novel would have been put on the stage. She wrote back saying she would need time to reread the book which she had totally forgotten. Having familiarized herself anew with *Indiana*, she wrote to Meurice (13 June 1867): 'Pour un premier ouvrage c'est assez bien analysé en effet. Mais y a-t-il un drame possible à coudre, avec les situations jetées çà et là au hasard de la plume?' – and the project appears to have been dropped.

It was the elderly dramatist Pixérécourt who, in association with Cornu, produced a version of Sand's *Valentine* at his own theatre, the Gaîté, in 1834, only a year before it burned down leaving him a shattered invalid. As usual with these adaptations, certain concessions were deemed necessary so as not to offend the susceptibilities of a mixed audience; in particular, the sub-plot involving Valentine's sister Louise, living in hiding after having given birth to an illegitimate child, was dropped completely. Perhaps to fill the gap and restore the balance between the sexes, an important new character, Bénédict's sister Perrine, was introduced, though her function in the play was hardly more than to comment sardonically on the behaviour of the other characters. Most of the important incidents in the book figure in this adaptation: Bénédict's first visit to the château to tune Valentine's piano; his rescue of Valentine from a watery death; and in Act III, the rather daring scene taking place in her bedroom, constituting a quite adequate dramatization of chapter 23. At this point Valentine's *mariage de convenance* to Lansac (renamed here Robsay and turned into a cold-blooded, calculating Englishman) has been celebrated but not consummated, and Bénédict's purpose is that it should remain so, if necessary by assassinating the bridegroom as he enters the bridal chamber; hence the scene when, armed with two loaded pistols, he hides himself nearby prepared to commit murder rather than allow Lansac/Robsay to exercise his conjugal rights. For Robsay, however, the marriage is simply a pretext for getting control of Valentine's dowry; he is content to let her be and leaves shortly afterwards to take up a diplomatic post in Russia.

In the fourth act Robsay has returned and, having discovered his wife's growing intimacy with Bénédict during his absence, extorts her signature on a deed conveying the estate to him so that he can promptly sell it off; here again, there is no divergence from the sequence of events in the novel. It is only in Sand's conclusion that the two adapters decided on a radical alteration. Robsay, challenged by Bénédict, does not deign to cross swords with him, whereupon Bénédict takes him by the throat and strangles him. This extremely violent ending was consonant with the two adapters' intention to present Sand's novel as a traditional melodrama, with Bénédict the hero, Robsay the villain, and Valentine the hapless victim. The work as she undoubtedly intended it to be understood was primarily an attack on male exploitation of women, particularly among the upper classes, by means of the marriage system, a message which would hardly commend itself to the majority of theatre-goers in 1834. Valentine is obliged, by her upper-class mother, to agree to marry Lansac while secretly in love with Bénédict; but this love remains platonic throughout, in the play as in the novel. George Sand gave it to Bénédict to voice the most violent denunciations of 'l'infâme tyrannie de l'homme sur la femme'; but this thesis is not allowed to surface in the play.

In all these dramatizations of her novels – none of them authorized by her, it seems – it was particularly the original denouement that was rejected by the adapters, as being presumably insufficiently theatrical or melodramatic for the tastes of contemporary audiences. Léon Halévy's version of *Leone-Léoni* is no exception; it had its first showing at the Ambigu-Comique on 6 May 1837, approximately three years after the novel was serialized in the *Revue des Deux Mondes* prior to being published in book form in 1835. Halévy discarded the frame-story, and the first act opens with the Shrove Tuesday masked ball in Brussels where Gabrielle (i.e. Juliette) is persuaded by her fiancé, the fascinating but mysterious Léoni, to elope with him before the banns are called; it is not impatience that drives him to this extraordinary course, but fear of the revelations that Wagner (i.e. Henryet) will be able to make to his discredit – and Wagner's return to Brussels is expected hourly.

What interest the novel has centres on the creation of the figure of Léoni himself, totally unscrupulous, a trickster and a thief, who yet is passionately in love with the girl he has disgraced and continues to humiliate, but whom he refuses to abandon even when pressed to do so by his boon companions; she is his Eloa, 'un ange que j'entraîne avec moi dans l'abîme', as he says. Eventually Wagner tracks her down to the palazzo where they are living in Venice and, in the stage version at least, persuades her to return with him to Brussels (in the novel, he is stabbed to death by Léoni and one of his ruffianly accomplices and that is only the first of a series of crimes which his protesting mistress finds herself suspected of helping him to commit). Restored finally to her family, Gabrielle is reconciled with her parents who are duly grateful to Wagner when he offers to marry her. This solution would seem to content everyone concerned, except Gabrielle who, asked if she consents, replies ambiguously: 'Ai-je le droit de refuser?' But Léoni reappears, to smuggle into the house a silk ladder with a note telling her to hang it from the balcony overlooking the main square; if by midnight she has failed to follow this instruction, a pistol shot will tell her that he has ended his life. Just before midnight, Gabrielle swallows a draught of poison and, hearing a pistol shot in the darkness, dies crying defiantly at the last: 'Ah! il m'aimait!' This gives the play a Romeo-and-Juliet ending, with both lovers committing suicide, whereas George Sand, conserving the almost mythological flavour of her tale, preferred to give it no denouement whatsoever: the last glimpse we are granted of the two infernal lovers is of them being swept down the Grand Canal in a gondola, on their way to Trieste and no doubt to fresh criminal exploits.

The failure of her play *Cosima* (1840) at the Comédie-Française seems to have discouraged Sand for the time being from making any further attempt to establish herself as an original playwright. Eventually, however, she offered her own adaptation of *François le Champi* to the Odéon where it had its first performance on 25 November 1849 and proved an outstanding success, reaching its fiftieth performance on 21 January 1850 and its hundredth on 20 March. The author had had so little confidence in her play that she did not even trouble to attend rehearsals: 'C'était d'une effrayante simplicité', she wrote to the actor-manager Bocage who had offered to stage it, 'et si j'avais été directeur, je crois que je ne l'aurais pas voulu'.[8] She had condensed her material by omitting all the earlier episodes: the first scene shows François's return to the mill after a six-year absence, having heard that the miller Blanchot had died and that his widow, François's foster-mother, is lying ill in bed with only the old servant Catherine to look after her. The play thus concentrates on the successful efforts of François to straighten out Madeleine's financial affairs, and her eventual agreement to marry him, her strongly maternal affection yielding to something warmer. It was presumably the very simplicity of the plot, together with Sand's idealized depiction of rustic manners, that struck audiences at the time as a welcome novelty and contributed to its abiding popularity.

Hoping no doubt to cash in on this unexpected success, a couple of professional playwrights, Anicet-Bourgeois and Charles Lafont, turned their attention to another of Sand's *romans champêtres*, *La Petite Fadette*, and put on their version a few months after the resounding triumph of *François le Champi*. But spectators at the Variétés were disappointed if they went along to the theatre expecting anything like a faithful dramatization of Sand's artless tale. At least one of the major themes of the novel, the close tie of affection between the two twin brothers, was totally eliminated, Sylvinet being cut out of the plot entirely. By way of compensation, the adapters introduced two other stories, presumably of their own invention, the first concerning a farmer's attempt to sell off his flock of sheep while concealing the fact that they are infected with sheep-pox; the second involving a complicated story of an inheritance left to Landry and Madelon on condition they marry each other. Although this *comédie-vaudeville* was billed as having been 'tirée du roman de George Sand', the formula by no means implied that she had approved the dramatization; in fact, it was the cause of a good deal of ill-feeling between her and the management of the Variétés. She had admittedly given Anicet-Bourgeois and Lafont her consent to use *La Petite Fadette* as the basis for a play, but had not thought it necessary to stipulate that her name should not appear as co-author. Nevertheless, the director of the Variétés, a certain Aimé Thibaudeau,

> publia partout, à l'avance, des réclames pour annoncer que la pièce était de moi. Le jour de la représentation venu, mon nom fut mis en grosses lettres sur l'affiche et celui des auteurs en caractères microscopiques. Même ficelle sur les couvertures de l'ouvrage en vente chez les libraires, et ficelle complète dans toutes les annonces et affiches des théâtres de province où la pièce fut jouée sous le nom unique de George Sand.[9]

This declaration, though contained in a private letter and given no wider publicity at the time, makes it clear that the first adaptation of *La Petite Fadette* is not to be regarded as a work for which she bore any responsibility, in spite of the fact that there are passages (such as that in Act II, scene 15, where Landry tries to make Fadette see that it is solely because she transgresses popular preconceptions of the proper distinction between the sexes that she is so disliked in the neighbourhood) which are textually almost identical to what Sand had written in the novel. But the firm line she took then on the vexed question of attribution seems to have wavered somewhat towards the end of her life when a new version of *La Petite Fadette* as a light opera was produced at the Opéra-Comique (11 September 1869). The libretto was actually the work of Adolphe de Leuven, who had shown it to her and obtained her approval; he had asked her to be present at a late rehearsal and accordingly she had turned up at the theatre 'sans y connaître un chat. Mais ils sont tous venus à moi comme si j'étais leur maman'. Writing to her daughter-in-law Lina after the first performance, which was well received, she mentions that after the final curtain fell, somewhat to her surprise she was proclaimed as the author: 'Tout le monde la croit mienne, moi, je crois qu'elle est de Leuven, et en somme je ne sais pas de qui elle est'. But she was paid the standard royalty, even that due to the composer Théophile Semet, though with her customary delicacy in financial matters she promptly passed his share on to him.

The high-handed action of Thibaudeau in commissioning two playwrights to dramatize *La Petite Fadette* and then billing it as Sand's work was not repeated: by the mid-century theatre directors had grown cautious and perhaps reluctant to face an action for breach of copyright. The dramatization of *Mauprat*, an earlier novel of hers published in 1837, was, it seems, her own work entirely. Offered to the Odéon, it was accepted with alacrity and proved a great draw not just during its first run (from November 1853 to January 1854) but at its numerous subsequent showings in the provinces. George Sand sacrificed certain episodes (Bernard's adventures in America during the War of Independence, and the trial he has to stand later for the attempted killing of Edmée), but basically she used the same sequence of events as she had in the novel. The oath that Bernard extracts from Edmée as the price for saving her from rape, when he gets her to promise 'de n'être à personne avant d'être à vous', is transferred to the play (Act I, scene 3) more or less as it stands, and Bernard's gradual transformation from the young savage he appears at the start to a mature man in control of his passions is traced, it may be thought, rather better in the dramatized version than in the original novel where it does seem agonizingly protracted.

Living in semi-retirement at Nohant, Sand was disinclined to work on further adaptations without the help and encouragement of someone based in Paris and having ready access to the theatres of the capital; she had always to overcome a certain reluctance to rehash a work of fiction so as to fit it for the footlights, and she would not undertake this tiresome work unless approached first by a man of letters known to her and trusted by her, who would do most of the donkey-work. The first of these was Paul Meurice, who had come to her notice as a left-wing journalist during the Second Republic and subsequently as one of Victor Hugo's most stalwart defenders during his years of exile. Meurice had apparently got in touch with her first with a suggestion he might attempt a dramatization of her novel *Les Beaux Messieurs de Bois-Doré*, of which he had read the first few instalments published in *La Presse* at the end of 1857. But having committed himself to undertake the work, he was taken aback when he came to read the exuberant developments in the latter part of the novel, more suited for the film, an as yet undreamed-of medium, than for the stage. He communicated his doubts to Bocage, the actor-director known to be an old friend of Sand, and was reassured on hearing that the novelist would be happy to give him carte blanche to make whatever changes and abridgements he deemed necessary.[10] His version was therefore confined to events in the first part of the novel: the discovery of the true identity of the boy Mario, D'Alvimar's pursuit of the beautiful heiress Lauriane, the confirmation of D'Alvimar's responsibility for the earlier assassination of Mario's father and Bois-Doré's brother, and the death of the murderous Spaniard in a duel with Bois-Doré; while Lauriane, at the end of the play, chooses Jovelin as her husband in preference to her three other suitors. By taking considerable liberties in this way with Sand's long and rambling, though far from tedious, historical novel, Meurice was able to reduce it to the dimensions of a run-of-the-mill melodrama, with all the traditional ingredients of the genre: a long-lost son and heir recognized at last, a pathetic heroine, and a villain unmasked and finally punished. But audiences at the Ambigu-Comique in the 1860s (Meurice's adaptation had its first performance there in 1862) still doted on the melodrama, and were to continue to do so for many years to come; what may be thought a little surprising is that this first run of *Les Beaux Messieurs de Bois-Doré* was followed by two successful revivals, one at the Odéon in 1867 and another at the Porte-Saint-Martin in 1887.

This dramatization was followed by that of *Le Marquis de Villemer*, possibly the most successful reworking of one of Sand's novels for the stage. The audience for the first night at the Odéon (29 February 1864) was glittering, including as it did all the adult members of the imperial family; Napoleon III was observed to be wiping his eyes at the end. The second performance was tumultuous; as the author herself reported: '[...] un triomphe inouï, une tempête d'applaudissements d'un bout à l'autre, à chaque mot, et si spontanée, si générale qu'on coupe trois fois chaque tirade'.[11] The play ran for the rest of the season, was resumed at the beginning of the next, and was not finally taken off until 23 January 1865. It received the highest accolade of all in 1877, when it entered the repertory of the Comédie-Française. To some extent, no doubt, it owed its unprecedented favour to its setting in upper-class society, with none of the main characters being other than blue-blooded, though the heroine, reduced in circumstances, has had to seek employment as lady's companion; but at least she ends by marrying the marquis.

The play had been advertised as a four-act comedy by George Sand, without any mention of a collaborator, though there were persistent rumours that Alexandre Dumas *fils*, known to be a close friend of hers, had had some part in its composition. He had read *Le Marquis de Villemer* when it was published as a novel in 1862, and at that time had been struck by its potentialities for the stage. He was already considered one of France's leading dramatists, and Sand was delighted to hear that he was hoping to use it as the basis for a new play, and correspondingly disappointed when, a year later, he wrote advising her he was abandoning the project. He did, however, enclose with his letter a draft of what he had written so far. In her reply (22 May 1863) she asked whether he would mind if she completed the task, to which of course he raised no objection. In September, he went down to Nohant to see how she was progressing; she reported on this visit in a letter to La Rounat, director of the Odéon since 1856, in which she informed him that 'en quelques heures de causerie, tout s'est bien débrouillé grâce à lui, de la façon la plus ingénieuse et bientôt j'aurai exécuté le plan qu'il m'a ébauché si admirablement'. But for reasons best known to himself, Dumas did not want his name to appear as co-author, and though she begged him to reconsider, he was adamant. It is not difficult to see his hand in the opening scene, involving a drily witty conversation between the mother of the marquis and a character who plays no part in the novel, the Comte de Danières, the legal guardian of the eminently marriageable Diane de Saintrailles. Similarly in Act II, one would guess that the scene between the Duke and Léonie d'Anglade, with its *badinage mondain* not unlike what one encounters in some of Musset's one-act comedies, was the work of Dumas rather than of Sand. But otherwise, with the exception of Caroline's escape from the house to take refuge with her wet-nurse in the mountain country round Le Puy, the events in the novel are for the most part faithfully reproduced in the play; both play and novel end with Caroline gracefully yielding to her former employer's abject pleading that she should let bygones be bygones and consent to marry the marquis.

Once it became the rule that novelists should be consulted before their work could be used as the basis for a play – and this did not come about until the mid-century – they had at least some say as to who should be entrusted with the task of dramatization. In cases when the author of the novel was also the author of the play, it occasionally happened that the stage version was at least as successful as the work of fiction. This was probably the case with Octave Feuillet's *Roman d'un jeune homme pauvre* and certainly true of Dumas's *Dame aux camélias* which worked so well in its dramatized form that the play shortly displaced the original novel entirely. Nearly every noteworthy nineteenth-century work of fiction had its authorized stage doublet: Zola's *L'Assommoir* (1879) and *Nana* (1881), Daudet's *Le Nabab* (1880) and *Jack* (1881), the

Goncourts' *Germinie Lacerteux* (1888) and *Charles Demailly* (1892). But there were exceptions. Was Julien's prediction in the last chapter of *Le Rouge et le noir* – 'Peut-être un jour vous me verrez le sujet d'un mélodrame' – ever fulfilled? Fortunately not, as far as we know. *Salammbô* was turned into an opera in 1892, but Flaubert, although approached more than once to authorize a stage version of *Madame Bovary*, steadfastly refused, '[...] trouvant qu'une idée est faite pour un seul moule, qu'elle n'est pas à deux fins'.[12] But he was exceptional in this respect. In general, authors of successful novels found it difficult to withstand the blandishments of the stage and to pass up the chance of having their work applauded by a visible and vocal audience.

Notes

[1] W. G. Hartog, *Guilbert de Pixérécourt, sa vie, son mélodrame, sa technique et son influence* (Paris: Champion, 1913), 168, 192.

[2] Jules Janin, *Histoire de la littérature dramatique* (Paris: Michel Lévy, 1855–1858), v 100.

[3] Balzac's letter of 7 January 1835, thanking him for the invitation and promising to be present, is reproduced in Roger Pierrot's edition of Balzac's *Correspondance* (Paris: Garnier, 1962), ii 616–617.

[4] *La Comédie humaine*, ed. Marcel Bouteron (Paris: Gallimard, 1951), ii 556.

[5] An illustration of this scene, published in *Le Charivari* (19–20 April 1835) has been reproduced in P.-G. Castex's edition of *Le Père Goriot* (Paris: Garnier, 1960).

[6] *Revue de Paris* (2 November 1834); reprinted in Balzac, *Œuvres diverses* (Paris: Conard, 1940), 643–655.

[7] Jules Lemaître, *Impressions de théâtre* (Paris: Boivin, 1888–1918), iv 327. The adapter was named as Clairville, a pseudonym used by Louis-François Nicolaïe.

[8] George Sand, *Correspondance*, ed. Georges Lubin (Paris: Garnier 1991), ix 361.

[9] Ibid., xiv 403.

[10] See Dorrya Fahmy, *George Sand, auteur dramatique* (Paris: Droz, 1935), 230–231, and Sand's letter to Paul Meurice, *Correspondance*, xiv 501.

[11] Sand, *Correspondance*, xviii 290.

[12] See E. and J. de Goncourt, *Journal: Mémoires de la vie littéraire* (Monaco: Éditions de l'Imprimerie Nationale, 1956–1958), iii 202.

'Voilà le poëte hystérique': Flaubert, Frédéric and Emma

NAOMI SEGAL

This article will look at two modes of the genealogical relation among art-for-art's-sake writers of the later nineteenth century in France. In the second, longer argument, I shall examine Flaubert's relation of quasi-paternity with his two protagonists Frédéric Moreau and Emma Bovary. I shall suggest that the author/character relation typified in the aesthetic of Flaubert is one that fantazises a loss of the body, a kind of paternity fraught by the wish to be a father without having a child, and is most clearly represented in the motif of gender ambiguity. If, borrowing from Flaubert's theoretical remarks, we take the authorial position in realism to be that of the invisible father-God, what is the latter's relationship with his characters? And then what is the reader's place half-in and half-out of that haunted world? Which of these figures of a fiction, if any, has a body? And how is that body gendered? Is there any hope of a habeas corpus in literary matters? And what do we mean, anyway, by the 'having' of a body?

The first genealogy could more properly be termed a relation among brothers, but there is a mode of derivation in it that suggests other kinds of heritage or debt. I am interested in tracing an origin for Flaubert's fantasy of realist authorship in writing of a different – in some schemes, antithetical – genre, one that explicitly makes of the human figure an object rather than a character. The genre is lyric poetry and the aesthetic which creates Flaubert, Frédéric and Emma is that of art for art's sake. It is Baudelaire who produced the provocative epithet of my title, referring not (ostensibly) to Flaubert but to Emma, in a review published six months after *Madame Bovary* appeared and four months after the publication of *Les Fleurs du mal*. The latter was dedicated to the 'parfait magicien ès lettres' Théophile Gautier, and it is with him as a kind of originator that I would like to begin.

The tenth poem of *Émaux et camées*, 'Contralto', was first published in 1849. It takes up the same theme of the inviting ambiguity of the double-sexed as in *Mademoiselle de Maupin* (1835–1836), but here the object of desire has no desire of its own. The poem opens with the description of a statue:

> On voit dans le musée antique
> Sur un lit de marbre sculpté,
> Une statue énigmatique
> D'une inquiétante beauté.
>
> Est-ce un jeune homme? est-ce une femme?
> Une déesse, ou bien un dieu?
> L'amour, ayant peur d'être infâme,
> Hésite, et suspend son aveu.
>
> Dans sa pose malicieuse,
> Elle s'étend, le dos tourné
> Devant la foule curieuse,
> Sur son coussin capitonné.
>
> Pour faire sa beauté maudite,
> Chaque sexe apporta son don.
> Tout homme dit: C'est Aphrodite!
> Toute femme: C'est Cupidon!
>
> Sexe douteux, grâce certaine,
> On dirait ce corps indécis
> Fondu, dans l'eau de la fontaine,
> Sous les baisers de Salmacis.
>
> Chimère ardente, effort suprême
> De l'art et de la volupté,
> Monstre charmant, comment je t'aime
> Avec ta multiple beauté!
>
> Bien qu'on défende ton approche,
> Sous la draperie aux plis droits
> Dont le bout à ton pied s'accroche,
> Mes yeux ont plongé bien des fois
>
> [...]

They have not, of course, because a statue cannot be penetrated by anything except the erotic imagination. Instead, as in most of the other poems of the collection, the aesthetic event here is a matter of the surface, of what Sartre calls in *L'Être et le néant* the appropriation by means of a 'glissement',[1] whether that of skiing, caressing or thought. Gautier's verses may tease the senses with the loveliness of flesh or silk, petal or cheek, the hesitation between pink and white; in each case it is the suspension of an uncertainty on a surface that makes the thing beautiful. And beauty, which is after all the single overt arbiter for the art-for-art's sake writer, is here explained not in terms of balance – a self-enclosed, 'classical', lateral relation – but of desire – a motion-towards, a wish for consummation, exchange, expenditure or gift. In 'Contralto', beauty is 'inquiétante', 'maudite', 'multiple', everything except stable. This is a world of excitement, action and frustration, not of the nicely resolved *mot juste*. The object of desire is a body that is no body. Like those of Gautier's frozen or posthumous women, it is both provocative and inaccessible. But the women of 'Le Poème de la femme' or 'Coquetterie posthume' are anything but passive – in accordance with the rules of masculine perversity, they are willed into life before (and after) they oblige the necrophiliac fantasy; they have movement. In 'Contralto', the statue teases by its very immobility, for only such solid drapery can promise the perfect refusal of sexual knowledge.

So much for the definition of the aesthetic object. Lolling between sexes, it has the capacity to awaken universal lust and make the eye an organ of appropriation – at the price of being (as in any pornography) strictly inaccessible. In *Mademoiselle de Maupin*, the feminine ideal turns out to be a man – and then again a woman – putting the complacent Romanticism of d'Albert into a deserved spin. D'Albert thinks he wishes to *have*, but more exactly he is concerned to *be*, the female body:

[...] je n'ai jamais rien tant souhaité que de rencontrer sur la montagne, comme Tirésias le devin, ces serpents qui font changer de sexe [...]

J'ai commencé par avoir envie d'être un autre homme; – puis, faisant réflexion que je pouvais par l'analogie éprouver à peu près ce que je sentirais et alors ne pas éprouver la surprise et le changement attendus, j'aurais préféré d'être femme; cette idée m'est toujours venue, lorsque j'avais une maîtresse qui n'était pas laide; car une femme laide est un homme pour moi, et aux instants de plaisirs j'aurais volontiers changé de rôle, car il est bien impatientant de ne pas avoir la conscience de l'effet qu'on produit et de ne juger de la jouissance des autres que par la sienne.[2]

D'Albert's motive is narcissism: being the body of the other – rather than being in it as an interloper who is not of it, penis or child – would be to feel the pleasure he alone can give; he seems to envy in women the Lacanian femininity which consists of having specularity and sensation at the same time, but (like Lacan or Ovid's Tiresias) he is imagining this from a position that becomes the other without ever ceasing to be itself, for if it did the pleasure in the mirror would be gone. In Madeleine de Maupin, we see a different version of the same wish; her desire takes on the doubleness of an androgynous epistemology:

> [...] je ne pourrai jamais aimer complètement personne ni homme ni femme; quelque chose d'inassouvi gronde toujours en moi, et l'amant ou l'amie ne répond qu'à une seule face de mon caractère [...]
>
> Ma chimère serait d'avoir tour à tour les deux sexes pour satisfaire à cette double nature: – homme aujourd'hui, femme demain, je réserverais pour mes amants mes tendresses langoureuses, mes façons soumises et dévouées, mes plus molles caresses, mes petits soupirs mélancoliquement filés, tout ce qui tient dans mon caractère du chat et de la femme; puis, avec mes maîtresses, je serais entreprenant, hardi, passionnné, avec les manières triomphantes, le chapeau sur l'oreille, une tournure de capitan et d'aventurier. Ma nature se produirait ainsi tout entière au jour, et je serais parfaitement heureuse, car le vrai bonheur est de se pouvoir développer librement en tous sens et d'être tout ce qu'on peut être.
> (p. 394)

We must not forget that this character is, no less than the females in 'Le Poème de la femme' and 'Coquetterie posthume', the embodiment of her author's d'Albertian fantasy. Madeleine/Théodore too is created to serve the man who is imagining how it is to be her. But in her we see the wish of female androgyny carried further than simple narcissism: she is no reflective object but, like God, wholly subject. Not reversal but doubleness is essential to her turn-by-turn androgyny. She recognizes that it is by the fetishes of surface – the hat, the swagger, the pouting or slavish gestures – that we are a man or a woman: the reality of self that 'se produit tout entière au jour' is its consciousness of being visible. What follows, though, is the loss of sensation as the price of knowledge; the two, in this system, cannot coexist. By the end, Madeleine can *only* be both a man and a woman, and cannot undress without loss. And so, after a night spent with both beloveds in turn, she must disappear into the sunset, leaving them with the *pis aller* of each other. What she might now feel and know is never available to the text. In both these positions, then – d'Albert's and Madeleine's – we see the fantasy of androgyny founder on the impossible simultaneity of pleasure and knowledge.

Mlle de Maupin is the androgynous statue given subjectivity; or rather (to respect chronology), the object of 'Contralto' is Mlle de Maupin denied it. It represents very exactly the freeze-frame of a masculine aesthetic – this body, despite its enigma, will not make a fool of you, you know just where you are with it – and if creating such things is not easy and requires the supreme effort, it is at least possible. Gautier is the opposite of Pygmalion, and would not make his mistake. Like Conrad Ferdinand Meyer, his near-contemporary, and Rilke, half a century later, he is fascinated by sculpture because of its opacity, that massiveness that is not so much solidity as the pure play of surface, the Medusan goal.

Medusa – or Midas? It is Baudelaire who introduces into the aesthetic of erotic petrification the image of the alchemist. If the material world offers only mud and shit, the true poet reaches in and brings forth a plum of gold. In his writing, the tease of the surface is more likely to be deadly than charming, and masks are so many skins ready to be stripped off. Despite his dandyish fascination with what is outside bodies (clothes, masks, make-up), Baudelaire reintroduces the concept of depth. And there is little that is cheerful in Baudelaire's desiring persona, just like Flaubert's. For both, authorship is a necessary trial. Where Gautier mocks at the hard work in creating what must be luxurious, Baudelaire and Flaubert emphasize the agony, the martyrdom, the (paternal) labour. It is clear, of course, that masculinity – like class – has an important part to play in this adaptation of an aesthetic of luxury. The kind of work that men may do must be visibly productive, not reproductive; yet reproduction haunts any creativity. The statuesque sterility of the object-woman (Sartre observed this too)[3] is one step towards the aesthetic of art for art's sake; the other is the peculiar fecundity which the male poet wants for himself.

In Baudelaire, instead of the mobile subjectivity of Galathea de Maupin, we have that of the creator-sufferer who slaves at her, Proserpine in her bed or a 'chœur de vermisseaux' attacking her cadaver.[4] How many times has he told us that *Les Fleurs du mal* is not a simple collection but an architectural structure? Modelled on autobiography, its story is that of the Oedipal son who, having lost the idyll of the archaic 'Géante', sets off on a quest for some other satisfaction; games of sado-masochism and various intoxications offer momentary relief, and the text ends teetering on a lonely version of the *Liebestod*. Right at the start, however, one poem, 'Élévation' raises interesting questions about the modes of masculine desire:

> Au-dessus des étangs, au-dessus des vallées,
> Des montagnes, des bois, des nuages, des mers,
> Par delà le soleil, par delà les éthers,
> Par delà les confins des sphères étoilées,
>
> Mon esprit, tu te meus avec agilité,
> Et, comme un bon nageur qui se pâme dans l'onde,
> Tu sillonnes gaiement l'immensité profonde
> Avec une indicible et mâle volupté.
>
> Envole-toi bien loin des miasmes morbides;
> Va te purifier dans l'air supérieur
> Et bois, comme une pure et divine liqueur,
> Le feu clair qui remplit les espaces limpides.
>
> Derrière les ennuis et les vastes chagrins
> Qui chargent de leur poids l'existence brumeuse,
> Heureux celui qui peut d'une aile vigoureuse
> S'élancer vers les champs lumineux et sereins;
>
> Celui dont les pensers, comme des alouettes,
> Vers les cieux le matin prennent un libre essor,
> — Qui plane sur la vie et comprend sans effort
> Le langage des fleurs et des choses muettes!   (p. 46)

'Élévation' is a special case of Baudelaire's aesthetics, for it typifies the central paradox of the Romantic theme of flight. Movement is repeatedly invoked in such phrases as 'au-dessus', 'par delà', 'tu sillonnes', 'envole-toi', 'va', 'et bois', 'derrière', 's'élancer', 'prennent un libre essor', in which the boyish imagination seems to be zooming towards some faraway goal. But the gestures are those of taking off rather than those of flying; as in a number of his other poems, it is the leaving that counts, arrival being always derisory. What happens in the last two lines is in startling contrast to the first eighteen. Here, suddenly, there is a fantasy of hovering, not zooming. The goal of desire is not penetrative consummation but suspension, distance, knowledge, power.

The equivalent in prose of the Baudelairean quest is the French *récit*, examples of which run from the eighteenth century until well into the twentieth, but which takes its shape in the Oedipal mirror-games of Romanticism. In these texts, a young man offers his story to a kindly or stern older man; confession is the price of Oedipal entry, but the real password is the death of the beloved, always a kind of mother and murdered in a slower repetition of an originating childbed death. Flaubert wrote a few such short texts that are counted among his juvenilia; but, however much sympathy of interests may have passed between him and Baudelaire, his is much more often the authorial fantasy of the last stanza of 'Élévation', the fantasy of realism. In his persona as implied author, and in the form of aesthetic practice which that persona represents, the propositions of art for art's sake and the mimetic imperative come together with the power of a new androgyny. Two figures stand at its poles: the bodiless author-God and the character of whom Baudelaire wrote: 'voilà le poëte hystérique'.

I want to begin my examination of the narrative posture in Flaubert's fiction with a discussion of *L'Éducation sentimentale*, in which gender ambiguity is not an issue but negative procreation is. The final version appeared, of course, twelve years after *Madame Bovary*, but it offers the initially simpler gender-relation of male author to male persona, and I want to set up that relation as a preamble to the question of the cross-gender generation of the earlier text.

Let us start by taking a little further the image of the author as bodiless. In two of his most famous definitions of authorship, Flaubert combines the unbodied, ungendered nature of the Judaic deity with the image of the perfectly disconnected phallus. Between them, these two images bring together the masculine phantasy of disincarnation as power:

> L'auteur dans son œuvre doit être comme Dieu dans l'univers: présent partout et visible nulle part.[5]

> Ce qui me semble beau, ce que je voudrais faire, c'est un livre sur rien, un livre sans attache extérieure qui se tiendrait de lui-même par la force interne de son style.[6]

These images recall that of the closure of 'Élévation': both the object and its creator are things that hover. Like God, they have no umbilicus; they are tied to nothing else by a reproductive dependency, and like the Lacanian phallus they are invisible and self-sustaining. This is at the price of castration, of course – but castration is the inevitable logic of the phallic idea of transcendence, whether in its zooming or its hovering mode.

Flaubert takes the aesthetic of art for art's sake into the 'lower sphere' of realism. I have called this a kind of androgyny because it brings together, like masculinity and femininity, the body and spirit commonly kept apart in the hierarchical politics of gender. The invisible author-God is naturally more powerful than an inert idol: hiding, he sees; shooting, he cannot be shot at; plurally claiming every gender, like the God of Genesis, he is nevertheless masculine both because language tends to its unmarked form and because the parent we cannot see is always the father.[7] The 'livre sur rien' is a paradox because it would be a text without referentiality – something perhaps like Gautier's 'Symphonie en blanc majeur' or Mallarmé's 'Le vierge, le vivace et le bel aujourd'hui', both poems blanched by their refusal of bodiedness, and which slide into the epithet of a colour everything that is sensuality without sentience. In prose fiction – at least in the mid-nineteenth century – matter was unavoidable; thus there must be flesh in the text, but that flesh will exist to desiccate, to end as a handful of dust. Flaubert claimed (reversing Baudelaire) that the writing of *Madame Bovary* was motivated by no more than the wish to 'faire quelque chose qui fût de la couleur de ces moisissures des coins où il y a des cloportes'.[8] The novelistic plot follows a grimly repetitious series of arcs: desire → disappointment, hope → loss. In the case of Frédéric Moreau, the protagonist does not even realize the pettiness of his aims. How does he serve his author as a disappointing progeny?

Frédéric is 'l'homme de toutes les faiblesses'.[9] In order to understand the use (beyond satire) of his feebleness, we can begin by comparing him with an older brother, the equally puerile but inspired Julien Sorel. Stendhal too creates a world in order to play with desire. Like any parent, he uses his child as a toy. Julien acts for him as the fairytale hero of the family romance,[10] setting off in quest of his fortune and a better *nom du père*. The author equips him with two magic gifts: the prodigious memory that will impress all the men, and the slender beauty that will touch the hearts of women.

This is what gives Stendhal's novels their idyllic feel: nothing falls out of the hands of the author's desire for happiness. In *Le Rouge et le noir*, Julien serves his creator as the ideal phallus, acting for him in a world that yields with just enough realist resistance to represent real flesh. But two problems arise with this phallic fantasy. First, as I have suggested earlier, it inevitably implies castration: as the character gets what the author wants, he exceeds and thus departs from him. To oppose this, the Stendhalian narrator stays close by Julien: this Pinocchio never loses his strings. And secondly, there is the problem of how the son is to have masculinity when that is as much the property of the father as he is; exactly as in the classical Oedipus complex, manhood cannot be shared between parent and child, rather first the latter and then the former concedes the right to potency. Put another way, if Julien serves 'Stendhal' as phallus, how can he have one of his own? To solve this problem, a drastic genealogical solution is found, adding weakness to weakness all down a line. There is another boy, Mme de Rênal's youngest child, and he is to Julien what the latter is to 'Stendhal': when the hero falls in love, Stanislas-Xavier falls ill.[11]

The crisis of the son's illness in *Le Rouge et le noir* is pivotal; during it, Mme de Rênal's sensual idyll is riven apart by guilt. It is not her husband or her legitimate duty that torments her, but the presence of a jealous God acting upon her through her child. We can glimpse here the vengeance of the author on the too-easy success of his surrogate. Julien suffers the panic of potential loss, seeing himself ousted as she slips away from him back into the anxious icon of the good mother. All his effort is to console and support, but guilt makes her masochistic, calling down a divine punishment on herself in order to save the child's life. Finally, just as the tension reaches its height, Julien is inspired to offer to adopt not the husband's place but that of the son: 'Ah! ciel, que ne puis-je prendre pour moi la maladie de Stanislas... / – Ah! tu l'aimes, toi, dit Mme de Rênal, en se relevant et se jetant dans ses bras'.[12] Julien Sorel does not founder on the motif of the sick son, and that is surely because Stendhal desires his success through weakness, not the crushing of his wishes. Flaubert, on the other hand, offers a similar theme with a very different outcome.

Let me reiterate the principle of this aesthetic phantasy. Flaubert wishes to exist in his text as its invisible maker: the characters must suffer beneath his eye and gratify him by their failures. Unlike the more direct persona of the desiring subject in Gautier or Baudelaire, the *récit* or even the realism of Stendhal, Flaubert's implied author is characterized by absence: there will be no look and no voice to catch him by. This scheme depends on a fixed relation of difference: on the one hand, the author who is invisible, bodiless, wise and male;

on the other the character, typified by a series of femininities, the visible body subject to others' gaze, the foolish mind trapped in a circularity of disappointment without disillusionment, the derivative indigestion of reading. (Later we shall look at this difference in action in the technique of *style indirect libre*.) Within such a difference, of course, the negative term serves to define the positive: a fictional world blighted by its depressing over-materiality *implies* the implacable divinity of its maker. In exactly this way, the mystery of paternity is evidenced by the blatancy of maternity – think of the plot of *The Scarlet Letter*. Flaubert, perhaps more horrible but certainly more discreet than Hawthorne, paints his narrative in greyish letters, but the logic is the same. This logic means that the quintessential other of the divine author must be a woman who gives birth to a daughter, doubled by a fatality of copying, condemned to be patriarchy's anti-icon. For the moment, let us see what happens to the male protagonist of Flaubert's plot.

Gilbert and Gubar have catalogued the dispiriting thematics of pen/penis in which male authorship is fantasized as a greater making than female reproduction.[13] Flaubert insisted that making a book resembles building a pyramid rather than gestating a child, but sexual generation returns repeatedly in the imagery of other letters. Here, in a letter to Louis Bouilhet comparing writing to sex, he describes impregnation as 'the real thing': 'Nous gamahuchons bien, nous langottons beaucoup, nous pelottons lentement, mais baiser! mais décharger pour faire l'enfant!'[14]

If style for its own sake is like petting, the real book is the child. A reproach seems to be implied here against the art-for-art's sake aesthetic understood as a perversion, the temptation of polymorphous pleasure which is true *zwecklose Zweckmäßigkeit*. For all his delight in perversity, Flaubert seems to be suggesting here that to grow up, a man has to leave behind the narcissistic bliss of merely Romantic creativity and show forth in a kind of flesh. But I hope I have suggested that the desire embodied in a project of realism produces additional problems for masculinity. For one thing, what sex would the child have to be? Flaubert seems to have found particular anguish in the thought of engendering a son:

> Moi, un fils! Oh non, non, plutôt crever dans un ruisseau écrasé par un omnibus... L'hypothèse de transmettre la vie à quelqu'un me fait rugir, au fond du cœur, avec des colères infernales...
>
> Oh oui, cette idée me torturait... Il faudrait tout un livre pour développer

d'une manière compréhensible mon sentiment à cet égard. L'idée de donner le jour à quelqu'un *me fait horreur*. Je me maudirais si j'étais père. – Un fils de moi, oh non, non, non, que toute ma chair périsse, et que je ne transmette à personne les embêtements et les ignominies de l'existence.[15]

The dread of reproduction seems directed here not only at the idea of being implicated in a bodily event but more significantly at the thought of causing the existence of another like himself. To make a second himself would, it seems, necessarily be to make a son. Such an incarnation would be an 'embêtement' not just in the everyday sense but in the sense of putting a bit more stupidity into the world. Whether utterly damned or capable of flashes of saintliness, 'bêtise' in Flaubert's thinking is always associated with repetition, reproduction, copying. Bouvard and Pécuchet are simply the *reductio ad absurdum* of this structure. The image of Frédéric and Deslauriers or Bournisien and Homais or Charles and Rodolphe sitting side by side sharing platitudes presages the copyists of the last novel.[16] All these pairs echo the 'deux bonshommes' that he claimed were to be found in his character[17] – no Faustian dialectic of the soul, just codgers, older of course but otherwise identical to the 'Garçon' he had both satirized and acted as a boy. Surrogacy combined with mockery allows the subject to reproduce himself doubled in the grotesque, establishing the fixed difference of a bodied and an unbodied position. The hierarchical relation of subject to object is necessary precisely as a rescue from the dangerous balance of a Dick und Doof, Didi and Gogo, me and him.

If the doubling of father and son is a terror, it is also a compulsion. Only the realist novel can put this under the control (as far as it goes) of conscious fantasy. As I have already suggested, Flaubert's extreme version of paternity as authorship produces an equally extreme anxiety about the theme of reproductive desire in his texts. In *L'Éducation sentimentale*, two sons are born, one to each of the two main women in Frédéric's life. Each of them has a bizarre gestation: the second Arnoux child springs into life three years old on the hero's return after two years away, and Rosanette's baby spends twenty-five months in the womb. Both children become at key moments the sick sons of the adulterous plot.

When he first glimpses Mme Arnoux, Frédéric becomes at once fixated to the charm of her orbit, traced out on the deck along the arc of her dress, measured by the dazzle of a gaze both directed and undirected – she looks up vaguely from some embroidery as he passes and he is dizzied by 'l'éblouissement que lui envoyèrent ses yeux'.[18] Like her occupation, she is both useful and luxurious: the wife desired with the Oedipal determination of adultery. Frédéric, of course, never 'has' and probably never really wants her; his is, instead, a derisory career shaped by fetishistic desire.[19] One fetish among others is her daughter, seen on the first day and used occasionally when her presence allows a simpering communication.[20] The son is born at a time when Arnoux's reputation has lost much of its glamour. But Frédéric stays doggedly by, listening to the beloved's complaints and enduring 'les bouderies de Mlle Marthe et les caresses du jeune Eugène, qui lui passait toujours ses mains sales sur la figure' (p. 171).

After a series of tragi-comic peripeteias, Frédéric declares his passion. Horrified at first, Mme Arnoux gradually gains confidence in his humility. They walk in the gardens at Auteuil and exchange banalities. Frédéric allows himself to hope – for what exactly? Then the child falls ill.

> Une après-midi (vers le milieu de février), il la surprit fort émue. Eugène se plaignait de mal à la gorge. Le docteur avait dit pourtant que ce n'était rien, un gros rhume, la grippe. Frédéric fut étonné par l'air ivre de l'enfant. Il rassura sa mère néanmoins, cita en exemple plusieurs bambins de son âge qui venaient d'avoir des affections semblables et s'étaient vite guéris.
> – « Vraiment? »
> – « Mais oui, bien sûr! »
> – « Oh! comme vous êtes bon! »
> Et elle lui prit la main. Il l'étreignit dans la sienne. [*sic*]
> – « Oh! laissez-la! »
> – « Qu'est-ce que cela fait, puisque c'est au consolateur que vous l'offrez!... Vous me croyez bien pour ces choses, et vous doutez de moi... quand je vous parle de mon amour! »
> – « Je n'en doute pas, mon pauvre ami! »   (p. 275)

Catching her in this mood, Frédéric asks for a simple proof: to meet the following Tuesday on the corner of the rue Tronchet. Before she has time to reconsider, she has agreed.

But the ungenerous author puts two obstacles in the way of consummation: the outbreak of the 1848 Revolution and the almost mortal illness of the woman's son. While Frédéric paces the pavement, Mme Arnoux undergoes an ordeal much more severe than that of Mme de Rênal, since she suffers it entirely alone. The narrative begins with the account of a dream:

> Elle avait rêvé, la nuit précédente, qu'elle était sur le trottoir de la rue Tronchet depuis longtemps. Elle y attendait quelque chose d'indéterminé, de considérable néanmoins, et, sans savoir pourquoi, elle avait peur d'être aperçue. Mais un maudit petit chien, acharné contre elle, mordillait le bas de sa robe. Il revenait obstinément et aboyait toujours plus fort. Mme Arnoux se réveilla. L'aboiement du chien continuait. Elle tendit l'oreille. Cela partait de la chambre de son fils. Elle s'y précipita pieds nus. C'était l'enfant lui-même qui toussait. Il avait les mains brûlantes, la face rouge et la voix singulièrement rauque. L'embarras de sa respiration augmentait de minute en minute. Elle resta jusqu'au jour, penchée sur sa couverture, à l'observer. (p. 280)

This fits Freud's first and simplest category of dreams precipitated by external stimuli. The subject wishes above all to go on sleeping, so the stimulus is incorporated into the events of a dream. In this case, Mme Arnoux's agoraphobia allows her to streetwalk at the price of not knowing whom or what she is waiting for, and also at the price (here the author bends down over her as she will over her conscience incarnate) of the guilt rhythmically calling her to wakefulness. This is not the first importunate little dog in an *Éducation sentimentale* by Flaubert,[21] and in a sense both animals may be saying the same thing. The characters are being warned of the horror of the flesh. Indeed, during the course of his agony, Eugène will be likened to a cardboard dog – as the grotesque turns, via the mechanical, into the uncanny.

The child suffers with gothic precision all day long. The famous style is dedicated cruelly to the representation of a blighted maternity. Doctors come and go, one old, one young, both ineffectual, while the mother submits to the despair of being able to do nothing but witness. When the boy finally and suddenly coughs up the croupous membrane – unexplained, resembling 'un tube de parchemin' (p. 282), it could be seen as the rendition of the phallus in an Oedipal drama that never reached sexuality – she falls on her knees and offers up to God 'comme un holocauste, le sacrifice de sa première passion, de sa seule faiblesse'.

In the meantime, the briefly bruised Frédéric has found consolation by taking the *lorette* to the love nest prepared for the *madone*. But Rosanette too is to be punished through a son, this time the offspring of the hero. When she discovers she is pregnant, the Maréchale is of course delighted. She plans to name him Frédéric. The father-to-be falls into a reverie: what if this had been Mme Arnoux's child, a little girl, 'brune et blanche, avec des yeux noirs, de très grands sourcils, un ruban rose dans ses cheveux bouclants! (Oh! comme il l'aurait aimée!)' (p. 362). But the baby is doubly misplaced – wrong sex, wrong womb:

> Rosanette se mit à sourire ineffablement; et, comme submergée sous les flots d'amour qui l'étouffaient, elle dit d'une voix basse:
> « Un garçon, là, là! » en désignant près de son lit une barcelonnette.
> Il écarta les rideaux, et aperçut, au milieu des linges, quelque chose d'un rouge jaunâtre, extrêmement ridé, qui sentait mauvais et vagissait.
> « Embrasse-le! »
> Il répondit, pour cacher sa répugnance :
> « Mais j'ai peur de lui faire mal? »
> « Non, non! »
> Alors, il baisa, du bout des lèvres, son enfant.
> « Comme il te ressemble! »   (pp. 387–388)

While maternal love here is both genuine and grotesque, paternity is only the latter. Whatever the resemblance, neither party is flattered by it. After a short time, Rosanette brings the baby home from the wet nurse, his small body covered in patches of thrush which look, inside the mouth, like 'des caillots de lait' (p. 402). The same evening, the patches have spread '[pareille] à de la moisissure, comme si la vie, abandonnant déjà ce pauvre petit corps, n'eût laissé qu'une matière où la végétation poussait'. While Frédéric sleeps, Rosanette watches; by morning, the child is dead.

The final repulsion is that parody of a 'coquetterie posthume' in which the mother has the body laid out for a portrait in a bed of camellia petals. How much further can the stylist Flaubert go in avenging himself upon the stupid aesthetics of desire? It seems as though the humiliation of having created Frédéric must be punished not only through the latter's reduction to a two-dimensional puppet but also through the ugly suffering of women he has placed in the Oedipal icon. Unlike Julien and Mme de Rênal – or even Julien and Mathilde, whose child is at least left unborn at the close of *Le Rouge* – Frédéric has no way forward, even into death. He ends up in a double act with the equally spineless Deslauriers, digestively repeating the best days of their youth.

In his surrogate as woman, Flaubert offers a more complex version of the reproductive relation to a fictional body. We all know the anecdote of how he got the subject of *Madame Bovary* from his friends Bouilhet and Du Camp, who hated the byzantine *Tentation de Saint Antoine*. In a letter written four years later, he comments on the difference between two modes of creativity:

> Ce qui m'est naturel à moi, c'est le non-naturel pour les autres, l'extraordinaire, le fantastique, la hurlade métaphysique, mythologique. *Saint Antoine* ne m'a pas demandé le quart de la tension d'esprit que la *Bovary* me cause. C'était un déversoir; je n'ai eu que plaisir à écrire, et les dix-huit mois que j'ai passés à en écrire les 500 pages ont été les plus profondément voluptueux de toute ma vie. Juge donc, il faut que j'entre à toute minute dans des *peaux* qui me sont antipathiques.[22]

The sexual terms in which this author expresses the pleasures and pains of writing are already familiar; but the contrast tells us something new. If the saint's pained continence let him pour forth, this novel of adultery is repressive exactly as it represents the entry into the woman. Everything in *Madame Bovary* is a sexual-political relation: the author refuses the very entry he desires.

What manner of eroticism is meant by the image of 'getting inside the skin' of a character? Like d'Albert, Flaubert 'is' Mme Bovary because he is not her. Emma's beautiful body, which makes her the object of enjoyment of the author's voyeurism, is joined to a transcendent desire which he must disparage. She does not desire men, she desires what they may bring her, an unbraked flight towards a far-off goal: pleasure, glamour, Paris. Instead she will get only the chewed cud of bad literature to think with, and all the men she seeks as mediators will let her down. She will turn in the repetitious circle of her femininity, and miss out even on the dubious privilege of having a son. In a moment, I shall look at two aspects of Emma's circularity – the use of *style indirect libre* and her fictional relation to her daughter – but first I want to come back to the quotation of my title and the question of authorial gender.

Baudelaire begins his review by showing what a writer of Flaubert's stature had to do in order to make an impact on the reading public. 'Soyons ... vulgaire dans le choix du sujet', he advises, and 'prenons bien garde à nous abandonner et à parler pour notre propre compte. ... Nous étendrons un style nerveux, pittoresque, subtil, exact, sur un canevas banal' (p. 451). Already the difference between author and world is established in terms of a coefficient of subtlety to banality. Then he raises the issue of gender:

> Il ne restait plus à l'auteur, pour accomplir le tour de force dans son entier, que de se dépouiller (autant que possible) de son sexe et de se faire femme. Il en est résulté une merveille; c'est que, malgré tout son zèle de comédien, il n'a pas pu ne pas infuser un sang viril dans les veines de sa créature, et que Mme Bovary, pour ce qu'il y a en elle de plus énergique et de plus ambitieux, et aussi de plus rêveur, Mme Bovary est restée un homme. Comme la Pallas armée, sortie du cerveau de Zeus, ce bizarre androgyne a gardé toutes les séductions d'une âme virile dans un charmant corps féminin. (p. 451)

The symbiosis of two androgynies is posited; but we may easily become confused about the polarized genders meeting and blending here. 'Flaubert' is praised for his tour de force not because he has succeeded in unsexing himself but because he has not. That is the miracle, for Baudelaire – that *despite* his acting skills he has made himself a woman who is in every positive aspect a man. There follows (in a discursus that takes up much of the space and most of the passion of this short text) a list of the 'grâces du héros' and the 'qualités viriles' of Emma Bovary.

These are, in order: 'l'imagination, faculté suprême et tyrannique, substituée au cœur ... qui domine généralement dans la femme comme dans l'animal'; the 'énergie soudaine d'action, rapidité de décision' typical of men of action; a 'goût immodéré de la séduction ... dandysme, amour exclusif de la domination'; and the ability to give oneself: 'Mme Bovary se donne ... magnifiquement, généreusement, d'une manière toute masculine, à des drôles qui ne sont pas ses égaux, comme les poètes se livrent à des drôlesses'. Of these four characteristics, only one, the second, is normally attributed to men; the others, and especially the last two, are qualities assigned to the passive emotionality conventionally considered feminine. Baudelaire returns to these feminized virilities when he concludes, apropos of Emma's convent school days:

> Les bonnes sœurs ont remarqué dans cette jeune fille une aptitude étonnante à la vie, à profiter de la vie, à en conjecturer les jouissances – voilà l'homme d'action!
> Cependant la jeune fille s'enivrait délicieusement de la couleur des vitraux, des teintes orientales que les longues fenêtres ouvragées jetaient sur son paroissien de pensionnaire; elle se gorgeait de la musique solennelle des vêpres, et, par un paradoxe dont tout l'honneur appartient aux nerfs, elle substituait dans son âme au Dieu véritable le Dieu de sa fantaisie, le Dieu de l'avenir et du hasard, un Dieu de vignette, avec éperons et moustaches; voilà le poëte hystérique. (p. 452)

All Emma's masculinities, then, are qualities of the imagination, not of the body; each one stands for a sensuality disembodied into impressionism. The dandified God Baudelaire conjures up for her resembles no one so much as the swashbuckling side of Madeleine de Maupin. Finally, the hysteria of the poet is that mystery which 'se traduit chez les hommes nerveux par toutes les impuissances et aussi par l'aptitude à tous les excès'. Through the compliment of regendering that is offered to the poor character, in other words, a way has been found to feminize Flaubert in particular and the (male) poet in general without loss of dignity.

It would surely be superfluous to discuss the rightness or wrongness of Baudelaire's gender categories; equally so, I hope, to show how Emma's wearing a monocle, taking the sexual initiative, liking perversity or wanting a son can fit very comfortably into the series of expediencies available to the frustrated woman. Ion Collas's psychological study gives a good account of her feminine hungers.[23] The point of interest here is the cross-sexual reproduction attributed to the writer. Baudelaire joins Flaubert in that woman's body Gautier was the first to try on. In the guise of the adolescent girl who does not wish to decide whether to be a man or a woman, the geniuses of art for art's sake quietly practise hysteria.

So much for the poetic fantasy. I want to argue that Emma, as a novelistic creature, serves Flaubert slightly differently from this; and I shall end by taking two text-internal angles of approach to the question of style and the body. *Style indirect libre*, as it is used by Flaubert at least, is the quintessential ironic device: it demands of readers that they side with the wisdom of authors and against the stupidity of characters via an unreliable index of discourse. Technically the *style-indirect-libre* text is genuinely ambiguous: it runs on in the third person and the past tense exactly like the narratorial voice – but 'something tells us' it is Emma or Charles or Frédéric thinking, and that 'something' is attributed to the author. What actually happens is that we, as obedient implied readers, facilitate the author's politics of divide-and-rule. We sense a lack of sophistication, call it by a character's name and assign it as a device to the artfulness of 'Flaubert'. At every step, the implied author comes into being as that which would not use such words naïvely, which exceeds the language by knowing it as the character cannot. The desiring body comes into being as that which is always just below the level of linguistic control. Emma – like Joyce's Eveline or Gerty MacDowell – is the subject of another's discourse, and she is so with a feminine stupidity. She has consumed bad writing and can do nothing but regurgitate it; in inferring her in it, we release 'Flaubert' from anything so carnal.

The real fiction he wants to create here is the masculinity of the author-God who can leave the female husk behind infused with his spirit and ready to fall into dust. The better part of femininity remains with him as the Baudelairean imagination. As readers, we try to show an equal imagination in getting the hint; that would make us worthy of him. But irony catches us the same way. When we split apart the body and soul of Flaubert's text, we condemn ourselves to being creatures of flesh, readers, hysterics, fixed like Emma in the toils of repetitious narcissism – girls if we take it seriously, Romantic boys if we look to see our masculinity peeping back. Even Baudelaire fell for that one.

There is one scene, however, where it seems as though Emma escapes for a moment from the specular circuit where she is entrapped. Let us begin by observing what it means that she is the mother of a daughter. Women in male-authored fiction rarely give birth to daughters, and when they do it is usually as a punishment. They are nearly always already transgressors – murderers like Thérèse Desqueyroux, prostitutes like Nadja and a whole host of others, adulteresses like Emma, Hester Prynne, Anna Karenina, Effi Briest. The latter exist with their daughters in marginal spaces: a garden, a cell, a cottage. Here, it is implied, they turn inward with their superfluity for, unlike the iconic Jocasta, Mary or Venus, they have done nothing to perpetuate the patrilinear chain or carry the father's name. Remember why Emma wanted a boy:

> Elle souhaitait un fils; il serait fort et brun, elle l'appellerait Georges; et cette idée d'avoir pour enfant un mâle était comme la revanche en espoir de toutes ses impuissances passées. Un homme, au moins, est libre; il peut parcourir les passions et les pays, traverser les obstacles, mordre aux bonheurs les plus lointains. Mais· une femme est empêchée continuellement. Inerte et flexible à la fois, elle a contre elle les mollesses de la chair avec les dépendances de la loi. Sa volonté, comme le voile de son chapeau retenu par un cordon, palpite à tous les vents; il y a toujours quelque désir qui entraîne, quelque convenance qui retient.
> Elle accoucha un dimanche, vers six heures, au soleil levant.
> – C'est une fille! dit Charles.
> Elle tourna la tête et s'évanouit.[24]

This is familiar enough stuff: a good girl in Freudian terms, Emma seeks to have what she cannot have via the fit expedient of birth: she is ready (or thinks she is) to play Jocasta. But the author cannot countenance this hallowed version of cross-gender reproduction, for his own is more perverse and more urgent. Emma must be condemned to the copying he will thereby escape.

The disappointing child, saddled with a Romantic name, is sent to a wet-nurse, the mère Rolet; visits to her assist the first stage of the Léon affair. When Berthe is back, Emma, confused by Léon's slowness, is playing the virtuous wife and mother; but nothing stimulates the young man into action and, in the throes of frustration, Emma seeks the help of the priest Bournisien, who understands only bodily ailments and recommends her husband the doctor. Home again, Emma throws herself into a chair. There follows the most extended encounter in the text between the mother and her child:

> [...] entre la fenêtre et la table à ouvrage, la petite Berthe était là, qui chancelait sur ses bottines de tricot, et essayait de se rapprocher de sa mère, pour lui saisir, par le bout, les rubans de son tablier.
> – Laisse-moi, dit celle-ci en l'écartant avec la main.
> La petite fille bientôt revint plus près encore contre ses genoux; et, s'y appuyant des bras, elle levait vers elle son gros œil bleu, pendant qu'un filet de salive pure découlait de sa lèvre sur la soie du tablier.
> – Laisse-moi! répéta la jeune femme tout irritée.
> Sa figure épouvanta l'enfant, qui se mit à crier.
> – Eh! laisse-moi donc! fit-elle en la repoussant du coude.
> Berthe alla tomber au pied de la commode, contre la patère de cuivre; elle s'y coupa la joue, le sang sortit. Madame Bovary se précipita pour la relever, cassa le cordon de la sonnette, appela la servante de toutes ses forces, et elle alla commencer à se maudire, lorsque Charles parut. C'était l'heure du dîner, il rentrait. (p. 118)

Daughters in the novel of adultery do not fall ill, they fall down and bleed, testing their mothers by imitation rather than threat. Hester's Pearl, despite her ironic name, lives off the scarlet letter and reproduces it in her person; Effi Briest's daughter Annie causes the awful denouement by an innocent fall on the threshold of her parents' house. Emma's lies to Charles and he tends the wound, sticking on a plaster:

> Madame Bovary ne descendit pas dans la salle; elle voulut demeurer seule à garder son enfant. Alors, en la contemplant dormir, ce qu'elle

conservait d'inquiétude se dissipa par degrés, et elle se parut à elle-même bien sotte et bien bonne de s'être troublée tout à l'heure pour si peu de chose. Berthe, en effet, ne sanglota plus. Sa respiration soulevait insensiblement la couverture de coton. De grosses larmes s'arrêtaient au coin de ses paupières à demi closes, qui laissaient voir entre les cils deux prunelles pâles, enfoncées; le sparadrap, collé sur sa joue, en tirait obliquement la peau tendue.
– C'est une chose étrange, pensait Emma, comme cette enfant est laide!
(pp. 118–119)

What is both comic and shocking here is Emma's utter refusal of specularity: she will never be the good mirroring mother because she finds no narcissistic pleasure in her child. It is left to Charles to see them (like Frédéric, in fantasy) as doubles, mistaken for sisters on future sunny days, each in a wide-brimmed summer hat. For Emma, there is no such satisfaction in the idea of doubling. In this, perhaps, she comes the closest, while frustrating it, to equalling the fantasy of her creator. For one moment – and only negatively, of course – she exceeds the terms of her sexual politics.

In later parts of the text, the daughter is superseded by the unpleasant Mme Rolet whom we never see nurturing but always consuming: typically of the false mothers of fiction, she is given the role of *entremetteuse*, and it is through her house at the edge of the village that adultery is mediated. In her final despair, between the attempts on Lheureux, Léon and Binet and the last resorts of Guillaumin and Rodolphe, Emma runs to the feminine space:

– Mère Rolet, dit-elle en arrivant chez la nourrice, j'étouffe!... délacez-moi.
Elle tomba sur le lit; elle sanglotait. La mère Rolet la couvrit d'un jupon et resta debout près d'elle. Puis, comme elle ne répondait pas, la bonne femme s'éloigna, prit son rouet et se mit à filer du lin.
Oh! finissez! murmura-t-elle, croyant entendre le tour de Binet.
– Qui la gêne? se demandait la nourrice. Pourquoi vient-elle ici?
(p. 313)

We are not sure either. Emma stares vaguely at the walls and ceiling of the hovel. 'Une longue araignée' crawls above her head down a crack in the beam. All around her, people, animals and objects are spinning. This is a hiatus before suicide in which she seeks and loses the company of women, as depletedly as the author offers it. The system of hopeless copying here is no longer the masculine aimlessness of Binet or Bouvard and Pécuchet but the weaving/unweaving (lacing/unlacing) of women's work. The orphaned Berthe will end her days working in a spinning factory. Flaubert was Hugh Selwyn Mauberley's 'true Penelope',[25] not his Ulysses.

Notes

Throughout this article, references to a cited text appear after quotations; passages without page reference are from the last cited page. Unless otherwise stated, all italics are mine.

[1] Jean-Paul Sartre, *L'Être et le néant* (Paris: Gallimard, 1943), 672–673. My argument in this article, while not derived from it, owes a major debt to Sartre's *L'Idiot de la famille* (Paris: Gallimard, 1971–1972), 3 vols.

[2] Théophile Gautier, *Mademoiselle de Maupin*, ed. M. Crouzet (Paris: Gallimard, 1973), 127. The discussion of this and other *récits* takes up material used in my *Narcissus and Echo: Women in the French Récit* (Manchester: Manchester University Press, 1988).

[3] Jean-Paul Sartre, *Baudelaire* (Paris: Gallimard, 1963), 147 ff.

[4] All quotations from Baudelaire are from the *Œuvres complètes*, ed. M. Ruff (Paris: Seuil, 1968). This phrase is from 'Je t'adore à l'égal de la voûte nocturne' (p. 57).

[5] Gustave Flaubert, letter to Louise Colet of 9 December 1852, in *Correspondance*, ed. J. Bruneau (Paris: Gallimard, 1973, 1980), 2 vols., ii 204.

[6] Gustave Flaubert, letter to Louise Colet of 16 January 1852, in *Correspondance*, ii 31.

[7] After all, *pater semper incertus est*, see the section entitled 'The advance of intellectuality' from Freud's *Moses and Monotheism*, in A. Richards (ed.), *The Pelican Freud Library*, tr. J. Strachey *et al.* (Harmondsworth: Penguin Books, 1985), xiii 358–363.

[8] This statement is quoted by André Breton, *Nadja* (Paris: Gallimard, 1964), 13–14.

[9] Gustave Flaubert, *L'Éducation sentimentale*, ed. P. Wetherill (Paris: Garnier, 1984), 302. It was with this phrase that Flaubert marked his own edition of the text.

[10] See Freud, 'Family romances', in *The Pelican Freud Library*, vii 217–225.

[11] For a more detailed discussion of this material, see my *The Adulteress's Child: Authorship and Desire in the Nineteenth-Century Novel* (Cambridge: Polity Press, 1992).

[12] Stendhal, *Le Rouge et le noir*, ed. P. Castex (Paris: Garnier, 1973), 110.

[13] Sandra Gilbert and Susan Gubar, *The Madwoman in the Attic* (New Haven and London: Yale University Press, 1979).

[14] From *Correspondance*, i 627–628; quoted in Victor Brombert, 'Flaubert

and the status of the subject' in Naomi Schor and Henry F. Majewski (eds.), *Flaubert and Postmodernism* (Lincoln and London: University of Nebraska Press, 1984), 107.

[15] These two extracts are from *Correspondance*, ii 67, 205. They are quoted in Marthe Robert, *En haine du roman* (Saint-Amand: Balland, 1982), 14.

[16] See Lucette Czyba, *Mythes et idéologie de la femme dans les romans de Flaubert* (Lyon: Presses Universitaires de Lyon, 1983), 315. See also Mary Orr, 'Reading the Other: Flaubert's *L'Éducation sentimentale* revisited', *French Studies* 46 (October 1992), 412–423.

[17] Letter to Louise Colet of 16 January 1852, in *Correspondance*, ii 30.

[18] Gustave Flaubert, *L'Éducation sentimentale*, 6.

[19] See Diana Knight, 'Object choices: taste and fetishism in Flaubert's *L'Éducation sentimentale*' in Brian Rigby (ed.), *French Literature, Thought and Culture in the Nineteenth Century* (Basingstoke: Macmillan, 1993), 198–217.

[20] For a more extended analysis of the mother/daughter relations of Mme Arnoux and Elisa Schlesinger as represented in Flaubert's fiction, see *The Adulteress's Child*, 76–79.

[21] Gustave Flaubert, *La Première Éducation sentimentale*, ed. F.-R. Bastide (Paris: Seuil, 1963), 234. This episode has been much discussed by critics, but the connection to the later scene has not previously been noted.

[22] Letter to Louise Colet of 6 April 1853, *Correspondance*, ii 297.

[23] Ion Collas, *Madame Bovary: A Psychoanalytic Reading* (Paris: Droz, 1985).

[24] Gustave Flaubert, *Madame Bovary*, ed. C. Gothot-Mersch (Paris: Garnier, 1971), 91.

[25] Ezra Pound, 'Hugh Selwyn Mauberley', in *Selected Poems* (London: Faber, 1968), 173.

Flaubert and Semanalysis: Rereading *L'Éducation sentimentale*

BRIAN NELSON

L'Éducation sentimentale is, famously, a frustratingly opaque text. Flaubert's ironic narrative strategies have been seen as calling into question the entire mimetic and communicative project of the novel, subverting the signification of conventional fiction in a way that would inspire much twentieth-century writing. Readers have found it difficult to reconcile Flaubert's expressed desire to write a book 'about nothing', to give the novel autonomy of stylization, with his desire to portray the moral history of the men and women of his generation through the illusions and mediocrity of his protagonist, Frédéric Moreau, and the chaos and misplaced idealism of the 1848 Revolution. My purpose in this essay is to suggest how the work of Julia Kristeva, in particular her theories of the 'symbolic' and the 'semiotic', provides useful analytic tools for an integrated reading of Flaubert's novel in its psychological, social and narrative aspects.[1]

Kristeva

Kristeva claims that every theory of language is implicitly or explicitly based on a concept of the speaking subject. Her work is thus located at the point of intersection of psychoanalysis and semiotics. Arguably the two most powerful influences on her work are Derrida, and his modes of deconstructive reading, and Lacan, with his notion of the 'unconscious structured like a language'. She attempts to make psychoanalysis relevant to textual analysis, not through a psychoanalysis of either the author or the reader, but through the analysis of what texts or discourses must repress. In turn, she brings to theories of subjectivity an understanding of the crucial role that the organization of language and representation plays in the construction of a unified stable subject.

Kristeva embarks upon a project which she calls 'semanalysis'. It examines, not the processes of meaning production (that is, codes of signification), but the processes which break down or destroy meaning – a method that evaluates not only the 'great texts' of literature but also the transgressive, experimental writings of the avant-garde. Secondly, it analyses the role of the speaking subject in discourse – the ways in which the subject both produces and subverts the production of textual meaning. The speaking subject cannot be identified with consciousness or the Cartesian *cogito*; it refers to a subject split into an unconscious and consciousness. Kristeva is interested in the intervention of language in the constitution of the unconscious, and the irruptions of subjectivity in language.

Semanalysis involves the following processes: (a) the examination not of the sign in itself, but of the processes and practices producing signs – the mode of production of signs; (b) focus not on the signifier or the signified, but on the relation both have to the speaking subject; (c) literature as the privileged object of analysis, particularly the literature of the avant-garde, where the specificities of the signifying act are most clearly manifested (though semanalysis could be applied just as well in the study of other representational systems, such as art, painting and film); (d) her semanalysis of literary and artistic texts opposes dominant models of linguistic and textual analysis, which are primarily concerned with language as truthful, referential and rational or as expressive and imaginative; (e) semanalysis thus subjects the foundation of all knowledges based on the sign, including philosophy, to a radical critique, subverting knowledge and science but making explicit the kinds of knowing subject they presume.

Kristeva's paper 'Signifying practice and mode of production' develops a distinction between two kinds of procedure involved in all signification and their relation to the constitution and deformation of the speaking subject. All sign systems rely on what Kristeva calls the procedures of 'setting in place', 'unity' or, more generally, the 'symbolic order'. This refers to the modality which sets up or establishes a signifying system, organizing it as a stable, ordered, regulated, law-abiding system. This unity is based on a conservative movement that maintains and consolidates existing forms of signification and social values – the realist novel, the Hollywood film, the romantic poem – signifying practices that naturalize or neutralize social, political and economic relations. Unity establishes order, stability and hierarchy. It can be identified with grammar, logic, syntax, as well as the use of a stable, cohesive 'I' in discourse – that is to say, with rule-governed, normative, representational relations. Unity occurs not only at the level of texts, but also at the level of the subject: unity is equated with the processes oedipalizing the child, ensuring that it accepts the social law against incest so that it gives up the mother and access to immediate gratification in exchange for a stable place and identity as a male or female subject. Unity, or the symbolic, is the site of law, the phallus and the rules of language.

Along with unity or the symbolic, Kristeva posits a much more subversive movement which she calls 'cutting through', 'traversing', 'process' or the 'semiotic':

> The traversing of the system takes place when the speaking subject is put in process and cuts across, at an angle as it were, the social institutions in which it had previously recognized itself. It thus coincides with the moments of social rupture, renovation and revolution.[2]

These two movements, the setting in place of a sign-system and the processes cutting through, the establishment of an ordered system of signification and the movement that disrupts it, are described by Kristeva as the interaction of the semiotic and the symbolic. Unity/ the symbolic indicates the stable forms of signification reproducing themselves; process/the semiotic is both what *precedes* unity, making it possible, and also what *exceeds* unity by overflowing it, threatening to disrupt it and throw it into disorder. Process precedes unity both logically and chronologically, providing unity with its raw materials. It constitutes the necessary raw ingredients for all systems of representation, the matter which these systems must order and control in order to have meaning. At the level of the speaking subject, it can be identified with the pre-Oedipal infantile sexual stages and processes, which are dominated by and directed to the figure of the mother. Unity is unable to accept or acknowledge its relation to process; process must remain unspoken. As necessary but unacknowledged, process or the semiotic threatens to traverse and break down unity once it is established (like the return of infantile repressed wishes in the form of dreams, symptoms, jokes and other unconscious manifestations). It threatens to break down the order upon which unity relies.

Kristeva argues that not only do the two terms 'unity'/'the symbolic' and 'process'/'the semiotic' describe signifying systems and the organization of sexual drives in the individual; they also refer to the ways in which social institutions, such as the family, the state and the Church, function:

> The state represents this unifying instance in relation to the process of contradiction which traverses the forces and relations of production. The family ensures unity in the face of the process of drives and of pleasure-overflow. This unity, of state and family, is achieved at the price of a murder and a sacrifice – that of the *soma,* the drive and the process.[3]

The distinction between unity and process thus simultaneously designates the functioning of signifying systems, psychic relations and social institutions. In the context of the individual's psychic and sexual development, unity is the Oedipal organization of drives, subsumed under the domination of the phallus, the law of patriarchy. Underlying (that is, preceding) the symbolic and overflowing it (that is, disruptively returning it to disorder) are those processes of the semiotic that are pre-Oedipal, free-flowing, disorganized, pleasure-seeking and feminine (in so far as they are maternally dominated). The pre-Oedipal is pre-phallic, a non-unified period in each individual's life which is closely associated with the mother, and in particular with the mother's body; by contrast, the Oedipal is phallic, hierarchically unified, governed by the rule of the paternal, an order requiring the child's renunciation of sexual desire for the mother and the mother's body.

The symbolic is thus Oedipal, and the semiotic is pre-Oedipal in the case of the individual. Kristeva claims that there is an analogous interaction between the symbolic and the semiotic in all signifying practices. Unity or the symbolic depends on the subject's ability to follow law and to take up a stable speaking position: the following of rules and codes (for example, the rules of sequence, continuity, editing, framing in realist narrative cinema; the demands of pitch, harmony and rhythm in music; the use of the norms of meaning, grammar, syntax in writing) which guarantee a comprehensible and recognizable text, in which the stable subject is able to recognize itself. Process or the semiotic, on the other hand, is required by the symbolic but cannot be acknowledged by it: pre-Oedipal bodily rhythms, pleasures, movements, spasms, cycles, etc. provide the libidinal energies and drives behind what will become speech in the child. In this sense, the semiotic precedes unity. But it is also what exceeds unity or the symbolic, particularly in the 'return' of these pre-Oedipal processes in the form of rhythms, intonations, and lexical, syntactic and rhetorical transformations. The semiotic in this second sense is the play on and subversion of the symbolic. The symbolic establishes the limits of any sign-system, while the semiotic is what forces these limits to be transgressed and stretched beyond their normal function.

Kristeva's analysis of the speaking subject and its role in the production of signification makes clear the *price* of discourse, the cost of coherence: a repression (or sacrifice) of the pre-Oedipal sexual drives and the maternal love-object. Signification is possible only with the repression of the excess needed to produce it. This pre-Oedipal, feminine, libidinal excess can be spoken only at the cost of introducing an irreducible, irrational and unknowable element into all language.

The Kristevan notion of symbolic-conservative and semiotic-transgressive processes should not be seen as ahistorical or merely structuralist; on the contrary, what is considered transgressive or revolutionary is relative to the historical norms and conventions it challenges. Today's radical, subversive or avant-garde practice is tomorrow's convention. No process is inherently incapable of unification; the ordering, symbolization or unification is a form of political control involving the reharnessing of semiotic energies back into a new symbolic norm. Norm and rupture work in dialectical tension.

Frédéric Moreau: Love and Identity

The most important thing in the life of Frédéric Moreau is his 'grand amour' for Mme Arnoux. But it is, above all, the *image* of Mme Arnoux that he loves:

> – Vous me faisiez l'effet d'un clair de lune par une nuit d'été, quand tout est parfums, ombres douces, blancheurs, infini; et les délices de la chair et de l'âme étaient contenues pour moi dans votre nom, que je me répétais, en tâchant de le baiser sur mes lèvres. Je n'imaginais rien au-delà. C'était Mme Arnoux telle que vous étiez, avec ses deux enfants, tendre, sérieuse, belle à éblouir, et si bonne! Cette image-là effaçait toutes les autres.
> (p. 503)

The image of Mme Arnoux evoked here is that of a mother:

Frédéric soupçonna Mme Arnoux d'être venue pour s'offrir; et il était repris par une convoitise plus forte que jamais, furieuse, enragée. Cependant, il sentait quelque chose d'inexprimable, une répulsion, et comme *l'effroi d'un inceste*... et tout à la fois par prudence et pour ne pas dégrader son idéal, il tourna sur ses talons et se mit à faire une cigarette. (p. 504, my italics)

From a Kristevan perspective, Frédéric's construction of a maternal image is significant, for entry into the symbolic order entails renunciation of unity with the mother, and therefore repression of all desire for her. The question thus arises of whether Frédéric's love for Mme Arnoux represents a repressed desire for his mother or an attempt to return to the semiotic, to escape from the anguish of living in the symbolic order and of maintaining a unified, independent identity.

As Michel Brix has shown,[4] although Frédéric's mother appears only fleetingly in the narrative, she is always present in his thoughts. His political ambitions and his concern for his appearance in the eyes of others derive from her. Moreover, despite his mother's virtual absence (which is similar in some respects to that of Mme Arnoux) and his apparent rejection of her advice, the image he constructs of Mme Arnoux is based on the desires, ambitions and characteristics of Mme Moreau.[5] This suggests a repressed desire for his mother, but it does not in itself mean that he feels anguish at living in the symbolic order and wishes to retreat into pre-symbolic existence. Thus it is necessary to explore the nature of Frédéric's identity and how it is reflected in his behaviour and in his attachment to Mme Arnoux.

Although Frédéric is the novel's protagonist, and we see nearly everything through his eyes, his identity remains unstable. He eludes all professional or political categorization in a bourgeois world in which identity is always determined by one's role in society: Deslauriers the would-be politician, Arnoux the entrepreneur and speculator, Rosanette the courtesan, M. Dambreuse the aristocratic financier-politician, Hussonnet the journalist and drama critic, and so on. Frédéric inhabits this society but never has a fixed role within it: he studies law but does not manage to find a job in the legal profession; he dreams of becoming a writer or a painter but his interest does not last; and his political 'ambitions' are abortive. His lack of ambition and his continual oscillation between various roles reveals an aversion to assuming a symbolic identity, that is, an identity constructed by the demands of bourgeois society. And since life in the social (that is, symbolic) order cannot satisfy his need for a stable identity, he would like to renounce this order and return to unity with his mother, to a state (the semiotic) in which he did not know the anguish of an independent existence. He tries to find a stable, unified identity by defining himself in relation to Mme Arnoux, a surrogate mother, rather than in relation to the external world. But, as Julia Simon Ingram has shown in a stimulating psychoanalytic study of *L'Éducation sentimentale*,[6] this is impossible, for it would mean renouncing language and his independent identity; this renunciation would make life in society impossible, and he would risk psychosis.[7] In Lacanian terms identity is only achieved by self-differentiation from the mother, and if Frédéric had succeeded in (re-)establishing unity and wholeness with Mme Arnoux, he would have lost his independence and identity as a separate person.[8] This is why he is afraid to consummate his desire for her.

The interaction in Frédéric of the semiotic and the symbolic thus helps to explain his lack of ambition, his indecision, and his obsessive love for Mme Arnoux – or rather, his attachment to an ideal which he is so careful not to degrade.

Revolution: Energy and Order

The political world of *L'Éducation sentimentale* is characterized by a state of conflict between the energy of the semiotic and the order of the symbolic. The social order as it exists under the July Monarchy – the order of the bourgeois state – is, from the moment Frédéric arrives in Paris, unstable and incapable of responding to the needs of the people; among Frédéric's friends there is constant talk of socialism and revolution, and even before February 1848 there are numerous riots. The climax comes in February, at the beginning of the third part of the novel; the government is no longer able to contain the energy and frustration of the people, which erupt with the sack of the Tuileries (pp. 357–363). This episode represents a moment when the energy of the semiotic overturns and breaks free from the order imposed by the symbolic. The mob takes possession of the Palace and ransacks everything that represents the monarchy:

> Et poussés malgré eux, ils entrèrent dans un appartement où s'étendait, au plafond, un dais de velours rouge. Sur le trône, en dessous, était assis

un prolétaire à barbe noire, la chemise entrouverte, l'air hilare et stupide comme un magot. D'autres gravissaient l'estrade pour s'asseoir à sa place.
– Quel mythe! dit Hussonnet. Voilà le peuple souverain! (p. 359)

But this is more than an appropriation of the palace and the throne; it is an overturning of everything that signifies power. The palace and the throne are signs of the king and his power, and thus represent the bourgeois state; it is this structure that reinforces the stability of the social order. The image of the bearded, half-clad worker on the throne disrupts this structure, reducing the throne – and thus the king and the state – to an object of ridicule. The intrusive worker, by sitting on the throne, forms a new chain of signification linking the people, power and the state, thus destabilizing the symbols that maintained the order of the bourgeois monarchy of Louis-Philippe.

The supreme example of the overturning of the existing symbolic order is the Club de l'Intelligence episode (pp. 373–380). The Club is intended to be a forum for the debate of revolutionary ideas, and Frédéric goes there to seek support for his candidature in the elections; what ensues, however, is not a meaningful discussion but a babble of voices and incompatible opinions, culminating with the incomprehensible speech of a Spaniard who drowns out Frédéric:

> Frédéric encore une fois voulut se faire entendre:
> – Mais citoyens! ...
> L'Espagnol continuait:
> – El martes próximo tendrá lugar en la iglesia de la Magdalena un servicio fúnebre.
> – C'est absurde à la fin! personne ne comprend!
> Cette observation exaspéra la foule.
> – A la porte! à la porte!
> – Qui? moi? demanda Frédéric.
> – Vous-même! dit majestueusement Sénécal. Sortez!
> Il se leva pour sortir; et la voix de l'Ibérien le poursuivait... (p. 380)

This absurd episode represents a rupture of the system of political discourse, which is no longer able to give order to the expression of opinions; the system seems to be evacuated of all meaning (the symbolic), and what remains is pure energy (the semiotic). Language becomes looser (it is even permitted to speak in Spanish) and signification is lost (no one at the Club understands a word of Spanish).

Kristeva notes that the overturning of the symbolic never lasts, and that the system always re-emerges, albeit in a different form. The new popular 'order' that emerges in February 1848 is even more unstable than the old one, which begins almost immediately to reimpose itself – by the suppression of the insurrection of June 1848, and finally by the *coup d'état* of Louis-Napoléon; even the former socialist Sénécal, who presided over the Club de l'Intelligence and expelled Frédéric when he protested against the absurdity and chaos that reigned there, becomes a policeman in the service of the Bonapartist regime as it brutally reimposes order.

Signification

This interaction between the semiotic and the symbolic, energy and order, process and structure, which is manifest in the character of Frédéric and in the course of the Revolution – that is to say, in the *content* of the novel – is also reflected in its *form*. The reader of *L'Éducation sentimentale* feels a sense of frustration similar to that of Frédéric and his generation. We have seen that Frédéric is constantly seeking lost unity with his mother by attaching himself to Mme Arnoux, but does not wish to renounce his independent identity; he wants to return to the semiotic realm, but cannot leave the symbolic. The revolutionaries succeed in overturning the old order, but what they do and say has no signification – they overturn the symbolic, but the semiotic that remains cannot last without order, and since the revolutionaries are incapable of imposing their own form of order, the old order is re-established. The reader's frustration derives from the fact that s/he wants to impose unity and coherence on Flaubert's moral history of the men and women of his generation, but, as Jonathan Culler has shown,[9] whether s/he tries to find a centre of coherence at the level of description, narration, character or theme, the text rejects his or her attempts to impose meaningful structures. In the Balzacian novel, the description of events and things is intended to represent reality, to create referential connections between these representations and aspects of the readers' reality, and to help them to a better understanding of life and society by offering a commentary on this 'reality'. But the novels of Flaubert 'demoralize' the reader by blocking the secondary processes; the reader may recognize the world described in the novel, but since this world lacks coherence and unity, the reader is unable to extract from it the meaning of his or her own world.[10] Even the descriptive passages which seem the most susceptible of symbolic interpretation resist it. For example, in the forest at Fontainebleau:

> [...] en se renversant la tête, on apercevait le ciel, entre les cimes des arbres. Quelques-uns, d'une altitude démesurée, avaient des airs de patriarches et d'empereurs, ou se touchant par le bout, formaient avec leurs longs fûts comme des arcs de triomphe; d'autres, poussés dès le bas obliquement, semblaient des colonnes près de tomber. (p. 398)

This passage has provoked various contradictory interpretations, most of which, however, affirm that it refers to the June insurrection, which occurs at the same time. It might be argued that the trees which 'avaient des airs de patriarches et d'empereurs, ou [...] formaient avec leurs longs fûts comme des arcs de triomphe', symbolize the value of the old order, or that they show the permanence of nature in relation to human affairs. On the other hand, those which 'semblaient des colonnes près de tomber' would shatter this interpretation. The systematic pursuit of symbolic interpretations produces a whole series of contradictions, and it must be recognized that the description contains elements of self-parody.[11]

Earlier, at Rosanette's costume dinner party, Frédéric, watching the women dancing, interprets the scene in terms of images of desire; but the images are not his – they are Romantic clichés, codes imposed by society, and Frédéric's interpretation becomes a parody of the interpretative process, subverting symbolic representation:[12]

> [...] toutes passaient dans le même éblouissement, et chacune avec une excitation particulière selon le genre de sa beauté. La Polonaise, qui s'abandonnait d'une façon langoureuse, lui inspirait l'envie de la tenir contre son cœur, en filant tous les deux dans un traîneau sur une plaine couverte de neige. Des horizons de volupté tranquille, au bord d'un lac, dans un chalet, se déroulaient sous les pas de la Suissesse, qui valsait le torse droit et les paupières baissées. Puis, tout à coup, la Bacchante, penchant en arrière sa tête brune, le faisait rêver à des caresses dévoratrices, dans des bois de lauriers-roses, par un temps d'orage, au bruit confus des tambourins. (p. 175)

When Frédéric goes to bed that night, he dreams of the dinner party, and the individual women become fragmented and fused in his mind: '[...] dans l'hallucination du premier sommeil, il voyait passer et repasser continuellement les épaules de la Poissarde, les reins de la Débardeuse, les mollets de la Polonaise, la chevelure de la Sauvagesse' (p. 183). The objects of Frédéric's desire are no longer individual women (if they ever were), but fragments of their (erotic) bodies; they lose their stable identities. The interpretative structure of desire established by Frédéric, which had provided an ordering principle helping him to establish coherent images of the women, collapses. The representational system of the symbolic is parodied, subverted and finally displaced by the semiotic.

Thus, for both the reader and the fictional characters, the world of *L'Éducation sentimentale* is demoralizing and confusing, a fluid, heterogeneous world it is impossible to unify and make sense of; each time it appears that a certain proposition is true, it is revealed that its 'truth' can never be trusted. Having spent several evenings watching a window which he thought was that of Mme Arnoux, Frédéric learns that she lives elsewhere (pp. 70, 90). Similarly, during the fighting in February 1848, 'on attaquait [...] le poste du Château-d'Eau, pour délivrer cinquante prisonniers, qui n'y étaient pas' (p. 356). The 'plot' is perplexing. Events arise and disappear without a sense of causality or purpose, so that in spite of constant agitation, nothing seems to happen. And when Frédéric and Deslauriers meet again at the end and look back over their lives, what they remember is an episode that occurred before the novel begins (pp. 508–510), as if everything that takes place during the previous 500 pages signifies nothing.

Flaubert's famous aims of writing 'un livre sur rien' and of expressing his feeling that 'la bêtise consiste à vouloir conclure' reflect a desire to deliver writing from the necessity of signifying and representing, and to displace interest from representation to the writing process itself. And here we return to the paradox of *L'Éducation sentimentale*: how can the novel both signify nothing and yet say something about the sentimental education of Frédéric and the moral history of the generation of 1848? The answer lies in the novel's remarkable unity of form and content. Kristeva's theories unite language, the functioning of signifying systems, psychic relations, the identity of the individual, social institutions and the social order; and Kristevan analysis of *L'Éducation sentimentale* shows that the psychology of Frédéric (above all, the question of his identity), the Revolution of 1848, and the indeterminacy of the text are all aspects of the dialectic between the symbolic and the semiotic, thus providing a suggestive framework for a unified reading of the novel and of its apparent contradictions.

Notes

[1] See Julia Kristeva, 'Signifying practice and mode of production', *Edinburgh Review* 1 (1976), 64–75, and Toril Moi (ed.), *The Kristeva Reader* (Oxford: Blackwell, 1986). All page references to *L'Éducation sentimentale* are to the Garnier-Flammarion edition, ed. Claudine Gothot-Mersch (Paris, 1985).
[2] Kristeva, 'Signifying practice', 64.
[3] Ibid., 64–65.
[4] Michel Brix, 'Portrait d'un jeune homme "entortillé par sa maman": le personnage de Frédéric Moreau dans *L'Éducation sentimentale*', *Les Lettres Romanes* 44 (1990), 297–313.
[5] Ibid., 305–309.
[6] Julia Simon Ingram, 'The aesthetics of fragmentation: *L'Éducation sentimentale*', *Nineteenth-Century French Studies* 18 (1989–1990), 112–132.
[7] See Elizabeth A. Grosz, *Sexual Subversions: Three French Feminists* (Sydney: Allen & Unwin, 1985), 56–57.
[8] See Ingram, 'Aesthetics', 113–114.
[9] Jonathan Culler, *Flaubert: The Uses of Uncertainty* (Ithaca: Cornell University Press, 1974).
[10] See ibid., 85–86.
[11] See ibid., 100–101.
[12] See ibid., 98.

Description et psychologie: génétique et poétique de l'indice dans *L'Éducation sentimentale*

ÉRIC LE CALVEZ

La topographie contribue certes à *montrer* le lieu qu'elle décrit, mais *faire voir* n'en est peut-être pas l'attribut primordial ou la finalité immédiate. Flaubert a insisté à plusieurs reprises sur la *motivation diégétique* de la description, s'interrogeant sur sa fonctionnalité. Selon ses termes mêmes, l'utilité de la description relève de son association avec le personnage : « Il n'y a point dans mon livre une description isolée, gratuite; toutes *servent* à mes personnages et ont une influence lointaine ou immédiate sur l'action »,[1] a-t-il répliqué à Sainte-Beuve pour justifier les descriptions de *Salammbô*, dont le critique avait reproché le nombre et surtout l'aspect *superflu*.[2] Il faut cependant aller plus loin, car de manière implicite un double jeu semble alors se dessiner : soit la description *sert* l'action en étant asservie par le personnage,[3] soit elle *influence* l'action d'une façon ponctuelle ou plus large, apparaissant ainsi comme une composante majeure du mode narratif.

Un aspect essentiel de la fonction diégétique des descriptions que je vais étudier ici à partir de *L'Éducation sentimentale*[4] concerne les signes descriptifs qui, selon Barthes, sont des *indices* ayant « toujours des signifiés implicites ».[5] La *description indicielle* est donc de l'ordre de la connotation, et les détails sont affectés « d'une valeur fonctionnelle indirecte, dans la mesure où, s'additionnant, ils reconstituent quelque indice de caractère ou d'atmosphère, et peuvent être ainsi finalement récupérés par la structure ».[6] Je me consacrerai ici aux indices de caractère, c'est-à-dire à ces éléments qui, tout en étant topographiques, participent pourtant de la construction de l'état d'esprit du personnage.[7]

Indice et Psychologie

Le rôle psychologique de la description indicielle, corrélat fonctionnel des principes métonymiques, bien connus, qui relient description et personnage, n'est pas nouveau dans *L'Éducation sentimentale*.[8] Néanmoins, le problème consiste à dépasser une intuition herméneutique pour s'interroger sur les spécificités textuelles qui régissent ce passage de l'atmosphère au personnage, et du personnage à l'atmosphère; elles sont souvent peu manifestes. En fait, c'est le contexte qui favorise cette transposition du sens. La description topographique possède un signifié second, psychologique, car elle est insérée dans un contexte lui-même psychologique. Mais le parcours métonymique de la relation indicielle emprunte deux voies différentes : soit l'espace influence le personnage, soit, réciproquement, l'état d'âme du personnage se reflète dans le paysage, et en influence la représentation.

Il est rare en effet chez Flaubert que, pour signifier l'effet de l'espace sur le personnage qui lui est conjoint, le lien soit aussi direct que dans cette séquence, postérieure à la description de l'atmosphère au café Anglais : « Ce parfum et cette fraîcheur détendirent ses nerfs ».[9] Les deux détails topographiques, « moires » et « magnolia », sont ici paraphrasés par deux sujets (« parfum », « fraîcheur ») d'un énoncé de *faire* (« détendirent »), dont l'objet est, précisément, le personnage (« ses nerfs »). Généralement, la frontière entre topographie et psychologie est plus opaque, même quand le lien demeure littéral, comme pour la description de Creil,[10] où la connexion sémiotique introduit dans la description le *faire interprétatif* du personnage (« lui semblait »), tandis que l'espace contemplé en modifie le comportement (« il en conçut plus de respect pour Arnoux »), et plus encore si le texte établit un double *faire* interactif, comme à la clausule de la description de Paris:[11] « [...] et les fumées de leurs pipes tourbillonnaient dans l'air pur, qui rafraîchissait leurs yeux encore bouffis; ils sentaient, en l'aspirant, un vaste espoir épandu ».

Les relations de l'espace et du personnage ne sont pas toujours autant explicites, loin de là. La présence intradescriptive d'un actant anthropomorphe n'en est pas moins perceptible parfois dans la succession même des informations. Considérons la description des sables d'Arbonne et le récit qui la suit :

> Ils arrivèrent un jour à mi-hauteur d'une colline tout en sable. Sa surface, vierge de pas, était rayée en ondulations symétriques; çà et là, telles que

des promontoires sur le lit desséché d'un océan, se levaient des roches ayant de vagues formes d'animaux, tortues avançant la tête, phoques qui rampent, hippopotames et ours. Personne. Aucun bruit. Les sables, frappés par le soleil, éblouissaient; — et tout à coup, dans cette vibration de la lumière, les bêtes parurent remuer. Ils s'en retournèrent vite, fuyant le vertige, presque effrayés. (p. 328)

L'énoncé narratif psychologique (« vertige », « effrayés ») paraît la conséquence de l'énoncé descriptif; le *vertige* est le résultat de cette « vibration de la lumière » où les bêtes « parurent remuer ». Comme l'indique le verbe (« parurent ») et le *faire* fallacieux (« éblouissaient »), les personnages sont bien l'objet, implicite, de la description.[12]

A la clausule d'une description du salon des Dambreuse est juxtaposée une autre de ces séquences psychologiques sous-entendant la relation personnage-décor :

Il traversa une antichambre, une seconde pièce, puis un grand salon à hautes fenêtres, et dont la cheminée monumentale supportait une pendule en forme de sphère, avec deux vases de porcelaine monstrueux où se hérissaient, comme deux buissons d'or, deux faisceaux de bobèches. Des tableaux dans la manière de l'Espagnolet étaient appendus au mur; les lourdes portières en tapisserie tombaient majestueusement; et les fauteuils, les consoles, les tables, tout le mobilier, qui était de style Empire, avait quelque chose d'imposant et de diplomatique. Frédéric souriait de plaisir, malgré lui. (pp. 130–131)

Aucun lien n'est établi entre cet intérieur, où abonde le luxe, et le « plaisir » qu'éprouve soudain le personnage, sinon celui, métonymique, qui transforme la succession des notations en implication. Par le biais de la description, à la fois médiateur et actant, s'inscrit dans la diégèse (sans qu'elle soit dite pour autant) la réalisation du programme narratif annoncé pour introduire la scène. C'est en effet par désir de luxe que Frédéric se rend chez les Dambreuse : « Puis, voulant connaître enfin cette chose vague, miroitante et indéfinissable qu'on appelle *le monde*, il demanda par un billet aux Dambreuse s'ils pouvaient le recevoir » (p. 130). Si *le monde* est inconnu, vague et indéfinissable, l'euphorie du personnage résulte directement de la description, qui en donne simultanément la connaissance et la définition.

Il en va de même quand la sémiosis est orientée en sens inverse, du personnage vers le paysage cette fois. Une des descriptions de Paris en donne une illustration exemplaire. Comme si sa longueur exigeait un surcroît de précisions et de justifications préalables, elle est insérée dans le récit par une surenchère de notations psychologiques extrêmement imbriquées (et non seulement par la focalisation et la position en surplomb du personnage) :

> Alors commencèrent trois mois d'ennui. Comme il n'avait aucun travail, son désœuvrement renforçait sa tristesse. Il passait des heures à regarder, du haut de son balcon, la rivière qui coulait entre les quais grisâtres, noircis de place en place par la bavure des égouts, avec un ponton de blanchisseuses amarré contre le bord, où des gamins quelquefois s'amusaient, dans la vase, à faire baigner un caniche. Ses yeux, délaissant à gauche le pont de pierre de Notre-Dame et trois ponts suspendus, se dirigeaient toujours vers le quai aux Ormes, sur un massif de vieux arbres, pareils aux tilleuls du port de Montereau. La tour Saint-Jacques, l'Hôtel-de-Ville, Saint-Gervais, Saint-Louis, Saint-Paul se levaient en face, parmi les toits confondus, — et le génie de la colonne de Juillet resplendissait à l'orient comme une large étoile d'or, tandis qu'à l'autre extrémité le dôme des Tuileries arrondissait, sur le ciel, sa lourde masse bleue. C'était par derrière, de ce côté-là, que devait être la maison de Mme Arnoux. (p. 64)

L'état d'âme (« ennui ») est renforcé par la durée (« trois mois »), expliqué par l'inactivité de Frédéric (« aucun travail », « désœuvrement ») et dénoté par la répétition de l'information psychologique (« renforçait sa tristesse »). Le dédoublement de la durée même, pour introduire la description (« Il passait des heures ») associe cette dernière à l'énoncé psychologique, tandis que la représentation de Paris accentue réciproquement et de manière implicite la tristesse du personnage : elle reflète à la fois le contexte dysphorique (saleté des quais et de l'eau) et le personnage qui en est la cause directe, comme l'indique la clausule, point de convergence de l'énumération des monuments et de la signifiance du passage : « C'était par derrière, de ce côté-là, que devait être la maison de Mme Arnoux ». Le texte avouera d'ailleurs peu après le principe métonymique qui le régit : « Paris se rapportait à sa personne, et la grande ville, avec toutes ses voix, bruissait, comme un immense orchestre, autour d'elle » (p. 68).

Le contexte oriente à la fois le sens, la fonction et le mode représentatif de la description. Avant le départ de Frédéric pour Nogent, à la fin du cinquième chapitre de la première partie, le récit dénote à plusieurs reprises le bonheur du personnage : « Il s'y montra gai », « Tous étaient heureux » (p. 86). La description des boulevards de Paris, où flâne alors Frédéric, est peut-être la plus euphorique du roman :

> Des nuages roses, en forme d'écharpe, s'allongeaient au-delà des toits; on commençait à relever les tentes des boutiques; des tombereaux d'arrosage versaient une pluie sur la poussière, et une fraîcheur inattendue se mêlait aux émanations des cafés, laissant voir par leurs portes ouvertes, entre des argenteries et des dorures, des fleurs en gerbes qui se miraient dans les hautes glaces. La foule marchait lentement. Il y avait des groupes d'hommes causant au milieu du trottoir; et des femmes passaient, avec une mollesse dans les yeux et ce teint de camélia que donne aux chairs féminines la lassitude des grandes chaleurs. Quelque chose d'énorme s'épanchait, enveloppait les maisons. Jamais Paris ne lui avait semblé si beau. Il n'apercevait, dans l'avenir, qu'une interminable série d'années toutes pleines d'amour. (p. 87)

L'espace paraît nimbé de la même béatitude que le personnage : « Des nuages roses, en forme d'écharpe, s'allongeaient au-delà des toits », « fraîcheur inattendue », « argenteries », « dorures », « des fleurs en gerbes qui se miraient dans les hautes glaces », comme le précise du reste la séquence qui suit la description : « Jamais Paris ne lui avait semblé si beau. Il n'apercevait, dans l'avenir, qu'une interminable série d'années toutes pleines d'amour ». Le transfert sémantique qui résulte de la conjonction du personnage et du décor subvertit la représentation de ce dernier, au profit d'un signifié psychologique. La clausule de la description non seulement synthétise la valeur euphorique de l'espace, mais de plus s'humanise, la polysémie du verbe *s'épancher* en témoigne : « Quelque chose d'énorme s'épanchait ».

Au contraire, il est impossible de déceler une quelconque orientation du vecteur sémiotique quand la conjonction des actants prend une forme *sylleptique*. Après la scène du dîner chez les Arnoux rue de Choiseul, l'euphorie de Frédéric (« son cœur débordait ») est déplacée dans le paysage qui s'empare du personnage (« un air humide l'enveloppa ») et que réciproquement le personnage accapare (« il aspirait l'air ») :

> Un air humide l'enveloppa; il se reconnut au bord des quais.
> Les réverbères brillaient en deux lignes droites, indéfiniment, et de longues flammes vacillaient dans la profondeur de l'eau. Elle était de

couleur ardoise, tandis que le ciel, plus clair, semblait soutenu par les grandes masses d'ombre qui se levaient de chaque côté du fleuve. Des édifices, que l'on n'apercevait pas, faisaient des redoublements d'obscurité. Un brouillard lumineux flottait au-delà, sur les toits; tous les bruits se fondaient en un seul bourdonnement; un vent léger soufflait.

Il s'était arrêté au milieu du Pont-Neuf, et, tête nue, poitrine ouverte, il aspirait l'air. Cependant, il sentait monter du fond de lui-même quelque chose d'intarissable, un afflux de tendresse qui l'énervait, comme le mouvement de l'onde sous ses yeux. (p. 49)

La séquence psychologique qui suit la description des quais indique plutôt une interaction. A la *profondeur* de l'eau (« de longues flammes rouges vacillaient dans la profondeur de l'eau ») répond le *fond* (métaphorique) de Frédéric, et les sémèmes *aquatiques* relevant de la représentation de la Seine envahissent le récit psychologique (imbrication qu'explicite l'*afflux* de tendresse, ainsi que la comparaison diégétique : « comme le mouvement de l'onde sous ses yeux »).

Cette fusion, qui permet la circulation du sens d'un énoncé à l'autre, ici topographique, là psychologique (voir du reste la séquence : « tous les bruits se fondaient en un seul bourdonnement ») sera inversée dans la scène qui répétera allusivement celle-ci, au cinquième chapitre. Le *bourdonnement* sylleptique, à la fois anthropomorphe et atmosphérique, était dans le premier contexte introduit dans l'énoncé descriptif, mais symétriquement il se retrouve alors dans l'énoncé psychologique, tandis que le verbe conjonctif *se mêler* fait écho au verbe *se fondaient* du contexte précédent :[13]

> Le vent, en de certains endroits, secouait le tuyau de tôle d'une cheminée; des sons lointains s'élevaient, se mêlant au bourdonnement de sa tête, et il croyait entendre, dans les airs, la vague ritournelle des contredanses. Le mouvement de sa marche entretenait cette ivresse; il se trouva sur le pont de la Concorde.
>
> Alors, il se ressouvint de ce soir de l'autre hiver, — où, sortant de chez elle, pour la première fois, il lui avait fallu s'arrêter, tant son cœur battait vite sous l'étreinte de ses espérances. Toutes étaient mortes, maintenant!
>
> Des nues sombres couraient sur la face de la lune. Il la contempla, en rêvant à la grandeur des espaces, à la misère de la vie, au néant de tout. (p. 76)

Quand, plus rarement, la description indicielle est associée au personnage par l'intermédiaire d'un connecteur qui introduit dans l'énoncé une contradiction, la conjonction, tout illusoire, est en fait disjonctive.

La première description des Champs-Élysées appartient à un contexte qui, d'euphorique, devient dysphorique, et elle participe de cette transformation :

> Les jours de soleil, il continuait sa promenade jusqu'au bout des Champs-Élysées.
>
> Des femmes, nonchalamment assises dans des calèches, et dont les voiles flottaient au vent, défilaient près de lui, au pas ferme de leurs chevaux, avec un balancement insensible qui faisait craquer les cuirs vernis. Les voitures devenaient plus nombreuses, et, se ralentissant à partir du Rond-Point, elles occupaient toute la voie. Les crinières étaient près des crinières, les lanternes près des lanternes; les étriers d'acier, les gourmettes d'argent, les boucles de cuivre, jetaient çà et là des points lumineux entre les culottes courtes, les gants blancs, et les fourrures qui retombaient sur le blason des portières. Il se sentait comme perdu dans un monde lointain. Ses yeux erraient sur les têtes féminines; et de vagues ressemblances amenaient à sa mémoire Mme Arnoux. Il se la figurait, au milieu des autres, dans un de ces petits coupés, pareils au coupé de Mme Dambreuse.
>
> — Mais le soleil se couchait, et le vent froid soulevait des tourbillons de poussière. Les cochers baissaient le menton dans leurs cravates, les roues se mettaient à tourner plus vite, le macadam grinçait et tous les équipages descendaient au grand trot la longue avenue, en se frôlant, se dépassant, s'écartant les uns des autres, puis, sur la place de la Concorde, se dispersaient. Derrière les Tuileries, le ciel prenait la teinte des ardoises. Les arbres du jardin formaient deux masses énormes, violacées par le sommet. Les becs de gaz s'allumaient; et la Seine, verdâtre dans toute son étendue, se déchirait en moires d'argent contre les piles des ponts. (pp. 23–24)

Frédéric rêve de revoir Mme Arnoux (« son cœur battait vite, espérant la rencontrer »), et l'atmosphère s'accorde à ses espérances (« les jours de soleil », avant la description), tout comme le tableau des femmes (« dont les voiles flottaient au vent ») et des voitures, où le luxe est récurrent. Une séquence narrative et psychologique établit cependant une première distanciation entre le personnage et le spectacle qu'il contemple : « Il se sentait comme perdu dans un monde lointain ». Il est notable que les deux détails connotant précédemment l'euphorie de l'atmosphère sont réintroduits dans la description qui apparaît alors, où ils sont quasiment dégradés : « le soleil se couchait », tandis que le vent est « froid », et la liquidité métaphorique du verbe *flotter* (relatif tout d'abord aux *voiles*) se métamorphose en des « tourbillons de poussière ». Certes, les couleurs s'assombrissent (« teinte des ardoises », « violacées ») voire se salissent (« verdâtre »), mais visiblement le passage n'est pas doté d'un simple sens mimétique (représentation d'un coucher de soleil); il est régi par sa signifiance diégétique. La conjonction *mais* (« mais le soleil se couchait ») signale l'organisation contradictoire de l'énoncé, et partant la transformation de l'euphorie en dysphorie.[14] Pour interpréter la clausule de la description (« se déchirait en moires d'argent contre les piles des ponts »), on doit anticiper et transposer dans le paysage le désespoir de Frédéric qui sera illustré par les trois paragraphes suivants. Le verbe *déchirait*, contenant un sémème *textile*, légitime l'intrusion de la métaphore (« moires d'argent », réitérant par ailleurs le luxe), toutefois le cliché qui sous-tend le syntagme descriptif permet simultanément l'association de ce *déchirement luxueux* à un *désespoir déchirant*, celui que semble précisément impliquer la description disjonctive.

Dans la longue description des faubourgs de Paris, l'effet disjonctif est plus manifeste, car le *mais* s'interpose entre la clausule et la séquence psychologique qui la suit immédiatement :

> La plaine, bouleversée, semblait de vagues ruines. L'enceinte des fortifications y faisait un renflement horizontal; et, sur les trottoirs en terre qui bordaient la route, de petits arbres sans branches étaient défendus par des lattes hérissées de clous. Des établissements de produits chimiques alternaient avec des chantiers de marchands de bois. De hautes portes, comme il y en a dans les fermes, laissaient voir, par leurs battants entr'ouverts, l'intérieur d'ignobles cours pleines d'immondices, avec des flaques d'eau sale au milieu. De longs cabarets, couleur sang de bœuf, portaient à leur premier étage, entre les fenêtres, deux queues de billard en sautoir dans une couronne de fleurs peintes; çà et là, une bicoque de plâtre à moitié construite était abandonnée. Puis, la double ligne de maisons ne discontinua plus; et, sur la nudité de leurs façades, se détachait, de loin en loin, un gigantesque cigare de fer-blanc, pour indiquer un débit de tabac. Des enseignes de sage-femme représentaient une matrone en bonnet, dodelinant un poupon dans une courte-pointe garnie de dentelles. Des affiches couvraient l'angle des murs, et, aux trois quarts déchirées, tremblaient au vent comme des guenilles. Des ouvriers en blouse passaient, et des haquets de brasseurs, des fourgons de blanchisseuses, des carrioles de bouchers; une pluie fine tombait, il faisait froid, le ciel était pâle, mais deux yeux qui valaient pour lui le soleil resplendissaient derrière la brume. (p. 104)

Cette fois, la description établit une antithèse particulière. De par la laideur des détails représentés, et la dysphorie qui y est partout connotée, voire dénotée, elle s'oppose directement à la joie fébrile de Frédéric retournant à Paris. Le même procédé se répète tout de suite après, dans la description de la Seine, quoique selon des modalités différentes : « La Seine, jaunâtre, touchait presque au tablier des ponts. Une fraîcheur s'en exhalait. Frédéric l'aspira de toutes ses forces, savourant ce bon air de Paris qui semble contenir des effluves amoureux et des émanations intellectuelles » (p. 105). Du fait que le connecteur n'est plus contradictoire, le désignateur (« ce bon air ») et l'action stéréotypée de *humer l'air* conjoignent apparemment espace et personnage. Pourtant, comme le sous-entend l'apparition du *faire interprétatif* du personnage (« qui semble »), Frédéric se trompe; rien de tel n'est visible dans l'espace qu'il investit et lisible dans la description de la sorte désignée.[15]

Dans la perspective d'une *poétique* du descriptif, le problème théorique que pose la fonction indicielle des descriptions concerne l'*orientation* des informations. En effet, à cause de son appartenance à un contexte somme toute régulateur, la description indicielle tend à avoir une situation textuelle bien cloisonnée. Il est donc impossible de localiser la source voire la motivation d'un tel procès sémiotique. De par l'aspect nécessairement vectorisé du récit, et les relations métonymiques établies entre espace et personnage, on interprétera bien entendu la description comme le simple *reflet* subsidiaire d'un état d'âme; elle peut en paraître le médiateur, certes pas le générateur. Considérer l'élaboration de l'indice dans les brouillons permet toutefois de déplacer cette impasse causaliste.

De l'Explicite à l'Implicite

Comme l'on peut s'y attendre, les relations de la description avec son contexte sont sensiblement différentes dans les manuscrits,[16] car elles évoluent parallèlement aux transformations du texte lors de la rédaction. L'espace prend consistance par rapport au personnage dès la germination de la description, cette dernière acquiert une dimension diégétique grâce à la multiplicité des liens métonymiques qui sont tissés, lentement ou rapidement selon les cas. Il semble pourtant que, au stade préliminaire de l'énumération scénarique des détails, Flaubert ait souvent besoin de dénoter littéralement leur statut indiciel. L'évolution génétique de la description indicielle confond métonymiquement topographie et psychologie; l'état d'âme du personnage s'imprime dans la représentation de l'espace qu'il semble orienter. Toutefois, dès que l'énoncé a acquis la stabilité isotopique et l'interaction métonymique nécessaires à sa signifiance, de tels liens explicites sont gommés ou effacés de la description pour n'être maintenus que dans le récit, seul à contenir un signifié psychologique. Voici quelques exemples de ce phénomène.

Les plaines que Frédéric contemple pendant son voyage vers Creil (p. 192)[17] sont simultanément « vertes et bêtes » sur le scénario (17604 f° 76 v°) et, lorsque la séquence est rédigée, elle prend la forme suivante : « la campagne recommençait. plate, ennuyeuse » (17604 f° 91 v°). Dans la version publiée, l'ennui du personnage, qui était tout d'abord intradescriptif (il s'agissait bien d'un attribut de la campagne) sera narrativisé : « Frédéric, seul sur sa banquette, regardait cela, par ennui » (p. 192).

Il en va de même pour les prédicats qui décrivent l'atmosphère de l'hôtel de Fontainebleau sur le scénario (p. 322) : « paix et confortable » (17611 f° 48), progressivement associés aux personnages : « impression de rafraîchissement et de calme après le tumulte de Paris » (17607 f° 124), jusque dans le texte définitif (pp. 322–323) :

> L'hôtel où ils logèrent se distinguait des autres par un jet d'eau clapotant au milieu de sa cour. Les portes des chambres s'ouvraient sur un corridor, comme dans les monastères. Celle qu'on leur donna était grande, fournie de bons meubles, tendue d'indienne, et silencieuse, vu la rareté des voyageurs. Le long des maisons, des bourgeois inoccupés passaient; puis, sous leurs fenêtres, quand le jour tomba, des enfants dans la rue firent une partie de barres; — et cette tranquillité, succédant pour eux au tumulte de Paris, leur causait une surprise, un apaisement.[18]

La présence d'un détail anthropomorphe dans les descriptions de la version publiée est donc la cicatrice, le résidu surfaciel de la transformation des informants en indices connotatifs. Dans les brouillons de la description de la fabrique d'Arnoux (p. 196), la mention des *patouillards* est immédiatement suivie d'un prédicat qui n'est pas tant topographique que psychologique:[19] « broyage. patouillards. machines <ennuyeuses> » (17604 f° 83 v°, premier scénario) et la phase de rédaction en renforce un instant l'effet : « le mouvement était continu et Frédéric ne tarda pas à s'ennuyer » (17604 f° 118, quatrième brouillon). La version publiée préférera l'adjectif verbal *agaçante*,[20] qui seul indique la fonction indicielle de la séquence.[21]

L'étroitesse de la relation paysage-personnage est telle, que l'élaboration de la description indicielle peut contribuer à la formation de l'énoncé psychologique, comme si l'espace était le générateur de la transformation qui affecte le personnage, et donc le stimulus de ses sentiments. Prenons l'exemple d'une des descriptions de la campagne, au premier chapitre, insérée dans le récit du voyage vers Montereau. En voici le texte définitif :

> Un peu plus loin, on découvrit un château, à toit pointu, avec des tourelles carrées. Un parterre de fleurs s'étalait devant sa façade; et des avenues s'enfonçaient, comme des voûtes noires, sous les hauts tilleuls. Il se la figura passant au bord des charmilles. A ce moment, une jeune dame et un jeune homme se montrèrent sur le perron, entre les caisses d'orangers. Puis tout disparut.
> La petite fille jouait autour de lui. Frédéric voulut la baiser. (p. 9)

A l'origine, sur le premier scénario, quelques brèves informations sont simplement juxtaposées : « rêves de vie avec elle. un château de briques — deux tourelles carrées — terrasse — immenses charmilles — taillis... émotion. veut baiser la petite fille » (17599 f° 73 v°).

Signes descriptifs (ce sont du reste les plus développés) et narratifs (« rêves de vie avec elle », « émotion », « veut baiser la petite fille ») établissent les premiers jalons de la scène. Plus encore que leur succession, leur juxtaposition même recèle apparemment une implication sous-entendue. En effet, les « rêves de vie » semblent concrétisés par la description qui apparaît alors, l'espace étant le support de l'émotion de Frédéric qui, attendri, veut embrasser Marthe.

Lors de la rédaction, l'expansion du passage élabore cette interaction qui, initialement, demeure embryonnaire et somme toute peu perceptible. On peut voir transcrit le second brouillon, où le texte est tout à fait détaillé déjà (17599 f° 83 v°, transcription 1). L'*émotion* y prend la forme d'un fantasme, dont la description est le médiateur indispensable et sans aucun doute l'agent germinatif : « Il se la figura passant au bord des charmilles. Elle le cherchait, dans la peur vaguement, en marquant sur le sable la forme de ce pied qu'il contemplait maintenant. Elle avait quelque chose à lui dire ». Il est suivi d'une phrase (introduite d'ailleurs par l'adverbe *alors*, soulignant l'implication) qui oppose les personnages situés dans l'espace représenté au désir de Frédéric pensant à Mme Arnoux :

                                                         legeremt
[Alors] /il/*Il* se la figura passant au bord des charmilles
               en l'appelant /*par son nom*/
elle le cherchait - [dans la peur vaguement - en marquant
sur le sable la forme d/u/*e* ce pied qu'il contemplait
maintenant. elle avait qq chose [qque] à lui dire]
                                /*vaguement*/ *α* ils se rencontraient.
             α comme   *mieux*
Alors p\ [irriter] mieux preciser son desir α irriter son
desespoir, [au moment où tout disparaissait, le hasard
Mais à ce moment-là   *α*   *dame*
voulut] [qu']une jeune [femme] en robe blanche α qu'un
jeune homme en veste nankin, se montr/ass/*èrent* [au detour]
                        le   *entre les caisses d'orangers*
sur [le seuil du] perron - [α ce n'etait pas lui. ce n'etait
pas elle, Comme il y a des gens heureux, pensait-il. ?]
             /*ce ne serait jamais eux.*]   /α] puis tout
disparut.

Transcription 1: campagne, p. 9 (extrait de 17599 f⁰ 83 v⁰, deuxième brouillon)

> Alors pour mieux préciser son désir et irriter son désespoir, au moment où tout disparaissait, le hasard voulut qu'une jeune femme en robe blanche et qu'un jeune homme en veste nankin, se montrassent sur le seuil du perron — et ce n'était pas lui, ce n'était pas elle. Comme il y a des gens heureux, pensait-il.

Flaubert supprime dès ce folio tous les liens explicites associant entre eux les énoncés. Ce retour à l'implicite aboutira au texte squelettique de la version publiée, où seule la séquence « il se la figura passant au bord des charmilles » demeure la trace allusive de l'émotion de Frédéric contemplant et réinterprétant le paysage.

De même, Frédéric et Deslauriers doivent au second chapitre « arriver à l'exaltation poétique <impersonnelle> » (17599 f⁰ 85 v⁰, premier scénario). Ils y parviendront par l'intermédiaire de l'espace, comme l'indique l'interligne : « excités par la nuit — et leurs événements présents privés », et plus précisément grâce à l'apparition du paysage de Nogent :[22] « La conversation reprend, et excités par la nuit, le paysage (le Livon, le moulin, etc.) et leurs événements intimes arrivent à une *grande exaltation impersonnelle* » (17599 f⁰ 68 v⁰, deuxième scénario).

Éric Le Calvez: Description et Psychologie 125

```
                          α ils continuèrent à Causer. en marchant sur les ponts.
                                           minuit sonna   Les vannes des moulins etaient fermé
                          La nuit etait douce.  α claire - la chute du Livon
                 de la prise d'eau qui fait une ile factice
[La rivière α le canal    interrompait   seule  le  silence  -  un  roulement
coulaient son courant     sourd continu. -  un gros bruit doux  -  l'ile se
sous deux ponts           levait audessous d'eux - peupliers à gauche - route de Paris
qui s'appuient sur        en face - senteur d'automne ........ excités par tout cela -
l'ile]
```

Transcription 2: Nogent, p. 16 (extrait de 17599 f° 140 v°, premier brouillon)

Quand il élabore la description, Flaubert maintient sur plusieurs folios des indices explicites : « route de Paris en face — senteur d'automne... excités par tout cela » (17599 f° 140 v°, transcription 2; voir aussi « et excités par la solitude, par le silence, et par le bruit même de leurs paroles, ils épanchaient leurs cœurs abondamment, comme deux sources jumelles qui se versent l'une dans l'autre », clausule de la description sur 17599 f° 124 v°, huitième brouillon) mais il finit par les supprimer; la conjonction espace-personnages est encore présente dans la version publiée (dans la séquence qui suit la représentation de Nogent), cependant le rôle psychologique de la description n'y est plus littéral.

Alors que la fonction indicielle est généralement inhérente aux balbutiements de la description, quelquefois au contraire la conjonction, élaborée après coup, vient se greffer tel un prétexte stratégique sur les séquences topographiques. Si, dans les brouillons de la description du brouillard (p. 67), la disjonction est présente dès le premier jet : « temps affreux, humide. pavé gras.[23] mais sensation exquise » (17601 f° 132), il n'en va pas de même pour la description des faubourgs de Paris (p. 104), dont la sémiosis est pourtant identique, nous l'avons vu.

Sur les premiers scénarios, la laideur des détails n'est pas soulignée. Le seul effet disjonctif est établi, depuis le Carnet contenant les informations que Flaubert a prises sur place, par une séquence narrative dilatoire : « Frédéric avait eu de la joie à Charenton, mais la campagne recommença ».[24] Dans la marge du sixième brouillon en revanche apparaît une séquence qui désigne l'ensemble du paysage et vient donc en souligner l'effet : « tout cela [était laid] <offrait ce que les capitales ont de plus hideux> mais n'importe » (17602 f° 32 v°). L'insertion de la disjonction « mais

                                                            α [la] une
                                               [une] pluie fine tombait - [une pluie]
                                                le [ciel] temps etait froid, le ciel gris
                                                      [ses plaisirs]   pâle
[C'etait tout ce que la capitale avait de pire.] ses vices, ses mensonges
                    toute   [Fred]
Sa misère [a] sa hideur.   Mais il n'eprouvait ni degout ni
              Mais   .   brillaient
tristesse. deux yeux qui valaient pr lui le soleil <,> [etaient]
là bas, derrière   [tout à l'heure]
[dans] la brume.   [il allait les revoir.]

Transcription 3: Paris, p. 104 (extrait de 17602 f° 59, cinquième brouillon)

n'importe » nécessite sans doute une explication et légitime l'élaboration progressive de la connexion contradictoire (que l'on peut voir sur l'extrait de 17602 f° 59, transcription 3). L'explication topographique et psychologique est ensuite raturée, implicite dans le *mais* disjonctif.

Dans les brouillons de la scène du dîner chez Arnoux, les modifications du récit permettent d'établir la conjonction du plaisir de Frédéric et de la représentation de la salle à manger. En voici le texte définitif :

> La compagnie, les mets, tout lui plaisait. La salle, telle qu'un parloir moyen âge, était tendue de cuir battu; une étagère hollandaise se dressait devant un râtelier de chibouques; et, autour de la table, les verres de Bohême, diversement colorés, faisaient au milieu des fleurs et des fruits comme une illumination dans un jardin. (p. 46)

Cette conjonction demeurait, sur le premier scénario, topographique et isolée de la séquence euphorique : « Tout plaît à Frédéric. La salle à manger » (17600 f° 147 v°, transcription 4). La mention du *milieu*, sur le troisième brouillon, semble alors expliciter l'euphorie (d'ailleurs dédoublée) et la description l'illustrer : « Tout plaît à Frédéric. Il se trouve bien dans ce milieu. La salle à manger » (17600 f° 126 v°). Par la suite, la rédaction du passage associe directement espace et psychologie : « La compagnie, l'ameublement, la conversation, les plats, tout lui plaisait » (17600 f° 146 v°).

Une fois encore la conjonction littérale disparaîtra. Le terme *ameublement* est supprimé sur le sixième brouillon (17600 f° 157) et

```
                                              ⎛ plafond à
                                              ⎜ caissons - α
                           (2) tendue         ⎝ xxxx avec⎞
 - [entrée dans la Salle à manger.] - tapisserie - deux
                   sur l'une                           chiffres
 etagères sculptés. l'argenterie descend en amphithéâtre -
 - sur l'autre le dessert.
                 La table a l'aspect d'un jardin où on
                             morceaux
 aurait laissé tomber des [plaq] d'argent - Verres de couleur
 en quantité   effet d'illumination
            pas un pareil. (3)
           Pr aller dans la salle à manger⎞     du Vieux
                              prend le bras [de Dittmer]  α⎞
             Me Arn fait asseoir à sa gauche [Dittmer]
             à sa droite une place reste vide - c'est pr Pellerin A
             [le vieux]. D Il arrive. « vous voyez que je n'ai
             pas fait la bête. » Hussonnet est à coté de la petite
             fille.
                 Tout plait à Fr. La salle à manger (1)
```

Transcription 4: salle à manger, p. 46 (extrait de 17600 f⁰ 147 v⁰, premier scénario)

la séquence indicielle, à l'incipit de la description (« La salle à manger, tendue de cuir battu, avait un air moyen âge qui le ravissait »), sur le quatrième (17600 f⁰ 146 v⁰). Seule la juxtaposition des énoncés, dans la version définitive, demeure le témoin muet de ce dialogue sémantique.

L'Indice Affecté

Le passage de l'explicite à l'implicite, solidaire de l'élaboration de la description indicielle, relève certes d'une technique, mais aussi, et peut-être surtout, d'une esthétique (il faut *montrer* en *suggérant* plutôt qu'en *expliquant*), car les corrections ou les suppressions ne sont jamais attribuables alors au rejet de répétitions (qui préoccupent toujours Flaubert quand il travaille son texte).[25] Bien sûr, opacifier l'indice consiste déjà à le modifier; néanmoins, la rédaction aboutit à une description dont la fonction diégétique est

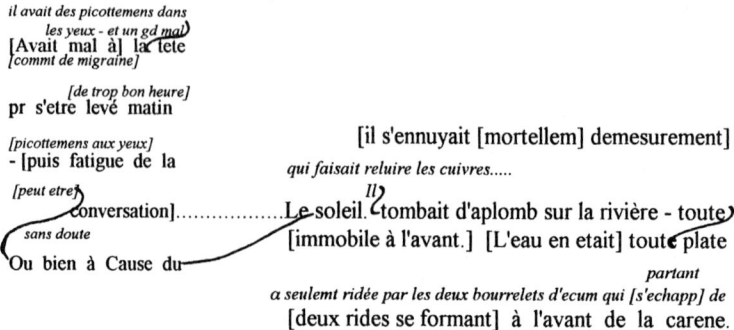

Transcription 5: campagne, p. 5 *(extrait de 17599 f⁰ 39 v⁰, premier brouillon)*

interprétable grâce aux liens métonymiques et connotatifs établis entre les personnages et les détails topographiques. Dans d'autres cas, plus rares et plus particuliers, les transformations affectent le statut indiciel même de la description. Nous allons considérer successivement deux exemples de ce phénomène.

Les transformations du contexte d'une des descriptions de la campagne, dans le premier chapitre, révèlent les diverses possibilités que Flaubert aménage successivement pour diégétiser la description. Voici tout le passage dans sa version définitive :

> Frédéric avait vu ce titre-là, plusieurs fois, à l'étalage du libraire de son pays natal, sur d'immenses prospectus, où le nom de Jacques Arnoux se développait magistralement.
> Le soleil dardait d'aplomb, en faisant reluire les gabillots de fer autour des mâts, les plaques du bastingage et la surface de l'eau; elle se coupait à la proue en deux sillons, qui se déroulaient jusqu'au bord des prairies. A chaque détour de la rivière, on retrouvait le même rideau de peupliers pâles. La campagne était toute vide. Il y avait dans le ciel de petits nuages blancs arrêtés, — et l'ennui, vaguement répandu, semblait alanguir la marche du bateau et rendre l'aspect des voyageurs plus insignifiant encore. (p. 5)

Sur le premier jet du premier brouillon, la description est tout d'abord encadrée par deux séquences indicielles (17599 f⁰ 39 v⁰, transcription 5). L'une d'elles dénote l'état d'âme de Frédéric, « il s'ennuyait démesurément », l'autre résume de façon explicite l'effet du paysage (c'est-à-dire la fonction de la description dans le récit) et le rapport, non moins explicite, que sa représentation entretient avec le tableau des voyageurs qui la suit : « et la monotonie du paysage se reflétait sur le bateau — dans leur costume et dans leur mine ». Emprisonnée par deux séquences dénotant l'ennui, la description de la campagne se conforme donc à celui de Frédéric (auquel elle succède), que redouble ensuite la description du pont du bateau. La succession syntagmatique et la cohésion sémantique sont telles, qu'il n'est pas possible de connaître la source du signifié psychologique (rappelons qu'il s'agit du premier brouillon du passage).[26] L'ennui de Frédéric est-il primordial et trouve-t-il un répondant, quasi illustratif, dans celui que dénote la description de la campagne, et que renforce celle du pont? Ou bien au contraire l'image des voyageurs pousse-t-elle Flaubert, en cascades rétroactives, à épandre de l'ennui dans le paysage et dans les sensations de Frédéric? On ne saurait trancher avec certitude; puisque toutes les informations sont synchroniques, sur le folio, la motivation de leur association est indécidable.

Il est toutefois possible d'aller plus loin. En effet, la brièveté de la séquence relative à l'état d'âme de Frédéric (« il s'ennuyait démesurément ») laisse croire qu'il s'agit d'un simple prétexte transitoire pour introduire ce qui est, précisément, essentiel et d'ailleurs bien plus développé déjà. De plus, lors de la correction de ce premier jet, les sentiments de Frédéric sont tout d'abord mis entre crochets, et ensuite raturés, sans doute parce que Flaubert souhaite transformer la *monotonie* du paysage en *ennui* (il lui faut en effet éliminer la répétition), plusieurs essais interlinéaires en témoignent. Un nouvel énoncé indiciel s'élabore alors dans la marge, tout à fait différent de celui auquel il se substitue : cette fois Frédéric a « mal à la tête » et ressent « des picotements dans les yeux ». Or Flaubert relie directement ces séquences psychologiques à la description du paysage, insérant un connecteur qui fait du *soleil* l'agent de ces nouvelles sensations de Frédéric : « ou bien à cause du soleil. Il tombait d'aplomb sur la rivière ». Cette nouvelle construction s'éloigne de celle du texte d'origine; si la description est toujours indicielle, elle l'est différemment, du fait même que les sentiments du personnage sont interchangeables (*migraine* vs *ennui*).

Sur le brouillon suivant, la description gagne en autonomie (17599 f° 38 v°, voir la transcription 6). En effet la conjonction grammaticale *migraine-soleil* est supprimée, seule leur succession syntagmatique connote encore la conjonction des actants : « Il avait un commencement de migraine pour s'être levé trop matin sans

```
                              avait      un commencement de migraine
                         [Il se sentait] [un picottement dans les yeux avec un gd mal de tête]
                                      [de]      [bonne heure]  sans doute     ou bien à cause
[pr n'av. pas]           pr s'etre levé [de] trop [bon matin sans [p] doute, ou bien à cause
  [sans doute]                         Le soleil       matin                  [reluire]
[du soleil]              du soleil qui] dardait d'aplomb, en faisant [briller les cuivres
        [qui maintenant]                                              [briller]
                         [[le cuivre du]     ]reluire
                         [du] [bastingage α] les gabillots [de fer,] autour des mâts. La rivière
```

Transcription 6: *campagne, p. 5 (extrait de 17599 f° 38 v°, deuxième brouillon)*

```
                         ( Il etait content de l'avoir vu. Puis en songeant qu'il ne le reverrait peut-etre jamais
                         (une tristesse singulière l'envahit[|] ]       [les gabillots de fer autour des mats]
                                                                         bastingage
                         Le soleil dardait d'aplomb, en faisant reluire les plaques du bordage α la surface de l'eau
à chaque detour de la    immobile. Elle se coupait à la proue du navire, en deux sillons qui se deroulaient
rivière le même rideau   jusqu'au bord des prairies. La campagne etait toute vide.  Il y avait dans le ciel
de peupliers pâles       de petits nuages blancs arrêtés - α l'ennui vaguement epandu semblait allanguir
[se representait.]       la marche [du p] du bateau, α rendre l'aspect des voyageurs plus insignifiant
                         encore.
```

Transcription 7: *campagne, p. 5 (extrait de 17600 f° 75 v°, huitième brouillon)*

doute. Le soleil dardait d'aplomb, en faisant reluire les gabillots autour des mâts. » Leur lien est devenu si ténu qu'une nouvelle modification du sentiment (le « picotement dans les yeux » est ensuite raturé) n'affecte en rien la construction de l'énoncé, voire sa signifiance.

Quand la séquence concernant la *migraine* est elle-même raturée (17599 f° 46, septième brouillon), la description est alors immédiatement juxtaposée à celle qui la précède, relative cette fois à un autre état d'âme de Frédéric, sa *tristesse* après la conversation avec Arnoux. On peut voir transcrit le résultat de cette transformation; notons que Flaubert s'interroge alors sur le statut de cette juxtaposition (17600 f° 75 v°, transcription 7). Dans ce cas, la répétition du verbe (*vu, reverrait*, non soulignée par Flaubert peut-être du fait qu'elle n'entraîne pas une assonance) ne paraît pas exiger la disparition de l'ensemble de la séquence psychologique, qui s'effectue pourtant sur la copie autographe (B.H.V.P. f° 4; Flaubert n'a pas tenté auparavant de modifier l'un des deux verbes). Il semble plutôt que le refus de toute explication, qui dans *L'Éducation sentimentale* implique généralement l'opacité des enchaînements narratifs, motive la réduction progressive de l'énoncé psychologique,

> Fouet en main α secouant les rênes il sifflait
>   *α*
> entre ses dents un air de bravoure italienne. *il humait*
>   *doux*
> [le vent] avec delices le vent qui lui passait dans
> *sur le corps comme un large baiser*
>   [les cheveux.] [il] [perdait] [ses regards dans l/es/*a*
>   *dorés* ⎫
> *gde couleur [de pourpre]*   *le ciel à l'occident*
> nuages] empourpr/és/*ait* [qui s'étalai/en/*t* au couchant
> sur la campagne]. - [il y perdait] [ses regards
> s'y perdaient.]

Transcription 8: campagne, pp. 10–11 (extrait de 17599 f° 58 v°, premier brouillon)

d'autant plus, sans doute, qu'il est connoté par la description indicielle, prioritaire et indifférente à ces bouleversements successifs.

    Une autre des descriptions de la campagne, à la fin du même chapitre, subit sans doute la transformation la plus étonnante au cours de sa rédaction. En voici le texte définitif, avec son contexte :

> A Bray, il n'attendit pas qu'on eût donné l'avoine, il alla devant, sur la route, tout seul. Arnoux l'avait appelée « Marie. » Il cria très haut « Marie! » Sa voix se perdit dans l'air.
>   Une large couleur de pourpre enflammait le ciel à l'occident. De grosses meules de blé, qui se levaient au milieu des chaumes, projetaient des ombres géantes. Un chien se mit à aboyer dans une ferme, au loin. Il frissonna, pris d'une inquiétude sans cause. (pp. 10–11)

L'origine de cette description est problématique. Sur le premier brouillon (17599 f° 58 v°, transcription 8), non seulement elle est située dans un contexte antérieur (Frédéric n'y est pas encore descendu de la calèche) mais de plus son système représentatif est différent (seul le coucher de soleil germe, sans doute parce que la séquence décrivant les *meules* appartient à ce moment à la description précédente, représentant la campagne accompagnant le voyage).[27] Enfin, elle est euphorique, comme le souligne la conjonction du personnage et de l'espace, établie à plusieurs reprises (« il humait le vent avec délices » ou « il humait le vent <doux> qui

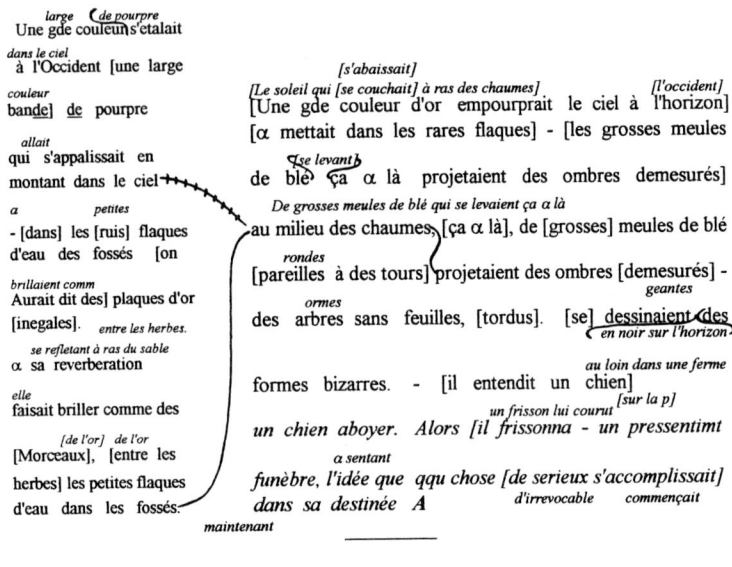

Transcription 9: campagne, pp. 10–11 (extrait de 17599 f° 77 v°, deuxième brouillon)

lui passait <sur le corps comme un large baiser> », « il perdait ses regards dans les nuages »).

Il est possible que la transformation contextuelle résulte de la ressemblance sémantique qui se profile entre une première séquence, « il perdait ses regards dans les nuages », et une seconde, « sa voix se perdit dans l'air », qui apparaît après le cri de Frédéric. En effet, sur le brouillon suivant, la description, déplacée, lui est juxtaposée (17599 f° 77 v°, transcription 9). D'une part, elle n'est plus introduite dans le récit par une séquence conjonctive, d'autre part, sa mimésis est modifiée (le coucher de soleil est cette fois accompagné d'une description des champs et des fossés bordant la route). Sa sémiosis aussi : son statut indiciel a changé, puisqu'elle est maintenant dysphorique, connotant la *souffrance*, à la fois par l'intermédiaire de certains détails (« petites flaques d'eau dans les fossés », « des arbres sans feuilles, tordus, dessinaient en noir sur l'horizon des formes bizarres ») et de la séquence clausurale qui s'élabore : « il entendit un chien aboyer. Alors il frissonna — un pressentiment funèbre, l'idée que quelque chose d'irrévocable commençait dans sa destinée », et, plus bas sur le folio : « qu'était-ce donc? quel malheur allait venir ».

 Peut-être Flaubert souhaite-t-il utiliser l'*humanité* des nuages *empourprés* pour en déplacer le sens, en même temps qu'il replace la description dans un contexte où l'euphorie paraît tout illusoire, comme le laissent pressentir les connotations du verbe *se perdre* (« sa voix se perdit dans l'air »). La conjonction du décor et du personnage, qui suit maintenant la description, ne laisse subsister aucun doute sur son effet dysphorique : « Alors il frissonna ». Dans la version publiée, l'implication a disparu et la conjonction demeure implicite : « Il frissonna, pris d'une inquiétude sans cause ». Tel un clin d'œil, le récit du texte final dénote une absence de causalité que produit, justement, sa rédaction régressive; dans les brouillons l'espace est bien la *cause* indirecte de cet *effet* psychologique.[28]

Circulation de l'Indice

L'interférence métonymique entre description et récit est d'autant plus manifeste, dans les brouillons, que la contextualisation progressive de la description permet quelquefois la libre circulation de l'indice d'un énoncé à l'autre. C'est le dernier phénomène, mais non le moindre, qui concerne la fonctionnalisation génétique de la description indicielle; nous allons en considérer quelques exemples.

 Voici la version définitive de la description de l'extérieur du château de Fontainebleau:[29]

> Le matin, de bonne heure, ils allèrent visiter le château. Comme ils entraient par la grille, ils aperçurent sa façade tout entière, avec les cinq pavillons à toits aigus et son escalier en fer à cheval se déployant au fond de la cour, que bordent de droite et de gauche deux corps de bâtiments plus bas. Des lichens sur les pavés se mêlent de loin au ton fauve des briques; et l'ensemble du palais, couleur de rouille comme une vieille armure, avait quelque chose de royalement impassible, une sorte de grandeur militaire et triste. (p. 323)

Comme la séquence indicielle située à la clausule de la description le laisse entendre, l'importance du château n'est pas seulement documentaire. Ce phénomène est visible dès son expansion scénarique : « le lendemain, visite au château. Cour des adieux <pavé, escalier. Physionomie grave du château> » (17607 f⁰ 22 v⁰). Les détails qui amplifient le lieu, dans l'interligne, participent d'une part de la topographie (*pavé*, *escalier*), mais d'autre part résument l'effet général du château en le dotant d'attributs singulièrement humains : « physionomie grave ».[30] Sur le folio suivant, l'adjectif est transposé du lieu aux personnages, qui deviennent donc objets du *faire* descriptif : « le grand air du monument les rend tout d'abord graves » (17607 f⁰ 93 v⁰). Cette construction sera encore maintenue sur deux scénarios, puis elle sera modifiée sur l'esquisse, lors du passage à la rédaction. En effet, de par la métonymie qui régit le fonctionnement indiciel de la description, les prédicats apparaissent interchangeables; Flaubert réintègre l'adjectif dans la description, si bien que l'énoncé psychologique se dédouble temporairement : « [le grand air] <air solennel, grave> du monument les rend graves » (17607 f⁰ 120 v⁰). L'effet indiciel sera implicite dès le brouillon suivant (17607 f⁰ 118), où Flaubert supprime l'« aspect grave du monument » et l'impression de Frédéric et Rosanette (« Un sentiment de respect les saisit à voir la façade »); notons que c'est aussi à ce moment qu'il commence à élaborer la clausule indicielle de la description, qui ne participe plus dès lors d'un *effet* explicite sur les personnages (elle est d'ailleurs très proche déjà du texte définitif) : « tout cet ensemble couleur de rouille comme une vieille armure, avait quelque chose d'impassible, une grandeur militaire et triste ».

Le même phénomène se produit dans les manuscrits d'une description de la Seine, au premier chapitre. En voici la version définitive :

> Les cordes vibraient; et leurs sons métalliques semblaient exhaler des sanglots et comme la plainte d'un amour orgueilleux et vaincu. Des deux côtés de la rivière, des bois s'inclinaient jusqu'au bord de l'eau; un courant d'air frais passait; Mme Arnoux regardait au loin d'une manière vague. Quand la musique s'arrêta, elle remua les paupières plusieurs fois, comme si elle sortait d'un songe. (p. 7)

Sur le troisième brouillon, « le vent faisait frissonner les glands rouges de la bordure de la tente » (17599 f⁰ 51 v⁰). Ce *frisson* atmosphérique devient celui de Frédéric, sur le brouillon suivant, où la description apparaît maintenant après une séquence psycho-

```
                                                      [en amphithéâtre]
  sanglots α comme  la plainte [dithyrambique] d'un amour
  orgueilleux α vaincu. ⌈Frederic du moins [y sentait cela -] [α il]
   α fremissait                                              fond    ⌉
  [II] frissonnait dans le saisissement d'une melancolie sans [bornes]⌋
       sur        (2])   [Seine]     bois      [en amphithéâtre]
      [Des] deux côtés de la rivière, ⌊des [feuillages] descendaient jusqu'au
      Des 2 cotés
      bord de l'eau.
```

Transcription 10: rivière, p. 7 (extrait de 17599 f° 66, quatrième brouillon)

logique : « il frissonnait dans le saisissement d'une mélancolie sans bornes » (17599 f° 66, transcription 10). En fait, la réversibilité sémantique est telle que les catégories relatives au paysage s'insèrent même dans l'énoncé qui dénote l'état d'âme du personnage. La mélancolie est sans *bornes* alors que les bois descendent jusqu'au *bord* de l'eau; de plus, pour supprimer la répétition, Flaubert substitue aux *bornes* psychologiques un *fond* étrangement *aquatique*. Cet *écoulement* sémantique, juste avant la description de la rivière, révèle une fois de plus l'imbrication génétique des énoncés, propre à l'élaboration contextuelle de toute description indicielle, même si dans ce cas la version publiée n'en portera plus aucune trace (sinon, de façon allusive, dans le récit).[31]

Au contraire, l'indice est maintenu dans la description du boudoir de Mme Arnoux, dont on peut lire le texte définitif :

> Il n'éprouvait plus aucun trouble. Les globes des lampes, recouverts d'une dentelle en papier, envoyaient un jour laiteux et qui attendrissait la couleur des murailles, tendues de satin mauve. A travers les lames du garde-feu, pareil à un gros éventail, on apercevait les charbons dans la cheminée; il y avait, contre la pendule, un coffret à fermoirs d'argent. Çà et là, des choses intimes traînaient : une poupée au milieu de la causeuse, un fichu contre le dossier d'une chaise, et, sur la table à ouvrage, un tricot de laine d'où pendaient en dehors deux aiguilles d'ivoire, la pointe en bas. C'était un endroit paisible, honnête et familier tout ensemble. (p. 45)

Dès le premier scénario se manifeste une tentative de fonctionnalisation : « moment de recueillement de Frédéric. impression de luxe doux — ... contrastant avec l'intérieur du bureau » (17600 f° 148 v°). Bien sûr, il s'agit tout d'abord d'opposer le domicile d'Arnoux à son lieu de travail, mais cette opposition prend immédiatement la forme d'un *effet* psychologique (auquel elle cédera du reste la place;

136 Narrative Voices in Modern French Fiction

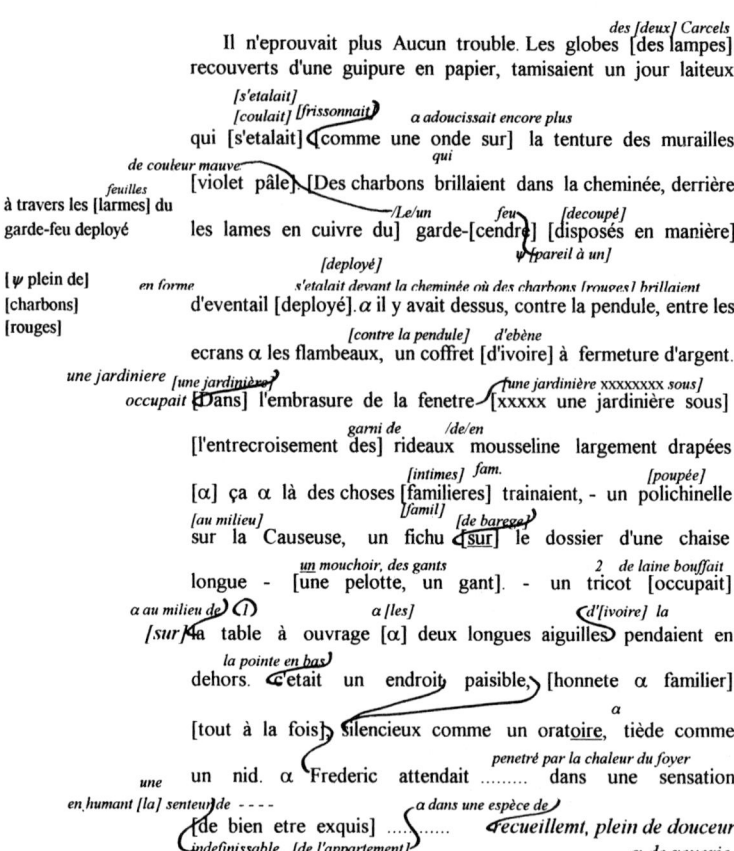

Transcription 11: boudoir, p. 45 (extrait de 17600 f° 153, quatrième brouillon)

l'opposition des lieux n'est pas littérale dans le texte final, et seule une mise en rapport des deux scènes permet de la déceler) : le lieu et les sensations de Frédéric sont associés, l'impression que produit le milieu (*luxe doux*) n'est autre que celle que ressent le personnage, en proie à un « recueillement » ou même à un « recueillement exquis » (17600 f° 120 v°, brouillon suivant).

Il est toujours un moment, dans la rédaction de telles descriptions indicielles, où la séquence psychologique est raturée mais réapparaît pourtant, transposée dans la description même et transformée, nœud sémantique qui signale le passage de la mimésis à la sémiosis. Ainsi, la séquence représentant la lumière, « les globes des lampes recouverts d'une guipure en papier, tamisaient un jour laiteux qui s'étalait comme une onde sur la tenture des murailles violet pâle », est modifiée quand la clausule psychologique (par ailleurs redondante) est biffée : « Frédéric attendait ... dans une sensation de bien-être exquis, en humant la senteur indéfinissable de l'appartement, et dans une espèce de recueillement, plein de douceur et de rêverie » (17600 f° 153, quatrième brouillon, transcription 11). Les lampes en effet tamisent maintenant « un jour laiteux qui adoucissait encore plus la tenture des murailles de couleur mauve »; l'état d'âme de Frédéric quitte le récit et impressionne rétroactivement la séquence, et partant l'ensemble de la description, dotée d'un *faire* dont l'objet demeure implicite. Ce phénomène est encore perceptible dans la version publiée, puisque le verbe *adoucissait* y est devenu *attendrissait* (dès le cinquième brouillon, 17600 f° 155).[32]

La métonymie dote la description topographique de détails et prédicats anthropomorphes, connotatifs, qui pourraient tout aussi bien se trouver insérés dans le récit et y être dénotatifs, si Flaubert l'avait organisé en un énoncé psychologique. Tel n'est pas le cas cependant dans la plupart des exemples abordés ici. Il l'avait souvent fait au préalable, comme s'il avait besoin, lorsqu'il commence à rédiger, de disposer les énoncés, leur enchaînement et leur association de manière explicite. Les brouillons le révèlent, qui témoignent de nombreux processus d'effacement; si bien que, au vu des manuscrits, l'indice de la version publiée apparaît comme le résultat, voire le résidu, des interactions sémantiques qui ont entraîné ou cautionné l'élaboration de la description psychologique. L'*humanit*é, récurrente, ne conserve que la mémoire des processus qui en ont assuré la sémiosis.[33]

Mais, plus encore que le simple passage de l'explicite à l'implicite, les brouillons dévoilent des phénomènes transformationnels qui soulignent l'instabilité de l'indice en formation : le statut indiciel de la description peut être affecté au cours de la rédaction du texte et l'indice circuler indifféremment de la description au récit, du récit à la description. Ce mode spécifique de signifiance, qui semble à première vue se fonder tout entier sur des processus de *substitution*,[34] ne saurait donc être isolé des phénomènes plus généraux de textualisation qu'une *poétique génétique* a pour tâche de définir (les modifications de la sémiosis du coucher de soleil, pp. 10–11, le démontrent de façon éclatante); il relève de choix esthétiques plutôt que purement narratologiques (voire stratégiques), où se devine la distance qui sépare le dit du non-dit.

Notes

[1] Henri Mitterand fait une remarque similaire à propos des descriptions de Zola : « [...] l'espace intervient dans l'action comme une force non inerte; non pas comme un simple décor, mais comme un élément actif qui se joue entre les ambitions et les désirs des personnages », « Le temps et l'espace », *Genèse, structure et style de « La Curée »* (Paris : CDU-Sédès, 1987), 150.

[2] Lettre à Sainte-Beuve, 23–24 décembre 1862 in Proust, *Correspondance*, éd. Jean Bruneau (Paris : Gallimard, 1991) iii 278.

[3] Voir d'ailleurs Gérard Genette, pour qui la description est une « esclave toujours nécessaire, mais toujours soumise, jamais émancipée », *Figures II* (Paris : Éditions du Seuil, 1969), 57.

[4] Gustave Flaubert, *L'Éducation sentimentale*, éd. Peter Michael Wetherill (Paris : Garnier, 1984). Toutes les références, données dorénavant entre parenthèses seulement, renvoient à cette édition.

[5] Roland Barthes, « Introduction à l'analyse structurale des récits », repris dans *L'Aventure sémiologique* (Paris : Éditions du Seuil, 1985), 182.

[6] Roland Barthes, « L'Effet de réel », repris dans *Le Bruissement de la langue* (Paris : Éditions du Seuil, 1984), 167.

[7] Pour d'autres valeurs fonctionnelles des indices (notamment la *socialité* des personnages), voir mon étude « Description, construction : L'espace du texte (à propos de *L'Éducation sentimentale*) », *Rivista di letterature moderne e comparate* 49 (1996), 83–102.

[8] Voir par exemple Jean Bruneau, *Les Débuts littéraires de Gustave Flaubert, 1831–1845* (Paris : Armand Colin, 1962), 561, et Geneviève Bollème, *La Leçon de Flaubert* (Paris : Julliard, 1964).

[9] Voici le texte de toute la description : « Par les deux fenêtres ouvertes, on apercevait du monde aux croisées des autres maisons, vis-à-vis. De larges moires frissonnaient sur l'asphalte qui séchait, et un magnolia posé au bord du balcon embaumait l'appartement. Ce parfum et cette fraîcheur détendirent ses nerfs; et il s'affaissa sur le divan rouge, au-dessous de la glace » (p. 210).

[10] Pp. 192–193. Il y est dédoublé, tout d'abord intradescriptif : « La ville, construite au versant de deux collines basses (dont la première est nue et la seconde couronnée par un bois), avec la tour de son église, ses maisons inégales et son pont de pierre, lui semblait avoir quelque chose de gai, de discret et de bon » (p. 192), et enfin clausural : « Un moulin tournait, barrant dans toute sa largeur le second bras de l'Oise, que surplombe la manufacture. L'importance de cette construction étonna grandement Frédéric. Il en conçut plus de respect pour Arnoux » (p. 193).

[11] En voici le texte complet (p. 53) : « Le matin, ils se promenaient en

manches de chemise sur leur terrasse; le soleil se levait, des brumes légères passaient sur le fleuve, on entendait un glapissement dans le marché aux fleurs à côté; — et les fumées de leurs pipes tourbillonnaient dans l'air pur, qui rafraîchissait leurs yeux encore bouffis; ils sentaient, en l'aspirant, un vaste espoir épandu ».

[12] Ce phénomène se rencontre également dans les descriptions où le *faire* prend la forme d'un simple adjectif verbal : « De larges courroies filaient d'un bout à l'autre du plafond, pour s'enrouler sur des tambours, et tout s'agitait d'une façon continue, mathématique, agaçante » (description des patouillards dans la fabrique d'Arnoux, p. 196); « La voiture roulait, et les chèvrefeuilles et les seringats débordaient les clôtures des jardins, envoyaient dans la nuit des bouffées d'odeurs amollissantes » (atmosphère à Auteuil, p. 85).

[13] Cette étroite collaboration métonymique voire sylleptique de l'espace et du personnage a été fort bien exprimée par les Goncourt (à propos de *Salammbô*), qui se sont pourtant empressés de la condamner : « Il y a une grande fatigue dans ces descriptions [...]; les robes marchent sur les visages, les paysages sur les sentiments », *Journal*, 6 mai 1861 (Monaco : Imprimerie Nationale, 1956), iv, 190.

[14] Selon Guy Larroux, du reste, la signification du *mais* est solidaire de résonances affectives dans la description; voir « Grammaire d'un paragraphe flaubertien », *Poétique* 76 (1988), 477.

[15] Voir aussi la description du brouillard, bâtie sur un dispositif identique (p. 67) : « [...] un lourd brouillard, estompant la façade des maisons, puait dans l'air. Frédéric le humait avec délices ». L'antithèse *puait* vs *humait avec délices* indique le fonctionnement disjonctif de la description indicielle. La suite du texte dénonce d'ailleurs l'allure fantasmatique des notations : « L'éclat des lumières, sur le boulevard, le remit dans la *réalit*é » (je souligne).

[16] Les manuscrits de *L'Éducation sentimentale* (scénarios et brouillons) sont conservés au Département des Manuscrits de la Bibliothèque Nationale, sous la cote Nouvelles Acquisitions Françaises (N.A.F.), volumes 17599–17611 (je ne reproduirai pas ici le signe N.A.F.); le manuscrit autographe est conservé à la Bibliothèque Historique de la Ville de Paris (abrégé ici en B.H.V.P.). Le code de transcription adopté est diplomatique, respectant la disposition du manuscrit et l'orthographe de Flaubert. Tous les ajouts sont en italique et, quand ils sont interlinéaires, se trouvent en caractères plus petits, rapprochés de la ligne sur laquelle ils viennent se greffer. Les signes de ponctuation ajoutés sont situés entre soufflets : <,>. Les mots ou phrases entre crochets, [...], sont raturés; les surcharges sont indiquées par / ... / (entre les barres figure le passage surchargé et à droite, en italique, celui qui surcharge); les passages non déchiffrés sont indiqués par xxxxx; le signe α est souvent utilisé par Flaubert pour remplacer la conjonction *et*.

[17] Dont voici le texte définitif (p. 192) : « A droite et à gauche, des plaines vertes s'étendaient; le convoi roulait; les maisonnettes des stations glissaient comme des décors, et la fumée de la locomotive versait toujours du même côté ses gros flocons qui dansaient sur l'herbe quelque temps, puis se dispersaient ».

¹⁸ Voir aussi la description du salon des Dambreuse déjà citée (p. 130); elle contient à l'origine une séquence psychologique : « il se sentait à l'aise, chez lui », tandis que la marge du folio renchérit : « délectation. aucun trouble. c'est en rapport avec sa nature » (17602 f° 63 v°). Il en va de même pour la description de la Seine à Fontainebleau (p. 329) : « moment exquis » et dans l'interligne : « apaisement, béatitude » (17607 f° 157). La séquence qui décrit la Seine se charge ensuite d'un sens psychologique, temporairement : « elle était platé comme un miroir et si tranquille qu'elle semblait ne pas couler » (17607 f° 156 v°).

¹⁹ Pour les extraits des brouillons cités dans le corps du texte, les soufflets <...> indiquent une addition, les crochets [...] une suppression.

²⁰ Le même phénomène se produit pour la description de l'atmosphère à Auteuil (p. 85) : « des odeurs de seringats et de chèvrefeuilles venaient par bouffées. Son cœur se fondait en tendresses » (17601 f° 257). Les *molles odeurs* deviennent, quand la séquence psychologique est biffée, « amollissantes » (17601 f° 262).

²¹ Il ne faudrait pas croire cependant que Flaubert s'empresse d'opacifier le statut indiciel des descriptions. Quelquefois au contraire la conjonction des actants, initiale, se multiplie au cours de l'élaboration du passage, comme le montre par exemple la clausule de la description euphorique de Paris déjà citée auparavant (p. 53). L'effet indiciel est noté dès le scénario : « sentiment de vie et de fraîcheur » (17600 f° 60 v°), et est tout à fait accentué, non sans redondance d'ailleurs, lors du passage à la rédaction : « le grand air rafraîchissait leurs yeux encore bouffis de sommeil. Il entrait dans leur poitrine à pleins poumons et leur apportait une sensation de fraîcheur et comme des gonflements d'espérance » (17601 f° 17).

²² Dont voici la version définitive :

> Quand ils allaient du côté de Nogent, ils avaient, en face, un pâté de maisons s'inclinant quelque peu; à droite, l'église apparaissait derrière les moulins de bois dont les vannes étaient fermées; et, à gauche, les haies d'arbustes, le long de la rive, terminaient des jardins, que l'on distinguait à peine. Mais, du côté de Paris, la grande route descendait en ligne droite, et des prairies se perdaient au loin, dans les vapeurs de la nuit. Elle était silencieuse et d'une clarté blanchâtre. Des odeurs de feuillage humide montaient jusqu'à eux; la chute de la prise d'eau, cent pas plus loin, murmurait, avec ce gros bruit doux que font les ondes dans les ténèbres. Deslauriers s'arrêta, et il dit :
> — « Ces bonnes gens qui dorment tranquilles, c'est drôle! Patience! un nouveau 89 se prépare! » (p. 16).

²³ Notons par ailleurs que le *pavé gras* est un indice dysphorique stéréotypé; on le trouve également dans la description des rues du Quartier Latin : « le pavé était gras » (p. 24).

²⁴ Carnet 13, f° 5. Voir Flaubert, *Carnets de travail*, éd. Pierre-Marc de Biasi (Paris : Balland, 1988), 333. Voir aussi mon article « Notes de repérage et descriptions dans *L'Éducation sentimentale* (étude de genèse) », *Neuphilologische Mitteilungen* 94 No. 3/4 (1993), 359–360.

²⁵ Voir par exemple mon étude « La Description modalisée. Un problème

de poétique génétique (à propos de *L'Éducation sentimentale*) », *Poétique* 99 (septembre 1994), 350–351.

[26] Notons cependant que l'ennui n'est pas évident ou littéral dans le paysage, excepté peut-être dans la représentation répétitive de la rivière, « toute immobile à l'avant » et « l'eau en était toute plate ». Il semble que ce soit plutôt la séquence suivant la description qui, résumant la *monotonie* du paysage, demande d'en redéfinir *a posteriori* le sens.

[27] En voici la version définitive : « Des champs moissonnés se prolongeaient à n'en plus finir. Deux lignes d'arbres bordaient la route, les tas de cailloux se succédaient » (p. 10).

[28] On peut relever un phénomène similaire, quoique moins spectaculaire, pour la description du parterre du château de Fontainebleau. En voici le texte définitif suivi de son contexte (p. 325) :

> C'est un vaste rectangle, laissant voir d'un seul coup d'œil ses larges allées jaunes, ses carrés de gazon, ses rubans de buis, ses ifs en pyramide, ses verdures basses et ses étroites plates-bandes, où des fleurs clairsemées font des taches sur la terre grise. Au bout du jardin, un parc se déploie, traversé dans toute son étendue par un long canal.
>
> Les résidences royales ont en elles une mélancolie particulière, qui tient sans doute à leurs dimensions trop considérables pour le petit nombre de leurs hôtes, au silence qu'on est surpris d'y trouver après tant de fanfares, à leur luxe immobile prouvant par sa vieillesse la fugacité des dynasties, l'éternelle misère de tout […].

Or, dans les brouillons, l'effet indiciel est immédiatement littéral : « parterre et parc. mélancolie des châteaux et jardins royaux » (17607 f° 93 v°, premier scénario ponctuel), et sera précisé davantage : « régularité embêtante des jardins à la française. allées trop larges, plates-bandes trop plates » (17607 f° 130), ou encore : « on s'ennuie vite au milieu de ces larges allées qui s'étendent rectangulairement » (17607 f° 129). La *mélancolie* voire l'*ennui* quittent ensuite la description pour investir le récit qui résume l'impression générale que donnent « les résidences royales ». Pourtant, dans l'édition de 1869, le lien entre description et récit était encore explicite, et légitimait la succession des énoncés : « Les résidences royales, *du reste*, ont en elles une mélancolie particulière » (je souligne).

[29] A propos de la genèse de cette partie de l'épisode, voir mon étude « Visite guidée (genèse du château de Fontainebleau dans *L'Éducation sentimentale*) », *Genesis* 5 (1994), 99–116.

[30] De même, dans les brouillons de la description de Paris déjà citée (p. 64), la « longueur de l'été à Paris » (17601 f°s 119 et 37 v°) devient brusquement la « langueur de l'été à Paris » (17601 f° 119 v°), car la *langueur* découle de la tristesse de Paris à ce moment, mais plus encore de celle de Frédéric, obsédé par l'absence de Mme Arnoux.

[31] Voir aussi l'organisation de la description euphorique du jardin de Frédéric (p. 188) : « On était aux premiers jours d'avril. Les feuilles des lilas verdoyaient déjà, un souffle pur se roulait dans l'air, et de petits oiseaux pépiaient, alternant leur chanson avec le bruit lointain que faisait la forge d'un carrossier ». Sur le premier scénario les syntagmes « temps doux.

oiseaux chantent » ont un répondant immédiat dans le récit psychologique qui les suit : « Frédéric est porté à l'espérance, à l'attendrissement » (17604 f° 20 v°). Sur le second brouillon la séquence représentant le ciel répète l'attendrissement du personnage : « le ciel d'un bleu tendre, semblait d'une douceur infinie » (17604 f° 70), tandis que le « souffle [de printemps] » sera tour à tour « caressant » (17604 f° 71) et « doux » (17604 f° 69).

[32] Le même phénomène se produit pour la description du bureau de Dambreuse. En voici la version définitive (p. 385) : « Les cartons, les tiroirs étaient ouverts pêle-mêle, les livres de comptes jetés de droite et de gauche; un rouleau de paperasses ayant pour titre : « Recouvrements désespérés », traînait par terre; il manqua tomber dessus et le ramassa ». Dans les brouillons, la description topographique, « tout est sens dessus dessous dans le bureau. les coffres-forts sont défoncés — les cartons ouverts. elle a fouillé partout » (17609 f° 22 v°) devient soudain psychologique dès ce premier scénario, se conformant au *bouleversement* de Mme Dambreuse (anéantie par la certitude d'être ruinée), lui-même raturé et déplacé : « Tout est sens dessus dessous, <bouleversé> dans le bureau » répond à « Il l'y trouve [bouleversée] <atterrée> ».

[33] On pourrait appliquer à certaines descriptions flaubertiennes cette remarque de Greimas : « L'espace ainsi instauré n'est qu'un signifiant, il n'est là que pour être pris en charge et signifie autre chose que l'espace, c'est-à-dire l'homme, qui est le signifié de tous les langages », A. J. Greimas, « Pour une sémiotique topologique », *Sémiotique et sciences sociales* (Paris : Éditions du Seuil, 1976), 130.

[34] Geneviève Bollème assurait par exemple (sans avoir eu recours aux brouillons, il est vrai) : « C'est la description qui est le récit parce qu'elle est analyse et expression des sentiments que les choses symbolisent ou supportent, se confondant avec eux et eux avec elles », *La Leçon de Flaubert*, op. cit., 268.

Dressed/Undressed: Objects of Visual Fascination in Zola's *L'Assommoir*

SUSAN HARROW

Les chemises de Mademoiselle Remanjou [...] fournissaient des commentaires interminables.[1]

Clothes tell their own story and bodies speak through their clothes. In *L'Assommoir* the processing of clothes (they are repeatedly itemized, laundered, exchanged, selected, combined, discarded) is central to the plot dynamics. With the decline of Gervaise Macquart measured by the swell of dirty linen, by laundry which becomes increasingly muddled and spoiled, clothes are made to bear a significant narrative charge. The stock-in-trade of the novel's protagonist, clothes form a nexus of meanings which draw primarily on material, commercial, economic and social values. The focus of this study is those less conspicuous moments where the production of culturally authorized meanings is disrupted by a narrative suddenly arrested by a set of erotic possibilities.

As Gervaise struggles to defend her excessive starching and stiffening of Goujet's collars, her blush reminds us that clothes are a means of access to the erotic body, that laundering affords commercially sanctioned intimacy with the body of the other: 'Elle craignait de laisser voir le *plaisir* qu'elle prenait à repasser elle-même les chemises de Goujet. Bien sûr, elle n'avait pas de pensées *sales*; mais elle n'en était pas moins un peu honteuse' (p. 539) (my italics).[2]

Clothes are a substitute for the absent body, a channel for desire (hence the blush), and the object of its sublimation (cleansing those 'sales pensées'). Professional zeal may explain Gervaise's over-starching of Goujet's shirts but subtending this is the urge to write her desire on Goujet's body (in blood!) and thus claim that body for herself. It is a desire in which Goujet is complicit: ' "Tenez, c'est du carton ... Mon fils ne se plaint pas, mais ça lui coupe le cou ...

Demain, il aura le cou en sang, quand nous reviendrons de Vincennes"' (p. 539).

The narrative of the dressed/undressed body – at its most legible in *Nana*[3] – has been obscured in *L'Assommoir* by the broader, more explicit themes of social deprivation, heredity, alcoholism, work, 'a woman's life', and environment.[4] I would like to suggest that this forgotten narrative is of central importance in *L'Assommoir* and connects intimately with questions of identity and the construction of self and other. My particular focus is those instances where the narrative veers from the economic and cultural meanings of clothes to engage a discourse on the body, crucially the eroticized body of visual curiosity. The starting-point is the legibility of clothes and their significance in the domestic and professional economies of Gervaise Macquart. From there I shall move on to objects of viewing, dressed and undressed, examining the topos of male narcissism (Lantier's appropriation of female patterns of self-viewing) and exploring the narrative preoccupation with 'body-gazing' through scenes of visual fascination involving a male viewer and a female body viewed (Lantier/Amanda; Goujet/Gervaise).

The story of Gervaise gives rise to a text obsessed with clothing, its narrative possibilities and its legibility. The laundress's shop is central to the production of a clothes fiction. Clémence, the hapless laundry-assistant, is an unstoppable narrator of the stories imprinted upon clothes by their wearers. For Clémence, it is all about turning dirt into dirty stories: 'à chaque pièce, cette grande vaurienne lâcha un mot cru, une *saleté*, elle étalait les misères des clients, les aventures des alcôves, elle avait des plaisanteries d'atelier sur tous les trous et toutes les taches qui lui passaient par les mains' (p. 507). Clémence exposes the intimate life of the body readable in each item of soiled linen, and so she reveals the rich potential of clothes for story-telling. As Madame Putois tries to censor Clémence's attempts to turn clothes into fiction, her protests merely confirm the legibility of clothing, conveying a sense of the indelicacy of stories which 'undo' (and make public) the secret, sexual life of the body: 'c'est un de ces *déballages* qu'on évite de faire chez les gens comme il faut' (p. 507). But, the narrative possibilities of clothing are unsuppressible as Gervaise's interpretative activity makes clear. This activity effectively duplicates the Naturalist project, for it involves observation, recognition, identification, naming, conjecture, and deduction – deploying the methods of her creator, the protagonist appropriates, in the process, something of his authority:

[...] elle suivait les pièces *d'un regard attentif*, pour les *reconnaître* au passage; et elle ne se trompait jamais, elle *mettait un nom* sur chacune, au flair, à la couleur. [...] Les chemises de Mademoiselle Remanjou, par exemple, *fournissaient des commentaires interminables;* elles s'usaient par le haut, la vieille fille *devait avoir* les os des épaules pointus; et jamais elles n'étaient sales [...] ce qui *prouvait* qu'à cet âge-là on est quasiment comme un morceau de bois, dont on serait bien en peine de tirer une larme de quelque chose [...] à chaque triage, on *déshabillait* ainsi tout le quartier de la Goutte-d'Or. (pp. 507–508)[5]

Clothes are a multi-layered text inviting interpretation, a palimpsest through which the reader glimpses a body demanding to be made narrative. Interpretation is the act of stripping away ('déshabiller', 'déballer'), the uncovering of hidden layers of meaning and secret surfaces. Clothes (as objects of narrative exposure and concealment) are central to story-telling and the production of narrative. While the interpretative activity of Zola's laundresses offers a model for the reader, critics have tended to overlook the narrative potential of clothes and the body in *L'Assommoir* (and more generally), stressing instead the functionality of description and the economy of detail with which Zola approaches clothes and the bodies they cover. Thus Philippe Hamon situates the description of clothes and the body within the narrow limits of the classificatory project: 'La description de l'habit reste réduite à une ou deux notations à fonction classificatoire: le prêtre a sa soutane, la fille sauvage a un habit de 'bohémienne', etc.'[6] For Hamon, clothes are the unremarkable stock-in-trade of the Naturalist writer. For Gervaise and company, clothes are singularly 'remarkable'. Repeatedly scrutinized, picked over, viewed and reviewed, clothes are the focus of endless conjecture. I want to argue here that clothes and the bodies which they cover (and continually, and more interestingly, expose) are no mere adjunct to fiction. I want to ask *how* clothes signify in the narrative, in what precise ways they come into meaning, and how clothes absorb the fascinated gaze of the spectator, turning the viewer into a dreamer of the private body.

Clothes are the major props of Gervaise's domestic and professional economies. Clothes provide a crucial source of the hard cash-currency upon which the laundress's economic success, indeed her material survival, depend. Early in the text, the pervasiveness of the market-place, the precariousness of exchange, and the erosion of commodity value are hinted at: as Gervaise surveys the room at the Hôtel Boncœur, her gaze falls upon furniture draped with clothes which can no longer be exchanged, traded, or transformed into cash, clothes which have reached the end of their circulation – 'les *dernières* nippes dont les marchands d'habits ne voulaient pas' (pp. 375–376).

Clothes are put into circulation through the distinct but structurally comparable processes of laundering and of pawning. Clothing is subject to endless recycling, the repetition and repeatability of the laundering and pawning processes providing factors of (provisional) stabilization in what are pressured economies. The business of laundering turns clothes into objects of endless traffic between Gervaise and the countless 'pratiques' she services. The constant shuttling of laundry-items from shop to unnamed clients and back again positions Gervaise, at any given moment, as sender and recipient of clothes, source and destination of laundry. The circulation of clothes around the central figure of the laundress mimes the circulation of signs in the narrative, while the processes of sorting, itemizing, accumulating and transforming the laundry parallel those processes of metonymization, metamorphosis, 'brouillage', differentiation and classification which define the technical repertory of the Naturalist writer.

The homogeneous, undifferentiated 'linge' is the object of processes of categorization which include itemizing/metonymizing ('mouchoirs', 'chemises', 'gilets', 'serviettes', 'torchons', 'pantalons'); individual labelling ('le paquet de Mme Gaudron'); inscription ('Quand une pièce d'un nouveau client lui passait entre les mains, elle la marquait d'une croix au fil rouge pour la reconnaître', p. 505); gendering ('jupons', 'bas', 'jupes de soie', 'pantalon de *femme*', 'pantalon d'*homme*'); enumeration (counting and entering in the register (' "Ça fait trente-deux mouchoirs [...] et deux autres, trente-quatre" ', p. 507); valuation ('les chemises d'homme cinq sous, les pantalons de femme quatre sous, les taies d'oreiller un sou et demi, les tabliers un sou, ce n'était pas cher, attendu que bien des blanchisseuses prenaient deux liards ou même un sou de plus pour toutes ces pièces', p. 539); and hierarchization (clothes are indicators of domestic values and practices that allow the laundress-reader to differentiate between hyper-clean and squalid families). The categorial system is thrown into confusion when carelessness and, later, indifference take a hold, resulting in the non-differentiation of clothes and laundry-chaos (laundry is delayed, laundry marks cease to signify, the identification of clothes breaks down and their provenance is blurred).[7] Items of linen are spoiled and mutilated as buttons are torn off or the fabric is burned (pp. 639–640). Order veers towards disorder as the process breaks down and the system lurches out of control. Dirt is no longer banished but merely spread around, unambiguity is replaced by confusion ('brouille') as items are lost or muddled and circulation is interrupted. In short, 'elle s'abandonnait à un grand désordre' (p. 639). Now the interpretative activity passes from Gervaise to Madame Goujet who reads the unequivocal signs (holes, scorch-marks) of the laundress's slide into indifference – 'Madame Goujet se mit à examiner les pièces une à une' (p. 640). Gervaise is no longer an interpreting subject but an interpreted object. Losing control of the processing of clothes, Gervaise loses control of her own destiny.

The development of the narrative destabilizes the laundry-system in material and in mythic terms. Laundering is initially read as an unambiguous, unidirectional, transformative process whose constant repetition confirms the effort-achievement causality that defines Gervaise's life-view. Gervaise's laundry-shop is the powerhouse of positive transformation: there are some clear parallels between the laundry-shop in the early stages and the forge. Respectively gendered feminine and masculine, both are functional, efficient, productive, complex, and the site of heroic activity. In the same way as the blacksmith relentlessly hammers his formless lump of metal into a desired object, so the laundress manipulates her linen (beats, wrings, bleaches, blues, starches, presses it into shape). And where the blacksmith strives to outperform his rival at the forge, conscious of his spectator and of the imperatives of staging his prowess, Gervaise is no less intent on the visual enhancement of her output. Mindful that the whiteness of the finished linen is the measure of her performance, she uses blue wallpaper in her shop-window to '*faire valoir* la blancheur du linge' (p. 497). The activity of the laundress is mythically comparable with the transformative feat of the alchemist – Gervaise is the transformer of soiled laundry into clean, starched clothes. The purifier of her world, she turns squalor into salubriousness, the stained into the immaculate. The transformative order is, however, provisional, precarious, susceptible to reversal (just as the forge is dysfunctional, uncontrollable, fatal, mesmerizing, so is Gervaise's shop). The slide into laundry-chaos is anticipated in chapter 2. Here Gervaise defends 'son plan de vie bien arrêté tandis que Coupeau, qui ne lâchait pas son désir de l'avoir, plaisantait, *tournait tout à l'ordure*' (p. 407). In the midst of the narrative comes an early warning signal that Coupeau is a polluter, a producer of linguistic dirt, a pursuer of salacious innuendo, a purveyor of semantic impurity. This inscribes (in 'tournait') the idea of reverse transformation (the tainting of pure by impure, the lapse into soilure). The conjunction 'tandis que' structures and maintains the opposition, stressing the conflict of motivations between Gervaise and Coupeau, placing these in a precarious balance that endures until Gervaise's resolve weakens, distinctions blur, and the slide towards the opposing set of values accelerates into decline: '[...] elle s'accoutumait déjà aux ennuis et aux *saletés* de l'argent, ne gardant de ces embêtements-là que le bonheur d'en être sortie, jusqu'à la prochaine fois' (p. 541). And so, short-termism begins to replace deferred gratification as Gervaise's philosophy.

Pawning, as a process of repeatable and, ideally, revocable liquidation of personal effects, is narrativized from the beginning of the novel. Gervaise recounts how she pawned her skirt for three francs and spent the sum on food: ' "Tu sais bien que j'ai eu trois francs sur ma jupe noire. Nous avons déjeuné trois fois là-dessus" ' (p. 384). Pawning underscores the significance of clothes as exchange-value and provides the mechanism which affords Gervaise access to the local economy as a consumer. Gervaise is a practised liquidator, one who is conscious of the need to stabilize the process of exchange and transformation. However regular the process, it is *regulated* only as long as Gervaise controls the steadily accumulating pile of pawnbroker receipts (the 'reconnaissances' are symbolic reminders of the retrievability of the clothes; they represent the knowledge or, more modestly, the hope that the layer of tickets can be re-transformed into layers of clothes). The process is destabilized by Lantier's misappropriation of the tickets (at the end of chapter 1). Whilst Lantier's action has potentially disastrous implications for the central character, it is crucial for the development of the plot. Lantier's theft of the irreplaceable tickets breaks the notional contract between himself and Gervaise, disrupts the cycle of repetition and exchange, and launches the narrative.

Initially robbed of the sexual exclusivity of her relationship with Lantier, Gervaise experiences the loss of the pawnshop receipts as an ultimate violation of her trust in Lantier. In material terms, this spells the collapse of the family's strained economy, but Gervaise has already paid a high price in sexual terms. Forced by Lantier to pawn her every dress, Gervaise has suffered the loss of her beauty and desirability, an erosion of her sexual power and position ('[...] "tu ne me trouves plus assez bien depuis que tu m'as fait mettre toutes mes robes au mont-de-piété"', p. 382). At the end of chapter 1, Lantier's final rejection of Gervaise in favour of the publicly circulating, commodified body of ' "cette traînée d'Adèle [...] [qui] a couché avec tout le restaurant"' (p. 382) concludes the cruel realignment of sexual values.

Already, in this first chapter, the slippage between commercial (domestic) economy and erotic economy is marked by the swerve from outward signs (clothes) to the bodies that wear them. Gervaise's aspirations are functional, collective, family-led and active: ' "Si tu te mets avec ton ami de la Glacière, nous reviendrons sur l'eau avant six mois, le temps de *nous nipper* et de louer un trou"' (p. 382). The language of Gervaise stresses the notion of self-reliance (the reflexive form 'se nipper'), the combination of basic material aims ('se nipper', 'louer un trou') underscoring the tension between her own simple goals and the more complex desires of Lantier. These she perceives as individual, cultural, passive, and linked to narcissistic, erotic, and mimetic motivations: '[...] "tu voudrais être habillé *comme un monsieur* et promener des catins en jupes de soie"' (p. 382). Here the very order of the phrases mimes the swerve from socio-cultural values ('comme un monsieur') to erotic meanings ('promener des catins'). The semantic and grammatical selections which make up Gervaise's discourse on clothes expose the gap between her self-construction and her reading of the egotistical Lantier.

At this point I will take a closer look at Lantier's efforts at self-actualization and how these draw on the erotic, mimetic and narcissistic possibilities of clothes. Lantier views the world in terms of clothes and accessory objects. He spends lavishly on silk frocks, as Gervaise says (p. 389): decorating himself (' "une montre pour lui"') and dressing others (' "une jupe de soie pour moi"'). Clothes afford Lantier pleasure that is at once fetishistic and erotic, mimetic and narcissistic. Lantier's fixation with the repeatedly purchased silk frock marks a displacement from erotic body to fetishized clothes-object. He repeatedly reduces women to the clothes they wear ('il crevait d'aise parmi les jupes, se fourrait au plus épais des femmes', p. 608; 'une jupe lui trottait dans la tête', p. 747), and, inevitably, to their underclothes ('les jupons'). And so he avoids the kind of direct contact with the other that is precarious, complex, demanding, preferring the passiveness of substitute objects: '[...] tout ce coin pareil à une alcôve où traînait le déballage des dames du quartier semblait être pour lui le trou rêvé, un refuge longtemps cherché de paresse et de *jouissance*' (p. 608). The mass of soiled women's clothes is a guarantee of non-differentiation, a refuge from the problems of individuation, and a release from the need to engage with the other. At the same time, the clothes provide uncensored access to the desired body-imprinted object. Lantier's inclinations confirm Tony Tanner's reminder that ' "fetishized" objects are relatively safe, easily available, undemanding of reciprocity or commitment and thus (allow) a person whose feelings have been aroused to remain in a passive, spectator-consumer relationship to the other'.[8] Lantier is, of course, never happier than when he is spectator and consumer. His metaphorical status as a 'mangeur de boutiques' becomes a literal truth when, cramming himself with Virginie's sweets, he begins to exhaust her shop's stock. As for his spectatorship, he is a consummate viewer, one who exploits the potential of his gaze to signify: 'Il [...] fatiguait [Gervaise] de son regard, fixait sur elle des regards hardis, où elle lisait nettement ce qu'il lui demandait' (p. 613).

Like Gervaise (like Zola) Lantier knows that clothes tell a story. In other words, clothes are a focus for the interpreting practices of others (and are crucial in the construction of self as an object under the gaze of others). Lantier presents himself as a surface to be read in ways that he attempts to control by means of judicious selections from the set of available visual and verbal indicators: 'Lantier déclara, d'une voix grave, en choisissant les termes, que son cœur était mort, qu'il voulait désormais se consacrer uniquement au bonheur de son fils' (p. 600). Constantly transforming what *is* into what *is not*, Lantier converts tawdry truth into seductive illusion, turns raw nature into a dazzling cultural object (language, food, manners, costume) for the consumption of others.[9] Lantier's attitude to food is revealing: where Coupeau is partial to 'des ribotes dans le chic *bon enfant*' (p. 618) (an indication of the simple palate of the zinc-roofer which identifies Coupeau with the 'bon enfant' values of the uncultivated, naïve, powerless and natural), Lantier is the 'homme [...] si *difficile*' (p. 618), where the adjective embraces not only the sense of 'finicky' but extends into 'duplicitous', 'ambiguous', 'unfathomable', 'complex'. Tellingly expert at sauces, at what *garnishes* the plain meat, Lantier works along the axis of refinement and exclusiveness, effecting an implicit transformation of the everyday into the exceptional: '[il] trouvait sur la carte des noms de sauces *extra*ordinaires' (p. 618). His strategy is exposed and debunked by a nominal juxtaposition that points up the inappropriateness of elevated tastes to the modest status of a hatter, 'les goûts d'*aristo* du *chapelier*' (p. 618). The attitudes and practices of Lantier as regards food and clothes reveal a clear homology. His compulsion to dress things up (the dual function of which is to conceal and to refine) points to Lantier's fixation with surface at the expense of substance. He knows the mesmerizing power of appearances.

Freud defines narcissism as female, as the obsession of the viewed object. Lantier is an example of male narcissism. Conscious of himself as a body-object to be viewed by female subjects, he is concerned with precisely *how* he is viewed. He is keenly aware that clothes mediate between viewing subject and viewed object. As the gaze of the viewer criss-crosses the surface of its object, it fastens on a clothes-item which, originally an obstacle to desire, turns now into a focus for desire. Whilst Lantier's obsession implies a partial feminization of the character who puts himself willingly in the position of the viewed object, the feminization-effect is neutralized by a characteristically phallic concern with viewing (more precisely, with controlling the viewing practices of others), and with the visual construction of the object of both narcissistic and erotic desire (his own body). The desire to be seen and to control viewing activity may explain the mutual attraction of Lantier and Nana, who will become the consummate manipulator of her spectators, both on stage and off. As Nana steals a sideways glance at Lantier (watching him watching her), the narrative of *L'Assommoir* points up the prefigurative value of aspects of the adolescent Nana's behaviour: 'Cette merdeuse de dix ans marchait comme une dame devant lui, se balançait, *le regardait de côté*, les yeux *déjà* pleins de vice' (p. 610). Lantier has a taste for the exhibitionist practices at which Nana will excel in *La blonde Vénus*. Already at age 15, Nana is adept at staging her body for the delectation of others:

> L'été était la saison de ses triomphes [...] l'encolure du corsage, qu'elle ouvrait en cœur avec des épingles, [...] montrait la neige de son cou et l'ombre dorée de sa gorge [...]. Les dimanches furent pour elle [...] des journées de rendez-vous avec la foule, avec tous les hommes qui passaient et qui la reluquaient [...] Dès le matin, elle s'habillait, elle restait des heures en chemise devant le morceau de glace accroché au-dessus de la fenêtre. (pp. 709–710).

Nana and Lantier are avid viewers in turn. While Nana indulges her own precocious voyeuristic inclinations, spying on her mother's adulterous activity – '[...] la figure collée contre la vitre, elle resta là, à attendre que le jupon de sa mère eût disparu chez l'autre homme [...]. Elle avait de grands yeux d'enfant vicieuse, allumés d'une curiosité sensuelle' (p. 633) – Lantier is a keen patron of the café-concert, enticing Gervaise to Mlle Amanda's strip-show in chapter 8, an episode to which I shall return.

Lantier constitutes himself at the nexus of artifice, illusion and theatricality. The first indicator of the performative value Lantier attaches to clothes and their signifying potential is the black felt hat which he sends flying through the air (p. 380), a gesture which announces his anger, and arrogance, but perhaps most revealingly, his ostentation. Lantier channels his efforts into cultivating an appropriate physical appearance, focusing not only clothes but the body itself, or at least some body-part. The narrative inscribes the character's obsessive behaviour through the writing of repetition, through duplication of the same or similar images. The first sighting of Lantier homes in on his 'minces moustaches, qu'il frisait toujours d'un mouvement machinal de la main' (p. 380). Following Lantier's re-entry into the narrative, we learn that 'il soignait *toujours beaucoup* ses minces moustaches' (p. 597), the adverbial selections emphasizing the repetition and excess that are Lantier's signature. Lantier's obsession breaks down into a manic attention trained on the same limited set of part-objects. The repeated morsellization extends to attitudes towards food and personal health. His obsessive finickiness effectively morsellizes the food on his plate: '[...] il *discutait chaque fricot*, au point de vue de la santé, faisant remporter la viande lorsque'elle lui semblait trop salée ou trop poivrée' (p. 618). *Discuter* emphasizes processes of viewing, analysis and critical examination, processes which will allow Lantier to dissect the performance of Mlle Amanda, and, as Gervaise notes, the body of the performer: 'Lantier [donnait] des détails sur la personne en question de l'air d'un monsieur qui lui aurait compté les côtes en particulier' (p. 630). Lantier's tendency to morsellize, to itemize, to metonymize what is constituted in its wholeness and completeness (the bodies of self and other) speaks to something more than narcissism. It betrays an urge to break down what is powerful, threatening, desirable and unknowable. Anthony Giddens comments: 'What might appear as a wholesale movement towards the narcissistic cultivation of bodily appearance is in fact an expression of concern lying much deeper actively to "construct" and control the body'.[10] This is shown up most vividly by Lantier's preoccupation with his body-size. In a narrative where failure and fatness are strongly correlated (through Gervaise), remaining slim might predispose the character to success or, at least, survival. Lantier's obsession with neither gaining nor losing weight outdistances cultural and moral imperatives. It reveals a neurotic desire to stabilize and control: 'Il se soignait beaucoup, mesurait son ventre à la ceinture de son pantalon, avec la continuelle crainte d'avoir à resserrer ou à desserrer la boucle [...] il calculait tous les plats de façon à ne pas changer sa taille' (pp. 646–647).

The recurrence of the verb 'pincer' in descriptions of Lantier as well as in the character's own lexicon is telling.[11] The urge to constrain his own body, via 'une vieille redingote tachée qu'il pinçait à la taille' (p. 380), extends to a desire for power over the body of others (pinching Clémence, p. 601), and infiltrates his world-view: '"Je vais tâcher de pincer l'autobus"' (p. 598). In his attempts to define and contain the body, Lantier reveals an obsession with control (over self, others, the world) and with production, as a necessary instrument of control; he recognizes the freedom and power of the producer, '[...] le producteur n'est pas un esclave' (p. 608). Impelled by the demands of self-actualization, Lantier's desire to produce himself cannot be separated from the need to produce others, which ranges from turning them into a cultural object or eroticized body to provoking a certain reaction in others. His project is successful if we are to judge by the reactions of Coupeau. Lantier remains silent on the question of his income, he allows his clothes to do the talking, prompting Coupeau to (erroneous) conjecture based on his interpretation of the available sartorial signs:

> Ce gaillard-là [...] ne vivait pas de l'air du temps. [...] il savait s'arranger, il bibelotait quelque commerce, car enfin *il montrait une figure de prospérité*, il lui fallait bien de l'argent pour se payer du *linge blanc et des cravates de fils de famille*. (p. 598)

An accomplished exploiter of the transformative potential of the objects with which he surrounds himself, Lantier is an equally competent manipulator of the interpretative limitations of others, skills central to his project of self-actualization. The notion that the body is a surface to be read and to be 'named' in certain ways that Lantier endeavours to control is confirmed in '*son ancien titre de patron restait sur toute sa personne* comme une noblesse à laquelle il ne pouvait plus déroger' (p. 598).

The narrative deconstructs the image Lantier holds up for others to view. Certain linguistic selections draw attention to the discrepancy between appearance and expectation, as well as to the appropriation by Lantier of a set of signs (visual, verbal, gestural, linguistic) normally identified with a higher social status. Lantier is sartorially and visually distinctive because he wears (as a replacement for his stained, troublesome 'redingote') 'un paletot gros bleu *comme un monsieur*' (p. 598); because he sports 'des cravates de *fils de famille*'. The attribute implies that Lantier does not belong to the category of bourgeois 'fils de famille'. Likewise in 'il causait poliment, avec les manières d'un homme qui *aurait* reçu de l'instruction', the past conditional tense points up the gap between image and reality; by telling us that Lantier is *like* an educated man, the narrator reminds us that he is *not* one (p. 598). The attitude of leisureliness adopted by Lantier emphasizes the mimetic practices of an individual who, devoid of originality, grounds his attempts at self-actualization in the duplication of second-hand images: '[il] se promenait au soleil, les mains dans les poches, *ainsi qu'un bourgeois*' (p. 598). The concentration of rhetorical pointers (qualifiers, attributes, similes, analogies) exposes Lantier as an accomplished but transparent imitator 'gardant lui-même un langage *choisi*' (p. 608). His refined clothes/body-speak is paralleled in verbal language that reflects the same concern with production and selection. While Lantier consciously resists the pull of the spontaneous, uncultivated discourse which is natural to him, he provokes and relishes the lewdness of others, their verbal improprieties and oaths. We have, in *L'Assommoir*, a narrator intent on exposing the gap.

Lantier seeks to construct an image of himself as different, better, unique, a prince come among people. The success of his project depends on the lack of sophistication of a reader like Coupeau. The zinc-roofer is mesmerized by the glittering object Lantier holds before him, reads visual appearance for reality, confuses the part with the whole, surface with substance. But Gervaise, the professional clothes-reader, is competent in matters of differentiation. Inhaling the sickening and compelling odours which rise from Lantier's trunk,[12] she instantly seizes upon the gap between image and truth, surface and depth: 'Gervaise, penchée, sentait monter une odeur de tabac, une odeur d'homme malpropre, qui soigne seulement le dessus, *ce qu'on voit de sa personne*' (p. 605). Gervaise's ability to differentiate is not in question. It is her lapse into *indifference* which is critical.

L'Assommoir is a novel preoccupied with the body, particularly the body under pressure.[13] The oppressive architecture of the 'immeuble', the aggravated lameness of Gervaise, and the back-splitting toil of the laundresses identify the key pressure factors as environmental, genetic and professional.[14] Constrained and straining (expressed phenomenally as a series of breaks, cracks, splits, bursts of fabric and flesh),[15] the body is pressed to its physical limits in *L'Assommoir*. Central to the representation of human crisis, the body is the site of trial and failure, chaos and catastrophe. From disease, drunkenness, injury and poverty, to sadism, madness, death and decay, catastrophes of the flesh mark the *moments forts* of the novel, and the body is made to bear a substantial and sustained narrative charge.[16] Whether it be the savaged body of Lalie or the frenzied form of the delirious Coupeau, the progress of the narrative is arrested by visions of extreme suffering. The recurrence of the word 'tableau' frames a number of such events, focusing the body as a surface for visualization and interpretation by both reader and characters. In chapter 10 Gervaise enters the Bijards' home where she witnesses a scene of unrestrained sadism and brutality: 'Lalie, affolée, hurlante, sautait aux quatre angles de la pièce [...] mais la mèche mince du grand fouet l'atteignait partout, [...] lui pinçant la chair de longues brûlures [...]. Devant un pareil *tableau*, [Gervaise] fut prise d'une indignation furieuse' (p. 693).[17] Painfully aware that the story of the body is written on the body itself, Gervaise reads, in Lalie's martyred flesh, the signs of her own imminent brutalization. The narrative confirms the body as a site of recognition and locus for meaning, designating the body of the other as a mediating object in the construction of self.

Zola pursues a narrative that veers towards the body's abolition, towards utter dehumanization. This is signalled early in the text where the thud of Coupeau's body as it hits the ground is compared to 'le coup sourd d'un paquet de linge' (p. 482), or where Lalie's tiny form, under the lashes of Bijard's whip, is described as 'rebondissant d'elle-même ainsi qu'une balle élastique' (p. 693).[18] The discovery of the putrefying corpse of Gervaise marks the fall from language, the point at which the body escapes the power of language to construct it, bringing silence and the end of narrative. Zola's novel announces in this respect the postmodernist literature of silence which Ihab Hassan has so powerfully described.[19]

I want now to turn to the question of visual curiosity and the body. In Zola's novel, the body is a source of voyeuristic pleasure.

Two extreme instances of visual pleasure-seeking grip the reader's attention – in chapter 4 the old woman's riveted gaze seems to define (determine?) the trajectory of Coupeau's fall through the air; in chapter 9 Nana's morbid fascination with the corpse of her grandmother is satisfied only by the substitution of her own body for that of the corpse: '[...] pour avoir la paix, on finit par lui permettre de s'allonger à la place de maman Coupeau. [...] Cette nuit-là, elle dormit joliment bien, dans la bonne chaleur et les chatouilles du matelas de plume' (p. 671). These powerful scenes identify the body as an object of intense curiosity, a surface which attracts and absorbs the fascinated gaze of the spectator, and a focus for desire, however perverse. Disturbing and tantalizing, these scenes expose a narrative of looking, desiring and knowing, that resurfaces in moments of erotic curiosity.

There is, in *L'Assommoir*, nothing comparable to the staging of the female body that we find in *Nana*, with the single, telescoped exception of the nude performance of Mlle Amanda in chapter 8. Amanda prefigures Nana whose official name 'Anna' is pre-inscribed phonetically in '*Amanda*'. The evening spent by Lantier and Gervaise at the café-concert constitutes a minor but significant episode in the novel, for the nude performance raises the related questions of the female body and male spectatorship. The representation of nudity implies a female object and a male subject of desire (viewer, artist, spectator). The performance is a focus for a gaze that is phallic, and for desire, the appeasement of which is endlessly deferred. Gervaise's reaction, guided by the gaze of Lantier, is to project herself into the role of Mlle Amanda, to construct herself as that desired body, a process which provokes a mixture of wonderment and modesty: 'Jamais elle n'aurait osé se mettre nue devant le public' (p. 630). She recoils from the idea of her own performance whilst admiring this 'peau à faire envie' (p. 630): the body of the performer is a nexus of female envy and male erotic desire. The phallic gaze fragilizes the female body, denying unity, atomizing, objectifying, as Lantier recounts 'des détails sur la personne en question, de l'air d'un monsieur qui lui aurait compté les côtes en particulier' (p. 630). As the performer's body is renarrativized by Lantier, so Gervaise is made to assume the position of a male gazer, constrained to adopt phallic patterns of viewing, forced to see as men see. It is hardly surprising, then, if Lantier's narration of the body-story provokes Gervaise's 'curiosité sensuelle' (p. 630). Gervaise's viewing of Mlle Amanda through the mediating eyes of Lantier confirms the phallic gaze as the inescapable agent of knowing. It is on moments of eroticized curiosity about the body and on desire for the body that I now wish to focus.

In a novel where unsavoury linen, stuffed into every crack and crevice, comes spewing out of holes in the wall, where clothes threaten to swamp their wearers (here the swaddled figure of Mme Putois is a graphic hyperbole), where the protagonist risks total immersion in the chaos of soiled laundry – '[...] elle disparaissait entre les chemises et les jupons [...] une débâcle de malpropreté [...] cette mare grandissante' (p. 508) – sightings of the naked, and potentially erotic, body are exceptional. Those rare moments when the unclothed body is glimpsed are quickly censored by a reticent narrator or a modest character; Madame Putois, for example, reproaches Clémence for revealing too much flesh: '[...] "remettez votre camisole. Vous savez, je n'aime pas les indécences. Pendant que vous y êtes, montrez votre boutique. Il y a déjà trois hommes arrêtés en face"' (p. 504). If the naked body is the object of visual resistance (the object of obsessive dressing, or an object confined by the relatively safe parameters of stage-performance), those moments where the body comes into view have particular significance in a narrative of curiosity and knowing. I want to look at a particular scene in chapter 4 where the body of Gervaise is glimpsed by Goujet.

In this scene Gervaise's privacy is invaded (apparently unintentionally) by the gaze of the blacksmith. The glimpsing of the naked body extends narrative possibilities for it arouses desire without appeasing it. This is a significant moment of recognition for Goujet whose gaze constructs Gervaise as an erotic object and himself as the desiring subject. However, this moment of visual pleasure gives rise to visual repression, as Goujet seeks to deny the power of his own newly eroticized gaze. Goujet's refusal to see himself reflected in Gervaise's eyes constitutes a 'self-blinding', a denial of his position as desiring subject: '[...] de huit jours, il ne la regarda pas en face' (p. 474). Goujet's act of visual repression is 'copied' by a narrative intent on ellipsis and self-censorship; the description of the scene and its reverberations is confined to a single sentence, the details edited out. The blacksmith may deflect his gaze but his body refuses to be censored, instead it 're-signs' itself via a blush which confirms Goujet's emotional 'gêne' and offers a new surface for interpretation. Thus the body writes the story of desire, its mobile surface encoding psychological meanings which are reciprocated and duplicated by the other: '[...] il finissait par la faire rougir elle-même' (p. 474).[20] Goujet's embarrassment triggers Gervaise's awareness of herself as a sexual being for Goujet, and signals at the same time the transgressive value of the encounter. As Gervaise's flushed face registers this, so her body is made to signify, forced to tell its own story. This moment of viewing is crucial to knowledge, to the construction of self and of other, and particularly to consciousness of self as an object for the other (an instance of Sartrean 'I'm thinking you thinking me').[21] Goujet is conscious of Gervaise as an erotic body, but is more uncomfortably aware of himself as a desiring subject in the process of being 'thought' by Gervaise.

To return to the scene itself, what exactly does Goujet see? Zola is reticent here, exercising writerly modesty by means of a (partial) narrative cover-up. Gervaise is obliquely described as 'à moitié nue' (which half?) before the narrative swerves to the neck-scrubbing activity. This calls up some parallels with the painterly treatment of women bathing and washing: works by Degas, and later Sickert, focus a metonymized body, directing the attention of the viewer to body-part (hair, back, neck), the body viewed not as a coherent whole but fragmented. Gervaise's neck is the focus for Goujet's gaze and for the reader's gaze, both restricted by a censorial narrator. With the rest of the body factored out, invisible, the metonymized 'cou' is an alluring substitute for the half-naked body of Gervaise and the only available focus for erotic meaning. This brings into play Melanie Klein's notion of part-object where the gaze veers from body-whole to some morsellized body-part.[22] Just as the naked hand of Emma Bovary, emerging from the drawn blinds of the carriage that conceal her adulterous congress with Léon, 'bears the freight of what is denied to sight',[23] so the exposed neck of Gervaise Macquart absorbs the fascinated gaze of spectator, narrator and reader but, by deferring possibilities for knowing, exasperates desire.

Further aspects of this scene confirm its painterly nature. At the point where Goujet's gaze is arrested by the semi-naked body of Gervaise, narrative progress is interrupted. Non-verbal and defined exclusively by Goujet's gaze, this scene evokes the detachment and inwardness of a picture.[24] Goujet's intrusion turns Gervaise's body-privacy into an object of viewing, and turns the blacksmith into the visual producer of that body-object. The casting of Goujet in the role of visual creator should not surprise us, for we know his passion for cutting up pictures and producing *tableaux* for his bedroom wall, his preference for visual media over verbal media: '[...] des images de haut en bas, des bonhommes découpés, des gravures coloriées [...], des portraits de toutes sortes de personnages, détachés des journaux illustrés. [...] le soir la lecture le fatiguait; alors il s'amusait à regarder ses images' (pp. 473–474). Goujet's intrusion into what he constructs as a public space and what Gervaise's act of washing redefines as an exclusive and private sphere makes Goujet the viewer and Gervaise the body viewed and framed by an eroticized male gaze. Structures emerge here which are comparable to those identified by Philippe Hamon in his discussion of portraiture in Zola. While Hamon's concern is with *consciously* painterly scenes, the coincidence of structures suggests an equivalence between the criteria for narrativized aesthetic representation and Goujet's viewing activity: '[...] le modèle est muet, voire les yeux fermés, la parole est absente, regardant et regardés sont immobiles, à une certaine "distance", la scène est fixée sous le regard du peintre'.[25] The emphasis on silence, on distance, and on the immobility of gazing subject and gazed-upon object proposes a clear parallel between the status of painter and his model in other novels, and the relative positions of Gervaise and Goujet in this scene. This instance of spectatorship bears contrast with the forge-scene in chapter 6: here the plastic analogy returns, verbalized in terms which announce a sublimation imperative, as Zola confronts and swiftly deflects the question of female desire and a male object of eroticized curiosity. The gendered roles of viewer and viewed are reversed with Gervaise now in the position of viewing subject but with one significant difference: Gervaise is denied her real-life viewed object. The form she gazes upon is not Goujet 'in the flesh' but the safer, idealized image of 'Goujet' as an imaginary marble representation, a notional 'museum piece': '[...] un cou pareil à une colonne, blanc comme un cou d'enfant; une poitrine vaste, large à y coucher une femme en travers; des épaules et des bras sculptés qui paraissent copiés sur ceux d'un géant dans un musée' (p. 533).

The narrative implications of this intrusion upon Gervaise's bathing are considerable. New perspectives are brought to bear on the characters' perceptions of self and other and this produces a change in intersubjective relations that is profoundly felt and verbally inexpressible: 'Il y avait entre eux quelque chose de très doux qu'ils ne disaient pas' (p. 491). The opening-up of new perspectives on a familiar object is a Zolian practice which Hamon aligns with Impressionist technique. The writer is like the painter 'attentif à saisir le *même objet* (*Cathédrales* et *Meules* de Monet, par exemple) dans ses aspects différents, dans ses variations au cours des saisons ou moments de la journée, de le considérer chaque fois comme *nouveau*'.[26] Opening the door, Goujet expects to find 'Gervaise' (constructed socially and culturally, as 'laundress', as 'neighbour'). He glimpses instead her body in its physicality and, more disturbingly, in its erotic possibilities. Crossing the threshold between social and sexual meanings that is marked by modes of dress and undress, Goujet carries his memory of the socially constructed 'Gervaise' into his confrontation with the (newly revealed) erotic possibilities. This leads not only to embarrassment (the flushed faces signal and confirm sexual meaning which is grasped but remains unspoken),[27] but to confusion in the epistemological sense ('qu'est-ce que ça veut dire?'). Struggling to disentangle the *idea* of Gervaise from the *body* of Gervaise, Goujet faces 'the problem of negotiating between a particular and sexed body, and a generalized and idealized one'.[28] Whilst the door may present itself as unambiguously liminal, passing through that door involves rather less of an exchange of one set of meanings for another (the social for the sexual) than a problematizing of the reality of Gervaise for Goujet. For Goujet, Gervaise can no longer be read in the same way as before, but exactly how she should be read by him is problematic.

The consequence of body-gazing is to turn Gervaise into a hermeneutic object, to enigmatize her in the mind of Goujet. The visualization of an eroticized body disrupts formerly stable perceptions of self and other, precipitating the crisis of recognition and knowing that is the basis for the exploration of new subjective and intersubjective possibilities. The moment of viewing reveals the body of the other as crucial to the location of true meaning. This brings sharply into focus, by contrast, the self-absorption (and self-delusion) of Lantier, the perverse and manic product of a clothes-saturated narrative. Lantier's retreat into clothes is a form of resistance to knowledge and a substitute for contact. Repeatedly, in the clothes he selects, the soiled linen he hoards, or the fetid laundry he relishes, Lantier constitutes himself at the nexus of commodity and erotic fetishisms, perpetuating a culture of narcissism and endlessly deferring authentic engagement with others.

Notes

[1] Émile Zola, *Les Rougon-Macquart*, ed. Henri Mitterand (Paris: Gallimard, 1960–1967), 5 vols., ii 508. Subsequent page references to *L'Assommoir* are to this edition.

[2] Throughout this article all italics in quotations are my own.

[3] Two brilliant analyses of *Nana* are Janet Beizer, 'The body in question: anatomy, textuality, and fetishism in Zola', *L'Esprit Créateur* 29 No. 1 (1989), 50–60; and Naomi Schor, 'Smiles of the sphinx: Zola and the riddle of femininity' in *Breaking the Chain: Women, Theory and French Realist Fiction* (New York: Columbia University Press, 1985), 29–47.

[4] Critical interest in *L'Assommoir* is undiminished. Among the major studies of the last twenty years which include discussion of *L'Assommoir* are: David Baguley, *Naturalist Fiction: The Entropic Vision* (Cambridge: CUP, 1990); Chantal Bertrand-Jennings, *L'Éros et la femme chez Zola: de la chute au paradis retrouvé* (Paris: Klincksieck, 1977); Philippe Hamon, *Le Personnel du roman: le système des personnages dans les 'Rougon-Macquart d'Émile Zola* (Paris: Droz, 1983); Robert Lethbridge and Terry Keefe (eds.), *Zola and the Craft of Fiction* (Leicester: Leicester University Press, 1990). Recent monographs include Valerie Minogue's perceptive study *Zola: 'L'Assommoir'* (London: Grant & Cutler, 1991) and Roger Clark's informative *Zola: 'L'Assommoir'* (University of Glasgow French and German Publications, 1990). *Les Cahiers Naturalistes* (hereafter *CN*) 52 (1978) was devoted to *L'Assommoir* and includes articles on work, the working classes, realism, language and lexicon, and the theme of water. Other pertinent articles include David Baguley, 'Event and structure: the plot of *L'Assommoir*', *PMLA* 90 (1975), 823–833; R. Butler, 'Structure des récurrences dans *L'Assommoir*', *CN* 57 (1983), 60–73; P. Carles, '*L'Assommoir*: une déstructuration impressionniste de l'espace descriptif', *CN* 63 (1989), 117–125.

[5] The body is constantly speaking through its clothes, producing a logic of interchangeability which, at times, finds expression in the language of indifferentiation: '[...] elle roulait les pièces, après avoir plongé et secoué sa main sur *les corps des chemises et des pantalons*' (p. 504).

[6] Hamon, *Le Personnel du roman*, 167. From the same functionalist perspective, Hamon emphasizes Zola's minimalist treatment of the body: 'En ce qui concerne le physique de ses personnages, Zola se contente souvent d'une brève notation de la couleur des cheveux et des yeux, de la forme générale du visage, de la taille et de l'embonpoint général' (pp. 167–168).

[7] The progress of the narrative is marked by the aggravation of the structures of indifferentiation. Not only does Gervaise ultimately fail to differentiate between items of laundry belonging to her different customers, but whole identities become undone as difference is denied. Thus the rumour circulates that the bodies of Gervaise and Virginie are indistinguishable to Lantier (p. 675), that the hatter mistook one body for the other and only noticed the following day. If the story is apocryphal at the point where it is recounted by neighbours, it is justified by Lantier's repeated public denial of the significance of difference: 'Lorsqu'on venait demander Coupeau, on [...] trouvait [Lantier] toujours là [...] et il répondait pour Coupeau, il disait que c'était la même chose' (p. 647).

[8] Tony Tanner, *Adultery in the Novel* (Baltimore and London: Johns Hopkins University Press, 1979), 288.

[9] Lévi-Strauss identifies in primitive societies the need to overcome the opposition between nature and culture through mediation and transformation, be it in the act of marriage or in the cooking process; see *The Savage Mind* (London: Weidenfeld & Nicolson, 1966), and *The Raw and the Cooked* (London: Jonathan Cape, 1970). In order to be functional, such processes need to be visible and explicit. Lantier may be an accomplished transformer, but his implicit denial of nature, his cover-up of the processes of his self-production, and his presentation of himself as a finished object, actualize the disruptive and dysfunctional project of deception.

[10] Anthony Giddens, *Modernity and Self-Identity: Self and Society in the Late Modern Age* (Cambridge: Polity Press, 1991), 7.

[11] Étienne Brunet, *Le Vocabulaire de Zola* (Geneva and Paris: Slatkine-Champion, 1985), i, isolates 'pincer' as one of three verbs (the others are 'rigoler' and 'croquer') occurring with high relative frequency in *L'Assommoir*.

[12] The topos of quaint, compelling and nauseating odours, and the ambivalence these induce bring to mind Baudelaire's 'Spleen' poem 'Pluviôse, irrité contre la ville entière' with its pack of enticing and filthy cards 'plein de *sales parfums*'.

[13] *L'Assommoir* is the story of the flawed body and this is emblematized by Gervaise's lame leg. The play of Zola's onomastics ensures that she *becomes* the defective leg (La Banban). The fracturing of the body brings with it the atomizing of identity. Other nicknames and sobriquets identify characters in terms of significant body-parts or body functions – Bec-Salé, Bois-sans-soif. The body (or some discrete part thereof) narrativizes family history, registers moral position, or indicates emotional reaction (Gervaise's joy at obtaining her own laundry-shop alleviates her lameness). The everyday (and often humorous) narrative of bodily deficiencies and symptoms in *L'Assommoir* ranges from colds and indigestion to vomiting, sciatica, and noisy 'plumbing'.

[14] Degas's painting of the two laundresses ('Les Repasseuses', c.1884) is a study of the body under strain. The lowering of the head and partial obscuring of the face of the figure on the right direct the viewer's attention from the straining back and shoulders of the laundress, down the extended arms to the doubled-over hands as they push down determinedly on uncooperative fabric. Zola's powerful and focused description of the exertions of the women at the washhouse in the opening chapter anticipates Degas's style and subject-matter: 'Des fumées montaient de certains coins, s'étalant, noyant les fonds d'un voile bleuâtre [...] il y avait des files de femmes, les bras nus jusqu'aux épaules, le cou nu, les jupes raccourcies [...]. Elles tapaient furieusement, riaient, se renversaient pour crier un mot dans le vacarme, se penchaient au fond de leurs baquets' (p. 386).

[15] The text abounds with examples of clothes and bodies pressured, straining, fragilized: '[...] sa gorge puissante de belle fille crevait sa chemise, ses épaules faisaient craquer les courtes manches' (p. 504); ' "Donne ta peau que j'en fasse des torchons" ' (p. 399); 'Elle entra, [...] grasse à crever son corsage' (p. 581); '[...] le corsage, trop étroit, tirait sur les boutonnières, la

coupait aux épaules; et la jupe, taillée en fourreau, lui serrait si fort les cuisses, qu'elle devait marcher à tout petits pas' (p. 439).

[16] The dystopic vision of the body that prevails in this novel is at times alleviated by idealized representation (in the heroic body of the blacksmith). This signals not so much a lapse into comforting dualism, but an attempt to locate the body as the point of intersection of opposites, reinforcing the idea of the body narrativized *in extremis*.

[17] The topos of viewing and framing is reaffirmed when Gervaise first visits Coupeau at Sainte-Anne: ' "Ah! mon Dieu! quelle vue!" ' (p. 782); and on her return the next evening when his condition has worsened: 'Dire que, la veille au soir, chez les Boche, on l'accusait d'avoir exagéré le *tableau*' (p. 786).

[18] This seems to prefigure existentialist images of the objectified body, cf. J.-P. Sartre, *La Nausée* (Paris: Gallimard, 1938), where Roquentin is aware of the 'paquet tiède' (a card-player next to him), while he notes of his own head that it is 'toute molle, élastique', and continues: 'on dirait qu'elle est juste posée sur mon cou; si je la tourne, je vais la laisser tomber' (p. 36).

[19] Ihab Hassan, *The Dismemberment of Orpheus: Towards a Postmodern Literature* (New York: Oxford University Press, 1971), considers the development of the literature of silence to its high point in postmodernism through the work of Sade, Kafka, Beckett and Hemingway.

[20] Peter Brooks, *Bodywork* (Cambridge, MA, and London: Harvard University Press, 1993) studies the body as signifying process in English and French literature (including *Nana*), in painting and in photography. Brooks raises questions of spectatorship, visual curiosity and 'body-writing' central to the present study.

[21] See J.-P. Sartre, *L'Être et le néant: essai d'ontologie phénoménologique* (Paris: Gallimard, 1943) for the conceptual elaboration of the ideas explored in *La Nausée*.

[22] Klein's theory of 'part-objects' is discussed by Brooks, *Bodywork*, 19.

[23] Ibid., 93.

[24] The separateness and inwardness of the *tableau* are enhanced by the sense of privacy which defines the scene. While Goujet's entrance disrupts Gervaise's intimate activity, it also brings into focus the notion of privacy and a condition largely obscured in a narrative which so relentlessly focuses the collective sphere (that of work, family, couple, leisure).

[25] Hamon, *Le Personnel du roman*, 84.

[26] Ibid., 79.

[27] Tanner, *Adultery*, 354.

[28] Brooks, *Bodywork*, 138–139.

Hitting the Mine: Modulations in Narrative Voice in Proust's *A la recherche du temps perdu*

ROBIN MACKENZIE

> Considerations of voice have invariably been understood as expressions of identity, and thus subordinate to it. Voice has thus always led to claims of formal unity for the immense *Recherche* through recourse to identity. (Margaret Gray)[1]

> Elle [l'aventure] est racontée du point de vue de l'expérience et de la sagesse, elle est écoutée du point de vue de l'ordre. [...] Le narrateur opère sur l'événement humain ce travail que, selon Meyerbeer, le savant du 19ᵉ siècle a opéré sur le fait scientifique: il réduit le divers à l'identique. (Jean-Paul Sartre)[2]

Narrative voice has traditionally been associated with the twin themes of identity and authority. Stylistic unity and the single identifiable point of view are read as an indication, even a guarantee, of the fundamental unity and coherence of a narrating self. Proust's narrator formulates this idea, albeit in slightly different terms:

> [Le style] est la révélation, qui serait impossible par des moyens directs et conscients, de la différence qualitative qu'il y a dans la façon dont nous apparaît le monde [...] Par l'art seulement nous pouvons sortir de nous, savoir ce que voit un autre de cet univers qui n'est pas le même que le nôtre. (iv 474)[3]

Style is the expression of vision, and vision is specific to the individual. This is as clear a formulation as one could want of the indissoluble link between voice and interiority, style and the self.

There has been much speculation about the temporal position (or positions) of the narrator of *A la recherche*. Muller, in an influential study, parsed the narrative voice into seven instances, differentiated by style and/or by temporal position in relation to the events of the narrative (and the younger self who is protagonist of that narrative).[4] Genette, however, has taken issue with Muller's complex but not perhaps entirely convincing schema, arguing that there is no evidence to suggest that the act of narration is anything other than instantaneous.[5]

The exact temporal position(s) of the narrator in relation to his narrative is less important for my argument than the possible implications of retrospective narration. Sartre, in the second epigraph to this article, indicates in broad outline some of the assumptions underlying the use of the retrospective narrator in nineteenth-century fiction. This retrospective narrator occupies a position of intellectual authority: he interprets, explains and passes judgement on character and event, and acts as the reader's guide and mentor. Sartre is in fact referring to the work of Maupassant, an author in most ways entirely unlike Proust. But the point holds good – to some extent at least – for the retrospective narrator in *A la recherche*, who frequently appears (and on occasion claims) to be narrating from a position of understanding and insight about himself (his past self). At one point in *La Prisonnière*, for example, we find the narrator claiming knowledge of 'la vérité subjective' of his younger self: '[...] les images qui me faisaient agir [...] étaient à ce moment-là fort obscures; je ne connaissais qu'imparfaitement la nature suivant laquelle j'agissais; aujourd'hui j'en connais clairement la vérité subjective' (iii 850). This belief in the possibility of discovering 'la vérité subjective' underlies the *moraliste* discourse adopted at times by the narrator. Malcolm Bowie contrasts this discourse with a more discontinuous, disrupted mode of writing which – in its syntactical structures and its lexical textures – seems to show traces of unconscious activity and desire.[6] The claims to lucidity and epistemological authority implicit in the *moraliste* position are of course incompatible with the psychoanalytic model of interpretation favoured by Bowie. The psychoanalytic critic rejects the epistemological claims of introspection, and sees discourse as a site of semantic conflict between the conscious and the unconscious mind.

The assumptions about the unity of the self and the authority of the narrator in *A la recherche* have been challenged by a number of critics. The notion of the 'moi multiple' was central to the work of as early a critic as Jacques Rivière; indeed it formed the basis of his comparison of Proust and Freud as analysts of 'le cœur humain'.[7]

More recently, the authority of the retrospective narrator has been under assault since the emergence of *la nouvelle critique*, with its propensity for reading *A la recherche* against the grain of the narrator's explanations and 'lois générales'.

Several critical approaches have proved particularly fruitful for the thematics of voice and identity. First there are the stylisticians, in particular Jean Milly, whose work on the Proustian sentence isolates two major 'phrases-types' in *A la recherche*.[8] This kind of attention to the detail of Proust's text tends to challenge received ideas of stylistic homogeneity, and (as we have seen) if the style – the narrative voice – is not unified, then the unity of the self behind the voice is called into question.

Another intellectual tendency which combines close attention to the detail of the text with an interest in broad questions of identity and authority is psychoanalysis. Lejeune, Weber and Doubrovsky point out condensations and displacements of meaning in the text, and trace their implications for the mapping of the narrator's psyche.[9] Fractures and fissures in the text suggest that the identity of the narrator is similarly fragmented, that unconscious desire and affect emerge at key moments to disrupt the apparent unity of the narrator's self.

An interesting and potentially very fertile approach which to some extent bridges the divide between stylisticians and psychoanalysts is that of A. Piette, in an as yet unpublished thesis on prose rhymes in Proust, Joyce and Beckett.[10] Piette identifies and comments on various instances of rhyme and phonetic recurrence in passages of *A la recherche*, reading them as traces of affect (especially anxious affect) which resurface in the narrator's prose as a result of involuntary memory. Piette is careful to eschew psychoanalytic vocabulary or forms of explanation; but the mechanics of his analysis, the ways in which he relates textual patterns to (putative) psychic events, show striking parallels to psychoanalytic modes of reading.

Perhaps the most subversive and searching close reader of all is Paul de Man, whose chapter on Proust in *Allegories of Reading* lays bare the aporia, the unresolvable contradictions, which are generated by the figurative language of *A la recherche*.[11] De Man's analysis implies that the narrator can never be 'in control' of his meaning, that the structures of metaphor and figuration necessarily subvert his (naïve but inescapable) urge to articulate an internally coherent set of meanings. The narrator's rhetoric – his voice – is therefore riven with contradictory meanings: no single unified self can be inferred.

These recent explorations of the problematics of voice in *A la recherche* provide the backdrop for this article, which is however much more modest in its aims. It is an analysis of one particular passage which seems to me to shed some light on the complexity of narrative voice, its shifts and inflections, in Proust's novel. The episode in question occurs in the early part of *La Prisonnière*, before the Verdurin soirée, at the start of what Milly calls the 'deuxième journée'.[12] Marcel wakes up to find that the weather has changed completely since the previous day, and his resolve to begin work has correspondingly vanished. There follows a long passage, in the course of which the narrator traces (and comments upon) the movements of Marcel's consciousness – perceptions, memories, imaginings – as he meditates upon the meteorological conditions outside his window. The passage opens on a familiar note, with Marcel's oft-expressed resolve to start writing:

> J'avais promis à Albertine que si je ne sortais pas avec elle, je me mettrais au travail. Mais le lendemain comme si, profitant de nos sommeils, la maison avait miraculeusement voyagé, je m'éveillais par un temps différent, sous un autre climat. On ne travaille pas au moment où on débarque dans un pays nouveau, aux conditions duquel il faut s'adapter. Or chaque jour était pour moi un pays différent. (iii 589)

The ordering activity of the narrator is evident straight away: the principal theme of the passage (work, or the opposition between the resolve to work and the pleasure of procrastination) is introduced in the first sentence, and the main metaphor (of the 'navigation') appears in the second. The rhetorical form, or agenda, is likewise presented from the start: Marcel is concerned to find reasons (or pretexts) to justify his idleness, his reluctance to embark on the project he has set himself. He is desperately trying to persuade himself (and us) that his indolence and procrastination are justified, indeed beneficial and necessary. This is a rhetoric of evasion, of self-deception. The narrator's silence, the absence of any comment or judgement, creates an effect of gentle, but unmistakable, irony. 'On ne travaille pas au moment où on débarque dans un pays nouveau': the ironic gap between Marcel and the narrator is perceptible in the extremely questionable equation of the new day with a newly discovered land, which serves as a premise of Marcel's argument.

The 'navigation' metaphor suggests that Marcel's passivity, his 'paresse', is actually a form of adventurous activity, that his immobility is purposeful movement, an exploration of (perhaps uncharted) regions. This metaphorical slippage is compounded by the pronominal shift, from 'je' to the impersonal 'on': the observation is couched in the form of a maxim, a 'loi générale' of human behaviour, thus lending a spurious universality to Marcel's propensity for procrastination. He is dressing up, or disguising, a personal weakness as a general law of human behaviour, thus sidestepping any responsibility for his inability to work. Gustavo Pellon has argued that such pronominal shifts, from 'je' to 'nous' or 'on', are in fact akin to Albertine's use of anacoluthon, which Marcel interprets as an index of her mendacity: 'Surprisingly, throughout *A la recherche du temps perdu*, the narrator himself makes widespread use of Albertine's mode of evading the truth. [...] "On" and "nous" act as mediators from his subjective experience to a deceptive objectivity'.[13] Here, however, it is Marcel rather than the retrospective narrator whose evasions are disguised in pseudo-objective form. The self-deceiving discourse of the protagonist seems to invite an ironic reading, though there is no overt ironic comment by the narrator. However, as description of the varying weather conditions takes over from argument, the tone becomes more lyrical, and the implicit ironies begin to fade: 'Tantôt, par des jours irrémédiablement mauvais, disait-on, rien que la résidence dans la maison située au milieu d'une pluie égale et continue avait la glissante douceur, le silence calmant, l'intérêt d'une navigation' (iii 589). The stylistic shift here is quite noticeable: a more lyrical voice emerges, characterized by conspicuous phonetic patterning and a profusion of sensory notations. The sound echoes and repetitions are particularly striking: the recurrent 'u', 'eu' and 'i' sounds in 'située au milieu d'une pluie égale et continue'; the sibilants, liquids and nasals in 'la glissante douceur, le silence calmant'. This is dense, poetic prose: its harmonious quality, its aesthetic appeal, lull the reader into a predominantly sensuous response and distract attention from Marcel's (sophistical) argument.

Nevertheless, the 'jours irrémédiablement mauvais' sentence quoted above, and the following one ('une autre fois [...] tronc d'arbre'), still play a definable role in that argument: they function as examples, illustrations of the exciting variety of weather conditions which distract Marcel from his writing. But as the passage continues, the meteorological description seems increasingly to be there for its own sake. The following sentence seems redundant from the point of view of the argument; the descriptive voice is beginning to overwhelm the discursive:

> D'autres fois encore, aux premières cloches d'un couvent voisin, rares comme les dévotes matinales, blanchissant à peine le ciel sombre de leurs giboulées incertaines que fondait et dispersait le vent tiède, j'avais discerné une de ces journées tempétueuses, désordonnées et douces, où les toits, mouillés d'une ondée intermittente que sèche un souffle ou un rayon, laissent glisser en roucoulant une goutte de pluie et, en attendant que le vent recommence à tourner, lissent au soleil momentané qui les irise, leurs ardoises gorge-de-pigeon. (iii 590)

This sentence is as good an example of Proust's descriptive virtuosity as many passages in 'Combray', with its complex hypotactic structure, its series of surprising and slightly dissonant adjectives, its striking phonetic patterning, its wealth of sensuous detail. The narrator is by this stage largely caught up in Marcel's enthusiasm; critical distance has been overcome by poetic afflatus, any demonstrable trace of irony has disappeared. This is a mode of writing associated – both syntactically and lexically – with involuntary memory. Syntactically, we see the narrator's endeavour to seize the totality of the impression in a complex architecture of phrases and clauses, a procedure which John Porter Houston identifies as characteristic of Proust's writing: 'Proust's sentence structure is intended to bind together the most varied material into new wholes, new total impressions, where the accessory is as essentiel as the main object of contemplation'.[14] Lexically, the sentence not only displays a vivid, predominantly concrete, vocabulary; the words are also charged with intratextual associations, echoes of previous passages in the novel. The clearest echoes are of an earlier evocation of the Parisian cityscape in *Le Côté de Guermantes*:

> Un matin, après quelques semaines de giboulées et de tempêtes, j'entendis dans ma cheminée – au lieu du vent informe, élastique et sombre qui me secouait de l'envie d'aller au bord de la mer – le roucoulement des pigeons qui nichaient dans la muraille: irisé, imprévu comme une première jacinthe. (ii 440–441)

Here we find a series, a cluster of elements which recur in our text:

'giboulées', 'tempêtes', 'roucoulement', 'irisé'. There is of course no suggestion that Marcel in *La Prisonnière* is consciously remembering the earlier episode; but the structural similarities, the lexical affinities between the two texts suggest that there may be some unarticulated, subliminal memory trace – at what level of awareness it is difficult to judge – in the mind of the narrator.

The traces of involuntary memory – or of its textual correlatives – in the lyrical, descriptive voice bring about a clear, if subtle, shift in our attitude towards Marcel's 'paresse'. In the opening sentences, we are clearly supposed to be critical, if indulgently so, of Marcel's procrastination and the rather far-fetched excuses he finds to justify it. But as the sensuous richness and beauty of the meteorological evocations, and their echoes of other passages, begin to affect us, it begins to seem as though Marcel's *rêveries*, his apparent time-wasting, may not be so futile and unprofitable after all. These descriptions, bearing all the hallmarks of a style informed by privileged moments of perception and involuntary memory, irresistibly suggest that Marcel's apparently aimless musings and observations as he looks out of his Parisian window provide precious reserves for the book he plans to write, and perhaps form part of the 'livre intérieur de signes inconnus' which he must decipher if he is to convert experience into art. Beyond the procrastination, beyond the ironic voice of the narrator, there is a creative impulse, an entelechy, informing Marcel's 'paresse'. Like the poet in 'Expostulation and Reply', he can feed that mind of his 'in a wise passiveness'.[15]

The passage continues with a sequence of syntactical segments – we can hardly talk of sentences, as they have no main clause – which stand in parallel to the sentence we have just examined, picking up on the phrase 'une de ces journées'. However, although there is a syntactical parallelism, the semantic focus shifts from a description of external conditions to an account of the feelings and behaviour of a series of hypothetical types: 'le paresseux', the truant schoolboy, the man preparing for a potentially fatal duel. Pellon's remarks about a similar rhetorical move in the dream passage in *La Prisonnière* are relevant here:

> At times he [the narrator] shifts into an 'objective' third person, 'le dormeur', thereby extending his statements to human nature in general. [...] Despite continued use of anacoluthon in an attempt to lend an aura of universality to his experiences, the narrator sinks deeper and deeper

into anecdote. The description of 'the sleeper' [...] is too subjective to permit the reader's identification.[16]

Anecdote certainly looms large in the account of the hypothetical duellist's actions and feelings – his thoughts on life and death, work and idleness, are given in detail, the focalization is internal, there is even a short passage of direct speech: 'Si je pouvais ne pas être tué, se dit-il, comme je me mettrais au travail à la minute même, et aussi comme je m'amuserais!' (iii 590). The immediacy of this, the lack of distance between narrator and the hypothetical figure of the duellist, inevitably lead the reader to identify that figure with the narrator (or Marcel): the duellist comes to seem a third-person disguise for the first-person narrator. So far, Pellon's analysis seems to apply. The rhetoric of 'objectivity' is further heightened by the generalizing comments, the maxims, which appear with some frequency at this point:

> La vie a pris en effet soudain, à ses yeux, une valeur plus grande, parce qu'il met dans la vie tout ce qu'il semble qu'elle peut donner [...] Il la voit selon son désir, non telle que son expérience lui a appris qu'il savait la rendre. (iii 590)

> Mais il retrouve les mêmes obstacles aux plaisirs, aux excursions, aux voyages, à tout ce dont il avait craint un instant d'être à jamais dépouillé par la mort; il suffit pour cela de la vie. (iii 591)

However, the generalizing rhetoric here is not, as at the start of the passage, a rhetoric of self-deception. The narrator here speaks without any perceptible trace of irony, claiming a position of understanding, of psychological insight: he sees through the self-deception of the other. This is the narrator as traditional *moraliste*: lucid, authoritative, the voice of intellectual mastery.

The impression of lucidity is, if anything, heightened in the next paragraph, when the first-person narrator humorously acknowledges the identity between himself and the hypothetical duellist: 'Je faisais comme lui, et comme j'avais toujours fait depuis ma vieille résolution de me mettre à écrire' (iii 591). The distance here between narrator and Marcel is considerable: this is the disabused voice of experience, explicitly debunking the illusions of his younger self. But this lucid, authoritative voice – whose presence in *A la recherche* it would be perverse to ignore or deny – is soon displaced again by the lyrical mode we saw in the earlier descriptive passages:

> Mais je n'y étais plus le même sous un ciel sans nuages; le son doré des cloches ne contenait pas seulement, comme le miel, de la lumière, mais la sensation de la lumière (et aussi la saveur fade des confitures, parce qu'à Combray il s'était souvent attardé comme une guêpe sur notre table desservie). Par ce jour de soleil éclatant, rester tout le jour les yeux clos, c'était chose permise, usitée, salubre, plaisante, saisonnière, comme tenir ses persiennes fermées contre la chaleur. (iii 591)

The salient features of the lyrical voice – sound patterns, sensuous details, vivid metaphors, adjectival series – are all in evidence here. Indeed, some of them are developed further than in the earlier passages: the phonetic repetitions are if anything more dense, and we find traces of the 'anagrams' which Milly identified as characteristic of the 'style Bergotte'. ('comme le *miel*, de la *lumière*').[17] The phonetic patterning foregrounds certain phrases – 'le son doré', 'miel/lumière', 'la saveur fade' – which are reminiscent of Combray scenes (and the link with Combray is, unlike in earlier passages, explicitly mentioned here). The 'son doré' in particular is evocative of the church in Combray: 'On avait devant soi le clocher qui, doré et cuit lui-même comme une plus grande brioche bénie, avec des écailles et des égouttements gommeux de soleil, piquait sa pointe aigüe dans le ciel bleu' (i 64). The interplay of metaphor and metonymy between the two texts is interesting: in the Combray text, it is the steeple which is 'doré', whereas in the later passage it is the *sound* of bells. This synaesthetic transfer of epithets could be read as reproducing on a textual level the way the original data of perception are transformed and recombined in the memory. There are of course other passages in 'Combray' which prefigure our text: the network of lexical correspondences and echoes is dense. The description of the chapel of Gilbert le Mauvais is an example: '[...] la chapelle où [Mme de Guermantes] suivait la messe était celle de Gilbert le Mauvais, sous les plates tombes de laquelle, dorées et distendues comme des alvéoles de miel, reposaient les anciens comtes de Brabant' (i 172). The connections here are particularly close: the association of 'doré(es)' and 'miel' is a metaphoric prefiguration of the anagrammatic link ('miel' and 'lumière') we found in the description in *La Prisonnière*. This offers further support for my earlier contention that the lyrical, descriptive voice is imbued with textual traces (or correlatives) of involuntary memory: the explicit link with Combray made by the narrator is reinforced by a series of lexical and metaphoric echoes, verbal translations of the analogies between past and present moments which are the substance of 'la mémoire involontaire'.

Reminiscences of Combray surround the text like a corona at this point; but a more powerful, or at any rate traumatic, resurgence of past perceptions is to follow. The Combray connection, placed in parentheses in the text, is articulated by the narrator, and may or may not be fully present in Marcel's consciousness, whereas the following link, between Paris and Balbec, clearly occurs to Marcel himself. From then on, the resurgence of Albertine's image in his mind is only a matter of time.

Ominously, the first mention of Albertine is rather complacent in tone, with Marcel (the narrator's voice recedes behind that of Marcel at this point) congratulating himself on his intimacy with Albertine: 'Combien je possédais plus Albertine aujourd'hui!' The text veers off into description and evocation again, culminating in the return of the 'navigation' metaphor, which this time refers to memory rather than *rêverie*:

> Remontant paresseusement de jour en jour comme sur une barque, et voyant apparaître devant moi toujours de nouveaux souvenirs enchantés, que je ne choisissais pas, qui l'instant d'avant m'étaient invisibles et que ma mémoire me présentait l'un après l'autre sans que je pusse les choisir, je poursuivais paresseusement sur ces espaces unis ma promenade au soleil. (iii 591–592)

The idyllic image of the sea journey, and the lulling sounds and rhythms, arouse in the reader deceptive feelings of security, reflecting Marcel's unsuspecting complacency. But what we could perhaps call the ruse of recollection is operating here: an unconscious current of memories and associations seems to be pushing Marcel's thoughts back towards Albertine. When Balbec is evoked for the second time, the tone of the passage changes abruptly:

> Ces concerts matinaux de Balbec n'étaient pas anciens. Et pourtant à ce moment relativement rapproché, je me souciais peu d'Albertine. Même les tout premiers jours de l'arrivée, je n'avais pas connu sa présence à Balbec. Par qui donc l'avais-je apprise? Ah! oui, par Aimé. Il faisait un beau soleil comme celui-ci. Brave Aimé. Il était content de me revoir. (iii 592)

The distance between Marcel and the narrator has well nigh disappeared at this point: the movement of Marcel's thoughts is recorded more or less directly, as the passage shifts into something very close to interior monologue. The style changes correspondingly: sentences are short and disconnected; there is asyndeton within as well as between sentences; questions appear which are not rhetorical, but express Marcel's genuine uncertainty and anxiety; interjected particles ('Ah! oui', 'Par qui *donc* [...]') heighten the impression of immediacy given by the interior monologue. And lexically, we find the rather edgy, obsessive repetition of words and short phrases which Bowie has noted in other passages in *La Prisonnière*.[18]

These lexical repetitions are primarily stylistic, or mimetic, in that they convey the impression of an obsessive and anxious voice. On another textual level, however, they can also be read as thematically revealing. The phonetic/lexical series of 'Aimé', 'aime', 'aimer', followed later by 'amie', 'Aimé', perhaps foregrounds those themes of love and jealousy (of the hypothetical 'amie') which are the focus of Marcel's anxiety here. Likewise, the repetition of 'personne' in the following passage carries some semantic charge: 'Mais j'avais beau me le demander, la personne qui se posait la question et la personne qui pouvait offrir le souvenir n'étaient, hélas, qu'une seule et même personne, moi, qui se dédoublait momentanément, mais sans rien s'ajouter' (iii 592). This repetition – insistent enough to invite analysis – could be taken as underlining the narrator's contention that Marcel is in a sense 'one and the same', a subject identical to himself, containing no potentially productive duality. The doubling, or splitting, of the self into the one who questions and the one who should (but in fact cannot) answer, adds nothing: there is no access to some other level or 'scene' of subjectivity which might bring surer knowledge of the Other (Albertine), and hence reassurance to Marcel. The other conspicuous repetition is mimetic in a more precise sense, in that it records an expression which presumably haunts and torments Marcel's consciousness (rather than the narrator's), and acts as a leitmotif of his jealousy:

> Il m'avait dit qu'il l'avait rencontrée, qu'il lui avait trouvé mauvais genre. Qu'avait-il voulu dire par mauvais genre? J'avais compris genre vulgaire, parce que pour le contredire d'avance j'avais déclaré qu'elle avait de la distinction. Mais non, peut-être avait-il voulu dire genre gomorrhéen. (iii 592)

It is the ambiguity, the semantic indeterminacy of 'mauvais genre', which triggers Marcel's access of jealousy here, bringing a mass of submerged doubts and suspicions to the surface of consciousness. Just before this, the voice of the retrospective narrator re-emerges, as the navigation metaphor makes its final, climactic appearance: '[...] ma pensée, qui jusqu'ici avait navigué en souriant sur ces eaux bienheureuses éclatait soudain, comme si elle eût heurté une mine invisible et dangereuse, insidieusement posée à ce point de ma mémoire' (iii 592). This is a powerful image, with profound implications. The 'mine' – submerged, menacing, unexpected – connects with a powerful current of imagery in *A la recherche*: metaphors of depth and surface, of re-emergence from the depths, often occur in the narrator's mapping(s) of the mind, especially of its unconscious/subconscious strata from which emerge dreams, involuntary memory, associations of ideas and images triggered by certain impressions. Key episodes in which metaphors of depth and surface appear are abundant: the madeleine, the trees at Hudimesnil, the 'intermittence' dream in *Sodome et Gomorrhe*, the 'livre intérieur' evoked in *Le Temps retrouvé*.[19] The 'mine' – an apparently innocuous memory reactivated by the jealous mind – originates, like the above, in the unconscious; it differs from all but the 'intermittence' dream, however, in triggering traumatic rather than euphoric feelings. In this respect, the closest parallels to the 'ruse of recollection' as it works here are probably to be found in the dream passages:

> [...] on atteint les premiers antres où les 'autosuggestions' préparent comme des sorcières l'infernal fricot des maladies imaginaires ou de la recrudescence des maladies nerveuses, et guettent l'heure où les crises remontées pendant le sommeil inconscient se déclencheront assez fortes pour le faire cesser. (ii 385)

After the clinching metaphor of the 'mine', the disjunctive, repetitive voice reasserts itself. Hypotheses multiply, as Marcel's jealousy begins to take over the text. There is a move from the semantic investigations triggered by 'mauvais genre' to imaginative (re-)construction: 'Né d'un soupçon nouveau, l'accès de jalousie dont je souffrais était nouveau aussi, ou plutôt il n'était que le prolongement, l'extension de ce soupçon; il avait le même théâtre, qui n'était plus Montjouvain, mais la route où Aimé avait rencontré Albertine' (iii 592). The hypothetical scenario solidifies into pseudo-certainty, 'peut-être' shifting imperceptibly into 'sans doute':

> C'était peut-être une certaine Elisabeth, ou bien peut-être ces deux jeunes filles qu'Albertine avait regardées dans la glace au Casino, quand elle n'avait pas l'air de les voir. Elle avait sans doute des relations avec elle, et d'ailleurs aussi avec Esther, la cousine de Bloch. (iii 593)

This marginally resembles *style indirect libre,* with Marcel's perspective predominating: the retrospective narrator, in his persona of *moraliste* formulating general laws of feeling and behaviour, is aware of the unreliability, the fictionality of the jealous protagonist's speculations: '[...] le même jaloux n'hésite pas à former des soupçons atroces à propos de faits innocents, à condition, devant la première preuve qu'on lui apporte, de se refuser à l'évidence' (iii 593). This is virtually an admission that the scenarios recounted are in fact fabrications, inventions, and that Marcel has no means of access to the truth of Albertine's feelings, desires or even actions. The metaphoric tone of the passage has changed by this point, with the traditionally 'poetic' metaphor of the voyage, the navigation, giving way to metaphors drawn from medicine, couched in technical language:

> On arrive, sous la forme de soupçons, à absorber journellement à doses énormes cette même idée qu'on est trompée, de laquelle une quantité très faible pourrait être mortelle, inoculée par la piqûre d'une parole déchirante. [...] D'ailleurs, l'amour est un mal inguérissable, comme ces diathèses où le rhumatisme ne laisse quelque répit que pour faire place à des migraines épileptiformes. (iii 593)

This of course reiterates the predominant metaphor of love in *A la recherche* – love as malady – though with a new twist, since inoculation (which one would normally associate with healing) is here potentially fatal, whereas much larger quantities of the same dangerous idea can be absorbed if self-generated, as it were. It is the incursion from outside which is so especially traumatic.

The transition from lyrical voice to jealous voice, then, is signalled by the 'mine' metaphor, but initiated largely by the phrase 'mauvais genre', with its semantic (and referential) indeterminacy. The 'mine invisible et dangereuse' is a phenomenon of verbal memory, which is shown to have the power to generate large amounts of anxiety; this anxiety in turn issues forth in hypothesis and speculation. There are frequent instances, especially in the later sections of *A la recherche,* of the intimate links between memory, affect and language: language frequently acts as a channel, a conduit, along which emotionally charged memories pass.

A particularly interesting case is provided by the Buttes Chaumont. In *Albertine disparue*, after the death of Albertine, Marcel is assailed by memories of her: it seems as though everything – every object, every perception – carries a trace of the dead woman. As Marcel is reading the newspaper, seemingly inoffensive names set off chains of associations which – unlike the predominantly sensory associations which lead to the phrase 'mauvais genre' in our passage – work through verbal and semantic connections:

> Le titre de la mélodie de Fauré *le Secret* m'avait mené au *Secret du Roi* du Duc de Broglie, le nom de Broglie à celui de Chaumont. Ou bien le mot de Vendredi Saint m'avait fait penser au Golgotha, le Golgotha à l'étymologie de ce mot qui, lui, paraît l'équivalent de *Calvus mons*, Chaumont. Mais par quelque chemin que je fusse arrivé à Chaumont, à ce moment j'étais frappé d'un choc si cruel que dès lors je pensais bien plus à me garer contre la douleur qu'à lui demander des souvenirs. Quelques instants après le choc, l'intelligence qui, comme le bruit du tonnerre, ne voyage pas aussi vite, m'en apportait la raison. (iv 123)

The ruse of recollection is working here through verbal repetition (with variation), cultural allusion, etymology; and as in the 'mine' passage, it causes trauma ('un choc si cruel') when it reaches its destination, as it were. It is clear here – even more so than in the 'mine' passage – that we are dealing with a mental operation, and quite a complex one, which takes place to a great extent below the threshold of consciousness. These apparently random, aimless movements of associative thought have in fact a definite *telos:* emotionally charged memories of Albertine which will trigger Marcel's jealousy.

Of course, words which arouse Marcel's suspicions are not always the product of memory. In *La Prisonnière*, when Albertine is still living with Marcel, he frequently picks up on phrases, verbal tics, which she uses and which seem to him to be potentially revelatory. An example, typical in its banality, is Albertine's habit of asking 'C'est vrai?' on any and every occasion, which Marcel suspects is a residue, a precipitate, of the frequent compliments addressed to Albertine in the past.[20] As with 'mauvais genre' in the 'mine' passage, Marcel's jealous imagination constructs a complete scenario around an apparently banal and throw-away phrase.

This capacity of words to haunt, to re-echo in the mind, is of interest to us here primarily in relation to narrative voice, the narrator's discourse. This discourse is of course the product of recollection and reordering of phenomena: it has a different discursive and enunciatory status from the utterances of characters in the novel. But we can nevertheless look to the dialogue in *A la recherche*, and the narrator's comments on it, for the occasional clue, or insight, into the workings of the narrator's rhetoric – especially in those passages where the calm mastery of the retrospective narrator is replaced by a more anxious, disjointed, 'spoken' style.

What implications, then, do the modulations in narrative voice which we have traced in the 'mine' passage hold for those themes of identity, memory and interpretative authority which loom so large in *A la recherche*?

The simplest and most obvious observation to be made is that the narrative voice in the passage shows clear shifts of tone, considerable stylistic variation. The ironic voice of the opening sentences gives way to a more lyrical tone, which is superseded by a generalizing, *moraliste* narrative persona, which in turn gives way to a more disjointed, oral style. These shifts, often quite dramatic, suggest that the narrator's theories of style as vision, as the relatively unified expression of a unified self, do not really do justice to the complexity of the narrator's discourse. Stylisticians, especially more recent ones like Milly, have of course been acutely aware of this. The self recreated in memory and expressed in language would seem to be much more shifting and protean than a simple 'style as vision' equation might suggest. Together with this stylistic variation in the narrative voice, we also find considerable variation in the degree of distance between narrator and protagonist. The narrator is not always in evidence in the text, at least not overtly and explicitly. At times his voice is clearly perceptible, in the generalizing *moraliste* tenor of the descriptions of the duellist; at times we sense an implicit, unstated irony, as in the opening section of the passage; elsewhere the narrator seems to efface himself before the thoughts, perceptions and rêveries of Marcel, as we see at times in the descriptive passages, and more strikingly in the virtual interior monologue of Marcel the jealous lover. It is certainly the case that the kind of narrator whom Sartre sees as typical of the nineteenth-century novel – the voice of wisdom and understanding, the lucid and trustworthy interpreter of the action he relates – does appear in *A la recherche*; but this retrospective lucidity, this interpretative mastery, is not always the dominant note, and there are indications that what Genette calls 'l'extase de la réminiscence' does at times – indeed quite frequently – overwhelm the ostensibly controlling metalanguage of the narrator.[21]

This brings us to what is perhaps the crux of the matter: the interaction of memory and discourse, the ways in which the narrator's voice is modified under the pressure of different modes of reminiscence. There is obviously an element of interpretation, of inference, here, as we can reconstruct modes of memory only by an examination of textual signs, of the words on the page. However, it would seem plausible to argue that those passages in the text which bear verbal traces of involuntary memory (the description of weather conditions, with their textual echoes of Combray) and of other more traumatic forms of affective memory (the recollection of Aimé's words about Albertine) are characterized by an eclipse, an effacement, of the commenting voice of the retrospective narrator. His authoritative discourse is challenged, and sometimes overwhelmed, by the immediacy and emotional impact of certain forms of memory. This in fact concurs with some of the narrator's descriptions in *Le Temps retrouvé* of the effects of involuntary memory on the present-tense self:

> [...] ces résurrections du passé, dans la seconde qu'elles durent, sont si totales qu'elles n'obligent pas seulement nos yeux à cesser de voir la chambre qui est près d'eux. [...] Elles forcent [...] notre personne toute entière [...] à trébucher entre eux [les lieux lointains] et les lieux présents, dans l'étourdissement d'une incertitude pareille à celle qu'on éprouve parfois devant une vision ineffable, au moment de s'endormir. (iv 454)

The 'mine invisible et dangereuse', the re-emergence of Aimé's words into Marcel's consciousness, is certainly an involuntary memory of a sort. But our passage indicates that the distinction which the narrator makes between voluntary and involuntary memory is rather too neat, too exclusive, to do justice to the complexities of reminiscence as described and enacted in *A la recherche*. What we see in the 'mine' passage is the working of a form of associative memory: one image triggers another, apparently at random; but this seemingly random process moves unerringly towards a memory charged with traumatic force, which explodes into consciousness. The obvious hypothesis is that some hidden, unconscious current of desire or obsession is operating in Marcel's thought processes. The effects of this are very different from the euphoric experience of involuntary memory, triggered by the similarity of two sensations, but equally so from the willed, conscious recollection of past impressions which constitutes voluntary memory. Moreover, unlike the main occurrences of involuntary memory in the novel, the associative process in the 'mine' passage culminates in the recollection of a phrase ('mauvais genre'). Words – heard, read or remembered – have a particular capacity to haunt and torment Marcel in *La Prisonnière* and *Albertine disparue*. These words and phrases – Albertine's 'C'est vrai?', the name 'Buttes Chaumont' – are often relatively banal, stylistically unexceptional, and quite unlike the vivid or unusual lexis of many of the descriptive passages in the novel. But they do bear witness to the affective impact of language on consciousness, and carry potentially far-reaching implications for the narrator's style and discourse. The obsessive recurrence of words in Marcel's mind has as a textual correlative the lexical repetitiveness which Bowie has identified as a salient feature of the style of many passages in *La Prisonnière*. Once again, we find the narrative voice permeable to the impact of the events narrated: it is as though the narrator absorbs, imitates, reproduces the anxious repetitions which characterize Marcel's thoughts when he is tormented by his obsessive jealousy of Albertine.

Proust's narrator is not – or not always – the voice of unperturbed mastery and lucidity which Sartre describes in the epigraph at the beginning of this article. The mastery he shows is perhaps more akin to that of a mental navigator, plotting his course through the eddies and cross-currents of remembered experience, in the realization that there will be reefs, tempests and sunken mines, to be negotiated with the help of the rhetorical instruments of syntactical construction and metaphorical connection.

Notes

[1] Margaret Gray, *Postmodern Proust* (Philadelphia: University of Pennsylvania Press, 1992), 45.

[2] Jean-Paul Sartre, *Qu'est-ce que la littérature?* in *Situations II* (Paris: Gallimard, 1948), 55–330 (p. 181).

[3] The edition of *A la recherche du temps perdu* used is the new Pléiade edition in 4 volumes, under the general editorship of Jean-Yves Tadié (Paris: Gallimard, 1987–1989). Volume and page numbers refer to this edition.

[4] Marcel Muller, *Les Voix narratives dans 'A la recherche du temps perdu'* (Geneva: Droz, 1965), 9–22.
[5] Gérard Genette, *Figures III* (Paris: Seuil, 1972), 234–235.
[6] Malcolm Bowie, 'Proust, jealousy, knowledge' in *Freud, Proust and Lacan: Theory as Fiction* (Cambridge: CUP, 1987), 45–64 (p. 57).
[7] Jacques Rivière, *Quelques progrès dans l'étude du cœur humain*, Cahiers Marcel Proust 13 (Paris: Gallimard, 1985).
[8] Jean Milly, *La Phrase de Proust* (Paris: Champion, 1983), 205.
[9] Philippe Lejeune, 'Écriture et sexualité', *Europe* 49 (1971), 113–143; Samuel Weber, 'The Madrepore', *Modern Language Notes* 87 (1972), 915–961; Serge Doubrovsky, *La Place de la Madeleine* (Paris: Mercure de France, 1974).
[10] A. C. Piette, 'Rhyme and Memory in the Prose of Proust, Joyce and Beckett' (unpublished Ph.D. dissertation, University of Cambridge, 1988).
[11] Paul de Man, 'Reading (Proust)' in *Allegories of Reading* (New Haven and London: Yale University Press, 1979), 57–78.
[12] See Milly's Garnier-Flammarion edition of *La Prisonnière* (Paris, 1984).
[13] Gustavo Pellon, 'Giving the lie to liars: a note on anacoluthon in *A la recherche du temps perdu*', *Modern Language Notes* 95 (1980), 1347–1352 (p. 1349; p. 1351).
[14] John Porter Houston, *The Traditions of French Prose Style* (Baton Rouge: Louisiana State University Press, 1981), 248.
[15] William Wordsworth, 'Expostulation and reply' in *Lyrical Ballads 1798*, ed. W. J. B. Owen (Oxford: OUP, 1969), 103–104:

Nor less I deem that there are powers,
Which of themselves our minds impress,
That we can feed this mind of ours,
In a wise passiveness.

[16] Pellon, 'Giving the lie', 1351.
[17] Milly, *La Phrase*, 57–58.
[18] Bowie, 'Proust, jealousy and knowledge', 57–58.
[19] *A la recherche*, i 45; ii 77–78; iii 157–159; iv 458.
[20] *A la recherche,* iii 531.
[21] Genette, *Figures III*, 189.

Proust and Politics

MALCOLM BOWIE

It would be unwise to think of *A la recherche du temps perdu* as a documentary record of the Third Republic, or as the fictional re-creation of a characteristically French political process. Thiers, Gambetta, Clemenceau and Jaurès flit through the pages of the novel as wraiths thrown up by salon conversation or by the narrator's reverie. They have no policies worth specifying; they are not the authors of events or the instigators of legislation; and their grip upon the crisis- and scandal-laden texture of current affairs is no tighter than that of Louis XIV, Napoleon or Talleyrand, whose ghosts are also astir in Proust's book. Political parties and factions are named but not described. Upheavals within the Church, the army or the judiciary are notable only for the shock waves and the ripples of curiosity they send through dinners and receptions. And the First World War, which provides the backcloth to the closing stages of the narrative, is as inscrutable as the Fronde or the Congress of Vienna. Politics, one might wish to say, fascinates Proust only in extreme dilution. It matters to him when it adds a new spice to social relationships or to his narrator's self-analysis, but is otherwise lacking in character and complexity.

Yet if we return to Proust's writing armed with a somewhat extended notion of what politics is, we can see the book as imbued with political awareness and concern. Class relations, for example, are anatomized at length by the narrator himself and by Charlus, Norpois, Saint-Loup and the duc de Guermantes. Working-class, bourgeois and aristocratic characters all have developed views on the mechanisms of class society, and nice distinction-making between social positions is a conversational sport available to all comers, irrespective of the positions they themselves occupy on the class spectrum. The narrator serves a long apprenticeship in the discrimination between classes, and addresses his reader as one eager learner to another.

The aristocracy is particularly favoured by the narrator as an object of socio-political inquiry, for it has the merit of complexity. The timeless and unified character that the aristocracy possesses for the hasty observer soon breaks down, on closer inspection, into a fluid array of sub-species, each with its own animated history. The reader is reminded at great length, during the Doncières episode in *Le Côté de Guermantes*, that the Napoleonic aristocracy is not at all the same thing as the *ancien régime* aristocracy, whose titles had in many cases simply been 'confirmed' by the emperor. Le prince de Borodino and Robert, marquis de Saint-Loup-en-Bray, are brought together by military service, but a wide gulf continues to separate the nobilities to which they belong and to create coolness between these comrades-in-arms (ii 427).[1] The Courvoisiers and the Guermantes belong to the same social caste, are different branches indeed of the same family, but differ from each other in countless points of behaviour, sensibility and intelligence. In *La Prisonnière*, the aristocratic Charlus, who has now dwindled into an adviser on matters of status and rank to the bourgeois Mme Verdurin, schools her at length in the shadings that persist even within the 'old' aristocracy, and seeks with increasing exasperation to refashion one of her guest-lists accordingly:

> Je vois dès les premiers mots que nous ne parlons pas la même langue, puisque je parlais de noms de l'aristocratie et que vous me citez le plus obscur des noms des gens de robe, de petits roturiers retors, cancaniers, malfaisants, de petites dames qui se croient des protectrices des arts parce qu'elles reprennent une octave au-dessous les manières de ma belle-sœur Guermantes, à la façon du geai qui croit imiter le paon. (iii 739)

Charlus's lofty scorn and sarcasm speak of a class system that is already in terminal disarray. The system ought to be intelligible, even to Mme Verdurin. It ought above all to have a neatly stratified pyramidal structure, but a variety of factors – including intermarriage, the buying of titles and the invention of genealogies – has caused the strata to buckle and to leak one into the next. To make matters still more difficult, all Proust's commentators speak with the bias of their own desires for social dominance or advancement, and are hugely unreliable as sociological observers. Charlus rewrites his insider's account of aristocratic manners to suit his own caprice, and recomposes his letters of credence in accordance with his latest campaign of sexual conquest. Ambitious hostesses compete for the favours of the nobility, who in their turn have an unillusioned sense of their own market value. The preservation of class boundaries calls for strenuous policing, yet the task is already a futile one. The legitimacy of the Guermantes now exists only in the narrator's youthful dreams of a glorious feudal past. In the present, the family offers a sorry spectacle. Their battles and tournaments are now played out indoors, on the salon floor, in the faubourg Saint-Germain. The 'regard perforateur' and the 'salut scrutateur' that they bring to the newcomer in their midst are the last residue of their former valour, a final bloodless feat of arms (ii 736–737).

If there is a simple initial lesson to be drawn from Proust's handling of the pseudo-politics of aristocratic society, it is perhaps that wishful fantasy is a potent political force, and one which needs to be acknowledged inside as well as outside the institutions of state. It is certainly a conviction of this kind that provides anchorage for the narrator's protracted meditations on the Dreyfus affair:

> Quand les systèmes philosophiques qui contiennent le plus de vérité sont dictés à leurs auteurs, en dernière analyse, par une raison de sentiment, comment supposer que, dans une simple affaire politique comme l'affaire Dreyfus, des raisons de ce genre ne puissent, à l'insu du raisonneur, gouverner sa raison? (ii 593)

The narrator seeks to supply, as a complement to the documented public events which give the affair its visible contours, a map of its subterranean evolution as feeling. Beneath a history of accusations, counter-accusations, cover-ups and courts-martial, there is a history of visceral emotion, and the two are more than contingently connected. The nobility of the faubourg, for example, almost unanimously adopting the anti-*dreyfusard* cause, bring damage upon themselves even as they shore up their traditional allegiances. They welcome into their circle, for the purposes of the crusade against Dreyfus, individuals who have nothing to recommend them apart from an appropriate intensity of anti-Semitic and xenophobic passion. When the case is over and Dreyfus has been freed and rehabilitated, these social upstarts do not obligingly melt back into the obscurity from which they had emerged. They have taken up a new social position during the state of emergency and are not now to be dislodged. An aristocratic war against one group of outsiders has ended with another group quietly claiming victory. An embattled caste, in its crazed attempt to refortify itself, has opened itself up to invasion; it has willed yet another irreversible movement in its own long, slow destruction.

For Proust, then, the social and political topography of the Dreyfus case cannot be coherently mapped or modelled without making continuous reference to the habits of feeling that typify the main groups involved in the case. But in addition to these dynamic portraits of collective emotion, he provides a gallery of individual studies, and these too are reconnected to the world of public affairs. Charlus, for example, rehearses an entire chronicle of anti-Semitic commonplaces in *Le Côté de Guermantes*, and subjects Bloch to a sadistic *ad hominem* attack. Yet the scenarios of torture and cruelty that are the copper coinage of the anti-Semitic imagination and casually re-emerge in Charlus's talk soon give way to a profound personal fascination: Charlus is charmed by Bloch, excited by him, driven by him into a state of sexual and political disarray. Such are the unruly fantasies and obsessions from which entrenched political doctrines grow, the narrator proposes, and the Dreyfus events are remarkable only for the variety and urgency of the libidinal energies which they mobilize. Only the war is to provide an equivalent series of semi-public adventures for the sexual appetite. Saint-Loup, surrounded by his troops, relishing his life in a closed order of fighting males, is described as living out sexual desires that are 'ennuagés d'idéologie' (iv 325), clinging to an outmoded chivalric ideal. But the relationship between sex and ideology in this novel is forever one of reciprocal 'enclouding'. So much so that the politics of sexual intimacy to be observed inside the relationships between Swann and Odette, the narrator and Albertine, or Charlus and Morel, have the same underlying structure as the politics of the salon or that of the ministries whose margins we glimpse from time to time. Power-play in each of these arenas may be described in a single language of gesture: feint, subterfuge, conspiracy, tactical lying, the deferral of gratification by mere eloquence and indirection are the very grammar of politics and bring the bedchamber and the Chamber of Deputies into piquant proximity.

There is one appealingly straightforward way of coming to terms both with the density of political reference in Proust's novel and with the wilful thinness with which it characterizes statecraft, parliamentary democracy and public administration. The novel is a panoramic account of an individual's subjectivity, and catches up within itself, as the instrument of that individual's self-understanding, a dizzying profusion of alternative selves. The narrator spawns the relentless procession of 'not-me's over and against which his 'me' comes tenuously into being. It would well suit the purposes of such a book for the public domain in its turn to be submitted to the rule of subjectivity, and for society to be understood not as a durable set of suprapersonal institutions and arrangements but as the sum of the interpersonal exchanges taking place within a given community. The competing claims of republicanism and monarchism, or of the old and new aristocracies, for example, would in this view result from the solidification, and the reconfirmation generation upon generation, of what were originally personal dispositions and the spasmodic upheavals of individual desire. Understanding any social institution would not then involve looking for the system of which it was part, but would demand that detailed attention be paid to the characteristic rhythms and intensities of individual experience from which the institution itself was fashioned and into which it constantly threatens to dissolve again. Proust's narrator seems himself to be lending his support to such a view when he says in *Le Temps retrouvé*: 'Je sentais cette influence capitale de l'acte interne jusque dans les relations internationales' (iv 492).

If we look at Proust's novel through this sort of lens, many of its seeming oddities do indeed begin to make sense. The displacement of the political process as an object of inquiry by a powerful flow of personal impressions and affective states is no longer simply a long-range consequence of the Romantic emphasis on the feeling individual. It is the mainspring of a new critical and satirical vision. This novelist who places himself inside a subjectivity and on the margins of the political world is able to represent politics as a cruel dreamlike charade. But he does this not simply to press the claims of the individual and his much-vaunted 'inner life', and not simply to reduce the study of politics to a branch of social psychology. Out of the narrator's estrangement from the political sphere comes a sabre-toothed style of political critique. Having no other public role than that of a lesser courtier in a superannuated court, he develops a lucid rage against politics at large. He needs victims, and finds them everywhere.

Proust's account of an ailing aristocracy miraculously re-energized by the Dreyfus affair resembles Musil's hilarious history of the 'Collateral Campaign' in *The Man Without Qualities* (1939–1942). For Musil as for Proust, countless pages of savage comedy are to be derived from a single grandiose disproportion: that between the cant and ceremonial to which political agents are devoted and the simplistic ideas which sustain them. The Collateral Campaign is an eleventh-hour attempt to rescue some last shred of coherence, some valedictory sense of past glory, from the wreckage of the Austro-Hungarian empire. This campaign is doomed to failure, yet pursued with cunning, deliberation and an exquisite sense of protocol. The imperial substance has already rotted away, but how self-importantly its shadows continue to dance. The key 'idea', early in Musil's novel, is simply that a Prussian should take over the spiritual leadership of the great Austrian campaign, but this is mockingly introduced in the language of a new Copernican revolution:

> [...] what distinguishes an overwhelmingly great idea from an ordinary, perhaps even incomprehensibly ordinary and mistaken one, is the fact that it is in a kind of molten state, as a result of which the ego enters into infinite expanses and the expanses of the universe enter into the ego, whereby it ceases to be possible to recognise what belongs to oneself and what to the infinite. Hence overwhelmingly great ideas consist of a body, which, like the human body, is compact but perishable, and of an eternal soul, which is what lends them their significance, but which is not compact – on the contrary, at every attempt to get hold of it in cold words it evaporates into nothingness.[2]

Proust's narrator dreams as a child that a fabulous feudal system has survived by an improbable grace of history into the modern era, and then, as a young adult, wakes up to an aristocracy that has long been a phantasmagoria and is now on the point of extinction. Dreyfus provides the *mondains* with the last semblance of a common cause, and brings their rituals and ceremonies back into apparent alignment with the affairs of society at large. The question 'is he or she one of us?', asked of an unknown visitor to the salon, dramatizes an otherwise insignificant social occasion. Loyalty, duty, patriotism and decency can no longer be taken for granted: they are everywhere to be tested, and protected when threatened. An entire social edifice can be made to tilt and lurch by a single unguarded word. In the dying moments of their history, the aristocracy has discovered a last delusional sense of historical mission.

Proust's political comedy is nowhere closer to Musil's 'Kakania' – that hyper-ironical re-creation of *fin-de-siècle* Austria – than in his fantasticated portrait of Théodose II who is the king of a nameless Eastern country. If we were invited to treat *A la recherche du temps perdu* as a *roman-à-clef*, we could say that Théodose is Tsar Nicholas

II and leave matters there. His numeral gives the reader a clue, and the diplomatic events evoked in the novel map so closely on to the contemporary chronicle of Franco-Russian relations that the identification seems unanswerably neat and convincing. But to look at the matter simply in these terms would be to leave Proust's astonishing powers of derision out of account. For although Théodose's visits to Paris are a talking point during a number of separate episodes in the novel, the reader's main source of information about him is the former ambassador Norpois, whose diplomatic and oratorical skills enjoy their finest hour in the effulgence of the king's first visit. Reporting, at the beginning of *A l'ombre des jeunes filles en fleurs*, on the toast proposed by the visitor at the Élysée, Norpois is entranced by a single well-chosen word:

> C'est tout simplement un coup de maître; un peu hardi je le veux bien, mais d'une audace qu'en somme l'événement a pleinement justifiée. Les traditions diplomatiques ont certainement du bon, mais dans l'espèce elles avaient fini par faire vivre son pays et le nôtre dans une atmosphère de renfermé qui n'était plus respirable. Eh bien! une des manières de renouveler l'air, évidemment une de celles qu'on ne peut pas recommander mais que le roi Théodose pouvait se permettre, c'est de casser les vitres. Et il l'a fait avec une belle humeur qui a ravi tout le monde, et aussi une justesse dans les termes où on a reconnu tout de suite la race de princes lettrés à laquelle il appartient par sa mère. Il est certain que quand il a parlé des 'affinités' qui unissent son pays à la France, l'expression, pour peu usitée qu'elle puisse être dans le vocabulaire des chancelleries, était singulièrement heureuse. Vous voyez que la littérature ne nuit pas, même dans la diplomatie, même sur un trône, ajouta-t-il en s'adressant à moi. La chose était constatée depuis longtemps, je le veux bien, et les rapports entre les deux puissances étaient devenus excellents. Encore faut-il qu'elle fût dite. Le mot était attendu, il a été choisi à merveille, vous avez vu comme il a porté. Pour ma part j'y applaudis des deux mains. (i 451–452)

Théodose is conjured into being by Norpois's prolix commentary: the king is the author of an empty phrase, and this draws forth from the former ambassador an answering cascade of further vacuities. Proust's dark satirical genius takes wing here. Théodose is kingship become hot air. This is no longer the strong verbalization – that of oaths, edicts and treaties – by means of which a king might perform his functions and reassert his legitimacy, but the enfeebled afterlife of power finding expression in toasts, rumours and reportage.

Théodose's kingdom without name is the *nulle part* from which no diplomatic envoy ever returns. What better way of celebrating this low-water mark of the monarchical principle than with Norpois's 'two-handed' applause?

In episodes like this, and there are many of them, Proust's political imagination plunges with abandon towards the abyss. The delirium of Norpois and the nullity of Théodose spread as a contagion through the social order. The many-voiced world of opinion goes unanimously mad, and universal darkness, for a while, buries all. Yet Proust has constructed a narrator who can do many things and espouse many viewpoints. In one of his guises he thrills to danger and seeks an apocalyptic end to the posturings of the political animal, but in another he reinstates judgement and proceeds with caution. Dreyfus in particular slows him down, and prompts him to a step-by-step reconstruction of individual political choice.

While the narrator is clearly more reserved in his *dreyfusard* sympathies than Proust himself was, it is apparent from the first detailed discussions of the affair, which occur during the Doncières episode in *Le Côté de Guermantes*, that the Dreyfus case is to be a privileged site for political and moral discussion, a place where the hidden underworld of political commitment may be studied in laboratory conditions. Saint-Loup parts company with his aristocratic peers on the question of Dreyfus's innocence or guilt, and finds in the Doncières barracks a single like-minded officer: 'Saint-Loup m'avait parlé d'un autre de ses camarades qui était là aussi, avec qui il s'entendait particulièrement bien, car ils étaient dans ce milieu les deux seuls partisans de la révision du procès Dreyfus' (ii 404). The narrator describes himself as readily sharing in this atmosphere of fraternal warmth during his stay, and by numerous small complicit touches later in the novel identifies himself with the *dreyfusard* cause. ',M. de Cambremer avait conclu que j'étais dreyfusard', the narrator says in *Sodome et Gomorrhe* (iii 355), supplying no evidence to the contrary. The rhetoric of the pro- and anti-Dreyfus camps may be similar in certain respects, as may their campaign tactics and their appeals to this or that honourable tradition, but thereafter there is no equilibrium between them: on the one side is justice, and on the other infamy. In *Sodome et Gomorrhe* Swann tells the narrator that the prince de Guermantes has changed his mind on the question of Dreyfus's supposed crime: he had discovered new facts about the case and could then no longer sustain his former view. Swann's admiration for the uprightness of the prince is echoed and amplified by the narrator in his own voice. The truth must be told, and justice done (iii 108–110).

The narrator casts a merciless eye upon the myths and superstitions of the anti-*dreyfusards*. He holds their follies up to ridicule and, in the ironic play of his own monologue, exposes their rigidities. A perplexing question arises, however, as in all accomplished demythologizing performances of this kind. Where does the critic speak from? Where can he discover a vantage point, a system of values or a set of criteria that will not themselves fall victim to his critique? The anti-*dreyfusards* settle for error while truth is at hand, but the narrator cannot simply ground his attack upon them in the superiority of truth-telling to mendacity, for lying has already been shown to have its charms and even its virtues. Yet, without anchorage of this sort, how can the observer of an animated political scene avoid being swept along in the flux of other people's views? In *A l'ombre des jeunes filles en fleurs*, the narrator states the problem in an aggravated form, using a familiar visual image:

> [...] pareille aux kaléidoscopes qui tournent de temps en temps, la société place successivement de façon différente des éléments qu'on avait crus immuables et compose une autre figure. Je n'avais pas encore fait ma première communion, que des dames bien pensantes avaient la stupéfaction de rencontrer en visite une Juive élégante. Ces dispositions nouvelles du kaléidoscope sont produites par ce qu'un philosophe appellerait un changement de critère. L'affaire Dreyfus en amena un nouveau, à une époque un peu postérieure à celle où je commençais à aller chez Mme Swann, et le kaléidoscope renversa une fois de plus ses petits losanges colorés. Tout ce qui était juif passa en bas, fût-ce la dame élégante, et des nationalistes obscurs montèrent prendre sa place.
> (i 507–508)

Society seems to be an impersonal mechanism for the production of political change, and to have irony built into it. No sooner has one familiar form of anti-Semitism begun to dissolve, removing from Jews certain of their accustomed disabilities, than another form begins to gather strength. Within a generation, a prominent set of social attitudes has changed and changed again, and responsibility for these shifts cannot be clearly assigned to individual agents or even to groups propelled by a common purpose. The notion that irony is immanent in social change, and need not therefore be officiously superadded by the outside observer, continues to be employed by the narrator in his report on the later stages of the Dreyfus affair, and on its aftermath. At the start of *Le Temps retrouvé*, yesterday's traitors and scoundrels have become today's solid citizens. A profusion of late-blooming *dreyfusards* has transformed the entire political landscape: 'Toute la Chambre étant à un certain moment devenue révisionniste, c'était forcément parmi d'anciens révisionnistes, comme parmi d'anciens socialistes, qu'on avait été obligé de recruter le parti de l'ordre social, de la tolérance religieuse, de la préparation militaire' (iv 305). The political kaleidoscope has turned again, and with no responsible agent anywhere in sight.

The distinguishing mark of this narrator as a chronicler of his times is that, while being caught up in local events from day to day, he is able to take a long historical view of things. He expects recurrences, volte-faces and reversals of fortune. He launches his commentaries not from an extraterrestrial viewpoint but from the position of one who has inhabited the turmoil of society for a long time and grown accustomed to its tricks of perspective. However, his knowledge of the world, his expectation that new events will conform to old patterns, or that new patterns will be assembled from old building-blocks, produces disenchantment but not depression. Discovering that irony is in history anyway has a tonic rather than a debilitating effect on the narrator's own ironic style. Far from waiting passively for the next echo of things already said, or the next fulfilment of a destiny long ago foretold, he is able to model his own perceptions and his own narrative on the sameness-in-difference, the surprising predictability, of social life. By the mid-point of the novel, he has seen everything before, yet is eager to continue looking. An intellectual passion propels him. He measures tensions and stresses within systems. He points to the gaps and flaws that the proponents of those systems would generally wish to conceal. He values the moment when values begin to seem insecure, or when strong-minded criteria begin to go slack. Proust as a political commentator is an ironist's ironist. For him there is no bedrock, no stable map or measuring-rod, and no viewpoint from which all other viewpoints can be made to make sense. There is instead a continuous dialectical trajectory in his thinking, and a disinterested scrupulousness in his handling of divergent political passions. Yet he knows also that certain of those passions, the darkest and deadliest of them, must be repudiated. In speaking of the guiltless Dreyfus and the multitude of his accusers, Proust's narrator offers us his own version of Zola's 'J'accuse'.

Here, surely, is the programme of the European Enlightenment given a zestful, fleet-footed and thoroughly modern form. And here is a writer who can scarcely fail to gratify the Western liberal consensus, for he not only calls infamy by its name, exposes delusions and rejects reactionary views, but he speaks with such intellectual gaiety and with such *style*. How could principled high spirits of this kind ever be politically suspect?

Yet nothing in Proust's novel is as simple as this question makes it sound. I have spoken already of the taste for risk and extremity that Proust ascribes to his narrator. This expresses itself in an occasional reduction to absurdity of political meaning and in the creation of catastrophic social scenes. But the narrator takes everyday risks too. He has an everyday power of provocation about him, and a promiscuous will to imitate the views of other people. These qualities bring him at times into brutish and illiberal company. The anti-Semitism, for example, that is so firmly dismantled in certain episodes of the novel, is gleefully reinvented in others. In the following passage from *A l'ombre des jeunes filles en fleurs*, the narrator describes the absence of communication between Jews and non-Jews during the holiday season at Balbec:

> Or cette colonie juive était plus pittoresque qu'agréable. Il en était de Balbec comme de certains pays, la Russie ou la Roumanie, où les cours de géographie nous enseignent que la population israélite n'y jouit point de la même faveur et n'y est pas parvenue au même degré d'assimilation qu'à Paris par exemple. Toujours ensemble, sans mélange d'aucun autre élément, quand les cousines et les oncles de Bloch, ou leurs co-religionnaires mâles ou femelles se rendaient au Casino, les unes pour le 'bal', les autres bifurquant vers le baccara, ils formaient un cortège homogène en soi et entièrement dissemblable des gens qui les regardaient passer et les retrouvaient là tous les ans sans jamais échanger un salut avec eux, que ce fût la société des Cambremer, le clan du premier président, ou des grands et petits bourgeois, ou même de simples grainetiers de Paris, dont les filles, belles, fières, moqueuses et françaises comme les statues de Reims, n'auraient pas voulu se mêler à cette horde de fillasses mal élevées, poussant le souci des modes de 'bains de mer' jusqu'à toujours avoir l'air de revenir de pêcher la crevette ou d'être en train de danser le tango. Quant aux hommes, malgré l'éclat des smokings et des souliers vernis, l'exagération de leur type faisait penser à ces recherches dites 'intelligentes' des peintres qui ayant à illustrer les

Evangiles ou les *Mille et Une Nuits*, pensent au pays où la scène se passe et donnent à saint Pierre ou à Ali-Baba précisément la figure qu'avait le plus gros 'ponte' de Balbec. (ii 98)

This passage could be politely described as a phenomenology of anti-Semitic feeling, and a descriptive catalogue of the images and 'ideas' on which such feeling rests. The Jews who visit Balbec annually are colonizers rather than members of a simple *colonie de vacances*; they are assimilated, yet self-proclaimingly different; they are foreigners in demeanour if not in fact, and bring a disturbing breath of Eastern European or Oriental air to the otherwise bracing Normandy coast; they are a homogeneous and exclusive group; their womenfolk are a 'horde', and their menfolk draw attention to themselves by the uncanny glare of their apparel; they are an affront to Christianity, whether by refusing to conform to the statuary of a great cathedral or by sacrilegiously re-judaizing the gospels; their social behaviour brings upon itself, by its exaggeration and immodesty, the unanimous disapproval of French society; they are themselves to blame for whatever afflictions they continue to endure.

The narrative voice in this paragraph is of course much more nuanced than this bald enumeration of anti-Semitic motifs would suggest: the opinions of the Cambremers are always to be distrusted, and in so far as that family is associated with the charge of Jewish 'exclusivism', the charge must itself be an object of suspicion; the Parisian grain-merchants too, with their statuesque daughters, are unreliable arbiters in matters of taste and social conduct. Yet there is still something alarming about the cornucopian generosity with which this list unfolds and the seeming warmth with which the narrator embraces each vindictive vignette. Xenophobia has expanded to fill the entire social field. Its characteristic assumptions explain everything in sight, and provide the space of casino or ballroom or beach with a cogent geometry. In its monothematic accumulation of detail, if not in its undercurrents and inflections, the rhetoric of this passage is close to the pamphleteering style of Drumont in *La France juive* (1886) or of Céline in *Bagatelles pour un massacre* (1937).

It would be unsatisfactory to say of such writing simply that it represents one voice in a polyphony of voices in the book as a whole, and that its venom is amply neutralized by the narrator's sympathetic accounts elsewhere of Bloch and his family, and of the beleaguered Jewish community at large. The extremity of this writing deserves to be heard, and its searing aggression felt, before the problem of its presence in Proust's book is 'solved'.

During a later episode, in *Le Côté de Guermantes*, a remarkable dialogue is established between Charlus, whose cruelty is deplored by the narrator, and the narrator himself, who finds his own cruelty by imitation of his conversational partner. Charlus has just claimed that Dreyfus cannot be called a traitor because, being a Jew, he cannot be thought of as French, or as having responsibilities towards France; and he has sketched for the narrator a fantasy scene in which Bloch would appear as David to the Goliath of his own father:

> Cela composerait une farce assez plaisante. Il pourrait même, pendant qu'il y est, frapper à coups redoublés sur sa charogne, ou, comme dirait ma vieille bonne, sur sa carogne de mère. Voilà qui serait fort bien fait et ne serait pas pour nous déplaire, hein! petit ami, puisque nous aimons les spectacles exotiques et que frapper cette créature extra-européenne, ce serait donner une correction méritée à un vieux chameau. (ii 584–585)

The narrator recoils from Charlus at this point and from his 'hideous and almost mad' ravings, but the report he then interpolates on a conversation between Bloch senior and Nissim Bernard ends upon this cadence:

> S'attristant du malheur des Juifs, se souvenant de ses amitiés chrétiennes, devenant maniéré et précieux au fur et à mesure que les années venaient, pour des raisons que l'on verra plus tard, il [Bernard] avait maintenant l'air d'une larve préraphaélite où des poils se seraient malproprement implantés, comme des cheveux noyés dans une opale. (ii 586)

Some of the grotesquerie here is designed to give a foretaste of Nissim Bernard's sexuality, which is to be unveiled later in the novel: homosexuality is an incongruity and a pollution inside the jewel-like consistency of the procreative heterosexual group. But the image, which on the surface resembles such *fin-de-siècle* inventions as Odilon Redon's eye-flower or decapitated cactus-man, has another disturbing dimension too. *Larve* retains its classical Latin sense of 'mask' or 'ghost', but has a more modern meaning in the field of natural history. The Jew as larva, surreptitiously invading and devouring the body of Christian society, already had a long European history by this point, and had been given new currency by the biologizing tendency of much anti-Semitic writing in the later part of the nineteenth century. Wagner, to name only the most celebrated pamphleteer within this tradition, had spoken in such terms in his essay 'Judaism and Music' (1850). Proust's image, sweetened somewhat by its nod towards pre-Raphaelite painting, then switches 'almost madly' towards a further vision of corruption: Nissim Bernard, from having been a larva becomes an opal. Hair that had previously sprouted from a surface is now trapped inside a volume. It stands out as clearly and indissolubly against the surrounding radiance of the precious stone as the procession of Bloch family members had stood out against the pure concentrations of Frenchness gathered together in the Balbec casino. Fantasies of this kind have the peculiarity that they remove fears of uncleanness and contamination from the unruly inner world of feeling and project them into a stable, measurable outside space: 'foreigners', strangers, dirt and invasive organisms are material presences in an otherwise clear and unspoilt material medium. Social hygiene, like bodily hygiene, then becomes a simple art of repositioning matter.

The language of calumny in modern France is for the most part inert and formulaic, and what novelty it has comes more often from the discovery of a new target individual or group than from the display of unusual verbal invention. Proust is a true innovator, in this as in so much else: he has discovered, for long moments, a vilifying diction that unmistakably sings and dances. Writing like this does not belong to, say, an adolescent developmental phase in the narrator's personal history, and its presence in *A la recherche du temps perdu* cannot be explained as a feature of the growth and maturation that the novel traces in the long term. The states of heightened awareness and self-awareness that the narrator eventually reaches in *Le Temps retrouvé* are presented as the finest flowering of an always restless and experimental mind, and as a worthy destination for a long tale of mental strife. But on his way towards this happy outcome, the narrator does not simply slough off earlier and less perfect mental states in favour of the later and more perfect states that they prefigure. He does not gradually purge himself of his delinquencies. He darts about, improvises, regresses, anticipates, and becomes in one incarnation what he most opposes in another. This Dreyfus sympathizer suddenly seeks consensus with members of the opposing camp. This enlightened and debonair ironic voice suddenly seeks to know hatred from within. Indeed, the book has been put together in such a way as to allow the narrator to be delinquent whenever he chooses, and after as well as before his late moments of illumination.

If there is an irony governing Proust's entire account of the Dreyfus case, it is irony of a recklessly careering, self-overtaking kind – rather like that of Erasmus's *Praise of Folly* or Swift's *A Tale of a Tub*. One value system is used to expose another to ridicule, but the relation is a reversible one: the instrument of ridicule may become its object as the satirical text presses manically ahead. One of the hallmarks of the Proustian political vision is to be found in this extreme instability, in this resistance to all principles of social order and continuity. And this instability is jealously protected by Proust's text, even if this means giving house room from time to time to reprehensible views.

Outside the grand experimental laboratory that the Dreyfus case represents for the narrator, it is in his account of the working class that his relish for contradiction is most clearly on display. The narrator's attitudes towards the working class are sketched in considerable detail, and trenchantly enough to counterbalance his still more detailed portraits of the bourgeoisie and the aristocracy. On the one hand, workers, and especially family servants, are of interest to the narrator for what they tell of the past. They are embodiments of folk wisdom. They are a living link with feudalism, and their language, for all its malapropisms and faults of grammar, is a philological treasure-house, a rich layer of sedimented medieval forms. Through Françoise, or the street-traders whose cries echo in the opening pages of *La Prisonnière*, an otherwise lost antiquity continues to speak. On the other hand, however, certain workers have the glamour of modernity about them: electricians, mechanics, telephonists and employees in the rapidly expanding aviation industry are participants in a huge technological revolution and, however small their individual roles, they are seen collectively by the narrator as standard-bearers for enterprise and invention. The *mondains*, who would hesitate before visiting a bourgeois home for fear of meeting a republican there, would also as a matter of course wish to preserve oil-lamps and horse-drawn omnibuses in the face of modern machines (i 507). But the workers are alive to the poetry of the new.

If certain representatives of the working class are valued for the past they preserve and others for the bright future they seem to announce, we surely have an instructive contradiction, and the basis for a searching critical view of class society. The enlightened bourgeoisie, whose values the narrator often takes pains to reproduce, already knows, in Proust's account of it, that working-class identities are constructed and modified to suit the requirements of capitalist employers. The plasticity of this class during an era of social upheaval and rapid industrialization would seem to confirm the narrator's 'kaleidoscopic' view of social events and processes: the exact causes of change in the social order may be difficult to ascertain, but its effects are visible everywhere and, over the span of a generation, can radically alter the texture of daily living. Previously silent members of the community are starting to make a stir. Yet the narrator who comments in these terms on the passage of socio-historical time, and is often excited by the exploits of technocratic modernity, also looks back with unashamed nostalgia to an *ancien régime* of artisanal production methods and stable class relations. Perhaps silence was preferable after all to the new clamour.

The tension point between these two views is to be found in *Sodome et Gomorrhe*. Although the relationship between the narrator and Albertine is by now a very modern affair, receiving stimulus from the motor car and benediction from the 'aéroplane', the narrator is still positively chivalric in his protracted discussions of class:

> Car pour la chose, je n'avais jamais fait de distinction entre les classes. [...] je n'avais jamais fait de différence entre les ouvriers, les bourgeois et les grands seigneurs, et j'aurais pris indifféremment les uns et les autres pour amis, avec une certaine préférence pour les ouvriers, et après cela pour les grands seigneurs, non par goût, mais sachant qu'on peut exiger d'eux plus de politesse envers les ouvriers qu'on ne l'obtient de la part des bourgeois, soit que les grands seigneurs ne dédaignent pas les ouvriers comme font les bourgeois, ou bien parce qu'ils sont volontiers polis envers n'importe qui, comme les jolies femmes heureuses de donner un sourire qu'elles savent accueilli avec tant de joie. (iii 414–415)

As anti-bourgeois polemic goes, these remarks are far from inflammatory. Indeed, the familiar sins of the bourgeoisie – complacency, small-mindedness, self-interest, mercantilism, prudishness and the like – are omitted altogether, and the narrator stops short of complete absolution for members of this class because they occasionally behave badly towards their social inferiors. Exemplary politeness towards workers can, however, be expected from the aristocracy, as the narrator has already had occasion to note in his many sympathetic portrayals of Saint-Loup. The narrator thus projects himself, in two directions at once, away from his own class position: he identifies with the *grands seigneurs* as the givers, and with the workers as the receivers, of benevolence. Equality can be rediscovered between seeming non-equals, but only on condition that the bothersome bourgeois is removed from the scene.

This long discussion of the permeable and impermeable barriers between classes then takes a comparative turn. Where the narrator himself is a self-proclaimed strict egalitarian, his mother, though perfectly well disposed towards servants, mechanics and other working people, insists on observing certain physical and verbal boundaries: she would be reluctant to shake a working person's hand, and distressed to hear him address one of her own class equals in the second rather than the third person. What makes the entire passage so unusual as proto-sociology, however, is not the air of anxious gentility that hangs over it, but on the contrary its whiff of impending scandal. There is perhaps something promiscuous and narcissistic in the aristocratic cult of good manners, the narrator suggests, and an over-willingness to woo: the *grands seigneurs* are like pretty women whose smiles go everywhere. And again the mother's fear of a handshake between classes is perhaps a screen for the deeper fear of a transgressive sexual intimacy:

> Quand elle voyait un chauffeur d'automobile dîner avec moi dans la salle à manger, elle n'était pas absolument contente et me disait: 'Il me semble que tu pourrais avoir mieux comme ami qu'un mécanicien', comme elle aurait dit, s'il se fût agi de mariage: 'Tu pourrais trouver mieux comme parti'. (iii 415)

If mechanics are to be allowed into the dining-room, what can prevent them from making further improper advances? They will be marriage partners next, or worse.

These local injections of sexual fantasy into the narrator's account of class relationships are not at all unusual in the novel. Indeed, we glimpse briefly in this passage one of the organizing ideas of the book: beyond equality of the kind that radical politicians might campaign for – an equality which concerns, say, voting rights and citizenship – there lies an egalitarianism of desire in which the enfranchized and the disenfranchized alike share. A prince may look at a bellboy, and an electrician at a countess. The only problem with equality thought of in these terms is that it gives class politics a profoundly conservative tone. Class distinctions have to be retained rather than abolished in this world of indefinitely desiring individuals, for such differences are a powerful source of erotic stimulus. Rigidly stratified societies multiply the opportunities for pleasure that are available to sexual adventurers, and can enrich the fantasies of even the most austere stay-at-home.

This picture of social class as one erotogenic element in an encompassing libidinal economy culminates in *Le Temps retrouvé*, during the extended scene in Jupien's brothel. This brings together in a grandiose comic set-piece a number of bold reversals. War with Germany brings colour and animation to the capital: exotic military uniforms from the outposts of empire make Paris into a new Venice or Constantinople, and kilted Scotsmen send a tremor of excitement through the *demi-monde*. The nightly black-out offers freedom rather than restriction: in the shadows sexual contacts can be made without conversational preliminaries. Enemy bombing raids bring not terror but imposing drama to every street: daily life is lived out under the volcano and, in true Pompeian fashion, any embrace between lovers could prove to be their last. But by far the boldest reversal involves the status of the brothel itself. Anticipating Genet's *Le Balcon* or Buñuel's *Belle de jour* but already outstripping them in satirical exuberance, Proust turns Jupien's establishment into a model of class-bound society, and at moments into a social utopia. Professional and class identities must be preserved in order to be re-created in the sexual pantomime, but a sublime vision of classlessness still hovers over the scene: everyone is entitled to his desire, and entitled to exploit others in seeking outlet for it. The only blemish in what could otherwise have been a perfect circuit of sexual and monetary transactions is the hypocrisy that afflicts certain social groups. Where members of the higher social classes have an acquired nonchalance and candour in matters of sex, working people, who may also seek sado-masochistic adventures of the kind in which Jupien specializes, are constrained by the opinion of their fellows:

> Pour un employé d'industrie, pour un domestique, aller là c'était comme pour une femme qu'on croyait honnête, aller dans une maison de passe. Certains qui avouaient y être allés se défendaient d'y être plus jamais retournés et Jupien lui-même, mentant pour protéger leur réputation ou éviter des concurrences, affirmait : 'Oh! non, il ne vient pas chez moi, il ne voudrait pas *y* venir.' Pour des hommes du monde c'est moins grave, d'autant plus que les autres gens du monde qui n'*y* vont pas, ne savent pas ce que c'est et ne s'occupent pas de votre vie. Tandis que dans une maison d'aviation, si certains ajusteurs *y* sont allés, leurs camarades les espionnant, pour rien au monde ne voudraient *y* aller de peur que cela fût appris. (iv 415)

At this point the narrator, who appears throughout this scene as an excitable and not easily shockable observer, discovers the first glimmerings of a true political cause: aviation workers whose sexual wishes are thwarted in this way deserve to be emancipated. Their case is especially strong because, unlike the indolent, non-serving aristocrats who figure prominently among Jupien's customers, these plane-makers are active contributors to the common good and to the war effort. Where utopian thinkers would ordinarily attend first to the public rights and obligations that a successful civil society might prescribe for its members, and give sexual arrangements a subsidiary role in their planning, Proust's narrator places the demands of a dissident and unquenchable sexual drive at the centre of his scheme. Once overweening desire has been appropriately provided for, then lesser questions of economic and social policy can be decided in its wake. Honest toilers on the production line will then be able to pursue their pleasure without shame or ostracism.

Le Temps retrouvé brings class relationships, which have been unstable throughout the novel, to the brink of incoherence. The bourgeois Mme Verdurin re-emerges, twice widowed and twice remarried, as the princesse de Guermantes, and the narrator declaims an almost operatic lament for the lost worlds of poetry and enchantment that such usurpations leave behind them. Perhaps an ideal and indestructible princess, the purest distillation of class feeling, will rise up and haunt the procession of impostors that Mme Verdurin has unleashed:

> [...] et toujours, sans interruption, viendrait comme un flot de nouvelles princesses de Guermantes, ou plutôt, millénaire, remplacée d'âge en âge dans son emploi par une femme différente, une seule princesse de Guermantes, ignorante de la mort, indifférente à tout ce qui change et blesse nos cœurs, le nom refermant sur celles qui sombrent de temps à autre sa toujours pareille placidité immémoriale. (iv 533–534)

But it is in the brothel episode that Proust's reimagining of a class system in catastrophic decline reaches its most extreme and most ambiguous form. On the one hand, the flames of hell are to be seen lighting up the night sky, and premonitions of disaster are everywhere. Indeed, the *Titanic* has already gone down and Vesuvius has already erupted, although the bacchanal carries on in seeming unawareness under Jupien's benign supervision. The brothel, like Dante's inferno, is 'composite', cellular, divided up into separate scenes of punishment and degradation. Art history has become a collection of lascivious images, and philology has been reduced to the study of low-life sexual jargon. And most alarmingly of all, class characteristics have been turned into mere erotic accoutrements, and are valued, like whips, chains and spy-holes, only in so far as they produce or prolong arousal. On the other hand, the brothel is a place of refuge for desire. Many of Jupien's customers are on leave from the trenches, and all of them are the potential victims of bombing and bombardment. Where the crowned heads of Europe, and its politicians and generals, have produced carnage on a previously unimaginable scale, Jupien, who is 'intelligent comme un homme de lettres' (iv 394), devotes himself to altogether more civilized pursuits: he stages a restrained and playful form of belligerence, the outcome of which is not death or mutilation but pleasure and financial reward. The voice of Charlus is to be heard coming from inside one of the rooms as the narrator listens at the door: 'Je vous en supplie, grâce, grâce, pitié, détachez-moi, ne me frappez pas si fort, disait une voix. Je vous baise les pieds, je m'humilie, je ne recommencerai pas. Ayez pitié' (iv 394). This is the exultant sound of what we might call, paraphrasing a celebrated expression of Éluard's, 'le dur désir de désirer'. A prince, who can trace his ancestry beyond the Capetian kings, now seeks his pleasure at the hands of a brutish serf and, to enhance that pleasure, expects an array of antiquated torture instruments to be found for him. The transactions between torturer and masochist, and the playful reversal of master and slave relationships that these involve, are thus conducted in a self-consciously historical fashion: the aristocrat comes to terms with modernity, and with the dubious population of murderers and slaughtermen who, in his fantasies at least, crowd the back streets of the metropolis, by constructing for himself a medieval stage-set in which he can enjoy a paying victimhood. Class relationships have been exhaustively eroticized and commodified, and are now up for sale in a modern market economy, but the call of desire that is to be heard throughout this scene still has its dignity in the narrator's eyes and still manages to break free, at the last, from the taint of commerce: 'Or les aberrations sont comme des amours où la tare maladive a tout recouvert, tout gagné. Même dans la plus folle, l'amour se reconnaît encore' (iv 418). In the brothel, in wartime, love holds out against death. In the darkness, in the private rooms of this composite hell, in the farcical reinventions of an unequal society that Jupien stage-manages, love and fraternity have found their last stronghold.

This account of the working class is indeed contradictory, and part of a wider view in which politics itself is the science of contradiction in the social sphere. Working-class people, when they are not servants or artisans, are panders, spies and go-betweens. When they are not serving other people's sexual needs in these indirect ways, they are compliant small fry whose favours can be bought and sold at first hand. The fact that the narrator will share his table with a mechanic, and express solidarity with prostitutes during one extended episode, cannot do much to offset one's sense that, all in all, this self-proclaimed egalitarian would rather spend his time in other company. In the book as a whole, the abjection of the aristocracy weighs much heavier than that of the labouring poor. And although in part this emphasis flows from the superior absurdity of superior people, and from the freer rein this gives to Proust's satirical imagination, there are other reasons for it too. The narrator is presented as a bourgeois who has an affinity, and in due course a complicity, with the aristocrats whose company he seeks. Certain major elements in his own creative project seem to be reliant upon the inveterate inequalities that the class system embodies.

From an early stage in the novel it is clear that old and new aristocrats, even when risible in other respects, are to be valued for their sense of style, and that the excellences and excesses of their speech are particularly fascinating. Their dress, manners and deportment are all worthy of study, but their flamboyant verbal performances charm the narrator much more. Even the marquis de Norpois, who is introduced at the beginning of *A l'ombre des jeunes filles en fleurs* and is a figure of caricature during this and all subsequent appearances, brings a touch of genius to his unstemmable tirades. By the sheer force of his rhetoric he is able to transform clichés, proverbs, and fashionable phrases from the newspapers into a rich and strange delirium. In *Le Côté de Guermantes*, for example, he addresses Bloch torrentially on the need for caution among those who call for the Dreyfus case to be reopened:

> '[...] si, avant même que fût séchée l'encre du décret qui instituerait la procédure de révision, obéissant à je ne sais quel insidieux mot d'ordre vous ne désarmiez pas, mais vous confiniez dans une opposition stérile qui semble pour certains l'*ultima ratio* de la politique, si vous vous retiriez sous votre tente et brûliez vos vaisseaux, ce serait à votre grand dam. Êtes-vous prisonnier des fauteurs de désordre? Leur avez-vous donné des

gages?' Bloch était embarrassé pour répondre. M. de Norpois ne lui en laissa pas le temps. 'Si la négative est vraie, comme je veux le croire, et si vous avez un peu de ce qui me semble malheureusement manquer à certains de vos chefs et de vos amis, quelque esprit politique, le jour même où la Chambre criminelle sera saisie, si vous ne vous laissez pas embrigader par les pêcheurs en eau trouble, vous aurez ville gagnée. Je ne réponds pas que tout l'état-major puisse tirer son épingle du jeu, mais c'est déjà bien beau si une partie tout au moins peut sauver la face sans mettre le feu aux poudres [...]' (ii 542–543)

And so it goes on. In a sense, Norpois in spate has all the faults and none of the artistry that one might expect from professionalized political discourse. His language is by turns archaic and self-consciously modern, learned and exaggeratedly colloquial, circumlocutory and condescendingly plain-spoken. Whatever its register, it assiduously collects banalities and strings them together: the shortest route from one ready-made expression to another lies by way of a third such expression. Norpois's talk is all bluster, an accumulation of verbal waste-matter, an antidote to thinking.

Yet this is mastery of a kind. Norpois enjoys copiousness, puts pressure on his syntax to accommodate qualifications and grace-notes, and clearly believes that length is the soul of wit. His speech comes alive in its commonplaceness and reaches grotesquely towards a *bel canto* continuity of line. Just as Proust in his literary pastiches brings off the rare feat of sounding like Balzac, Flaubert or the Goncourts while continuing to sound like himself, so here he endows Norpois with certain of his own stylistic habits. Norpois in his harangues, like Legrandin in his over-embroidered accounts of silence and moonlight, speaks pidgin Proust. His language is ornate but not complex, expansive but intellectually undernourished. In displaying the absurdities of the Norpois verbal style Proust not only draws attention to the risks his own 'grand manner' willingly runs, but causes a current of fellow feeling to flow between his narrator and the aberrant linguistic performers whose portraits emerge from his pen. Norpois knows something important about language: that it abhors a vacuum and can muster huge forces with which to invade and occupy social space. Norpois's table-talk has gone irretrievably to the bad, but in certain major respects it remains exemplary. In his attention-seeking, his fondness for length and his inventive transformation of ready-made expressions, Norpois is rather like a novelist.

Norpois's class position and his profession license him to speak voluminously, and to tyrannize his social inferiors with opinions and reminiscences. But two other aristocratic figures, while enjoying the same privilege, exert a much more powerful influence on the narrator in the development of his literary vocation: Saint-Loup and Charlus. Both are prolific talkers on politics and international affairs, but their talk is more seductive than Norpois's for having a pronounced historical axis. Saint-Loup, during the Doncières episode, takes the narrator on a bold retrospective tour of European battles and traces a direct line of descent from the *Iliad* to the skirmishes of the modern day:

> On ne fait pas un atelier de peinture avec n'importe quelle chambre, on ne fait pas un champ de bataille avec n'importe quel endroit. Il y a des lieux prédestinés. Mais encore une fois, ce n'est pas de cela que je parlais, mais du type de bataille qu'on imite, d'une espèce de décalque stratégique, de pastiche tactique, si tu veux: la bataille d'Ulm, de Lodi, de Leipzig, de Cannes. Je ne sais s'il y aura encore des guerres ni entre quels peuples; mais s'il y en a, sois sûr qu'il y aura (et sciemment de la part du chef) un Cannes, un Austerlitz, un Rossbach, un Waterloo, sans parler des autres. Quelques-uns ne se gênent pas pour le dire. Le maréchal von Schlieffen et le général de Falkenhausen ont d'avance préparé contre la France une bataille de Cannes, genre Hannibal avec fixation de l'adversaire sur tout le front et avance par les deux ailes, surtout par la droite en Belgique, tandis que Bernhardi préfère l'ordre oblique de Frédéric le Grand, Leuthen plutôt que Cannes. (ii 410–411)

Saint-Loup's easy mastery of the historical archive and his ability to trace over long periods the migration of classic tactical or strategic devices speak directly to the narrator's own artistic ambitions: he too already has extensive tracts of time to manage, and inherits formal models from his predecessors ancient and modern. What is so impressive about Saint-Loup's historiography is that he seems to be the author rather than the mere chronicler of events. His family lost its place on the historical stage long ago, but Saint-Loup speaks as if they held it still. He is the originator of speech-events only, but in his witty, rhythmic, overflowing tirades he sustains the glorious illusion of political power.

Charlus dwells with comparable ease in historical time, and bases his claims to consideration both on his aristocratic titles and on the swagger with which he enumerates them. This is his response in *Sodome et Gomorrhe* to one who had presumed to draw attention to the modest-sounding rank of *baron*: 'Permettez, répondit M. de

Charlus avec un air de hauteur, à M. Verdurin étonné, je suis aussi duc de Brabant, damoiseau de Montargis, prince d'Oléron, de Carency, de Viareggio et des Dunes. D'ailleurs cela ne fait absolument rien. Ne vous tourmentez pas' (iii 333). There is an element of high farce in Charlus's self-fashioning, of course. His ancestry may reach far back into history and spread well beyond the confines of France, but Carency brings *carence*, or deficiency, into the picture, and *damoiseau* not only makes him improbably youthful but, by contagion from the far commoner *damoiselle*, feminizes him. For all his proud self-promotion, this male damsel is perhaps more remarkable for what he lacks than for what he has. A similar sense of ironic reservation pervades the narrator's description of Doncières: Saint-Loup's spontaneous exercises in military history reflect the youthful bravado of an officer cadet who has not yet made the transition from training camp to battlefield.

Aristocrats such as these can be made fun of for their arrogance, but at the same time admired for their boldness in exploiting history for their own ends. There is a resourceful and rapacious quality about their narrative performances, and from this the narrator eagerly learns. Earlier in the novel, Charlus had offered to take the narrator's worldly education in hand, and, as part of this process, to initiate him into the secret history of European political institutions. The emperor of Austria had recently praised Charlus for the depth of his knowledge and expressed regret that the last Bourbon pretender to the French throne had not had access to Charlus's advice: if he had had this good fortune, he would now be king. What the would-be king could so easily have enjoyed is now spread tantalizingly before the upwardly mobile narrator:

> J'ai souvent pensé, monsieur, qu'il y avait en moi, du fait non de mes faibles dons, mais de circonstances que vous apprendrez peut-être un jour, un trésor d'expérience, une sorte de dossier secret et inestimable, que je n'ai pas cru devoir utiliser personnellement, mais qui serait sans prix pour un jeune homme à qui je livrerais en quelques mois ce que j'ai mis plus de trente ans à acquérir et que je suis peut-être seul à posséder. (ii 583)

Such claims are preposterous, and the narrator has on numerous earlier occasions mocked Charlus for making them; there is always self-interest behind Charlus's professions of altruism, and a low motive beneath his high eloquence. Yet his vision of himself as a walking archive, a historical record in human form, is powerful enough to overcome certain of the narrator's scruples. There is a lesson to be had from Charlus, although not the one that he himself is eager to teach. For the narrator as novelist-in-waiting, Charlus points the way towards a necessary sense of the past. And the extreme plasticity that Charlus's views acquire as soon as they are pressed into the service of his erotic campaigns provides the spectacle not of promiscuity but of an ever-alert and ever-resourceful speculative intelligence. Charlus remakes the world to suit the passions of the moment, and in doing so acquires enviable lightness and dexterity. Again, any prospective novelist should take note.

Charlus and Saint-Loup share these qualities with Talleyrand, the exemplary political survivor, and in *Le Temps retrouvé* Charlus indeed compares himself with this illustrious aristocratic predecessor (iv 339). But where Talleyrand travelled lightly from one high office to another, adapting himself to the requirements of his successive political masters, Charlus and Saint-Loup have no masters and no power. They are a political irrelevance, yet move from one airy verbal fabrication to another with undiminished self-confidence and wit. Where Talleyrand had helped redraw the map of Europe at the Congress of Vienna, these latecomers merely talk, and their talk gains a special sinister brilliance as Europe descends into darkness. Talleyrand's disengaged political adroitness has become sublime *frivolity*. Proust's narrator insists upon the term, places a positive valuation upon it, and thinks of the mental quality it names as an inheritable characteristic. Saint-Loup's style is 'in the blood', and the inventiveness of Charlus also has a seeming genetic basis: '[...] il échafaudait volontiers en matière mondaine des théories où se retrouvaient la fertilité de son intelligence et la hauteur de son orgueil, avec la frivolité héréditaire de ses préoccupations' (iii 736). What aristocrats inherit, in the mental as well as in the material sphere, the bourgeois has to work for. Charlus and Saint-Loup have recourse to history and situate themselves in genealogical time, yet they glory in the gratuitousness of their inventions. The narrator, on the other hand, has no history and only the briefest of genealogies. He looks to the work of art, and to the exertions that it will require of him, to make good these deficiencies and to usher him into an enviably frivolous world.

The play of affinity and distance between the narrator and these aristocratic masters reaches its culmination in *Le Temps retrouvé*. Saint-Loup, on leave from the front and still fired by patriotic fervour, weaves witty verbal arabesques from the horrors of war. Even as he faces his own death, his nonchalance and intellectual disengagement are defiantly intact. Charlus and Saint-Loup, uncle and nephew, fellow customers in Jupien's establishment, grow more alike, in spite of the fact that Charlus's war is distinguished only by his suspected Germanophilia and by the consummate greed with which he continues to pursue his pleasures under the eye of the invader. But it is Charlus who has the greater originality, and who comes closer to being the supreme artist that the crazed and death-haunted tenor of the times seems to demand. The narrator defends Charlus in these terms against a fashionable society for whom his conversational style is now outmoded:

> En fait ils étaient ingrats, car M. de Charlus était en quelque sorte leur poète, celui qui avait su dégager de la mondanité ambiante une sorte de poésie où il entrait de l'histoire, de la beauté, du pittoresque, du comique, de la frivole élégance. Mais les gens du monde, incapables de comprendre cette poésie, n'en voyaient aucune dans leur vie, la cherchaient ailleurs, et mettaient à mille piques au-dessus de M. de Charlus des hommes qui lui étaient infiniment inférieurs, mais qui prétendaient mépriser le monde et en revanche professaient des théories de sociologie et d'économie politique. [...] Bref, les gens du monde s'étaient désengoués de M. de Charlus, non pas pour avoir trop pénétré, mais sans avoir pénétré jamais sa rare valeur intellectuelle. (iv 345–346)

How many more creative virtues can a would-be poet acquire and still not be a poet? To Charlus's historical sense and his frivolity, the narrator now adds comic and descriptive talents, a love of beauty, intellectual prowess and a happy freedom from professorial pedantry. The narrator is bringing Charlus uncomfortably close to the sort of poet he might himself become, and this means, within the logic of the narrator's self-creation, that Charlus must be discarded. Like Swann, Elstir, Bergotte and Vinteuil, he must be seen to be excellent and seen to fail. Only flawed role models can serve this bringing to birth of a new artist.

The repudiation of Charlus is completed during the brothel scene, and at a moment when the baron, coming closer still to the narrator himself, has almost become a novelist. The narrator has been listening to Jupien's compassionate account of Charlus's sexual needs, and in reaction to this arrives at a moment of cruelty as shocking as Prince Hal's rejection of Falstaff at the end of *Henry IV*:

Et en écoutant Jupien je me disais: 'Quel malheur que M. de Charlus ne soit pas romancier ou poète! Non pas pour décrire ce qu'il verrait, mais le point où se trouve un Charlus par rapport au désir fait naître autour de lui les scandales, le force à prendre la vie sérieusement, à mettre des émotions dans le plaisir, l'empêche de s'arrêter, de s'immobiliser dans une vue ironique et extérieure des choses, rouvre sans cesse en lui un courant douloureux. Presque chaque fois qu'il adresse une déclaration, il essuie une avanie, s'il ne risque pas même la prison.' Ce n'est pas que l'éducation des enfants, c'est celle des poètes qui se fait à coups de gifles. Si M. de Charlus avait été romancier, la maison que lui avait aménagée Jupien, en réduisant dans de telles proportions les risques, du moins (car une descente de police était toujours à craindre) les risques à l'égard d'un individu des dispositions duquel, dans la rue, le baron n'eût pas été assuré, eût été pour lui un malheur. Mais M. de Charlus n'était en art qu'un dilettante, qui ne songeait pas à écrire et n'était pas doué pour cela. (iv 410)

Everything is now in place for Charlus to become an artist. To the qualities that have already been listed the narrator now adds recklessness, an appetite for suffering, a willingness to be humiliated. Only a hair's breadth separates Charlus from the calling and the condition of the novelist, but the barrier is uncrossable. Charlus cannot write. The blow is delivered with offhanded insolence, and in the absence of its victim, but it strikes home as terribly as 'I know thee not, old man'. Charlus, like Falstaff, has outlasted his usefulness.

If the political dimension of *A la recherche du temps perdu* were to be articulated solely in terms of class conflict, we could say that it represents yet another Pyrrhic triumph for the professional bourgeoisie. The aristocracy is seen off by the narrator in his search for his own artistic vision and voice. Sometimes this process is brutal and peremptory, as when Mme de Surgis presents to Charlus her two sons, Victurnien and Arnulphe, who combine the twin perfections of beauty and stupidity (iii 96–98). And sometimes, as we have just seen in the case of Charlus himself, it is slow and filled with lingering admiration. The working class is often treated more charitably but is always at several removes from effective political action. Whereas aristocrats, in this social universe, have only the memory of power, and workers only the remotest foretaste of it, the narrator himself has the real thing. A reliable sign of his new-found potency is that he can offer himself both as a representative of the bourgeoisie in his daily habits and expectations, and as miraculously class-neutral and unaligned in his artistic endeavours. His tireless capacity for introspection and self-analysis is fed by unshakeable self-belief. He can lose himself in reverie and find himself again in sententious utterance which projects his personal experience towards mankind at large. He can lose himself in mimicry as he travels back and forth between the speech habits of different social groups, and find himself again in his own singular and obdurate vocal style. He triumphs where his fellow bourgeois Bergotte, Swann, Vinteuil and Elstir do not, for he has more staying power and single-mindedness than they have.

The price to be paid for this confident assumption of the artistic vocation is that of being a helpless bystander before real political events. The artistic ego can consume and transform everything in its path; it can look upon class wars and world war and not be shaken; it can assemble a ship of fools and yet rise clear of folly; it can even become an archive, a compacted mass of historical data given memorable artistic form. But although power converges upon Proust's artist from all these directions and heaps all these honours upon him, he still cannot either assume power in his own person or imaginatively reinvent the spheres in which it is exercised by others. The bourgeois artist cannot see the ground on which he himself is standing, or come to grips with the forces which make it possible for him to exercise freely his own inventiveness. He works hard to dissociate himself from a tribe of obsolete and gratuitous-seeming aristocrats, but a new gratuitousness, more terrifying than theirs, is his reward.

Yet this cannot be the whole story of Proustian politics. For although Proust's narrator skilfully negotiates his own release from the class identities by which others are bound, and blithely removes political parties and policies from the scene, he does not create for himself in the process a motionless observational platform. On the contrary, the particular virtue of this narrator, put together by Proust from so many competing loyalties, enthusiasms and antipathies within himself, is that he remains mobile and many-voiced throughout a very long novel. The political realm is alive with pretension, vanity and self-deceit. Intellectually, it produces paradoxes and absurdities in unstoppable profusion. The narrator is at home there, temperamentally, and wants his politics to be as complicated and inconsequential as possible.

The narrator's will to complication can produce dizzying short-term effects inside the narrative. Indeed there are passages where the personality of the narrator seems to come apart into an infinitely mischievous play of ironies. Where can he possibly ground his own observations and judgements when *all* classes and political groups, past and present, launch into a *danse macabre* before his eyes? A critical moment of this kind occurs in *Sodome et Gomorrhe*, when the narrator joins Saniette, Cottard, Brichot and other members of the Verdurin clan for a pilgrimage by train to La Raspelière. This property near Balbec, owned by the Cambremers but rented seasonally to the Verdurins, itself lacks secure social anchorage, and the narrator's journey to it is a stormy passage through troubled class feelings. Cottard is alarmed that princesse Sherbatoff might have to share a compartment with a farmer, Saniette fears a new peasants' revolt when he sees a railway platform crowded with members of the rural community, and Brichot tells the narrator of the pleasures that await him at their journey's end:

> 'Si ce sont vos débuts chez Mme Verdurin, monsieur, me dit Brichot, qui tenait à montrer ses talents à un "nouveau", vous verrez qu'il n'y a pas de milieu où l'on sente mieux la "douceur de vivre", comme disait un des inventeurs du dilettantisme, du je m'enfichisme, de beaucoup de mots en "isme" à la mode chez nos snobinettes, je veux dire M. le prince de Talleyrand.' Car, quand il parlait de ces grands seigneurs du passé, il trouvait spirituel et 'couleur de l'époque' de faire précéder leur titre de monsieur et disait monsieur le duc de la Rochefoucauld, monsieur le cardinal de Retz, qu'il appelait aussi de temps en temps: 'Ce *struggle for lifer* de Gondi, ce "boulangiste" de Marcillac'. (iii 268–269)

Brichot is the embodiment here of the social malady that Nietzsche had called *ressentiment*. Speaking from within a citadel of bourgeois complacency, he trains the full force of his erudition on those who enjoy a social and intellectual status superior to his own. His envy and animosity find expression in a heavy-handed teasing of the distinguished dead. In a single gesture, the Cardinal de Retz and La Rochefoucauld are reminded of what they were before they found fame, and transported abruptly into the modern world, the one becoming a crude social Darwinist and the other a supporter of General Boulanger, whose brief period of reactionary insurgency belongs to the late 1880s. What gives Brichot's pedantic fantasy its special air of dementia, however, is that he should proclaim Mme Verdurin's ascendancy while cutting Talleyrand down to size. *La douceur de vivre*, the celebrated phrase that Talleyrand had used, apocryphally, of the last years of the *ancien régime*, is now reapplied to the Verdurins' seaside residence, while Talleyrand himself becomes a vulgarian of the present day: *je m'enfichisme* or 'couldn't-care-lessery' was a coinage of the early 1890s, and even more up to date in Proust's France than, say, 'jingoism' in Britain at the same period.

The narrator's own position in all this criss-crossing of social perspectives is, to say the least, fragile and uncomfortable. He takes sides against Brichot, yet shares a great deal with him. The narrator, like Swann before him, has his own reasons for seeking temporary admission to the clan of which Brichot is an honoured member. Brichot's attack upon the aristocracy echoes the narrator's own resentful demythologizing of the Guermantes. Brichot in his time-travels through the history of France is a paltry and envious version of the all-knowing free spirit that the narrator aspires to become. His attention flickers between the peasants on the platform and the buffoonish bourgeois on the train, between the Verdurins and their aristocratic landlords, between low-grade, high-grade and purely imaginary princesses, and nowhere finds its point of rest. Class values are so much in crisis that an astute observer can do no more than conduct comparative measurements at chosen points in the social landscape, hoping to discover pockets of dignity, true feeling or intellectual probity hidden away in odd corners of the scene. Surviving in this world, and in due course perhaps breaking through into Talleyrand's *douceur de vivre*, is a matter of diplomacy and negotiation, of not insisting too much or trying too hard. The nascent artist must recognize that he too is a 'struggle for lifer', and that his essential gift is an indefinite power of adaptation.

What is true of episodes like the journey to La Raspelière is to some extent true of the novel as a whole. Proust aestheticizes politics, following the example of Saint-Loup, Charlus and other characters of his own invention. One is reminded at moments of Disraeli, for whom politics was uniformly dramatic and rhetorical whether played out at the hustings and in parliament or re-created in *Coningsby* and *Sybil*. Proust's political creatures are much given to rhetorical flights and to verbal displays bordering on madness. Salon discussion of contemporary politics is artfully whipped into a froth of fatuous opinions and slogans. The narrator has to a spectacular degree the adaptability and dexterity that in his youth he admired in Norpois and in Stendhal's Mosca, and, in addition, is master of an inexhaustible singing line that carries his narration through the din of divergent political voices.

Yet there is also something much more violent and dissonant in Proust's portrayal of the political life. All human situations are matters for negotiation, the narrator seems often to suggest, and inventiveness and adaptation should be watchwords for the artist quite as much as for the politician or the diplomat. But beyond this delicious play of possibility, real, non-negotiable conflicts and contradictions continue to exist, and these too find their way into the texture of Proust's novel. Here is a work which is in considerable part a pro-*dreyfusard* satire, and comparable in this to Anatole France's *L'Île des pingouins* (1908), yet one which incorporates into itself currents of visceral anti-Semitic feeling; a work which defends and celebrates the working class, yet offers a democratically improved form of prostitution as a cure for social ills; and a work which, while endlessly proclaiming the nullity of the aristocracy, locates and ingeniously exploits ever more sources of poetry in this discredited social class. This vision of politics has neither ease nor *douceur* in it, but offers at best a bracing pessimism. When even this breaks down, Proust's book leaves us with politics as an art of the impossible, and with ample reason for despair.

Notes

[1] All references to Proust's novel are to the 4 volumes of the new Pléiade edition, prepared under the general editorship of Jean-Yves Tadié (Paris: Gallimard, 1987–1989).

[2] *The Man Without Qualities*, tr. Eithne Wilkins and Ernst Kaiser (London: Secker and Warburg, 1954), i 126.

'Le Renégat': An Ironic Re-enactment of Camus's Djihad?

VALERIE HOWELLS

The plot of the 'Le Renégat' is fairly straightforward. A Catholic priest, driven by missionary zeal, sets out to convert a barbaric tribe living in the African desert, but he becomes their captive, and they beat him and cut out his tongue. Imprisonment, deprivation and torture lead him to deny his own faith and espouse their religion, worshipping the fetish, the guardian of evil. Overhearing plans to bring a replacement missionary to the settlement, the renegade priest escapes, steals a gun, and waits in ambush. After murdering the missionary, he is punished and left to die. In his agony, he reverts once more to his original beliefs.

Exploring Camus's narrative techniques, the careful reader is struck by the richness and density of texture which lie cloaked beneath an apparent and deceptive simplicity. In *L'Exil et le royaume*,[1] this richness is the result of probing the deep seams of the characters' 'secret selves'[2] and an equally secret universe. 'Le Renégat' invites us to share an even closer secret than its companion stories, but it is not one of easy access. In spite of the first-person narrative, 'Le Renégat' frustrates rather than facilitates the reader's desire for contact with the speaking 'I', shoring up dykes to protect Camus's vulnerability, all the while giving play to a polysemic flow and a temporal flux which re-create the disequilibrium of the confused mind from which this narrative supposedly emanates.

'Mystérieux à la lecture, "Le Renégat" le reste après étude critique'.[3] For Roger Quilliot, the text remains an enigma which will only be clarified if additional background material can be found. However, apart from material in *Carnets III*, little is known about the source or the genesis of the story.[4]

One of the earliest ideas for 'Un esprit confus' noted in the *Carnets* suggests a story built around the fundamental misanthropy of the central character.⁵ The 1956 version of the story is already much more complex, but the additions to the 1957 version, heightening as they do the emphasis on the opposition Europe/ Taghâsa, suggest that the narrative may encapsulate an ironic version of Camus's tortured response to the Algerian war.

As Camus himself stated: 'L'erreur de l'art moderne est presque toujours de faire passer le moyen avant la fin, la forme avant le fond, la technique avant le sujet'.⁶ Indeed, in my view, the key to 'Le Renégat' lies in the close relation of *forme* to *fond*, that is, in the expression of conflict and confusion experienced by the priest and its relation to autobiographical elements embedded in a fictional situation reflecting Camus's own moral and political dilemma during the Algerian war. That war led him seriously to question his moral and political standpoint, in a process of self-examination which caused him great torment. He knew that his support for the Arabs could make him indirectly responsible for the deaths of civilians, and possibly for harming his own family. This consideration made it impossible for him to endorse the actions of the FLN. The text of 'Le Renégat', on the contrary, pursues 'jusqu'au bout' the consequences of adopting a position which goes beyond desirable limits.

Between 1945 and 1958, Algeria witnessed an escalation of hostilities which affected Camus profoundly. In his articles in *Combat* and in *L'Express*,⁷ he made impassioned pleas for 'mesure' on both sides, arguing consistently for a negotiated compromise, but in August 1955, riots broke out in the north of Constantine, and brutal reprisals cost the lives of thousands of Algerians.⁸ Now it is almost inconceivable, in view of the scale of Camus's involvement in the Algerian troubles, and the fact that *L'Exil et le royaume* was composed during a period of growing crisis in Algeria, that his creative fiction should bear no trace of the effects of this harrowing ordeal, especially when we consider his comment in a letter written to Charles Poncet on 25 September 1955: 'Je suis bien angoissé devant les affaires d'Algérie ... et *ne puis penser à rien d'autre*' (my italics).⁹ For Victor Brombert the story is an allegory which 'deals with the drama of the mind', and the drama is the clash of humanist culture and totalitarian ideologies,¹⁰ but this is perhaps only part of the story. The mysterious nature of 'Le Renégat' is equally the protective cloak thrown around Camus's reaction to the Algerian crisis, and the text's harsh evocation of mental anguish and brutal torture bears the imprint of Camus's personal drama.

In his editorial notes for 'Le Renégat', Quilliot mentions that 'Camus aimait à dire, par boutade: "C'est le portrait du progressiste chrétien"' (*TRN*, p. 2044). For Van Nieuwenhuijze, in the context of cross-cultural relationships, progressivist thought is an attitude of enlightened colonialism which envisages the function of the ruling class as that of an agency for education and development.[11] Progressivism is sympathetic to nationalist claims for independence, but finds itself in a most critical position so far as loyalties and belonging are concerned. The vagueness of the progressivist's ideal produces the disadvantage of having no clear course to steer: 'Progressivism ends up in the clouds, not as an attitude bent upon practical implementation and institutionalization, but *as a missionary's attitude, regardless of its practical relevance*'.[12] Van Nieuwenhuijze's analogy of the missionary is strikingly similar to that chosen by Camus as the vehicle for 'Le Renégat'.

'Le Renégat' is a dialogic narrative which primarily sets out to convey the extent of the confusion in the protagonist's mind. Plunged *in medias res* at the beginning of the *nouvelle*, the reader is confronted by a text which verges on incoherence, finding himself, in the space of the first paragraph, bombarded with the essential problems of the text: the narrator's confusion, and his struggle to resolve it; the narrator's silence and isolation; a doubling of the narrative voice, and the interplay of past and present. As I hope to show in the detailed analysis which follows, each of these elements helps to express the particularly traumatic experience which Camus underwent during the Algerian crisis.

The *récit* begins with a dramatic expression of the fictional narrator's attempt to resolve his present state of confusion. The quotation marks which open the *nouvelle* suggest direct speech, leading the reader to anticipate an eventual movement in perspective which will allow him to identify the narrator, and situate him in the context of the fiction. With a sudden shock, the reader realizes that this direct speech is part of a curious interior monologue – the product of a tongueless mouth (p. 1579).

Complex thought processes invariably involve the formulation of language at a 'pre-speech level of consciousness',[13] and the literary technique of interior monologue can provide access to this inner world of the protagonist. In 'Le Renégat', however, focusing on the protagonist's ability to utter words causes the sophisticated reader to become even more conscious than in the case of conventional interior monologues that an unseen and unknown intermediary has to be intervening, to provide a vehicle for the text. Almost immediately, the problem of the author's relation to his fictional narrator is brought to the reader's attention. By inviting the reader's distrust of the narrative, does Camus wish to make it clear from the outset that his own political or moral view does not necessarily coincide with that of his fictional narrator? Or does the narrative's insistence on thoughts as they are conceived represent an attempt to convince the reader that he is witnessing the expression of ideas untainted by artifice? In any event, the central episode in the story – the cutting out of the priest's tongue – together with the text's recurrent reminders of the inarticulateness of the narrator and the silence imposed upon him, show Camus to be reinforcing the importance of words and the power of language in an interior monologue which could be seen as a fictional representation of Camus's own unvoiced internal struggle during the political crisis.

The political writings point to three main ways in which Camus was made to feel that silence would be his most appropriate response. First, the terrorist activities of the Arab nationalists had the effect of devaluing his arguments in their favour: '[...] le terrorisme [...] ne fait de surcroît que [...] *fermer la bouche* à l'opinion libérale française qui pourrait trouver et faire adopter la solution de conciliation'.[14] Secondly, Camus was advised by an associate to maintain silence on issues relating to the crisis in order to minimize serious risk to himself and his family. Thirdly, and most dramatically, threats of violence, kidnap and even death were issued to Camus in attempts to prevent him from addressing a public meeting in Algiers in January 1956.[15] The opening passage of Camus's 'Appel pour une trêve civile en Algérie' uses images of speech and its suppression to represent the effects of political constraints: 'Ce n'est pas la moindre de mes déceptions – et le mot est faible – d'avoir à reconnaître que [...] un homme, et un écrivain, qui a consacré une partie de sa vie à servir l'Algérie, s'expose, avant même qu'on sache ce qu'il veut dire, *à se voir refuser la parole*'.[16] Camus's political statements gained little support. As each faction strove for supremacy, both sides expected him to demonstrate his solidarity with them. The resulting *crise de conscience* is reflected in the form of the *nouvelle*. By revealing the protagonist's pre-speech consciousness, the interior monologue not only allows us to penetrate the realm of unresolved conflict, but it also imprisons us there.

Many devices contribute to the effect of disconcerting confusion.

A kind of suspect logic is suggested by processes of modification and substitution representing the unimpeded stream of thoughts coursing through the narrator's mind: '[Le curé] me faisait lire, il a fait rentrer le latin dans ma tête dure: "Intelligent ce petit, mais un mulet", [...] "Tête de vache" disait mon père ce porc' (p. 1580). Challenging or contradictory thoughts reflect mental and emotional confusion – 'mon père grossier, ma mère brute' (p. 1579); '[...] je les aimais peut-être' (p. 1582) – and shifts of subject maintain a rich play of ambiguity and a complex orchestration of symbols.

Against a background of confusion, Camus presents a narrator in the throes of self-examination, the effects of which are equally complex. One may admire the single-mindedness which refuses all complacency: 'Mon directeur ne comprenait pas quand je m'accablais: "Mais non, il y a du bon en vous!" Du bon! il y avait en moi du vin aigre, voilà tout' (p. 1580). But the admiration is tainted, at first by the bitterness of the protagonist's own retrospective irony – 'une seule idée et mulet intelligent j'allais jusqu'au bout' (p. 1580) – and then by a growing sense of disquiet, as the priest's fanaticism is revealed by self-castigation:

> Comment devenir meilleur si l'on n'est pas mauvais, je l'avais bien compris dans tout ce qu'ils m'enseignaient. Je n'avais même compris que cela [...] j'allais jusqu'au bout, j'allais au-devant des pénitences, je rognais sur l'ordinaire, enfin je voulais être un exemple, moi aussi, pour qu'on me voie, et qu'en me voyant on rende hommage à ce qui m'avait fait meilleur, à travers moi saluez mon Seigneur. (p. 1580)

A sequence of verbs in the first person underlines the supposed narrator's egoism and pride. Exclamation and emphasis convey mounting emotion: '[...] je ne détournais pas, moi, les yeux [...] l'offense et la souffrance étaient douces!' [p. 1580]); and the insistent repetition of 'meilleur' (four times in a single paragraph) becomes a crescendo, reaching its climax with the account of the priest's apotheosis, which Camus forcefully represents in the change from action to state and the switch from subject ('je') to object pronoun ('me', 'moi'), and culminating in the final imperative.

For the account of the priest's decision to go to Taghâsa, Camus shows the supposed narrator adopting a mocking tone of familiarity, using *discours indirect libre* to represent objections made to him by those at the seminary who tried, in vain, to prevent his foolhardy mission: 'Ils m'en ont fait des discours au séminaire pour me décourager et qu'il fallait attendre, ce n'était pas un pays de mission, je n'étais pas mûr, je devais me préparer particulièrement, savoir qui j'étais' (p. 1581). But Camus selects the same technique to present the comments of the would-be missionary, who persists in disparaging his own stubbornness and hubris: '[...] je secouais ma tête dure et je répétais la même chose [...] Puissant, oui, c'était le mot que, sans cesse, je roulais sur ma langue' (p. 1581).The narrator ironizes his earlier scorn for the limited ambitions of his mentors – 'Convertir des braves gens un peu égarés, c'était l'idéal minable de nos prêtres' (p. 1582) – and denounces his own misplaced arrogance: '[...] je voulais être reconnu par les bourreaux eux-mêmes [...] régner enfin *par la seule parole* sur une armée de méchants ... mon idée quand je l'ai, je ne la lâche plus' (p. 1582).

Parallels between the narrator's situation and that of Camus himself begin to emerge. In his early political writings, Camus confidently proclaimed his faith in the benefits to be derived from North Africa's acceptance of France's cultural heritage and ethical values, and in 1945 he wrote: 'Si nous voulons sauver l'Afrique du Nord, nous devons marquer à la face du monde notre résolution d'y faire connaître la France par ses meilleures lois et ses hommes les plus justes'.[17] Roger Quilliot suggests[18] that as late as January 1956, when organizing the meeting at which he would deliver his address 'Appel pour une trêve civile en Algérie', Camus still hoped that his intervention would achieve dramatic results. Like the renegade priest, he put his faith entirely in the power of words. Even so, Camus himself was not totally unaware of the irony of his situation, as the text of his address suggests: 'On peut rire sans doute à la mine que prend le prêcheur de réconciliation devant la réponse que lui fait l'histoire en lui montrant les deux peuples qu'il aimait embrassés seulement dans une même fureur mortelle'.[19] Both Camus and his protagonist become aware, in retrospect, of their misplaced belief in their own effectiveness as agents for political/religious change.

Using a characteristically ironic tone, Camus stresses the extent of the changes that the Taghâsan experiences have wrought in the narrator. He now has difficulty in comprehending his past ingenuousness: 'Et l'argent que le guide m'a volé, naïf toujours naïf je le lui avais montré' (p. 1582). Contact with the Taghâsans has radically altered his point of view: '[...] ils m'ont appris, oh oui' (p. 1582). In this context the description of the Taghâsan people is a particularly telling one, which emphasizes their isolation:

[...] dès le réveil ils commandent, ils frappent, ils disent qu'ils ne sont qu'un *seul* peuple, que leur dieu est le vrai, et qu'il faut obéir. Ce sont mes seigneurs, ils ignorent la pitié, et comme des seigneurs, ils veulent être *seuls*, avancer *seuls*, régner *seuls,* puisque *seuls*, ils ont eu l'audace de bâtir dans le sel et les sables une froide cité torride. Et moi ... (p. 1584)

This use of 'seul' perhaps echoes the demands for autonomy which the North African peoples continued to make throughout the period of confrontation, though the passage also underlines the power and cruelty of the Taghâsans. Essentially, what we have in the text of 'Le Renégat' is a reversal of situations. The young priest's pride has been replaced by humiliation. His dreams of subjugation have given way to a reality where the Taghâsans' mindless cruelty and tyranny cause him hesitation and doubt about the relevance of his mission, and a sense of irony with respect to his own situation.

In the account of his suffering and humiliation, the narrator appears to be launching a challenge, defying the belief that any other response would be possible under the circumstances: '... le visage tendu, la mémoire exténuée, oui, j'ai essayé de prier le fétiche' (p. 1586). Similar examples of emphatic affirmation recur in the story, suggesting perhaps an attempt at self-justification, as when Camus describes the effect of the woman's screams during her intercourse with the sorcerer: 'Et moi, à force de solitude, égaré, n'ai-je pas crié aussi; oui, hurlé d'épouvante vers le fétiche' (p. 1587). Eventually, bitter self-denunciation begins to colour the challenge: '... j'ai fait mieux que de le prier, j'ai cru en lui et j'ai nié tout ce que j'avais cru jusque-là' (p. 1589). The protagonist rejects all his former beliefs, as he reflects on the effects of an allegiance to the Taghâsans which would demand a betrayal of cultural and ethical values: '... à bas l'Europe, la raison et l'honneur et la croix. Oui, je devais me convertir à la religion de mes maîtres' (p. 1590). Camus added 'à bas l'Europe, la raison et l'honneur et la croix' after the 1956 edition of the *nouvelle*, that is, after his attempts to set up a dialogue to end the horrific events of the conflict. Perhaps it was a sense of shame which led him to pursue this criticism of European cultural values to its limit. Perhaps also, the text was a means of exploring an allegiance to the Arab population, which included acceptance of the methods of Arab extremists.

In the priest's telescoped account of his escape from Algiers and his journey through the Sahara towards the town of Taghâsa, description highlights a number of elements relating to the protagonist's consciousness and his state of mind. While the principal mode of Camus's writing is mimetic,[20] elements of the landscape also reflect the protagonist's view. Patricia Johnson convincingly argues that description in 'Le Renégat' represents the distorted vision of the first-person narrator:

> [...] l'auteur étend sa domination au-delà de la personnalité du narrateur [...] pour se livrer à un agencement plus subtil de l'univers extérieur qui s'insinuera, sans être analysé, dans l'esprit du narrateur percevant [...] le narrateur transforme à tel point la réalité extérieure – réalité déjà solicitée par le romancier pour lui faire refléter, inspirer, reproduire l'état d'âme du narrateur – que le prétendu décor devient essentiellement le prolongement du narrateur lui-même.[21]

These are pertinent observations about the role of description in 'Le Renégat', where the decor of the 'univers violent'[22] stresses inhumanity and cruelty, evoking the brutal reality of horrific experiences.

The hot, arid, stony landscape is described in images which emphasize its metallic, unyielding qualities – '[...] la montagne à nouveau, toute en pics noirs, en arêtes coupantes comme du fer' (p. 1582) – and the town of Taghâsa itself has a significantly geometric construction which has been the focus of two penetrating studies by Edward Hughes and Paul Fortier.[23] Already, in the earliest description of the town, the unyielding nature of the construction is underlined – 'murs droits' (p. 1583) – occurs twice within one sentence, and the dwellings are described as 'igloos cubiques' (p. 1583), but the predominant idea is that of an 'enfer blanc' where 'des terrasses blanches [...] semblaient se rejoindre toutes' (p. 1583). The choice of enclosed space is characteristic of Camus's use of decor to increase concentration and intensity. In 'Le Renégat', the angular constructs of the 'ville de l'ordre' represent 'le règne de la méchanceté qui était sans fissures' (p. 1589). For the renegade priest, 'la vérité est carrée, lourde, dense, elle ne supporte pas la nuance' (p. 1589), and it is this kind of rigorous order that Camus shows him attempting to impose in his own situation, as indicated at the beginning of the narrative: 'Il faut mettre de l'ordre dans ma tête [...] De l'ordre, un ordre [...] oui j'ai toujours désiré l'ordre' (p. 1579). However, Camus composes the narrative using a counterpoint of irreconcilables. Positioning the lyrical description of natural life outside the confines of the town almost parenthetically amid the sharply geometrical description of Taghâsa and its inhabitants, Camus stresses the aridity of exile, while at the same time highlighting the irrepressibility of those phenomena which resist any ordering process:

> [...] la ville stérile sculptée dans une montagne de sel, séparée de la nature, privée des floraisons fugitives et rares du désert, soustraite à ces hasards ou ces tendresses, un nuage insolite, une pluie rageuse et brève, que même le soleil ou les sables connaissent, la ville de l'ordre enfin, angles droits, chambres carrées, hommes roides. (p. 1589)

By making frequent allusions to a reality beyond the harsh inhuman world of Taghâsa, Camus suggests the longing for impossible tranquillity. As the sun rises over the renegade's ambush, heralding the searing heat of day, his language changes momentarily. There is a sudden outburst of nostalgia: '... le désert change, il n'a plus la couleur du cyclamen des montagnes, ô ma montagne, et la neige, la douce neige molle'; annulling this short-lived wave of lyricism almost immediately, Camus then reinstates the reality of the arid desert: '... non c'est un jaune un peu gris, l'heure ingrate' (p. 1581).

Building into the narrative a symbolism of colours, Camus reinforces descriptions of a land of extremes where men are condemned to solitude, whether by the intolerable heat of day or by the freezing polar night. Camus uses strong primary colours to heighten the impression of 'l'univers violent': the harsh blue sunlit sky, the yellow of the evening sky and the desert sand, the red sandals of the Taghâsans, and the red of the protagonist's blood. The most striking contrast, though, is that of black and white. Both extremes dominate the Taghâsan world, and Camus uses the black robes of the tribal masters as symbols of the evil of their repressive control. He introduces fleeting glimpses of muted colours (the mauve and grey of the desert before 'le grand éblouissement' (pp. 1581, 1591)) to convey a nostalgia for natural changeability (p. 1589) which momentarily undermines the priest's allegiance to the fetish and the order imposed by its domination, thereby suggesting a longing for some release from this intolerable situation.

When Camus presents the narrator's description of the trails of salt on the robes of the Taghâsan masters, likening them to the trails left by snails after the rain, this sudden recollection of the world outside the Taghâsan desert gives rise to a wave of anguish, expressed in a dramatic exhortation to annihilate the inhuman city and its malevolent tribes, and put an end to the protagonist's suffering: 'La pluie, ô Seigneur, une seule vraie pluie, longue, dure, la pluie de ton ciel! Alors enfin la ville affreuse, rongée peu à peu, s'affaisserait avec lenteur, irrésistiblement, et [...] emporterait vers les sables ses habitants féroces' (p. 1583). This statement of the opposition between water and the arid desert is characteristic of the way in which Camus infuses his descriptions with symbolic meaning, creating a network of linked images which work towards a metaphorization of the decor. Camus rarely uses decor in a simply connotative way. On the contrary, he tends to return to a series of oppositions which suggest, throughout the story, the antithesis of totalitarian order and natural mutability. He associates rain with the emotional security that may have surrounded the priest's past, representing the renegade's recollections of family closeness against a background decor which contrasts strongly with the physical and emotional climate of the present: 'frais comme les prés, comme la pluie du soir, autrefois, quand la soupe cuisait doucement, ils m'attendaient, mon père et ma mère, qui parfois me souriaient, je les aimais peut-être' (p. 1582). But it is when Camus intensifies the lyrical impulse of the priest's language to reach its peak in the description of night that water imagery becomes most compelling:

> Seule la nuit, avec ses étoiles *fraîches* et ses *fontaines* obscures, pouvait me sauver, m'enlever enfin aux dieux méchants des hommes, mais toujours enfermé, je ne pouvais la contempler. Si l'autre tarde encore, je la verrai au moins monter du désert et envahir le ciel, froide vigne d'or qui pendra du zénith obscur et où je pourrai *boire* à loisir, *humecter* ce trou noir et desséché que nul muscle de chair vivant et souple ne *rafraîchit* plus. (p. 1588)

Here, Camus's use of imagery underlines the emotional and moral polarization of the decor. He evokes memories of cool, endless expanses – 'l'eau de la nuit' (p. 1588) – with purifying and regenerating properties, presenting night as a symbol of freedom, solace and respite from the inexorable heat of the sun, and the oppressive monotony of psychological and physical suffering.

In the desert town of Taghâsa, however, water is never pure. It is contaminated by salt, which Camus links throughout the text with torture (the priest is beaten with ropes dipped in salt and water (p. 1586)) and with sterility: '[...] la ville stérile sculptée dans une montagne de sel' (p. 1589). Camus makes the salt seem ubiquitous: it marks the Taghâsans' robes, penetrates beneath fingernails and into the mouth, and contaminates the drinking water from the town's only well (p. 1583). Eventually, it will be spread over the world, a destructive element stifling youth – the embodiment of life and hope – and killing off all natural living things: '[...] mes maîtres [...] sèmeront leur sel sur le continent, toute végétation, toute jeunesse s'éteindra' (p. 1592).

Camus's concentration on the dominant factors of sun and salt relegates water to the memory and imagination or, worse, transforms it into a negative value: 'la haine est [...] la source de toute vie, l'eau fraîche, fraîche comme la menthe qui glace la bouche et brûle l'estomac' (p. 1590). Furthermore, when, ultimately, the priest is shown contemplating the night, Camus presents its liquid purity as providing no relief in a world of violence and hatred. Night does not quench the priest's thirst; on the contrary, Camus chooses darkness in place of sunlight as a backdrop to prolonged suffering, loneliness and pain: 'Que le désert est silencieux! La nuit déjà et je suis seul, *j'ai soif*, [...] mon corps brûle, la nuit plus obscure emplit mes yeux (p. 1593).

Camus builds his system of imagery around the extremes ordering the monotony of Taghâsan life: the torrid heat of day which gives way 'sans transition' (p. 1583) to polar night. At once a source of life and a harbinger of death, the sun frequently plays an important and ambiguous role in Camus's texts, but in 'Le Renégat', the extraordinary polyvalence of the image is symptomatic of a deliberate drive towards a more general polysemy indicating the complexity and perplexity of the protagonist's situation. The proliferation of meanings and associations allows Camus to suggest simultaneous discordant notions: this itself also reflects the 'esprit confus' of the narrator. At times, the imagery of 'Le Renégat' recalls that of *Le Malentendu*,[24] with the sun combining with water to symbolize life and freedom: '[...] je voulais partir, [...] commencer enfin à vivre dans le soleil, avec de l'eau claire' (p. 1579). But the sun here also represents religious faith – '[Le curé] me parlait d'un avenir et du soleil, le catholicisme c'est le soleil, disait-il' (pp. 1579–1580) – and in the renegade's mind, faith opens up the path to power. An allusion to the Napoleonic victory of 1805[25] uses the image of the sun of Austerlitz to increase dramatic intensity and suspense, drawing attention to the potential power of the protagonist. Training at the seminary takes place 'sous le soleil de Grenoble' (p. 1580) and, later, the priest's mission, as he envisions it, entails subjugation and the imposition of order by force, which is likewise represented by an image of the sun: '[...] je subjuguerais ces sauvages comme *un soleil puissant*' (p. 1581). However, the sun itself is also described as 'sauvage', and the positioning of this adjective creates confusion between the sun and the priest's 'seigneur': '[...] à travers moi saluez mon Seigneur. Soleil sauvage! il se lève, le désert change' (pp. 1580–1581). The use of the personal pronoun 'il' is ambiguous, its referent unclear. Camus creates further confusion when he repeatedly links the aggressive power of the barbaric tribe of Taghâsa with that of the sun: '[...] ils sont comme le soleil qui n'en finit pas de frapper' (p. 1582). Violent images colour the text: '[...] le soleil [...] qui me frappe [...] à coups de lances brûlantes soudain sorties du sol' (pp. 1582–1583). The full weaponry of a hostile world bursts in upon the narrator's consciousness with an intensity that recalls the murder scene in *L'Étranger*, where the light itself becomes 'glaive éclatant', 'épée brûlante', and 'longue lame étincelante'.[26] Equally, in 'Le Renégat', Camus highlights the consequences of totalitarian control by emphasizing physical suffering inflicted by the sun, and by using images drawn from weaponry and metal to underline those qualities shared by the sun and the barbarians' fetish: 'J'étais là jeté à genoux au creux de ce bouclier blanc, les yeux rongés par les *épées* de sel et de feu qui sortaient de tous les murs [...]. Sous les coups du soleil de fer, le ciel résonnait longuement, *plaque de tôle* chauffé à blanc' (p. 1584). The cruelty of the fetish is underlined a little later when the narrator notes that it has the shape of an axe, with metallic features ('j'ai vu le fétiche, sa double tête de hache, son nez de fer tordu comme un serpent', p. 1586).[27] Camus presents both the sun and the fetish as reigning over the kingdom of sterile violence in which the priest finds himself imprisoned: '[...] long jour sans âge où le fétiche régnait comme le soleil féroce sur ma maison de rochers' (p. 1588). The combination of metallic imagery and the figure of the sun consistently underlines violence, which Camus builds to a climax when the narrator identifies his own tongueless mouth with that of the sun:

> Maintenant, le soleil a un peu dépassé le milieu du ciel. Entre les fentes du rocher, je vois le trou qu'il fait dans le métal surchauffé du ciel, bouche comme la mienne volubile, et qui vomit sans trêve des fleuves de flammes au-dessus du désert sans couleur. (p. 1587)

Apart from its role in a rich pattern of images, the sun also functions as a temporal hinge in a highly complex structure which switches back and forth between the present, the recent and more distant past, and the future. References to the movement or stasis of the sun continually call the protagonist back to conflict and confusion, as Camus uses this temporal movement to intensify the dramatic anguish of the present, and to signal that retrospection provides no way out of the intolerable situation. Camus's temporal structure thus reinforces the impression of the protagonist's imprisonment simultaneously created by decor and imagery. The retrospective account (the young priest's ambitions, the flight from the seminary, the description of Taghâsa, and the first encounter with the barbaric tribesmen) is fragmented and interspersed with references to the sun which act as temporal shifters, always returning us to the present: 'Le soleil est encore monté, mon front commence à brûler' (p. 1582); '[...] le soleil [...] me frappe fort en ce moment, trop fort [...]. Oh! à l'abri, oui à l'abri, sous le grand rocher, avant que tout s'embrouille' (p. 1583); 'Quelle bouillie quand la chaleur monte [...] je sens le soleil' (p. 1584). Camus constantly interrupts digressions, forcing the inescapable torment of the moment on the consciousness of the protagonist. After the priest's tongue is cut out, his suffering is not allowed to be annulled by death: 'J'ai voulu me lever, je suis retombé, heureux, désespérément heureux de mourir enfin, la mort aussi est fraîche et son ombre n'abrite aucun dieu. Je ne suis pas mort' (p. 1589). Similarly, after his punishment for the murder of the missionary, he is subject yet again to the torture of the sun: '... je m'éveille, mais non, je vais mourir, l'aube se lève, la première lumière le jour pour d'autres vivants, et pour moi le soleil inexorable, les mouches' (p. 1593). The death he longs for eludes him still.

Camus's temporal swings also accompany changes in narrative mode. The lot of the renegade priest is a state of confusion which colours even his account of the past, rendering suspect his motives, and underlining the unreliability of this complex narrator. Very early on, the narrative moves from indications of the spatio-temporal present to indications which revolve around the present/past dichotomy. Using the word 'patiente' as a hinge – 'Patiente encore, sale esclave! Il y a si longtemps que je patiente' (p. 1579) – Camus swings the narrative focus to a different temporal perspective. The protagonist launches into an account of his early youth, and events anterior to the past alluded to at the beginning of the text: 'Depuis qu'ils m'ont coupé la langue [...]' (p. 1579). We now have a triple perspective, where the distant past is reflected and commented upon by the experiencing consciousness, which is itself the subject of reflection and comment in a different narrative mode. Nor is it always clear which voice is to the fore, so that the narrator's relation to his account is difficult to pinpoint. In a disjointed passage describing the stultifying atmosphere of the priest's childhood, a series of confused enumerations culminates in an expression of frustration and the need for escape: '[...] oh! je voulais partir, les quitter d'un seul coup et commencer enfin à vivre' (p. 1579). On the one hand, the strength of the priest's feeling is still perceptible, suggesting a reliving of experience; on the other hand, the intrusion of irony conveys that distance which indicates the reflective mode: '[...] ils m'ont vu arriver comme le soleil d'Austerlitz. Pâlichon le soleil, il est vrai, à cause de l'alcool, ils ont bu le vin aigre et leurs enfants ont des dents cariées' (p. 1580). But we are brought back to the present by the merging of the priest's father and the missionary he intends to murder: '[...] râ râ tuer son père, voilà ce qu'il faudrait, mais pas de danger, au fait, qu'il se lance dans la mission puisqu'il est mort depuis longtemps [...] alors il ne reste qu'à tuer le missionnaire' (p. 1580). A confused vindication of the priest's motive in setting out to kill the missionary, as a substitute for the dead father, is based on the illogical linking of 'père', 'mission' and 'missionnaire'. In the midst of this confusion, Camus introduces a strange, apparently nonsensical expression. 'Râ râ' becomes a recurrent motif in the text, and its function is multiple. The sound indicates the inarticulateness of the fictional narrator, and suggests the 'bruit de cailloux remués' which is all his tongueless mouth is capable of uttering. In addition, it recalls the mindless cries of football fans or members of extreme political parties. But the word also echoes the name of the ancient Egyptian sun-god, Ra, and by association, establishes a sense of the mental framework within which the narrative will unfold, indirectly prefiguring the introduction of the fetish god.[28] Consistently coinciding with a change in temporal perspective and a return to the preoccupations of the fictional present, 'râ' also indicates the change to the reflecting mode. The incantation of the articles of faith of the Catholic church, for instance, gives way to the critical, distanced view: 'Oui, j'ai cru, râ râ et je me sentais meilleur' (p. 1580). The focus then returns to the present as the priest looks in the direction of Taghâsa – 'Rien, rien encore jusqu'à l'horizon' (p. 1581) – but his present relative freedom causes his imprisonment to weigh upon his memory. In keeping with Camus's temporal strategy, the priest's account reaches once more back to the past. The association of Taghâsa with violence – 'Taghâsa dont le nom de fer bat dans ma tête' (p. 1581) – prepares the reader for the description of the cruelty of its inhabitants. As we read the account, however, we are struck by a significant change in tone. Confusion gives way to accuracy and clarity. The narrator reflects on the narrative even as he shapes it: 'Le premier à m'en parler a été le vieux prêtre [...] mais pourquoi le premier, il était le seul, et moi, ce n'est pas la ville de sel, les murs blancs dans le soleil torride qui m'ont frappé dans son récit, non, mais la cruauté des habitants sauvages' (p. 1581). At the same time, he sees himself across a span of years separating him from the experience he describes.

Further switches operate from past to present. In the account of the young priest's grandiose ambitions, there is a lingering sense of his exaggerated self-esteem which contributes to the reader's sense of unease: '[...] c'est ma force, oui, ma force à moi dont ils avaient tous pitié!' (p. 1582). The ensuing digression into the even more remote past is even more disturbing: 'Les pierres autour de moi crépitent sourdement, seul le canon du fusil est frais, frais comme les prés, comme la pluie du soir, autrefois, quand la soupe cuisait doucement, ils m'attendaient, mon père et ma mère, qui parfois me souriaient, je les aimais peut-être' (p. 1582). The uncertainty of even basic emotions reflects the way in which the voice constantly shakes any kind of stability. The cynical mode now comes to the fore, preventing any indulgence in nostalgia, so that the narrator forces himself to concentrate on the urgent task in hand: 'Mais c'est fini, un voile de chaleur commence à se lever de la piste, viens, missionnaire, je t'attends' (p. 1582). Brought suddenly back to the present moment, the narrative naturally resumes the account which, the reader anticipates, will provide an explanation for the projected murder.

The text is thus constantly moving between different levels, and the reader's vision continues to oscillate between the present of waiting, with its tension and its projection into the future, and the recent and more distant past. At the same time, there is an interweaving of different perspectives. The account of events leading up to the priest's mission to Taghâsa is laced with retrospective irony, while the distant past, evoked through the narrator's memory, projects images of family and emotional security which are constantly rejected. The result is an overwhelming sense of the narrator's mental confusion, countered only by the narrative being thrust back into the present – the domain of even more acute anguish.

After the account of the initiation, Camus builds to a dramatic and emotional climax with the description of the ritual coupling of the sorcerer and the young woman. This scene, with its combined elements of ritual music and dancing, the woman's cry, and the motif of sexual repression, heightens the impression of the narrator's alienation, bewilderment and horror: 'Et moi, à force de solitude, égaré, n'ai-je pas crié aussi, oui, hurlé d'épouvante vers le fétiche jusqu'à ce qu'un coup de pied me rejette contre le mur (p. 1587). Immediately, Camus brings the narrative back to the present, as before, by means of a striking parallelism in physical attitudes causing both moments of the narrative – past and present – to converge in a dramatic reminder of all the horrific elements of the fictional narrator's situation: '[...] jusqu'à ce qu'un coup de pied me rejette contre le mur, mordant le sel, comme je mords aujourd'hui le rocher, de ma bouche sans langue, en attendant celui qu'il faut que je tue' (p. 1587). The switch in temporal perspective maintains the dramatic tension of the present, so that the reader is never allowed to lose sight of the inescapable, unbearable conditions in which the protagonist must wait.

There are few glimpses of the future, but as the renegade priest prepares to contemplate the night, changes of tense effect a movement from negative – 'je ne pouvais la contempler' – to positive: 'je la verrai'; 'froide vigne d'or qui pendra'; 'je pourrai boire' (p. 1588). The whole passage represents the only expression of hope in the narrative which is neither corrected, contradicted, nor dismissed with irony. But it is short-lived, and is finally negated by reality, as night becomes the present moment of the narrative, prolonging physical and mental anguish: 'Que le désert est silencieux! La nuit déjà et je suis seul [...]. Tout est fini, j'ai soif, mon corps brûle, la nuit plus obscure emplit mes yeux' (p. 1593).

In order to convey conflict and contradictions Camus also introduces two narrative modes which are strikingly represented at the very beginning of the text:

> Depuis qu'ils m'ont coupé la langue, *une autre langue,* je ne sais pas, marche sans arrêt dans mon crâne, *quelque chose* parle, ou *quelqu'un* qui se tait soudain et puis tout recommence ô *j'entends trop de choses que je ne dis pourtant pas* [...]. De l'ordre, un ordre, dit la langue, et *elle parle d'autre chose en même temps.* (p. 1579)

The allusion to 'une autre langue' is not merely representative of the mental confusion of the protagonist, it is a reality of the text. The disjointed, feverish style of the opening of the narrative, with its lack of logical punctuation, and the frenetic pace of the language are soon superseded by a more lucid attempt to impose order. With an abrupt change in tone, the distance between the fictional narrator and his narrative widens, allowing his vision to coincide with that of the reader: '[...] j'attends le missionnaire qui doit venir me remplacer. Je suis là sur la piste, à une heure de Taghâsa, caché dans un éboulis de rochers, assis sur le vieux fusil' (p. 1579). Camus cuts short this impression of the narrator's distance from the fictional situation, forcing the decor upon the priest's sensibility, and using sense impressions to show how the walls of objectivity crumble. But each time the narrative is in danger of falling into relative inchoateness, a change of narrative mode saves the coherence of the text: '[...] il fait encore très froid, tout à l'heure il fera trop chaud, cette terre rend fou et moi, depuis tant d'années que je n'en sais plus le compte [...]. Non, encore un effort! Le missionnaire doit arriver ce matin ou ce soir' (p. 1559). Here, the interplay of two voices is clear. We have a narrator who is the performer of the narrative, and, at the same time, we are aware of a different narrative voice, undifferentiated by the use of new quotation marks, which comments on the narrative, correcting and judging it.

The fundamental duality of the narrative voice is strongly marked throughout the text, as, in a frequently repeated pattern, moments of weakness, anxiety or confusion on the part of the performing narrator draw a flashing, contemptuous retort as the cynical mode is reasserted: 'J'attendrai, j'attends, le froid, le froid seul me fait trembler. Patiente encore, sale esclave!' (p. 1579). The desperate prayer for rain to wash away the cruel town of Taghâsa is countered by a vigorous assertion of the omnipotence of the 'seigneurs' whose power replaces that of the Christian God to whom the appeal is made: 'Une seule pluie, Seigneur! Mais quoi, quel seigneur, ce sont eux les seigneurs' (p. 1583). Sometimes, the ironic, deflating mode is introduced without any indication of transition: '[...] c'est [le mal] qu'il faut servir pour installer son royaume visible, ensuite on avisera, ensuite qu'est-ce que ça veut dire, seul le mal est présent' (p. 1590). The commenting self-correcting voice of the narrator exerts a repressive control over the narrative, blocking emotional outbursts, stifling any tendency towards self-indulgence; but the anguished cry 'Quelle bouillie' returns (pp. 1579, 1584, 1588, 1590) as though to emphasize echoes of the intense confusion of the incipit – the perpetual conflict of an insoluble dilemma. The result is that it is impossible to trust either voice. The reader cannot empathize with the narrator, as Camus's use of the dialogic mode brings him sharply back to the awesome inhumanity which stifles human responses in this confusing and difficult character. As the reader lurches between extremes, Camus makes him experience from the inside the horror of confusion and indecision to which the protagonist is prey. Each time, the reader feels the contradictory impulses of the narrative, as the tone becomes more lyrical: '... je sens le soleil sur la pierre au-dessus de moi, il frappe, frappe comme un marteau sur toutes les pierres et c'est la musique, la vaste musique de midi, vibration d'air et de pierres sur des centaines de kilomètres' (p. 1584). This threatened lapse into lyricism is immediately cancelled out by an intervention heralded by the 'râ' of the ironic deflating mode: '[...] râ comme autrefois j'entends le silence' (p. 1584). There is no music: flights into the imagination are mere escapism. They attempt to divert attention from the starkness of reality.

After an account which stresses the inhumanity of his situation, the renegade's growing desire for violent action is represented in more frequent breaks in sentence construction, and a suddenly exclamatory tone:

'[...] je pleure de malheur et de désir, un espoir méchant me brûle, je veux trahir, je lèche le canon de mon fusil et son âme à l'intérieur, son âme, seuls les fusils ont des âmes, oh! oui, le jour où on m'a coupé la langue, j'ai appris à adorer l'âme immortelle de la haine!' (p. 1588)

This adoration of immortal hatred, into which Camus introduces the odd juxtaposition of 'lèche' and 'on m'a coupé la langue', signals a relapse into confusion, triggering the conflict of the two selves, in which the second voice, recognizing the confusion, attempts to restore order: 'Quelle bouillie, quelle fureur, râ râ [...]. Qui halète ici?' (p. 1588). As the narrative proceeds to recount the mutilation episode, the resurgence of the voice commenting on the narrative as it unfolds is signalled here, once again, by the expression 'râ' and the sudden interruption of the present tense: 'Mais, tout de suite après, râ le sorcier me guettait, ils sont tous entrés et m'ont arraché à la femme, battu terriblement à l'endroit du péché! quel péché, je ris, où est-il, où la vertu?' (p. 1589). The distinction between right and wrong is not only unclear; it is, to the cynical commenting voice, meaningless. The exclamation and question 'quel péché' echoes 'quel seigneur' (p. 1583) and emphasizes the clash of 'langues' as a result of which the Catholic language/tongue has been torn out, to be replaced by the language of cruelty and hatred: '[...] une jeune haine s'est mise debout un jour, en même temps que moi, a marché vers la porte du fond, l'a ouverte, l'a fermée derrière moi, je haïssais les miens' (p. 1589).

Camus aims to disconcert the reader, seeming to invite him at certain moments to empathize with the protagonist only to make him feel intimidated and alienated as the dialogic mode is brought into play. By confounding the reader's desire for a consistent psychological pattern, Camus promotes a confusion which is increased with the possible addition of a further voice when, after murdering the missionary, the renegade contemplates the scene around him, searching for the source of the words he hears: 'Qui parle, personne, le ciel ne s'entrouvre pas, non, non, Dieu ne parle pas au désert, d'où vient cette voix pourtant qui dit: "Si tu consens à mourir pour la haine et la puissance, qui nous pardonnera?"' (p. 1593). In this passage, the unattributed words are problematic, and the use of 'nous' enigmatic. It refers, perhaps, to 'toi et moi', that is, the dying missionary and his murderer, or to the two voices and 'moi'. However, throughout the narrative, Camus has not once used the second voice to refer to itself. The entire contribution of the second voice is negation (pp. 1581, 1587), even in the many questions it interjects (pp. 1583, 1589, 1590). The sudden intrusion of the first person plural and the 'tu' is completely unexpected. It suggests a community; but the text is striking for the absence of community, even among the solitary Taghâsans. Camus would seem to be indicating that the words issue from the voice of humanity, echoing Clamence's desperate recognition of man's lost innocence in *La Chute*: 'Oui, nous avons perdu la lumière, les matins, la sainte innocence de celui qui se pardonne à lui-même'.[29] Camus seems to propose in this text a comparison between ideologies. Christ died for man's redemption, whereas the renegade's death heralds war and destruction.

When, in a circular movement, the end of 'Le Renégat' returns to the problems of the exposition – 'Ah! Si je m'étais trompé à nouveau!' (p. 1593) – the words suggest the impossibility of a solution to the problems which preoccupy protagonist and author. Perhaps the only answer is a return to the status quo, and an entreaty to the brotherhood of man: 'Hommes autrefois fraternels, seuls recours, ô solitude, ne m'abandonnez pas' (p. 1593). René Godenne is right to question the sudden return to former values in the penultimate paragraph;[30] but what is most at issue is the renegade's sense of isolation. His primary objective has been to escape solitude, and the desirability of the triumph of evil rests on the guarantee that '[il] ne [sera] plus seul' (p. 1593). In fact, the renegade's choices confirm his isolation. This is underlined when the sorcerer reappears at the end of the story.[31] Still hoping to establish a sense of community, the renegade interprets the sorcerer's advance as a sign of fraternity: 'Quitte ce visage de haine, sois bon maintenant, *nous nous* sommes trompés, *nous* recommencerons, *nous* referons la cité de miséricorde [...]. Oui, aide-moi, c'est cela, tends ta main, donne' (p. 1593). His pleas are abruptly curtailed by the brusque intervention of the third-person narrative: 'Une poignée de sel emplit la bouche de l'esclave bavard' (p. 1593). Intratextually, the final sentence recalls the punishment meted out to the one missionary known to return from Taghâsa: 'Ils l'avaient fouetté et chassé dans le désert après avoir mis du sel sur ses plaies et dans sa bouche' (p. 1581). On a superficial level, this act of silencing is also a literal representation of rubbing salt into one's wounds. At the level of symbolism, the sterility of the salt suggests that the endless onslaught of words, and the changes of ideology provide no solutions. We are left, at the end of the text, with the sterility of silence. At a third level, in which the handful of salt synechdochically represents the country, the text suggests that it is the land itself which brings about the slave's silence and makes him redundant. At each level, a sense of Camus's anguish lies very close to the surface.

The sudden stepping outside the text surrounds the closure with ambiguity. Both Cryle[32] and Noyer-Weidner[33] suggest that the final comment is an adverse authorial judgement of the narrator. It is true that the intervention represents a final silencing of the narrator in favour of another, unattributable, narrative voice. The vacillations in the text, the representations of insoluble conflict in the double-voiced narrative, have not allowed the narrator to draw any closer to making a final choice. In a desperate final irony, demoting the protagonist from 'je' to 'il', the author imposes silence upon the narrator. Such is the outcome of this tale of conflicting loyalties and the desperate (failed) search for a sense of identity and community.

This is precisely the (non-)solution which Camus felt the need to impose on himself. At the height of the Algerian war, fearful that any statement he made might be used to encourage terrorism on both sides, Camus admitted his failure, bowed to external pressure, and ceased writing political articles.

Notes

[1] The edition used is Albert Camus, *Théâtre, récits, nouvelles* (Paris: Gallimard [Bibliothèque de la Pléiade], 1962). Page numbers in the text refer to this edition (*TRN*).

[2] In a letter to the painter Dorothy Brett written in 1921, Katherine Mansfield wrote of her objective as a short-story writer: '[...] one tries to go deep – to speak to the secret self we all have – to acknowledge that'. Quoted in Clare Hanson (ed.), *Re-reading the Short Story* (London: Macmillan, 1989), 4.

[3] *TRN*, 2043.

[4] *Carnets III* (Paris: Gallimard, 1989), 56–57, 93–94.

[5] *Carnets III*, 93–94.

[6] 'Dernière interview d'Albert Camus' (20 December 1959) in *Essais* (Paris: Gallimard, 1965), 1925–1928. The interview was first published in *Venture* 3 No. 4 (Spring–Summer 1960), 28–39.

[7] These articles are collected together in *Actuelles III* ('Chroniques algériennes 1939–1958') in *Essais,* 887–1018.

[8] For a detailed account of the Algerian crisis, see Yves Courrière, *La Guerre d'Algérie: le temps des léopards* (Paris: Fayard, 1969). The Constantine uprising is described on pages 187–189.

[9] The letter was published for the first time by Yves Courrière, *La Guerre d'Algérie,* 244. Throughout this article all italics in quotations are my own.

[10] Victor Brombert, '*The Renegade* or the terror of the absolute', *Yale French Studies* 25 (Spring 1960), 81–84 (p. 83).

[11] For information on progressivism, see C. A. O. Van Nieuwenhuijze, *Cross-Cultural Studies* (The Hague: Mouton, 1963), especially chapter 4, 'Post-colonial paternalism', 86–108.

[12] Ibid., 107.

[13] Dorrit Cohn discusses the appropriateness of the interior monologue as a means of conveying immediate responses, in other words the 'pre-speech' level of consciousness, in 'Narrated monologue: definition of a fictional style', *Comparative Literature* 18 No. 2 (Spring 1966), 97–122 (pp. 108–109).

[14] 'Lettre à un militant algérien' in *Essais,* 965.

[15] For an account of events evoking all the drama and intrigue of this episode in Camus's career, see Yves Courrière, *La Guerre d'Algérie,* 251–259. An abridged version of events is also presented by Roger Quilliot in the editorial notes to *Essais,* 1841–1842.

[16] Camus, 'Conférence à Alger, le 22 janvier 1956' in *Essais,* 991.

[17] 'Crise en Algérie' in *Essais,* 959. Camus's sense of justice in relation to Algeria contrasts with the renegade's emphasis on subjugation and 'puissance' – 'je subjuguerais ces sauvages comme un soleil puissant' (p. 1581)

– which Camus warned against in the 'Lettre à un militant algérien': '[...] le rêve d'une disparition subite de la France est puéril [...] le rêve d'une masse arabe annulée à jamais, silencieuse et asservie, est lui aussi délirant [...] J'ai défendu toute ma vie [...] l'idée qu'il fallait chez nous de vastes et profondes réformes. On ne l'a pas cru, on a poursuivi le rêve de la puissance qui se croit toujours éternelle' (*Essais*, 964).

[18] *Essais*, 1842.

[19] 'Appel pour une trêve civile en Algérie' in *Essais*, 992.

[20] The elements of his landscape may owe a great deal to the three-week visit to Algeria which Camus undertook in 1945, in order to write as objective an account as possible of the situation in Northern Africa. 'Crise en Algérie' was published in *Combat* in May 1945, 'à la suite d'une randonnée de 2.500 kilomètres sur les côtes et à l'intérieur de l'Algérie, jusqu'à la limite des territoires du sud' (*Essais*, 941).

[21] Patricia J. Johnson, *Camus et Robbe-Grillet: structure et techniques narratives dans 'Le Renégat' de Camus et 'Le Voyeur' de Robbe-Grillet* (Paris: Nizet, 1972), 77.

[22] Paul Fortier, *Une lecture de Camus* (Paris: Klincksieck, 1977), 104 ff.

[23] Edward Hughes, ' "La Vérité est carrée" – some reflections on Camus's '*Le Renégat ou un esprit confus*', *La Chouette* no. 10 (September 1983), 76–85 (pp. 80–81); Fortier, *Lecture*, 101.

[24] In *Le Malentendu*, Martha's longing to leave her present home and find life, liberty and happiness in sunnier climes near the sea is a central theme (*TRN*, 117, 120, 148, 149, 150).

[25] Napoleon's battle tactics at Austerlitz are well known: battle lines were drawn in the darkness and mist of early morning, but not until sunrise was the attack mounted which was to secure a great victory.

[26] *TRN*, 1167, 1168.

[27] Carina Gadourek likens the image of the fetish to the Nazi swastika in *Les Innocents et les coupables* (The Hague: Mouton, 1963), 207, but it is also reminiscent of the Italian fasces.

[28] Stephen Ullmann, in *The Image in the Modern French Novel* (Cambridge: CUP, 1960), 293, was the first to propose an association between 'Râ râ' and the Egyptian sun-god, though he suggests that 'Râ' is the actual name of the Taghâsan fetish. Philip Thody presents a similar view in *Albert Camus 1913–60* (London: Hamish Hamilton, 1961), 88. Subsequent critics have been unimpressed by this idea. Carina Gadourek, for example, in *Les Innocents et les coupables*, 211, rejects any link between the interjections 'râ râ' and the fetish. In my view, the word does have an associative value, even if not necessarily the name of the fetish.

[29] *TRN*, 1550.

[30] René Godenne, *Études sur la nouvelle française* (Geneva and Paris: Slatkine, 1985), 283–290. Godenne comments on the unexpected nature of the transformation (p. 284), but offers no critical evaluation, leaving others to judge whether the transformation is 'peu plausible' or 'maladroitement ou trop hâtivement exprimée' (p. 290 n. 2).

[31] Patricia Johnson's comments on hallucinatory doubling in 'Le Renégat' seem to confirm the sense of isolation. For Johnson, *Camus et Robbe-Grillet*, p. 46, the sorcerer is a version of the renegade's self, on whom as

narrator he has conferred certain of his own attributes in order to dissociate himself from the self. Here, the sorcerer's appearance suggests the mutilation and the cut-out tongue of the renegade. It would seem logical that the renegade's failure to integrate the two selves should increase his anguished sense of isolation.

[32] Peter Cryle, *L'Exil et le royaume d'Albert Camus: Essai d'analyse* (Paris: Minard, 1973), 87.

[33] A. Noyer-Weidner, 'Albert Camus in his short story phase' in Judith D. Suther (ed.), *Essays on Camus's 'Exile and the Kingdom'* (Mississippi: Romance Monographs, 1980), 45–87.

Le « je » durassien féminin: un miroir aux alouettes?

CATHERINE RODGERS

> From the beginning of my life the problem, for me, has been one of knowing who was speaking when I spoke in my books ... and if there is invention in my work, it is there.[1]

Peut-on dire « je » quand on est femme? Question qui peut de prime abord sembler singulière, mais que des féministes se sont posée, et qui exprime un malaise ressenti par de nombreuses femmes, qu'elles aient eu à prendre la parole ou la plume. Ce malaise confus s'est vu donner une explication par la psychanalyse et en particulier par les théories de Jacques Lacan, qu'Elizabeth Grosz résume de la façon suivante :[2]

> In one sense, in so far as she speaks and says « I », she too must take up a place as a subject of the symbolic; yet, in another, in so far as she is positioned as castrated, passive, an object of desire for men rather than a subject who desires, her position within the symbolic must be marginal or tenuous: when she speaks as an « I » it is never clear that she speaks (of or as) herself. She speaks in a mode of masquerade, in imitation of the masculine, phallic subject. Her « I », then, ambiguously signifies her position as a (pale reflection of the) masculine subject; or it refers to a « you », the (linguistic) counterpart of the masculine « I ».

Si les théories lacaniennes ont rationalisé la difficulté qu'éprouvent les femmes à parler et écrire au féminin, n'ont-elles pas aussi exacerbé cette difficulté, et ne l'ont-elles pas posée en une vérité immuable? Exilées au bord du langage, les femmes ne seraient-elles capables que de s'énoncer comme pâles réflexions du « je » masculin?

La question est d'autant plus pressante que le moi n'est plus, comme au temps de Descartes, compris comme entité non problématique, donnée d'emblée, cohérente et unifiée. Le moi est devenu avant tout un effet du langage et le « je » est le nœud où s'articulent différents discours et représentations. C'est ce sur quoi insiste Benveniste : « C'est dans et par le langage que l'homme se constitue comme sujet; parce que le langage seul fonde en réalité, dans sa réalité qui est celle de l'être, le concept d'ego ».[3] Ce décentrement du sujet, son inscription comme phénomène avant tout linguistique, ont du moins l'avantage d'éloigner le concept de subjectivité de l'idéologie humaniste et phallocrate. Mais on peut douter que la reformulation du problème de la subjectivité, placé comme il l'est désormais dans le langage, soit plus favorable à l'émergence d'un « je » au féminin quand, d'autre part, le symbolique, et le langage sont dominés par le Nom-du-Père.

Dans le courant des années 70, au moment de la prise de conscience féministe en France, plusieurs femmes écrivains ont cherché à faire émerger un « je » au féminin ou ont réfléchi sur les conditions qui permettraient une écriture féminine. Par exemple, Hélène Cixous dans « Le Rire de la Méduse » exhorte les femmes à écrire, à écrire leur corps, à montrer leurs « sextes »,[4] et Luce Irigaray, dans *Ce sexe qui n'en est pas un*,[5] montre à la fois la marginalisation des femmes, et travaille à créer un espace symbolique qui leur permette d'accéder à la représentation. Dans une perspective totalement différente, qui est celle de la destruction des genres, Monique Wittig marque l'impossibilité qu'éprouve la lesbienne à s'énoncer comme « je » unifié, en réécrivant le « je » comme j/e dans *Le Corps lesbien*.[6] Dans l'introduction au texte anglais, elle explique sa stratégie :

> J/e is the symbol of the lived, rending experience which is m/y writing, of this cutting in two which throughout literature is the exercise of a language which does not constitute m/e as subject. J/e poses the ideological and historic question of feminine subjects [...] if *I* [J/e] examine m/y specific situation as subject in the language, *I* [J/e] am physically incapable of writing « I » [Je], *I* [J/e] have no desire to do so.[7]

La recherche d'une énonciation féminine se place nécessairement dans une subversion, ou un dépassement de la théorie lacanienne, puisque pour celle-ci le plein accès au symbolique est dénié au féminin, et que tout « je » écrivant est nécessairement phallique. Au jeu de Lacan, le « je » féminin est nécessairement perdant.

Que se passe-t-il quand une femme écrivain cherche à inscrire et écrire ses propres expériences, son corps, ses désirs, et ses phantasmes, quitte à malmener la langue? Qu'en est-il de Marguerite Duras, qui depuis plus d'un demi-siècle écrit? De nombreux ouvrages critiques ont analysé les marques d'une écriture féminine dans la parole durassienne : dislocation de la phrase, de la syntaxe, présence du silence, du non-dit, de blancs dans ses textes sont autant de caractéristiques qui peuvent être comprises comme éléments subversifs des structures phallocrates du langage.[8] La plupart se sont attachés à étudier les représentations de l'expérience féminine que Duras nous donne à travers ses nombreuses protagonistes. Ce qui a été peu commenté par contre est le long itinéraire que Duras a parcouru de livre en livre pour tenter de produire une femme énonciatrice de son « je », et les structures narratives auxquelles elle a eu recours pour faire éclore ce « je ».

Que l'on ouvre *La Vie tranquille*,[9] le deuxième roman de Duras, et l'on est confronté à une narratrice autodiégétique : « Jérôme est reparti cassé en deux vers les Bugues. J'ai rejoint Nicolas [...] Je me suis assise à côté de lui » (*VT*, p. 11). *La Vie tranquille* s'annonce comme le récit fait par Françou d'une période décisive de sa vie. Tout événement est filtré par sa conscience et son écriture. Serait-on déjà arrivé à une énonciation au féminin? En surface, oui, et cependant, que l'on commence à pénétrer plus avant dans le texte, et l'on s'aperçoit que cette énonciation est un faux semblant, une mascarade, un acte qui recouvre un sujet fissuré et absent.

A plusieurs reprises Françou éprouve l'existence de son moi, sa cohérence et sa continuité comme une illusion, comme une chose qui lui est imposée par les autres mais non éprouvée par elle.

> J'étais couchée lorsque je me suis aperçue couchée dans l'armoire à glace; je me suis regardée [...] Je ne me suis pas reconnue. [...] Je n'ai plus su ce qui se rapportait le plus à moi, ce personnage ou bien mon corps couché, là, bien connu. Qui étais-je, qui avais-je pris pour moi jusque-là? Mon nom même ne me rassurait pas. (*VT*, p. 122)

Dans ce passage, l'identification de soi à l'image de soi vue dans le miroir, identification qui s'élabore normalement au tout début de la vie, lors du stade du miroir, est défaite. Est aussi remise en question l'unification du moi par le nom. Ceci aboutit non pas à une perte d'image de soi, mais à une duplication infinie de possibles images de soi.

Bien plus, celle du miroir une fois disparue à mes yeux, toute la chambre m'a semblé peuplée d'un cercle sans nombre de compagnes semblables à elle. Je les devinais qui me sollicitaient de tous côtés. Autour de moi c'était une fantasmagorie silencieuse qui s'était déchaînée. Avec une rapidité folle, — je n'osais pas regarder, mais je les devinais — une foule de formes devaient apparaître, s'essayer à moi, disparaître aussitôt, comme anéanties de ne pas m'aller. (*VT*, p. 123)

Françou essaye de se saisir de la forme dont elle a l'habitude pour se rendre compte que : « J'avais beau me remémorer les derniers événements des Bugues, c'était une autre qui les avait vécus, une qui m'avait remplacée toujours, en attendant ce soir » (*VT*, p. 123). Non seulement l'image du moi est multiple, mais discontinue. Au niveau de l'écriture, cette instabilité se traduit par une objectivation du « je » en « moi », en « elle » et en « on » : « Là, dans ma chambre, c'est moi. On croirait qu'elle ne sait plus que c'est d'elle qu'il s'agit » (*VT*, p. 121). Incapable de se connaître de l'extérieur (*VT*, p. 125), intérieurement elle s'éprouve comme une forme vide. Ce sentiment d'inexistence revient tout le long du texte; on peut citer : « Je n'étais personne, je n'avais ni nom ni visage. En traversant l'août, j'étais rien » (*VT*, p. 71), ou « Je suis une certaine forme dans laquelle on a coulé une certaine histoire qui n'est pas à moi » (*VT*, p. 36), et implicitement elle se compare à cette caisse vide ballottée par la mer (*VT*, p. 136). Forme creuse, à l'image de son sexe, gouffre vide qui se modèle sur la forme pleine du sexe de Tiène, Françou accepte l'apparence que les autres lui imposent. Ainsi, elle fantasme : « Plaire à Tiène comme une autre, toujours une nouvelle autre. Puisque je ne serais personne » (*VT*, p. 179).

Françou fait l'expérience de la nature illusoire du moi conventionnel, du moi unifié, continu et cohérent, et de l'oppression par laquelle il se constitue en rejetant tous les autres moi possibles. Son expérience cependant est ressentie comme une période de crise passagère, à surmonter, et elle n'envisage pas vraiment un autre mode de subjectivité, bien qu'elle soit consciente que la vie tranquille vers laquelle elle retourne est une vie de mort.

Le texte, dans son style et ses structures, reflète, crée le trajet subjectif de la narratrice. La première partie, située à la ferme des Bugues, en pleine terre, a la solidité d'un récit réaliste conventionnel, avec en particulier une progression causale et linéaire du temps. La deuxième partie qui se déroule au bord de la mer, correspond à la « crise existentielle » de Françou, et a par contre une structure nettement plus lâche où il est difficile de discerner un tel développement progressif : des impressions, des sensations, des réflexions se produisent dans un espace et un temps bloqués. Si structure il y a, elle est plus proche de celle communiquée par le mouvement de la mer. Dans la troisième partie, après le passage en italique qui reproduit les pensées fiévreuses de Françou lors de son retour, la narration retrouve le ton raisonné, posé et ordonné du début. Ce ton correspond au moment où Françou rejoint les Bugues, où elle va réintégrer la vie tout en moderato qu'on attend d'elle.

Deux questions ne manquent pas de se poser quant à l'organisation du texte : celle de la crédibilité de Françou comme narratrice de *La Vie tranquille* et l'omission dans le récit de l'acte d'écriture qui lui donne naissance. Comme Cismaru fut le premier à le remarquer, il est difficile d'admettre que Françou ait écrit *La Vie tranquille* : son peu d'éducation ne lui permettrait guère de produire un texte aussi sophistiqué.[10] Quant à la deuxième question, on pourrait objecter que cette omission est conventionnellement admise dans les récits à la première personne. Certes, cette réponse serait acceptable, mais il est quand même troublant qu'après *La Vie tranquille*, l'acte de narration, ou tout au moins une certaine réflexivité, soit toujours présent. C'est le cas des textes à la première personne qui succèdent à *La Vie tranquille : Le Marin de Gibraltar, Le Ravissement de Lol V. Stein, Le Vice-Consul*. Or ces textes ont tous pour narrateurs des hommes. Serait-ce que Duras sent confusément les freins qui existent à peindre comme énonciatrice et donc en partie créatrice de sa propre histoire, une femme qui, par bien des aspects, correspond aux stéréotypes de la passivité féminine? Le seul acte d'écrire confère un certain pouvoir; or dans *La Vie tranquille* ce pouvoir est gommé du texte. L'est-il parce que nous avons affaire à une narratrice? Dans les livres suivants il n'y aura pas de narratrice, Duras évitant ainsi le difficile problème de l'énonciation au féminin. Ses textes par contre ont pour centre d'intérêt un personnage féminin.

Dans *Le Marin de Gibraltar* la narration est assurée par un homme, même si le personnage principal est une femme, Anna — à moins que ce ne soit ce centre évanouissant autour duquel tout gravite qu'est le marin de Gibraltar. Plusieurs références sont faites par le narrateur à l'écriture projetée d'un texte, vraisemblablement *Le Marin de Gibraltar* lui-même, et l'acte narratif est donc en partie intégré à l'histoire. Son véritable pouvoir créateur est cependant dénié : Duras n'entrevoit pas encore le parti qu'elle peut tirer des déformations apportées par la sensibilité d'un narrateur. Le narrateur du *Marin* rapporte artificiellement des pans entiers de la parole d'Anna, et sa narration à lui est présentée comme objective.

Dans *Le Ravissement de Lol V. Stein* par contre, la puissance créatrice, déformatrice, destructrice de l'écrivain est représentée à travers Jacques Hold, en même temps que les risques encourus par l'écrivain dans l'acte d'écriture.[11] Dès le début du texte (*R*, p. 14) est établie la part d'invention générée par le narrateur, et donc la marque de son propre désir : « Voici tout au long, mêlés, à la fois, ce faux semblant que raconte Tatiana Karl et ce que j'invente sur la nuit du Casino de T. Beach. A partir de quoi je raconterai mon histoire de Lol V. Stein » (*R*, p. 14). A aucun moment nous ne sommes sûrs de la nature de ce que nous lisons : réalité découverte par Jacques Hold, fiction inventée par lui? Tout est perçu par lui, et nous, lecteurs, sommes à sa merci. Quand, page 120, il nous décrit ainsi son trouble aigu : « [...] je suis sorti en courant, je suis revenu sur mes pas, j'ai tourné en rond dans la chambre », nous sommes pris à sa narration et le croyons, pour découvrir, deux paragraphes plus tard, que ces mouvements ont été imaginés : « Je mens. Je n'ai pas bougé de la fenêtre, confirmé jusqu'aux larmes » (*R*, p. 121). Lol n'existe que comme personnage du récit de Jacques Hold, jamais nous n'avons un accès objectif à ses pensées. Dans ce cas, que croire des caractéristiques de Lol, de son absence, de sa différence, de sa supposée folie? Sont-elles réelles, ou un effet du désir de Jacques Hold? Quoi qu'il en soit, Jacques se laisse prendre au charme incertain de Lol et se trouve dangereusement happé par son univers, et ceci à deux niveaux, en tant qu'amant de Lol et en tant que narrateur. En tant que narrateur, Jacques, s'appuyant sur son travail objectif de détective, mais aussi remédiant au manque de faits objectifs grâce à son imagination, tente d'élaborer un texte cohérent, signifiant. Comme son nom en anglais l'indique, il tient, contrôle le texte, il en organise les fragments pour les unifier. Il tente d'asservir Lol : « Mes mains deviennent le piège dans lequel l'immobiliser, la retenir de toujours aller et venir d'un bout à l'autre du temps » (*R*, p. 107). Cette volonté correspond au côté sadique de sa personnalité qu'il exerce au plus haut point avec Tatiana (*R*, p. 167), mais aussi avec Lol dans la dernière scène qui les réunit (*R*, p. 187). Ce sadisme est contrebalancé par un net masochisme en lui, qui apparaît dans sa volonté d'être broyé, asservi par Lol (*R*, p. 106). En s'approchant de Lol, que ce soit par amour ou par l'écriture, Hold s'englue à elle : il se trouve enfermé dans son espace (*R*, p. 118), son temps (*R*,

p. 153), son souvenir (*R,* p. 180). Son récit s'en trouve modifié; imperceptiblement Jacques abandonne son but d'arriver à un récit conventionnel qui expliquerait et fixerait Lol, il renonce même à finir son texte :

> Je nie la fin qui va venir probablement nous séparer, sa facilité, sa simplicité désolante, car du moment que je la nie, celle-là, j'accepte l'autre, celle qui est à inventer, que je ne connais pas, que personne encore n'a inventée : la fin sans fin, le commencement sans fin de Lol V. Stein. (*R,* p. 184)

A la structure fermée du texte réaliste, il en vient à préférer une structure cyclique, qui se répète à l'infini, et qui s'ouvre sur le travail du lecteur. Il accepte donc de perdre le contrôle de son texte, et sa maîtrise de Lol.

Le choix par Duras d'un narrateur masculin répond à des motivations complexes, comme l'a montré Marcelle Marini au sujet du *Vice-Consul*,[12] où Duras reprend la structure narrative du *Ravissement* (écrivain femme, narrateur, et personnage féminin) mais en la compliquant puisque le narrateur doit partager l'espace du texte avec une autre voix narrative. Peter Morgan, le narrateur de l'histoire de la mendiante, peut être considéré comme la projection partielle de Duras, de l'aspect masculin de son être. Grâce à ce narrateur masculin, Duras peut tracer l'histoire de la construction (ou plutôt destruction) du féminin par la société. Elle peut écrire de la femme comme l'Autre.[13] En effet, il est clair que les hommes — Peter Morgan, mais aussi Charles Rosset et George Crawn — se constituent comme sujets en objectivant les femmes du récit (la mendiante, Anne-Marie Stretter) et finalement « elle », en projetant sur elles tout ce qu'ils rejettent pour eux et dont ils ont peur. En posant un narrateur masculin, Duras expose ce processus d'aliénation du féminin.[14]

Quelle que soit l'interprétation de ce choix de narrateurs masculins, ce qui ressort des textes de cette période, c'est l'impossibilité apparente pour Duras de représenter une énonciation au féminin. La phrase de Marini « Le roman [*Le Vice-Consul*] dit qu'il n'y a pas d'écriture-discours possibles au féminin sur le féminin »[15] résume bien la situation dans laquelle se trouve Duras à cette époque. Ses personnages féminins peuvent sembler puissants, mais leur pouvoir prend sa source dans leur position en tant qu'objets de désir, dans leur fétichisation.[16] La parole, et même souvent le regard, leur sont refusés : objectivées, aliénées, animalisées ou minéralisées, elles glissent vers la folie et la mort. Elles font leur le silence dans lequel on les enferme, et préfèrent l'authenticité de la dépossession de soi au moderato que la société leur propose. L'image la plus marquante de cette aliénation est peut-être la femme de *L'Amour* qui « ne sait pas être regardée » (*Ar*, p. 10).

Pourtant, de cet espace de non-être, progressivement, vont émerger une parole et une écriture au féminin. Deux facteurs peuvent peut-être expliquer cette émergence, et tous deux viennent de l'expérience cinématographique de Duras. Avec *La Femme du Gange* Duras commence à découvrir la possibilité de dissocier le film des voix de celui des images et dans *India Song* elle représente des voix sans corps, les voix 1, 2, 3 et 4, qui se rappellent, créent l'histoire centrale qui est une réécriture du *Vice-Consul*. Grâce à cette dissociation du texte entendu et des images, Duras se rend compte de la plus grande puissance évocatrice du texte par rapport à l'image. Graduellement, elle en vient à reconnaître la primauté du texte, et elle finit même par accorder un pouvoir quasi sacré à l'écriture — un pouvoir qui, on va le voir, va s'étendre jusqu'à la création par la narratrice de son propre corps et d'un moi pluriel et multiple.

Le deuxième facteur qui a peut-être contribué à l'apparition d'une énonciation au féminin est la présence de Duras dans le film *Le Camion*. Dans ce film Duras fonctionne pour le spectateur comme support imaginatif de la dame du *Camion*, cette femme âgée, déclassée qui chaque soir fait de l'autostop, monte dans un camion et « raconte sa vie pour la première fois » (*C*, p. 54) et invente sa vie (*C*, p. 107). Avec *Le Camion* Duras nous donne une timide tentative d'énonciation au féminin, et c'est comme si la personnalité même de Duras, telle qu'elle est connue des spectateurs et lecteurs — auteur de nombreuses œuvres — avait prêté caution à cette dame étrange du *Camion* et à sa capacité de fabulation, car la dame du *Camion* ressemble curieusement à Duras, se présentant même comme une image idéalisée de celle-ci. Toutes deux ont en commun la même description physique, leur appartenance passée au Parti Communiste, une enfance coloniale, un « gai désespoir », et surtout une grande disponibilité vers l'extérieur et une imagination infinie.[17] La dame du *Camion* est libérée de toute contrainte réaliste — comme Duras réalisatrice l'est — de toute idée préconçue ou reçue. Duras se serait donc appuyée sur sa propre expérience pour oser représenter une femme énonciatrice de son histoire, de son moi. Le moi que la dame du *Camion* se forge est loin d'être fixe et unique, au contraire il est changeant, variable selon ses humeurs et ses interlocuteurs. Les renseignements qu'elle donne au camionneur suspicieux sont « interchangeables » (*C*, p. 50) et ils n'aident pas à la situer socialement : elle est « déclassée » (*C*, p. 16). Cependant une certaine identité est assurée car Duras précise que si les éléments des histoires que la dame du *Camion* raconte sont variables, certains sont constants (*C*, p. 50). Et l'histoire que la dame élabore chaque soir peut nous renseigner sur ses désirs, sur son être profond plus justement que ne le ferait une carte d'identité. Plutôt qu'une identité bien définie, on est confronté à un champ d'identités, toutes variations sur un même modèle, ce qui nous renvoie à l'expérience de Françou dans la chambre, confrontée à toutes ces formes qu'elle aurait pu être. Mais la différence entre Françou et la dame du *Camion*, différence qui marque le travail accompli par Duras vers la réalisation d'une énonciation féminine, c'est que la dame du *Camion* revendique la multiplicité et l'incohérence de ses moi.

Duras poursuit le même travail au théâtre. Là aussi, elle affirme la suprématie du texte, de la lecture sur la représentation. Là aussi, on peut saisir les balbutiements d'une énonciation au féminin. Dans la pièce *Savannah Bay*, une autre femme, âgée elle aussi, actrice, joue, se joue, crée et se crée chaque soir, et dans son jeu, créateur de son « je », elle entraîne la jeune femme de la pièce. Toute sa vie Madeleine a joué des rôles, et elle a donc appris à se défaire de son identité pour devenir autre, le temps d'une représentation. Maintenant elle ne sait plus où s'arrête son je/jeu, où commence la fiction, où finit la réalité, elle a oublié quelles sont ces mémoires dont elle se souvient par bribes — est-ce que ce sont les siennes ou des textes qu'elle a appris? Cette confusion, elle la vit comme une libération, et comme une source de création. La Jeune Femme, qui est peut-être sa petite fille, vient en partie la voir pour essayer de connaître son passé : « c'est sur la mémoire défaillante de Madeleine qu'elle bâtit celle de son enfance, celle de sa naissance » (*SB*, p. 31). D'où son désespoir apparent par moments devant l'impossibilité de Madeleine à se rappeler (*SB*, p. 59) ou son refus à aller aussi loin que Madeleine dans la confusion des identités et souvenirs (*SB*, p. 57). Les distorsions opérées par Madeleine font que les trois figures féminines de la pièce se confondent et se recouvrent. Comme Susan D. Cohen l'a indiqué, il semble que la Jeune Femme vienne moins voir Madeleine pour découvrir son identité que « pour apprendre non seulement à jouer, mais à jouer pour (se) perdre ».[18] Cohen montre comment la Jeune Femme apprend progressivement à se défaire du « je » patriarcal, défini par « le patronyme qui fixe, classe et élimine ».[19] Ce détachement d'un moi fixe et donné est extrêmement libérateur et créateur; la nouvelle identité fluide et changeante sur laquelle il s'ouvre est cependant très fragile et à tout instant menacée d'anéantissement. Que le jeu de Madeleine s'arrête et son « je » cesse. Les efforts de la Jeune Femme pour faire parler Madeleine sont aussi un moyen de l'empêcher de sombrer dans un état d'entropie semblable à la mort. Dans la dernière partie de la pièce, Madeleine et la Jeune Femme jouent la légende des Amants. Toutes deux deviennent alternativement et sans ordre la jeune fille de l'histoire, qui est aussi Madeleine, et son amant. La Jeune Femme dit « je » pour Madeleine, et ce faisant, elle rend la présence charnelle de Madeleine superflue, et donc sa mort possible. Au théâtre, l'absence peut devenir présence sans avoir à passer par la présence d'un corps matériel. Ainsi la Jeune Femme dit à Madeleine : « Tu cries et la voici, elle, la petite morte, dans un éclair... le petit visage sous la houle, souriant d'aise, et le cœur éclate d'une abominable vérité » (*SB*, p. 70). La parole durassienne s'établit de plus en plus dans un espace d'absence-présence, où les « je » se font et se défont, où le « je » devient l'histoire qu'il crée, le texte qu'il choisit.

Ce processus est encore plus évident avec les *Aurélia Steiner*. Jusqu'ici, les personnages féminins qui s'énonçaient le faisaient oralement et étaient âgés, presqu'asexués. On pourrait alléguer que ces deux facteurs diminuent la spécificité féminine de l'énonciation ainsi représentée. L'oral ne porterait-il pas moins à conséquence que l'écrit, surtout quand il s'agit d'une femme, dont la parole peut toujours être ramenée à du « bavardage féminin »? Aurélia par contre est jeune, dix-huit ans, et affirme son désir et sa sexualité. Et Aurélia écrit. Et elle se nomme elle-même. Chaque version se termine par l'assertion de son nom, et de son écriture. Ainsi la fin d'*Aurélia Steiner Vancouver* :

> Je m'appelle Aurélia Steiner.
> J'habite Vancouver où mes parents sont professeurs.
> J'ai dix-huit ans.
> J'écris. (*AS*, pp. 165–166)

Serait-on en présence d'une énonciation de femme, mais qui revendiquerait un moi fixe, déterminé, arrêté par un nom? La fin du texte laisserait à penser qu'on pourrait avoir affaire à l'inscription d'un « je » patriarcal. Et pourtant, rien n'est moins sûr. Pour en juger, il faut suivre le cheminement de cette nomination à travers le texte. Bernard Alazet qui a étudié cet aspect d'*Aurélia Steiner Vancouver* explique que :

> Le nom [...] est [...] lié au père qui, à la fois dépositaire du nom [...] et son destinataire [...] entraîne par sa mort la nomination dans un espace impossible. On voit donc se profiler dans le texte un mouvement de quête autour du nom : non pas rechercher quel il est ... mais rechercher l'acte de profération qui lui permettrait d'appartenir.[20]

Et en effet Aurélia invente différents scénarios qui ont tous pour but d'obtenir la nomination par le père. D'abord, elle se regarde dans la glace, et à travers son image, elle voit celle de son père, et elle se dit son nom (on présume qu'elle veut ainsi voir son père la nommer), mais elle doit concéder que : « Vous n'êtes pas informé de mon existence » (*AS*, p. 142). Dans un effort désespéré pour faire surgir son père, elle tente de le créer ensuite à travers les jeunes marins du port : « Dans un monde où vous n'êtes pas en vie ils peuvent me tenir lieu de notre rencontre » (*AS*, p. 143). Sa première tentative fantasmée est un échec, le marin ne coïncide pas avec le père et quand il profère le nom Aurélia Steiner, ce dernier demeure un « nom sans sujet » (*AS*, p. 146). Alors Aurélia invente l'histoire de son origine, de sa naissance qui aurait coïncidé avec la mort de ses deux parents dans un camp de concentration. La mère, aussi appelée Aurélia, meurt en couches, et le père d'avoir volé de la soupe pour sa petite Aurélia. Une autre histoire, celle de la tempête, de l'amour mythique de la mer et du vent, vient entrecouper la première légende et s'y refléter, les deux étant liées par un ensemble de glissements métaphoriques et métonymiques. Allant se coucher sur la mer, Aurélia recrée sa naissance et l'union avec la mer/mère, mais la mère ne peut pas nommer. Finalement, un marin à l'image du père vient vers Aurélia, et il inscrit, en pénétrant Aurélia, son nom dans sa chair. Suite à cet acte se trouve le paragraphe déjà cité où Aurélia se nomme. D'après le mouvement du texte, il semblerait que pour Duras, la nomination doive venir du père, ou d'un homme lui tenant lieu, et que la fille/femme ne puisse que répéter un simulacre de nomination. Même si l'on considère que tout le récit d'Aurélia est inventé, il n'en demeure pas moins qu'Aurélia ressent la nécessité d'en passer par une nomination paternelle.

Mais pour répondre à la double question de la nomination et de la nature de l'énonciation dans ces textes, il faut considérer non plus seulement *Aurélia Steiner Vancouver* mais les différents textes dont le titre est *Aurélia Steiner*; alors on s'aperçoit que le même phénomène que pour la dame du *Camion* se répète : l'identité d'Aurélia devient variable, tout en passant par les mêmes points : la Judaïté, la mort tragique des parents, l'écriture, l'amour du « vous ». L'impression de fixité est défaite et la recherche de la nomination par le père n'est plus qu'un élément parmi d'autres. Ce qui émerge de tous les *Aurélia Steiner*, est l'image d'un moi qui est divers, variable, en constante évolution, d'un moi au féminin et d'une énonciation féminine. Comme le montrent les *Aurélia Steiner*, le « je » féminin semble ne pouvoir ou ne vouloir se créer que dans des récits partiels qui n'existent que l'un par l'autre. Cette structure narrative en miroir — par laquelle une histoire se crée par réflexion, réfraction d'une autre histoire, qui n'est elle-même à son tour que le reflet d'une autre histoire, parfois la même — semble être une condition de l'énonciation durassienne.[21]

Cette structure en miroir est particulièrement apparente dans *Moderato Cantabile* et dans le plus récent *Emily L*. Déjà, dans *Moderato Cantabile*, Anne et Chauvin se rencontraient pour parler entre eux de cet autre couple, sur lequel ils projetaient leurs désirs sadomasochistes, et ils finissaient par jouer eux-mêmes le scénario qu'ils avaient inventé pour les deux autres. Un subtil jeu d'identification s'opérait entre Anne et l'autre femme assassinée, qu'Anne, poussée par Chauvin, avait revêtue de son propre désir. Trente ans plus tard, Duras reprend la même structure en miroir dans *Emily L*.[22] Un couple formé d'un « je » (féminin) et d'un « vous » (masculin) se rend dans un café. Ils y trouvent « eux », le Captain et sa femme, Emily. D'abord perçus comme des formes privées de vie humaine — « on aurait dit des plantes, des choses comme ça intermédiaires » (*E*, p. 17) — graduellement ils s'animent sous les regards du « je »; leur histoire s'invente, vue par le « je ». Que le récit qu'on lit ait été produit par le « je » est indiqué à plusieurs reprises dans le texte. Il n'y a d'autre réalité que celle créée par le « je »; c'est ce dernier qui est dans la position de connaissance de cette histoire. Le « vous » questionne le « je », et reconnaît la vérité de ses dires sur l'autre couple. La nature des rapports entre le « je » et le « vous » est visible dans l'extrait suivant : « Vous me dites que vous voudriez savoir encore sur les gens de l'île de Wight. Je vous dis que je ne sais presque plus rien » (*E*, p. 146). Le rapport entre les sexes que l'on trouvait dans *Moderato Cantabile* où

Chauvin contrôlait la conversation et le récit, et en était le principal instigateur, se trouve donc inversé dans *Emily L*. C'est le « je » de la femme qui a le pouvoir d'énonciation et de création de l'histoire. Le « vous » de l'homme est en position d'objet dans le récit du « je », de même qu'il est l'objet de son regard : « je vous regarde » (*E*, p. 10). La structure en miroir s'est compliquée de *Moderato Cantabile* à *Emily L*. — dans le texte le plus récent, il ne s'agit plus seulement d'un récit se reflétant/se créant dans l'autre, mais de trois récits, se réfléchissant tous les uns dans les autres : celui du « je » et du « vous », d'Emily et du Captain, et d'Emily et du jeune gardien. Un semblant de l'histoire vécue entre le « je » et le « vous » se trouve capté dans les autres récits, comme le signale la narratrice : « ... ce que j'écris en ce moment, c'est autre chose dans quoi elle [notre histoire] serait incluse, perdue, quelque chose de beaucoup plus large peut-être... Mais elle, directement, non, c'est fini... je ne pourrai plus... » (*E*, p. 22–23). Duras joue des effets de réflexions dans son texte; l'insistance sur la glace au mur du café nous indique que nous sommes pris dans un prisme textuel et de nombreux paragraphes renvoient indifféremment d'un couple à l'autre, comme celui-ci :

> Leur âge, on ne peut pas le connaître. Ce qu'on voit, c'est qu'elle est sensiblement plus âgée que lui. Mais que lui il a rattrapé sa lenteur à elle. Qu'il refuse d'aller plus avant qu'elle ne le peut, ça depuis des années. Que c'est fini pour elle et que pourtant elle est encore là, dans les parages de cet homme, que son corps est encore à la portée du sien, de ses mains, partout, la nuit, le jour. (*E*, p. 20)

Le « elle » peut aussi bien se référer à la narratrice qu'à Emily, et le « il », au « vous », au Captain ou même peut-être au gardien. L'identité du « je » est réfractée entre le « elle » et le « je », mais aussi entre le « je » de l'énoncé et celui de l'énonciation, car leur non-coïncidence est soulignée par la distance temporelle instaurée entre le temps de l'histoire et celui de l'écriture : « Sur le moment j'avais cru qu'elle dormait, cette femme du bar. Maintenant je ne le crois plus » (*E*, p. 18). Cette complexité narrative, cet univers romanesque ambigu où les pronoms personnels ont des référents multiples, où les paragraphes renvoient indifféremment à un couple ou à un autre, sont-ils autant de marques de la difficulté de l'énonciation au féminin, ou plutôt témoins que l'énonciation au féminin appelle d'autres formes d'écriture, d'autres formes d'énonciation?

Si l'on continue la comparaison entre *Moderato Cantabile* et

Emily L., une autre caractéristique de l'énonciation durassienne apparaît, caractéristique que l'on avait déjà notée pour *Le Camion*, et qui est l'importance grandissante de l'élément autobiographique.[23] Duras a laissé entendre que *Moderato Cantabile* avait pour origine une expérience érotique très violente, mais qu'elle, Duras, était cachée derrière ce récit :

> Dans *Moderato Cantabile* — c'est la première fois que je dis cela! — j'ai essayé de relater une expérience personnelle vécue secrètement. Alors s'est posé un problème de pudeur. J'ai construit des murs autour de cette expérience. Et je l'ai entourée de glaces. J'ai choisi une forme d'autant plus rigoureuse que l'expérience avait été vécue violemment... Je suis cachée derrière *Moderato*.[24]

Elle est nettement moins cachée derrière le « je » d'*Emily L.*. Plusieurs détails assimilent le « je » à Duras : la location du récit à Quillebeuf — on sait qu'elle habitait un appartement tout près à Trouville — les longs voyages sur les bateaux, sa connaissance des Asiatiques, du Siam, ses écrits sur sa jeunesse en Indochine, l'alcool, les hallucinations nocturnes, et aussi plus généralement la relation du « je » au « vous » qui rappelle la relation de Duras à Yann Andréa. De plus dans l'émission de télévision *Au delà des pages*, elle a confié : « [...] ma parente profonde, ma sœur, c'est Emily L.. C'est moi, à un point que vous ne pouvez imaginer ».

Le trajet parcouru par Duras entre la dissimulation de l'expérience personnelle dans *Moderato Cantabile* et la mise en scène de sa propre relation avec Yann Andréa dans *Emily L.* illustre le mouvement d'une œuvre qui gravite de plus en plus autour de Duras elle-même,[25] et l'œuvre, telle une chambre d'échos, résonne de la voix de Duras. Ne demande-t-elle pas à Suzanne Lamy — dans une phrase qui est plus affirmative qu'interrogative : « Ma voix, tu dois l'entendre quand tu lis »?[26] Ces dernières années, les « je » de Duras ont envahi son œuvre. Où que l'on regarde dans l'œuvre durassienne, que ce soit *L'Amant*, *L'Amant de la Chine du Nord*, *La Douleur*, *Emily L.*, *La Vie matérielle*, *La Pute de la côte normande*, ou *Écrire*, on s'aperçoit, avec ravissement ou horreur, que de partout, les textes, tels des miroirs, nous renvoient tous une image de Duras, à la fois semblable et différente. Le lecteur est pris entre toutes ces images sans pouvoir s'arrêter à aucune.[27] Tout autour, le « je » durassien miroite; un « je » qui s'est d'abord voilé derrière d'autres protagonistes mais qui depuis les années 70 s'affiche comme énonciateur de sa propre histoire et son propre créateur. Ce que Duras avouait dans *Les Lieux* à Michelle Porte en 1977 à propos d'*India Song*, il semble qu'elle l'ait réalisé :

> [...] c'est moi partout, je crois, c'est... les deux femmes. Je ne peux pas être partout à la fois, voyez, quand j'écris mais pourtant j'ai envie de tout investir, je ne suis pas plurielle, et les voix, ça me parle partout, et j'essaye de... de quand même, de rendre compte un petit peu de ce débordement, et longtemps j'ai cru que c'étaient des voix extérieures, mais maintenant je ne crois pas, je crois que c'est moi si je n'écrivais pas, moi si je comprenais mieux, moi si j'aimais les femmes, voyez, ou si j'aimais une femme, moi si j'étais morte, moi si je comprenais, etc., c'est une sorte de multiplicité qu'on porte en soi, on la porte tous, toutes, mais elle est égorgée; en général, on n'a guère qu'une voix maigre, on parle avec ça. Alors qu'il faut être débordée. (*L,* pp. 102–103)

Abasourdi, ébloui, le lecteur est en passe de l'être, si en plus du « je » durassien qui se fait omniprésent dans ses œuvres, il se laisse méduser par les apparitions télévisées de Duras, soumettre à ses idées exprimées dans de nombreux interviews ou articles.

Le « je » durassien qui a émergé est certes celui d'une femme, qui met en scène ses désirs et ses fantasmes, mais c'est aussi un « je » dominateur, sadique qui n'hésite pas à apostropher et à subjuguer le « vous » de ses textes, qui est un homme,[28] ce qui pourrait conduire à souligner la position masculine, phallique adoptée par Duras.[29] Lors du passage à l'énonciation, la féminité du « je » durassien aurait-elle été réprimée, perdue? En recherchant au travers de la soixantaine d'ouvrages écrits par une femme, une énonciation féminine, nous serions-nous laissé attirer, puis piéger par un mirage? Et notre recherche n'aboutirait-elle qu'à fournir à la théorie lacanienne un autre exemple de l'impossibilité d'une énonciation féminine?

Certes Duras, d'abord en tant qu'écrivain, mais aussi parce que son « je » autobiographique fait preuve de désirs de domination, peut être considérée comme occupant une position phallique. Mais elle se joue de cette position et la sape. Quand elle dit : « La femme qui écrit se déguise..., en homme » (*P,* p. 38), c'est peut-être sur « déguise » que l'accent devrait être mis. Dans son texte le plus ouvertement autobiographique, *L'Amant,* pas plus que dans ses autres œuvres, elle n'accepte d'y figer son moi, ni de l'ériger en une entité monolithique, continue dans le temps. Dès le début de l'ouvrage, on peut lire : « L'histoire de ma vie n'existe pas. Ça n'existe pas. Il n'y a jamais de centre. Pas de chemin, pas de ligne. Il y a de vastes endroits où l'on fait croire qu'il y avait quelqu'un, ce n'est pas vrai il n'y avait personne » (*Am*, p. 14). Pour mieux empêcher toute tentation d'unification de la part du lecteur, de linéarité et de cohérence, elle choisit une organisation narrative qui procède par juxtaposition d'images, par association d'idées et non pas par développement linéaire ou dialectique. Surtout elle se refuse à l'illusion d'un « je » unifié. Son « je » se fissure en un « je » — où le « je » renvoie à un éventail de « Duras » — et en un « elle », un « elle » qui se décline en « l'enfant », « la petite », « la petite blanche », qui renvoie donc en général à Duras jeune, mais aussi à l'écrivaine de 70 ans.[30] Cette dissociation partielle de soi rappelle de nouveau la non-reconnaissance par Françou de son image dans la glace de l'armoire, mais cette fois-ci la non-coïncidence est assumée et affichée. L'enfant de *L'Amant*, mais aussi l'écrivaine au visage détruit, ne sont que reflets de Duras. Ces reflets, elle se les construit, et ils ne sont en aucun cas présentés naïvement comme copies d'une réalité en soi. Elle insiste d'ailleurs sur la part de désir qui entre dans cette construction de son image : « Ce jour-là je dois porter cette fameuse paire de talons hauts en lamé or. Je ne vois rien d'autre que je pourrais porter ce jour-là, alors je les porte. [...] Je me veux comme ça » (*Am*, pp. 18–19). Le jeu de réflexion autobiographique se continue avec *L'Amant de la Chine du Nord*. Et quand Duras, en 1991, termine un article pour *Libération* où elle donne ses propres goûts cinématographiques en parodiant elle-même la fin des *Aurélia Steiner*, que fait-elle, sinon dérober la référentialité de son nom et de son « je » en le projetant dans un espace fictionnel et fantasmatique?[31]

Ces exemples, mais aussi toute l'œuvre de Duras, montrent qu'elle est parvenue à rejeter l'idéal du « je » humaniste, réaliste, et phallocrate et qu'elle est arrivée à accepter une multiplicité de positions subjectives — y compris des positions masculines — qui est normalement réprimée; or cette multiplicité peut être considérée comme féminine.

Les propos que Cixous tient sur la femme dans *La Jeune Née* pourraient s'appliquer à Marguerite Duras : « [...] excédante, démesurée, contradictoire, elle détruit les lois, l'ordre « naturel », elle lève la barre qui sépare le présent du futur, brisant la loi rigide de l'inviduation [...] Elle vole ».[32] Et avec elle, envolons-nous du piège lacanien.

Abréviations

Dans cet article il est fait référence aux œuvres suivantes de Marguerite Duras. Dans le cas des œuvres dont des citations sont données, une abréviation du titre a été utilisée et celle-ci est indiquée en début de ligne.

Am	L'Amant (Paris : Éditions de Minuit, 1984)
	L'Amant de la Chine du Nord (Paris : Gallimard, 1991)
Ar	L'Amour (Paris : Gallimard, 1984)
AS	Aurélia Steiner, dans Le Navire Night — Césarée — Les Mains négatives — Aurélia Steiner — Aurélia Steiner — Aurélia Steiner (Paris : Mercure de France, 1979)
	Un barrage contre le Pacifique (Paris : Gallimard, 1950)
C	Le Camion (Paris : Éditions de Minuit, 1977)
	La Douleur (Paris : P.O.L., 1985)
	Écrire (Paris : Gallimard, 1993)
E	Emily L. (Paris : Éditions de Minuit, 1987)
	India Song (Paris : Gallimard, 1985)
	Des journées entières dans les arbres (Paris : Gallimard, 1954)
	L'Homme atlantique (Paris : Éditions de Minuit, 1982)
L	Les Lieux (Paris : Éditions de Minuit, 1974)
	Le Marin de Gibraltar (Paris : Gallimard, 1985)
	Moderato Cantabile (Paris : Éditions de Minuit, 1958)
ME	Le Monde extérieur (Paris : P.O.L., 1993)
	Nathalie Granger, suivie de La Femme du Gange (Paris: Gallimard, 1973)
P	Les Parleuses (Paris : Éditions de Minuit, 1985)
	La Pute de la côte normande (Paris : Éditions de Minuit, 1986)
R	Le Ravissement de Lol V. Stein (Paris : Gallimard, 1982)
SB	Savannah Bay (Paris : Éditions de Minuit, 1983)
	Le Vice-Consul (Paris : Gallimard, 1985)
	La Vie matérielle (Paris : P.O.L., 1987)
VT	La Vie tranquille (Paris : Gallimard, 1985)

Notes

[1] Marguerite Duras, cité dans Susan D. Cohen *Women and Discourse in the Fiction of Marguerite Duras: Love, Legends, Language* (London: Macmillan, 1993), 9.

[2] Elizabeth Grosz, *Jacques Lacan: A Feminist Introduction* (London: Routledge, 1990), 71–72.
[3] Emile Benveniste, *Problèmes de linguistique générale* (Paris : Gallimard, 1966), 259.
[4] Hélène Cixous, « Le Rire de la Méduse », *L'Arc* 61 (1975), 39–54 (p. 47).
[5] Luce Irigaray, *Ce Sexe qui n'en est pas un* (Paris : Éditions de Minuit, 1978).
[6] Monique Wittig, *Le Corps lesbien* (Paris : Éditions de Minuit, 1973).
[7] Monique Wittig, *The Lesbian Body*, tr. Peter Owen (New York : Avon, 1975).
[8] Il faut dire que dans les années 70, Duras elle-même a encouragé ce genre d'analyse, comme dans l'interview qu'elle a donnée à Susan Husserl-Kapit (*Signs* 1 No. 2 (1975), 423–434) ou dans ses conversations avec Xavière Gauthier (*Les Parleuses*, Paris : Éditions de Minuit, 1974). A contre-courant de la plupart des lectures féministes de l'œuvre de Duras, est celle de Trista Selous, *Feminism and Femininity in the Work of Marguerite Duras* (New Haven and London : Yale University Press, 1988). Selous refuse en particulier l'interprétation qui voit en les blancs du texte durassien une inscription du féminin.
[9] Une liste des œuvres de Marguerite Duras citées dans cet article se trouve ci-dessus.
[10] Alfred Cismaru, *Marguerite Duras* (New York : Twayne, 1971), 32.
[11] A en croire Julia Kristeva, il n'y a pas que le narrateur qui soit mis en danger par les histoires durassiennes et leurs protagonistes absentes, folles, perdues, le lecteur aussi y risque sa raison : « [...] il ne faut pas donner les livres de Duras aux lecteurs et lectrices fragiles [...] les livres [...] nous font côtoyer la folie » (*Soleil noir, dépression et mélancolie*, Paris : Gallimard, 1987, 235).
[12] Marcelle Marini, *Territoire du féminin avec Marguerite Duras* (Paris : Éditions de Minuit, 1977), 83–135.
[13] Duras a elle-même avoué qu'elle s'était trouvée dans l'impossibilité d'écrire l'histoire de la mendiante en son nom dans une interview accordée à Hubert Nyssen, « Marguerite Duras, un silence peuplé de phrases », *Synthèses* 254–255 (1967), 42–49 (p. 46).
[14] La lecture que fait Marcelle Marini de cette figure narrative ne me semble pas dépassée, malgré d'autres interprétations plus récentes; voir Maria Dibattista, « The clandestine fictions of Marguerite Duras » dans Ellen G. Friedman and Miriam Fuchs (eds.), *Breaking the Sequence: Women's Experimental Fiction* (Princeton: Princeton University Press, 1989), 284–297 (p. 289). Dibattista analyse cette figure comme « adroit acts of cultural sabotage » et elle explique que Duras « assumes not just the vestige and verbal mannerisms of another sex, but impersonates the narrative figure men have often arrogated for their own questionable ends, that classical figure of psychological and grammatical detachment — the third person ». Cette lecture réduit l'ambivalence de la position de Duras, transformant le malaise éprouvé par Duras à écrire en son nom en un acte purement critique, et elle néglige le fait que le narrateur — Jacques Hold ou Peter Morgan — ne sort pas indemne de son acte de narration, qu'il est loin

d'être détaché de l'histoire qu'il raconte. Pour pouvoir écrire sur la mendiante, Peter Morgan doit se laisser envahir jusqu'à un certain point par son expérience à elle, et ce faisant, lui aussi, risque de « se perdre ». Son mouvement est alternativement un mouvement de dissolution dans l'histoire de la mendiante et de répression de cette dernière pour pouvoir s'ériger en sujet. La lecture de Dibattista gagne donc à être juxtaposée à celle de Janine Ricouart qui envisage elle aussi le choix de narrateurs masculins comme un acte subversif, mais cette fois-ci de la position de connaissance et d'autorité de ces narrateurs : « Elle a l'air de donner le pouvoir ou le crayon, à un narrateur masculin, mais pour démontrer que ce narrateur se retrouve dans une position d'hystérie, de fragmentation tout comme les personnages féminins qu'ils (sic) essaient de circonscrire dans leur savoir/sans le savoir » (Janine Ricouart, *Ecriture féminine et violence : une étude de Marguerite Duras*, Birmingham, Alabama: Summa Publications, 1991, 133).

[15] Marini, *Territoire du féminin*, 96.

[16] Je rejoins ici l'analyse de Trista Selous, *The Other Woman: Feminism and Femininity in the Work of Marguerite Duras* (New Haven: Yale University Press, 1985), mais son interprétation n'est pas valable pour toutes les héroïnes durassiennes, comme le note aussi Cohen, *Women and Discourse,* 129.

[17] Duras a fait remarquer sa ressemblance à la dame du Camion : « La description physique de cette femme correspond à la mienne. Je la vois comme moi... je me suis vue. Avec cette valise. La banalité. J'ai pensé à moi ». (Interview avec Dominique Noguez, « La Dame des Yvelines », *Les œuvres cinématographiques de Marguerite Duras*, Éditions Vidéographiques Critiques, produites par le Ministère des Relations Extérieures, 1984, 47.)

[18] Susan D. Cohen, « La Présence de rien », *Cahiers Renaud Barrault* 106 (1983), 17–36 (p. 23).

[19] Ibid., 24.

[20] Bernard Alazet, « Je m'appelle Aurélia Steiner », *Didascalies* (avril 1982), 50–60. Alazet se place évidemment dans la logique d'Aurélia, au niveau de sa vie fantasmée, et non pas réelle où ses parents sont professeurs.

[21] L'œuvre de Duras est saturée de doubles, d'histoires qui en reflètent d'autres. Marie-Claire Ropars-Wuillemier dans « La Mort des miroirs : India Song, Son Nom de Venise dans Calcutta désert », *L'Avant-scène Cinéma* 225 (avril 1979), 4–12, a étudié le rôle important des miroirs dans le cinéma de Duras, et Julia Kristeva dans *Soleil noir* analyse ce qu'elle appelle le phénomène de réduplication dans les textes de Duras.

[22] Le lieu choisi, le port, le café — mais surtout le bac rouge — de la première page d'*Emily L.* forcent d'emblée le lecteur à établir un parallèle avec *Moderato Cantabile.*

[23] Même avant l'apparition du « je » quasi autobiographique, le lecteur averti avait pu établir la nature en partie autobiographique de nombreux textes de Duras, en particulier *Un barrage contre le Pacifique* ou *Des journées entières dans les arbres* (Paris : Gallimard, 1954). Dans *Les Parleuses,* 139, Duras avait d'ailleurs attiré l'attention de Xavière Gauthier sur l'aspect autobiographique d'*Un barrage.*

[24] Hubert Nyssen, *Les Voies de l'écriture* (Paris : Mercure de France, 1969), 129.

[25] Il est inutile de revenir ici sur la nature autobiographique des textes durassiens qui a été clairement établie par Aliette Armel dans *Marguerite Duras et l'autobiographie* (Bordeaux : Le Castor Astral, 1990).

[26] Dans *Marguerite Duras à Montréal*, textes réunis et présentés par Suzanne Lamy et André Roy (Montréal : Spirale, 1981), 57.

[27] Il suffit de parcourir *Le Monde extérieur*, collection d'articles journalistiques, de préfaces ou de textes non publiés qui s'étalent sur de nombreuses années, pour être frappée par le nombre de textes écrits à la première personne. D'ailleurs dans « Moi » (!) Duras reconnaît : « J'écris. Ce qui m'émeut c'est moi-même. Ce qui me donne envie de pleurer c'est ma violence, c'est moi » (p. 75).

[28] A titre d'exemple, voici le début de *L'Homme atlantique*, où le « je » féminin renvoie inévitablement à Duras, la réalisatrice du film et l'héroïne de l'histoire, et le « vous » masculin à Yann Andréa, l'acteur et « l'homme atlantique » :

> Vous ne regarderez pas la caméra. Sauf lorsqu'on l'exigera de vous.
>
> Vous oublierez.
> Vous oublierez.
>
> Que c'est vous, vous l'oublierez.
> Je crois qu'il est possible d'y arriver. (p. 7)

[29] J'ai par ailleurs (« Déconstruction de la masculinité dans l'œuvre durassienne » dans *Marguerite Duras, Rencontres de Cerisy*, Paris : Écriture, 1994, 47–68) évoqué le côté dominateur du « je » durassien nettement visible dans *L'Amant*. Et Trista Selous, « Marguerite and the Mountain » dans Margaret Atack et Phil Powrie (eds.), *Contemporary French Fiction by Women, Feminist Perspectives* (Manchester : Manchester University Press, 1990), 84–95, défend avec véhémence l'idée que Duras occupe une position masculine dans ses textes.

[30] Duras continue à s'objectiver en la troisième personne dans ses interviews. Ainsi dans la présentation de « Au delà des pages » (diffusé par TF1, juillet 1988), elle se présente ainsi : « Elle écrit. Elle écrit Marguerite Duras, M.D. Elle écrit ». Elle a commenté cette tendance : « J'aime bien parler de moi à la troisième personne. C'est une sorte de joke ... Y'a un clin d'œil, je me moque un peu. Mais en même temps c'est vrai ». (Interview conduite par Carole Sandrel, « Duras en liberté », *Télé 7 Jours* (26 juin 1988, 48–49.)

[31] Je m'appelle Marguerite Duras.
J'ai seize ans.
Ma mère est institutrice dans les postes du Mékong en Indochine française.
J'écris. (*ME*, 170).

[32] Hélène Cixous, *La Jeune Née* (Paris : Union Générale d'Éditions, 1975), 177–178.

List of Subscribers

The following have associated themselves with the publication of this volume through subscription:

Margaret Atack, Leeds
Richard Bales, Belfast
Mariette Ball, London
Susan Bassnett, Warwick
Gino Bedani, Swansea
Sheila M. Bell, Canterbury
William S. Brooks, Bath
A. J. L. Busst, Bangor
Marie-Claude Canova-Green, London
Brian Cainen, Swansea
Françoise Calin, Eugene (Oregon)
Bernice Cardy, Swansea
Graham Chesters, Hull
Francis Clarke, Swansea
Juliette Decreus, Mechelen (Belgium)
Armel Diverres, Swansea
Jean H. Duffy, Sheffield
Peter Dunwoodie, London
Carol Ann Evans, Swansea
Derek Gagen, Swansea
David George, Swansea

Chris Gossip, Armidale (NSW)
Marian Hobson, London
Edward Hughes, London
Penelope and Maxine Jacobs, Swansea
Jeremy Jennings, Birmingham
Gillian Jondorf, Cambridge
David Kinloch, Glasgow
R. C. Knight, Swansea
Mark Lee, Sackville (New Brunswick)
Philippe Lejeune, Fontenay-aux-Roses
Gerald Macklin, Jordanstown
Michael Moriarty, London
Howard Moss, Swansea
Annette Musker, Ystrad Meurig
Sabine G. Raffy, Cambridge (Massachusetts)
Philip Robinson, Canterbury
Christopher Rolfe, Leicester
Michael Sheringham, London
Edmund J. Smyth, Liverpool
Arthur Terry, Colchester
M. J. Tilby, Cambridge
John Trethewey, Aberystwyth
Julia F. Ward, Northampton
Margaret Whines, Sheffield
Tony Williams, Hull
Rhys W. Williams, Swansea

Bristol University Library
Durham University Library
Reading University Library
Department of French, University of Wales, Swansea